Lecture Notes in Computer Science 5114

Commenced Publication in 1973
Founding and Former Series Editors:
Gerhard Goos, Juris Hartmanis, and Jan van Leeuwen

Mladen Berekovic   Nikitas Dimopoulos
Stephan Wong (Eds.)

Embedded Computer Systems: Architectures, Modeling, and Simulation

8th International Workshop
SAMOS 2008, Samos, Greece, July 21-24, 2008
Proceedings

 Springer

Volume Editors

Mladen Berekovic
Institut für Datentechnik und Kommunikationsnetze
Hans-Sommer-Str. 66, 38106 Braunschweig, Germany
E-mail: berekovic@ida.ing.tu-bs.de

Nikitas Dimopoulos
University of Victoria
Department of Electrical and Computer Engineering
P.O. Box 3055, Victoria, B.C., V8W 3P6, Canada
E-mail: nikitas@ece.uvic.ca

Stephan Wong
Delft University of Technology
Mekelweg 4, 2628 CD Delft, The Netherlands
E-mail: stephan@ce.et.tudelft.nl

Library of Congress Control Number: Applied for

CR Subject Classification (1998): C, B

LNCS Sublibrary: SL 1 – Theoretical Computer Science and General Issues

ISSN	0302-9743
ISBN-10	3-540-70549-X Springer Berlin Heidelberg New York
ISBN-13	978-3-540-70549-9 Springer Berlin Heidelberg New York

Springer is a part of Springer Science+Business Media

springer.com

© Springer-Verlag Berlin Heidelberg 2008
Printed in Germany

Typesetting: Camera-ready by author, data conversion by Scientific Publishing Services, Chennai, India
Printed on acid-free paper   SPIN: 12437931   06/3180   5 4 3 2 1 0

Dedicated to Stamatis Vassiliadis (1951 – 2007)

Stamatis Vassiliadis

Professor at Delft University of Technology
IEEE Fellow - ACM Fellow
Member of the Dutch Academy of Sciences - KNAW

passed away on April 7, 2007.

He was an outstanding computer scientist and due to his vivid and hearty
manner he was a good friend to all of us.
Born in Manolates on Samos (Greece) he established in 2001 the successful series
of SAMOS conferences and workshops.
These series will not be the same without him.
We will keep him and his family in our hearts.

Preface

The SAMOS workshop is an international gathering of highly qualified researchers from academia and industry, sharing their ideas in a 3-day lively discussion. The workshop meeting is one of two co-located events—the other event being the IC-SAMOS. The workshop is unique in the sense that not only solved research problems are presented and discussed, but also (partly) unsolved problems and in-depth topical reviews can be unleashed in the scientific arena. Consequently, the workshop provides the participants with an environment where collaboration rather than competition is fostered.

The workshop was established in 2001 by Professor Stamatis Vassiliadis with the goals outlined above in mind, and located in one of the most beautiful islands of the Aegean. The rich historical and cultural environment of the island, coupled with the intimate atmosphere and the slow pace of a small village by the sea in the middle of the Greek summer, provide a very conducive environment where ideas can be exchanged and shared freely. The workshop, since its inception, has emphasized high-quality contributions, and it has grown to accommodate two parallel tracks and a number of invited sessions.

This year, the workshop celebrated its eighth anniversary, and it attracted 24 contributions carefully selected out of 62 submitted works for an acceptance rate of 38.7%. Each submission was thoroughly reviewed by at least three reviewers and considered by the international Program Committee during its meeting at Delft in March 2008.

Indicative of the wide appeal of the workshop is the fact that the submitted works originated from a wide international community that included Belgium, Brazil, Czech Republic, Finland, France, Germany, Greece, Ireland, Italy, Lithuania, The Netherlands, New Zealand, Republic of Korea, Spain, Switzerland, Tunisia, UK, and the USA. Additionally, two invited sessions on topics of current interest addressing issues on "System Level Design for Heterogeneous Systems" and "Programming Multicores" were organized and included in the workshop program. Each special session used its own review procedure, and was given the opportunity to include relevant work from the regular workshop program. Three such papers were included in the invited sessions.

This volume is dedicated to the memory of Stamatis Vassiliadis, the founder of the workshop, a sharp and visionary thinker, and a very dear friend, who unfortunately is no longer with us.

We hope that the attendees enjoyed the SAMOS VIII workshop in all its aspects, including many informal discussions and gatherings.

July 2008

Nikitas Dimopoulos
Stephan Wong
Mladen Berekovic

Organization

The SAMOS VIII workshop took place during July 21 − 24, 2008 at the Research and Teaching Institute of East Aegean (INEAG) in Agios Konstantinos on the island of Samos, Greece.

General Chair

Mladen Berekovic   Technical University of Braunschweig, Germany

Program Chairs

Nikitas Dimopoulos   University of Victoria, Canada
Stephan Wong   Delft University of Technology, The Netherlands

Proceedings Chair

Cor Meenderinck   Delft University of Technology, The Netherlands

Special Session Chairs

Chris Jesshope   University of Amsterdam, The Netherlands
John McAllister   Queen's University Belfast, UK

Publicity Chair

Daler Rakhmatov   University of Victoria, Canada

Web Chairs

Mihai Sima   University of Victoria, Canada
Sebastian Isaza   Delft University of Technology, The Netherlands

Finance Chair

Stephan Wong   Delft University of Technology, The Netherlands

Symposium Board

Jarmo Takala	Tampere University of Technology, Finland
Shuvra Bhattacharyya	University of Maryland, USA
John Glossner	Sandbridge Technologies, USA
Andy Pimentel	University of Amsterdam, The Netherlands
Georgi Gaydadjiev	Delft University of Technology, The Netherlands

Steering Committee

Luigi Carro	Federal U. Rio Grande do Sul, Brazil
Ed Deprettere	Leiden University, The Netherlands
Timo D. Hämäläinen	Tampere University of Technology, Finland
Mladen Berekovic	Technical University of Braunschweig, Germany

Program Committee

Aneesh Aggarwal	Binghamton University, USA
Amirali Baniasadi	University of Victoria, Canada
Piergiovanni Bazzana	ATMEL, Italy
Jürgen Becker	Universität Karlsruhe, Germany
Koen Bertels	Delft University of Technology, The Netherlands
Samarjit Chakraborty	University of Singapore, Singapore
José Duato	Technical University of Valencia, Spain
Paraskevas Evripidou	University of Cyprus, Cyprus
Fabrizio Ferrandi	Politecnico di Milano, Italy
Gerhard Fettweis	Technische Universität Dresden, Germany
Jason Fritts	University of Saint Louis, USA
Kees Goossens	NXP, The Netherlands
David Guevorkian	Nokia Research Center, Finland
Rajiv Gupta	University of California Riverside, USA
Marko Hännikäinen	Tampere University of Technology, Finland
Daniel Iancu	Sandbridge Technologies, USA
Victor Iordanov	Philips, The Netherlands
Hartwig Jeschke	University Hannover, Germany
Chris Jesshope	University of Amsterdam, The Netherlands
Wolfgang Karl	University of Karlsruhe, Germany
Manolis Katevenis	University of Crete, Greece
Andreas Koch	TU Darmstadt, Germany
Krzysztof Kuchcinski	Lund University, Sweden
Johan Lilius	Åbo Akademi University, Finland
Dake Liu	Linköping University, Sweden
Wayne Luk	Imperial College, UK
John McAllister	Queen's University of Belfast, UK
Alex Milenkovic	University of Utah, USA

Dragomir Milojevic   Université Libre de Bruxelles, Belgium
Andreas Moshovos   University of Toronto, Canada
Trevor Mudge   University of Michigan, USA
Nacho Navarro   Technical University of Catalonia, Spain
Alex Orailoglu   University of California San Diego, USA
Bernard Pottier   Université de Bretagne Occidentale, France
Hartmut Schröder   Universität Dortmund, Germany
Peter-Michael Seidel   SMU University, USA
Mihai Sima   University of Victoria, Canada
James Smith   University of Wisconsin-Madison, USA
Leonel Sousa   TU Lisbon, Portugal
Jürgen Teich   University of Erlangen, Germany
George Theodoridis   Aristotle University of Thessaloniki, Greece
Dimitrios Velenis   Illinois Institute of Technology, USA
Jan-Willem van de Waerdt   NXP, USA

Local Organizers

Karin Vassiliadis   Delft University of Technology, The Netherlands
Lidwina Tromp   Delft University of Technology, The Netherlands
Yiasmin Kioulafa   Research and Training Institute of
    East Aegean, Greece

Referees

Aasaraai, K.	Ehliar, A.	Hung Tsoi, K.
Aggarwal, A.	Eilert, J.	Iancu, D.
Andersson, P.	Ersfolk, J.	Iordanov, V.
Arpinen, T.	Evripidou, S.	Jeschke, H.
Asghar, R.	Feng, M.	Jesshope, C.
Baniasadi, A.	Ferrandi, F.	Juurlink, B.
Becker, J.	Fettweis, G.	Kalokerinos, G.
Berekovic, M.	Flatt, H.	Karl, W.
Bertels, K.	Flich, J.	Karlström, P.
Bournoutian, G.	Garcia, S.	Kaseva, V.
Burcea, I.	Gaydadjiev, G.	Katevenis, M.
Capelis, D.	Gelado, I.	Keinert, J.
Chakraborty, S.	Gladigau, J.	Kellomäki, P.
Chang, Z.	Goossens, K.	Kissler, D.
Chaves, R.	Gruian, F.	Koch, A.
Chow, G.	Guang, L.	Koch, D.
Dahlin, A.	Guevorkian, D.	Kohvakka, M.
Deprettere, E.	Gupta, R.	Kuchcinski, K.
Dias, T.	Hämäläinen, T.	Kuehnle, M.
Duato, J.	Hännikäinen, M.	Kulmala, A.

Kuzmanov, G.

Kyriacou, C.

Lafond, S.

Lam, Y.

Langerwerf, J.

Lankamp, M.

Lilius, J.

Lin, Y.

Liu, D.

Luk, W.

McAllister, J.

Meenderinck, C.

Milenkovic, A.

Milojevic, D.

Moshovos, A.

Mudge, T.

Nagarajan, V.

Navarro, N.

Nikolaidis, S.

Nowak, F.

O'Neill, M.

Orailoglu, A.

Orsila, H.

Papadopoulou, M.

Partanen, T.

Paulsson, K.

Payá-Vayá, G.

Pimentel, A.

Pitkänen, T.

Ponomarev, D.

Pottier, B.

Pratas, F.

Rasmus, A.

Salminen, E.

Sander, O.

Schröder, H.

Schuck, C.

Schuster, T.

Sebastião, N.

Seidel, P.

Seo, S.

Septinus, K.

Silla, F.

Sima, M.

Smith, J.

Sousa, L.

Streubühr, M.

Strydis, C.

Suhonen, J.

Suri, T.

Takala, J.

Tatas, K.

Tavares, M.

Teich, J.

Theodoridis, G.

Theodoropoulos, D.

Tian, C.

Tol, M. van

Truscan, D.

Tsompanidis, I.

Vassiliadis, N.

Velenis, D.

Villavieja, C.

Waerdt, J. van de

Weiß, J.

Westermann, P.

Woh, M.

Woods, R.

Wu, D.

Yang, C.

Zebchuk, J.

Zebelein, C.

Table of Contents

SoC

Application Specific

Special Session: System Level Design for Heterogeneous Systems

Special Session: Programming Multicores

Sensors and Sensor Networks

System Modeling and Design

Can They Be Fixed: Some Thoughts After 40 Years in the Business

Yale Patt

Department of Electrical and Computer Engineering
The University of Texas at Austin
patt@ece.utexas.edu

Abstract. If there is one thing the great Greek teachers taught us, it was to question what is, and to dream about what can be. In this audience, unafraid that no one will ask me to drink the hemlock, but humbled by the realization that I am walking along the beach where great thinkers of the past have walked, I nonetheless am willing to ask some questions that continue to bother those of us who are engaged in education: professors, students, and those who expect the products of our educational system to be useful hires in their companies.

As I sit in my office contemplating which questions to ask between the start of my talk and when the dinner is ready, I have come up with my preliminary list. By the time July 21 arrives and we are actually on Samos, I may have other questions that seem more important. Or, you the reader may feel compelled to pre-empt me with your own challenges to conventional wisdom, which of course would be okay, also.

In the meantime, my preliminary list:

- Are students being prepared for careers as graduates? (Can it be fixed?)
- Are professors who have been promoted to tenure prepared for careers as professors? (Can it be fixed?)
- What is wrong with education today? (Can it be fixed?)
- What is wrong with research today? (Can it be fixed?)
- What is wrong with our flagship conferences? and Journals? (Can they be fixed?)

M. Berekovic, N. Dimopoulos, and S. Wong (Eds.): SAMOS 2008, LNCS 5114, p. 1, 2008.

On the Benefit of Caching Traffic Flow Data in the Link Buffer

Konstantin Septinus[1], Christian Grimm[2],
Vladislav Rumyantsev[1], and Peter Pirsch[1]

[1] Institute of Microelectronic Systems, Appelstr. 4, 30167 Hannover, Germany
[2] Regional Computing Centre for Lower Saxony, Schloßwender Str. 5,
30159 Hannover, Germany
{septinus,pirsch}@ims.uni-hannover.de
{grimm}@rvs.uni-hannover.de

Abstract. In this paper we review local caching of TCP/IP flow context data in the link buffer or a comparable other local buffer. Such connection cache is supposed to be a straight-forward optimization strategy for look-ups of flow context data in a network processor environment. The connection cache can extend common table-based look-up schemes and also be implemented in SW. On the basis of simulations with different IP network traces, we show a significant decrease of average search times. Finally, well-suited cache and table sizes are determined, which can be used for a wide range of IP network systems.

Keywords: Connection Cache, Link Buffer, Network Interface, Table Lookup, Transmission Control Protocol, TCP.

1 Introduction

The rapid evolution of the Internet with its variety of applications is a remarkable phenomenon. Over the past decade, the Internet Protocol (IP) established being the de facto standard for transferring data between computers all over the world. In order to support different applications over an IP network, multiple transport protocols where developed on top of IP. The most prominent one is the Transmission Control Protocol (TCP), which was initially introduced in the 1970s for connection-oriented and reliable services. Today, many applications such as WWW, FTP or Email rely on TCP even though processing TCP requires more computational power than competitive protocols, due to its inherent connection-oriented and reliable algorithms.

Breakthroughs in network infrastructure technology and manufacturing techniques keep enabling steadily increasing data rates. For example, here are optical fibers together with DWDM [1]. This leads to a widening gap between the available network bandwidth, user demands and computational power of a typical off-the-shelf computer system [2]. The consequence is that a traditional desktop computer cannot properly handle emerging rates of multiple Gbps (Gigabit/s). Conventional processor and server systems cannot comply with up-coming demands and require special extensions such as accelerators for network and I/O

M. Berekovic, N. Dimopoulos, and S. Wong (Eds.): SAMOS 2008, LNCS 5114, pp. 2–11, 2008.

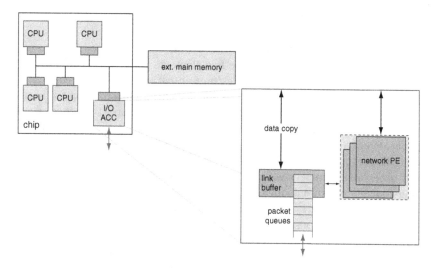

Fig. 1. Basic Approach for a Network Coprocessor

protocol operations. Fig. 1 depicts the basic architecture of a conceivable network coprocessor (I/O ACC).

One major issue for every component in a high-performance IP-based network is an efficient look-up and management of the connection context for each data flow. Particularly in high-speed server environments storing, looking-up and managing of connection contexts has a central impact on the overall performance. Similar problems arise for high-performance routers [3]. In this paper we denote our connection context cache extension rather for end systems than for routers. We believe that future requirement for those systems will increase in a way which makes it necessary for a high-performance end system to be able to process a large number of concurrent flows, similar to a router. This will become true especially for applications and environments with high numbers of interacting systems, such as peer to peer networks or cluster computing.

In general, the search based on flow-identifiers like IP addresses and application ports can possibly break down the performance caused by long search delays or unwanted occupation of the memory bandwidth. Our intention here is to review the usage of a connection context cache in the local link buffer in order to fasten up context look-ups. The connection context cache can be combined with traditional hash table-based look-up schemes. We assume a generic system architecture and provide analysis results in order to optimize table and cache sizes in the available buffer space.

The remainder of this paper is organized as follows. In section 2, we state the nature of the problem and discuss related work. Section 3 presents our approach for fastening up the search of connection contexts. Simulation results and a sizing guideline example for the algorithm are given in section 4. Section 5 provides conclusions that can be drawn from our work. Here, we also try to point out some of the issues that would come along with a explicit system implementation.

2   Connection Context Searching Revisited

A directed data stream between two systems can be represented by a so-called flow. A flow is defined as a tuple of the five elements {*source IP address, source port number, destination IP address, destination port number, protocol ID*}. The IP addresses indicate the two communicating systems involved, the port numbers of the respective processes, and the protocol ID the transport protocol used in this flow. We remark that only TCP is considered as a transport protocol in this paper. However, our approach can be easily extended to other protocols by regarding the respective protocol IDs.

From a network perspective, the capacity of the overall system in terms of handling concurrent flows is obviously an important property. From our point of view, an emerging server system should be capable to store data for multiples of thousand or even ten thousands flows simultaneously in order to support future high-performance applications. Molinero-Fernandez et al. [4] estimated that, for example, on an emerging OC-192 link, 31 million look-ups and 52 thousand new connections per second can be expected in a network node. These numbers constitute the high demands on a network processing engine. A related property of the system is the time which is required for looking-up a connection context.

Before the processing of each incoming TCP segment, the respective data flow has to be identified. This is done by checking the IP and TCP header data for IP addresses and application ports for both, source and destination. This identification procedure is a search over previously stored flow-specific connection context data. The size for one connection context depends on the TCP implementation, common values would be a size between $S = 64$ and $S = 256$ Byte. It is appropriate to store most of the flow data in the main memory. But how can fast access to the data be guaranteed?

Search functions can be efficiently solved by dedicated hardware. One commonly used core for search engines on switches and routers is a CAM (Context Addressable Memory). CAMs can significantly reduce search time [5]. This is possible as long as static protocol information is regarded which is typically true for data flows of several packets, e.g. for file transfers or data streams of some kilobytes and above. We did not consider a CAM-based approach for our look-up algorithm on a higher protocol level, because compared to software oriented implementations CAMs tend to be more inflexible and thus not well-suited for dynamic protocols such as TCP. Additionally, the usage of CAMs requires high costs and high power consumption. Our approach based on hash table is supposed to be a memory efficient alternative to CAMs with an almost equally effective search time for specific applications [6].

Using ideal values and hashes the search approaches $\mathcal{O}(1)$ time. During the past two decades there was an ongoing discussion about the hash key itself. In [7, 8] the differences in the IP hash function implementation are discussed. We believe the choice of very specific hash functions comes second and should be considered for application-specific optimizations only. As a matter of course, the duration of a look-up is significantly affected by the size of the tables.

Furthermore, a caching mechanism that enables immediate access to the recently used sets of connection contexts can also provide a speed-up. Linux-based implementations use a hash table and additionally, the network stack actively checks if the incoming segment belongs to the last used connection [9]. This method can be accelerated by extending the caching mechanism in a way that several complete connection contexts are cached. Yang et al. [10] adopted an LRU-based (Least Recently Used) replacement policy in their connection cache design. Their work provides useful insights of connection caching analysis. For applications with a specific distribution of data flows such a cache implementation can achieve a high speed-up. However, for rather equally distributed traffic load the speed-up is expected to be less. The overhead for the LRU replacement policy is additionally not negligible. This is in particular true when cache sizes of 128 and more are considered. Another advantage of our approach is that such a scheme can be implemented in software more easily. This is our motivation for using a simple queue as replacement policy, instead.

Summarizing, accesses on stored connection context data leads to a high latency based on delays of a typical main memory structure. Hence, we discuss locally caching of connection context in the link buffer or a comparable local memory of the network coprocessor. Link buffers are usually used by the network interface to hold data from input and output queues.

3   Connection Cache Approach

In this section we cover the basic approach of the implemented look-up scheme. In order to support next-generation network applications, we assume that a more or less specialized hardware extension or network coprocessors also will be standard on tomorrows computers and end systems. According to the architecture in Fig. 1, network processing engines parse the protocol header, update connection data and initiate payload transfers.

Based on the expected high number of data flows, storing the connection contexts in the external main memory is indispensable. However, using some space in the link buffer to manage recent or frequently used connection contexts provides a straight-forward optimization step. The link buffer is supposed to be closely coupled with the network processing engine and allows much faster access. In particular, this is self-explanatory in the case of on-chip SRAM. For instance, compare a latency of 5 with main memory latency of more than 100 clock cycles.

We chose to implement the connection cache with a queue-based or LRL (Least Recently Loaded) scheme. A single flow shall only appear once in the queue. The last element in the queue automatically pops out as soon as a new one arrives. This implies that even a frequently used connection pops out of the cache after a certain number of new arriving data flows, opposed to a LRU-based replacement policy. All queue elements are stored in the link buffer in order to enable fast access to them. The search for the queue elements is supposed to be functioned with an hash.

Let C be the number of cached contexts. Then, we assumed a minimal hash table size for the cached flows of $2 \times C$ entries. This dimensioning is more or less arbitrary, but it is an empirical value which should be applicable in order to avoid a high number of collisions. The hash table root entries are also stored in the link buffer. A root entry consists of a pointer to an element in the queue. After a cache miss, searching contexts in the main memory is supposed to be made over a second table. Its size is denoted by T. Hence, for each incoming packet the following look-up scheme is triggered: hash key generation from TCP/IP header, table access ①, cache access ② and after a cache, miss main memory access plus data copy ③ ④ – as visualized in Fig. 2.

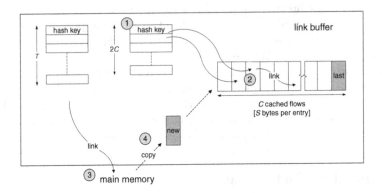

Fig. 2. TCP/IP Flow Context Look-up Scheme. Most contexts are stored in the external main memory. In addition, C contexts are cached in the link buffer.

We used a CRC-32 as the hash function and then reduced the number of bits to the required values, $\lceil \log_2(2 \times C) \rceil$ and $\lceil \log_2 T \rceil$ respectively. Once the hash key is generated, it can be checked whether the respective connection context entry can be found along the hash bucket list in the cache queue. If the connection context does not exist in the queue, the look-up scheme continues using the second hash table of different size that points to elements in the main memory. Finally, the connection context data is transferred and stored automatically in the cache queue.

A stack was used in order to manage physical memory locations for the connection context data within the main memory. Each slot is associated with one connection context of size S and its start address pointer leading to the memory location. The obvious advantage of this approach is that the memory slots can be stored from arbitrary positions in the memory. The hash table itself and even the stack can also be managed and stored in the link buffer. It is worth pointing out that automatic garbage collection on the traffic flow data is essential. Garbage collection is beyond the scope of this paper, because it has no direct impact on the performance of the TCP/IP flow data look-up.

4   Evaluation

The effectiveness of a cache is usually measured with the hit rate. A high hit rate indicates that the cache parameters fit well to the considered application. In our case the actual number of buffer and memory accesses were supposed to be the determining factor for the performance, since these directly correspond to the latency. We used a simple cost function based on two counters in order to measure average values for the latency. As summing up the counters' score with different weights, two different delay times were taken into account, i.e. one for on-chip SRAM and the other for external main memory. Without loss of generality, we assumed that the external memory was 20 times slower.

4.1   Traffic Flow Modeling

Based on available traces such as [11–13] and traces from our servers, we modeled incoming packets in a server node. We assumed that the combinations of IP addresses and ports preserve a realistic traffic behavior for TCP/IP scenarios. In Table 1, all trace files used through the simulations are summarized by giving a short description, the total number of packets $P/10^6$ and the average number of packets per flow P_{av}. Furthermore, P_{med} is the respective median value. Fig. 3 shows the relative numbers of packets belonging to a specific flow in percent.

Table 1. Listing of the IP Network Trace Files

Trace	Organization	Link	Date	$P/10^6$	P_{av}	P_{med}
LUH	University Hannover	GigEth	2005/01/12	8.80	37	10
AMP	AMPATH in Miami	OC12	2005/03/15	10.9	53	4
PUR	Purdue University	GigEth	2006/08/04	14.0	38	3
COS	Colorado State University	OC3	2004/05/06	2.35	13	3
TER	SDSC's Cluster	OC192	2004/02/08	3.25	1455	31

4.2   Sizing of the Main Hash Table and the Cache

On one hand, the table for addressing the connection contexts in the main memory has a significant impact on the performance of look-up scheme. It needs to have a certain size in order to avoid collisions. On the other hand, saving memory resources also makes sense in most cases. Thus, it is the question of how to distribute the buffer space the best way. In Eq. 1, the constant on the right side refers to the available space, the size of the flow context is expressed by S, a is another system parameter. This can be understood as an optimization problem as different T-C-constellations are considered in order to minimize the latency.

$$a\,T + S \times C = const \qquad (1)$$

For a test case, we assumed around 64K Byte of free SRAM space which could be utilized for speeding up the look-up. 64K Byte should be a preferable amount

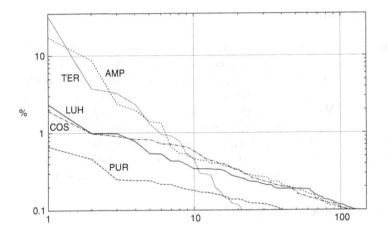

Fig. 3. Relative Number of Packets per Flow in a Trace File. The x-axis shows the number of different flows, ordered by the number of packets in the trace. On the y-axis, the relative amount of packets belonging to the respective flows is plotted. Flows with < 0.1% are neglected in the plot.

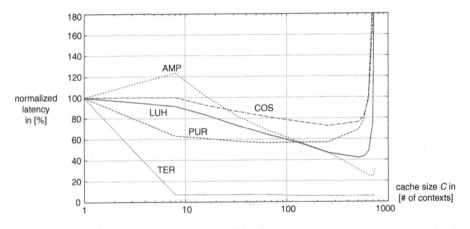

Fig. 4. Normalized Latency Measure in % for a Combination of a Hash Table and a Queue-based Cache in a 64K Byte buffer]

of on-chip memory. Moreover, we assumed that a hash entry required 4 Byte and a cached connection context $S = 88$ Byte. Based on these values, we evaluated different cache size configurations from $C = 0$ up to $C \approx 700$. The remaining space was used for the two hash tables as indicated in Fig. 2. Following Eq. 1, the value of T now depends on the actual value of C or verse visa.

Fig. 4 shows the five simulation runs based on the trace files, which were introduced in section 4.1. Each of the curves was normalized to run for $C = 0$. It can be seen that for larger C the performance is very much dominated by

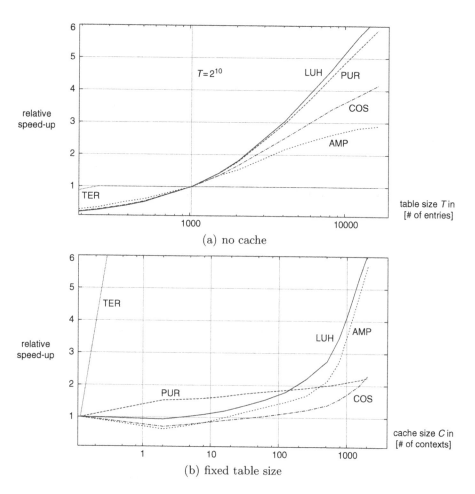

(a) no cache

(b) fixed table size

Fig. 5. Speed-up Factor for Independent Table and Cache Sizing. Referring to the performance of a table with $T = 2^{10}$, the possible speed-up that can be obtained with other T is shown above. In the diagram below, the speed-up for using different cache sizes C is sketched for a fixed $T = 2^{14}$.

the respective small size of the hash table. When the hash table size gets too small, the search time is significantly increased by collisions. In case of the TER-trace there is no need for a large cache. The main traffic is caused by very few flows, whereas they are not interrupted by other flows. Regarding to a significant speed-up of the look-up scheme for a broader range applications, the usage of a connection cache with e.g. $C = 128$ seems to be well-suited. This example can be extended with other constraints. Basically, the results are similar, showing an optimum region for T and C. Only if much more on-chip memory can be used for the scheme, such as a few Megabytes, the speed-up based on the a larger number of hash table entries will more or less saturate and consequently, much more flows can be cached in the buffer. However, it is remarkable that less than a Megabyte is excepted to be available.

Independent from a buffer space constraint it must be evaluated whether a larger size for the connection cache or hash tables is worth its effort. In Fig. 5 (a) configurations are shown, in which the cache size was set to $C = 0$, increasing only the table size T. Fig. 5 (b) shows cases for fixed T and different cache sizes. Again, the TER-trace must be treated differently, the reasons are the same as above. However, knowing about the drawbacks of one or the other design decision, the plots in Fig. 5 on page 9 emphasize the trade-offs.

5   Summary, Conclusion and Outlook

The goal of this paper was to improve the look-up procedure for TCP/IP flow data in high-performance and future end systems. We showed a basic concept of how to implement a connection cache with a local buffer, which is included in specialized network processor architectures. Our analysis was based on simulation of network server trace data from the last years. Therefore, this work provides a new look at a long existing problem.

We showed that a combination of a conventional hash table-based search and a queue-based cache provides a remarkable performance gain, whilst a system implementation effort is comparable low. We assumed that the buffer space was limited. The distribution of the available buffer space can be understood as an optimization problem. According to our analysis, a rule of the thumb would prescribe to cache at least 128 flows if possible.

The hash table for searching flows outside of the cache should include at least 2^{10} but preferably 2^{14} root entries in order to avoid collisions. We measured hit rates for the cache of more than 80% in average.

Initially, our concept was intended for a software implementation. Though it is possible to accelerate some of the steps in the scheme with the help of dedicated hardware, like the hash key calculation or even the whole cache infrastructure.

Acknowledgments

The authors would like to thank Sebastian Flügel and Ulrich Mayer for all helpful discussions.

References

1. Kartalopoulos, S.V.: DWDM: Networks, Devices, and Technology. Wiley-Interscience, John Wiley & Sons, Chichester (2003)
2. Shivam, P., Chase, J.S.: On the Elusive Benefits of Protocol Offload. In: Proceedings of the ACM SIGCOMM workshop on Network-I/O convergence (NICELI 2003), pp. 179–184. ACM Press, New York (2003)
3. Xu, J., Singhal, M.: Cost-Effective Flow Table Designs for High-Speed Routers: Architecture and Performance Evaluation. Transactions on Computers 51, 1089–1099 (2002)

4. Molinero-Fernandez, P., McKeown, N.: TCP Switching: Exposing Circuits to IP. IEEE Micro 22, 82–89 (2002)
5. Pagiamtzis, K., Sheikholeslami, A.: Content-Addressable Memory (CAM) Circuits and Architectures: A Tutorial and survey. IEEE Journal of Solid-State Circuits 41, 712–727 (2006)
6. Dharmapurikar, S.: Algorithms and Architectures for Network Search Processors. PhD thesis, Washington University in St. Louis (2006)
7. Broder, A., Mitzenmacher, M.: Using Multiple Hash Functions to Improve IP Lookups. In: Proceedings of the Twentieth Annual Joint Conference of the IEEE Computer and Communications Societies (INFOCOM 2001), vol. 3, pp. 1454–1463 (2001)
8. Pong, F.: Fast and Robust TCP Session Lookup by Digest Hash. In: 12th International Conference on Parallel and Distributed Systems (ICPADS 2006), vol. 1 (2006)
9. Linux Kernel Organization: The Linux Kernel Archives (2007)
10. Yang, S.M., Cho, S.: A Performance Study of a Connection Caching Technique. In: Conference Proceedings IEEE Communications, Power, and Computing (WESCANEX 1995), vol. 1, pp. 90–94 (1995)
11. NLANR: Passive Measurement and Analysis, PMA, http://pma.nlanr.net/
12. SIGCOMM: The Internet Traffic Archive, http://www.sigcomm.org/ITA/
13. WAND: Network Research Group, http://www.wand.net.nz/links.php
14. Garcia, N.M., Monteiro, P.P., Freire, M.M.: Measuring and Profiling IP Traffic. In: Fourth European Conference on Universal Multiservice Networks (ECUMN 2007), pp. 283–291 (2007)

Energy-Efficient Simultaneous Thread Fetch from Different Cache Levels in a Soft Real-Time SMT Processor

Emre Özer[1], Ronald G. Dreslinski[2], Trevor Mudge[2], Stuart Biles[1], and Krisztián Flautner[1]

[1] ARM Ltd., Cambridge, UK
[2] Department of Electrical Engineering and Computer Science, University of Michigan, Ann Arbor, MI, US

emre.ozer@arm.com, rdreslin@umich.edu, tnm@eecs.umich.edu,
stuart.biles@arm.com, krisztian.flautner@arm.com

Abstract. This paper focuses on the instruction fetch resources in a real-time SMT processor to provide an energy-efficient configuration for a soft real-time application running as a high priority thread as fast as possible while still offering decent progress in low priority or non-real-time thread(s). We propose a fetch mechanism, *Fetch-around*, where a high priority thread accesses the L1 ICache, and low priority threads directly access the L2. This allows both the high and low priority threads to simultaneously fetch instructions, while preventing the low priority threads from thrashing the high priority thread's ICache data. Overall, we show an energy-performance metric that is 13% better than the next best policy when the high performance thread priority is 10x that of the low performance thread.

Keywords: Caches, Embedded Processors, Energy Efficiency, Real-time, SMT.

1 Introduction

Simultaneous multithreading (SMT) techniques have been proposed to increase the utilization of core resources. The main goal is to provide multiple thread contexts from which the core can choose instructions to be executed. However, this comes at the price of a single thread's performance being degraded at the expense of the collection of threads achieving a higher aggregate performance. Previous work has focused on the techniques to provide each thread with a fair allocation of shared resources. In particular, the instruction fetch bandwidth has been the focus of many papers, and a round-robin policy with directed feedback from the processor [1] has been shown to increase fetch bandwidth and overall SMT performance.

Soft real-time systems are systems which are not time-critical [2], meaning that some form of quality is sacrificed if the real-time task misses its deadline. Examples include real audio/video players, tele/video conferencing, etc. where the sacrifice in quality may come in the form of a dropped frame or packet.

M. Berekovic, N. Dimopoulos, and S. Wong (Eds.): SAMOS 2008, LNCS 5114, pp. 12–22, 2008.

An soft real-time SMT processor is asymmetric in nature that one thread is given higher priority for the use of shared resources, which becomes the real-time thread, and the rest of the threads in the system are low-priority threads. In this case, implementing thread fetching with a round-robin policy is a poor decision. This type of policy will degrade the performance of the high priority (HP) thread by lengthening its execution time. Instinctively, a much better solution would be to assign the full fetch bandwidth to the HP thread at every cycle, and the low priority (LP) threads can only fetch when the HP thread stalls for data or control dependency, as was done in as done in [3], [4] and [5]. This allows the HP thread to fetch without any interruption by the LP threads. On the other hand, this policy can adversely affect the performance of the LP threads as they fetch and execute instructions less frequently. Thus, the contribution of the LP threads to the overall system performance is minimal.

In addition to the resource conflict that occurs for the fetch bandwidth, L1 instruction cache space is also a critical shared resource. As threads execute they compete for the same ICache space. This means that with the addition of LP threads to a system, the HP thread may incur more ICache misses and a lengthened execution time. One obvious solution to avoid the fetch bandwidth and cache space problems would be to replicate the ICache for each thread, but this is neither a cost effective nor power efficient solution. Making the ICache multi-ported [6,7] allows each thread to fetch independently. However, multi-ported caches are known to be very energy hungry and do not address the cache thrashing that occurs. An alternative to multi-porting the ICache, would be to partition the cache into several banks and allow the HP and LP threads to access independent banks [8]. However, bank conflicts between the threads still needs to be arbitrated and cache thrashing still occurs.

Ideally, a soft real-time SMT processor would perform the best if provided a system where the HP and LP threads can fetch simultaneously and the LP threads do not thrash the ICache space of the HP thread. In this case the HP thread is not delayed by the LP thread, and the LP threads can retire more instructions by fetching in parallel to the HP thread. In this paper, we propose an energy-efficient SMT thread fetching mechanism that fetches instructions from different levels of the memory hierarchy for different thread priorities. The HP thread always fetches from the ICache and the LP thread(s) fetch directly from the L2. This benefits the system in 3 main ways: a) The HP and LP threads can fetch simultaneously, since they are accessing different levels of the hierarchy, thus improving LP thread performance. b) The ICache is dedicated to the use of the HP thread, avoiding cache thrashing from the LP thread, which keeps the runtime low for the HP thread. c) The ICache size can be kept small since it only needs to handle the HP thread. Thus reducing the access energy of the HP thread providing an energy-efficient solution.

Ultimately, this leads to a system with an energy performance that is 13% better than the next best policy with the same cache sizes when the HP thread has 10x the priority of the LP thread. Alternatively, it achieves the same performance while requiring only a quarter to half of the instruction cache space. The only additional hardware required to achieve this is a private bus between the fetch engine and the L2 cache, and a second instruction address calculation unit.

The organization of the paper is as follows: **Section 2** gives some background on fetch mechanisms in multi-threaded processors. **Section 3** explains the details of how multiple thread instruction fetch can be performed from different cache levels. **Section 4** introduces the experimental framework and presents energy and performance results. Finally, **Section 5** concludes the paper.

2   Related Work

Static cache partitioning allocates the cache ways among the threads so that each thread can access its partition. This may not be an efficient technique for L1 caches in which the set associativity is 2 or 4 way. The real-time thread can suffer performance losses even though the majority of the cache ways is allocated to it. Also, the dynamic partitioning [9] allocates cache lines to threads according to its priority and dynamic behaviour. Their efficiency comes at a hardware complexity as the performance of each thread is tracked using monitoring counters and decision logic, which increases the hardware complexity and may not be affordable for cost-sensitive embedded processors.

There have been fetch policies proposed for generic SMT processors that dynamically allocate the fetch bandwidth to the threads so as to efficiently utilize the instruction issue queues [10,11]. However, these fetch policies do not address the problem in the context of attaining a minimally-delayed real-time thread in a real-time SMT processor.

There also have been some prior investigations on soft and hard real-time SMT processors. For instance, the HP and LP thread model is explored in [3] in the context of prioritizing the fetch bandwidth among threads. Their proposed fetch policy is that the HP thread has priority for fetching first over the LP threads, and the LP threads can only fetch when the HP thread stalls. Similarly, [4] investigates resource allocation policies to keep the performance of the HP thread as high as possible while performing LP tasks along with the HP thread. [12] discusses a technique to improve the performance by keeping its IPC of HP thread in an SMT processor under OS control. A similar approach is taken by [13] in which the IPC is controlled to guarantee the real-time thread deadlines in an SMT processor. [14] investigates efficient ways of co-scheduling threads into a soft real-time SMT processor. Finally, [15] presents a virtualized SMT processor for hard real-time tasks, which uses scratchpad memories rather than caches for deterministic behavior.

3   Simultaneous Thread Instruction Fetch Via Different Cache Levels

3.1   Real-Time SMT Model

Although the proposed mechanism is valid for any real-time SMT processor supporting one HP thread and many other LP threads, we will focus on a dual-thread real-time SMT processor core supporting one HP and one LP thread.

Figure 1a shows the traditional instruction fetch mechanism in a multi-threaded processor. Only one thread can perform an instruction fetch at a time. In a real-time SMT processor, this is prioritized in a way that the HP thread has the priority to perform the instruction fetch over the LP thread. The LP thread performs instruction fetch only when the HP thread stalls. This technique will be called *HPFirst*, and is the baseline for all comparisons that are performed.

3.2   Fetch-Around Mechanism

We propose an energy-efficient multiple thread instruction fetching mechanism for a real-time SMT processor as shown in Figure 1b. The HP thread always fetches from the ICache and the LP thread directly fetches from the L2 cache. This is called the *Fetch-around* instruction fetch mechanism because the LP thread fetches directly from L2 cache passing around the instruction cache. When the L2 instruction fetch for LP thread is performed, the fetched cache line does not have to be allocated into the ICache and it is brought through a separate bus that connects the L2 to the core and is directly written into the LP thread Fetch Queue in the core.

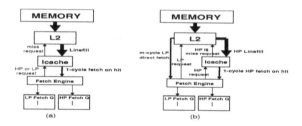

Fig. 1. Traditional instruction fetch in a multi-threaded processor (a), simultaneous thread instruction fetch at different cache levels in a soft real-time SMT processor (b)

This mechanism is quite advantageous because the LP thread is a background thread and an m-cycle direct L2 fetch can be tolerated as the HP thread is operating from the ICache. This way, the whole bandwidth of the ICache can be dedicated to the HP thread. This is very beneficial for the performance of the HP thread as the LP thread(s) instructions do not interfere with the HP thread, and therefore no thrashing of HP thread instructions occurs.

The *Fetch-around* policy may also consume less energy than other fetch policies. Although accessing the L2 consumes more energy than the L1 due to looking up additional cache ways and larger line sizes, the *Fetch-around* policy only needs to read a subset of the cache line (i.e. instruction fetch width) on a L2 I-side read operation from a LP thread. Another crucial factor for cache energy reduction is that the LP thread does not use the ICache at all, and therefore does not thrash the HP thread in the ICache. This will reduce the traffic of the HP thread to the L2 cache, and provide a higher hit rate in the more energy efficient ICache. Furthermore, the energy consumed by allocating L2 cache lines into the ICache is totally eliminated for the LP thread(s). Since the number of HP thread instructions is significantly larger than the LP, the energy savings of the HP thread in the ICache outweighs that of the LP threads increase in L2 energy.

In addition to its low energy consumption capability, the *Fetch-around* policy has the advantage of not requiring a large ICache for an increased number of threads. Since the ICache is only used by the HP thread, additional threads in the system put no more demands on the cache, and the performance remains the same as single threaded version. It is possible that a fetch policy such as round-robin may need twice the size of the ICache to achieve the same HP thread performance level as the *Fetch-around* policy in order to counteract the thrashing effect. Thus, the *Fetch-around* policy is likely to reduce the ICache size requirements, and therefore the static and dynamic ICache energy.

It takes approximately m-cycles (i.e. the L2 access time) to bring the LP thread instructions to the core from L2. This effectively means that the LP thread is fetched at every m cycles. One concern is the cost of the direct path between the L2 and ICache. This path does not have to be an L2 cache line size in width since the bus connects directly to the core and only need deliver the fetch width (2 instructions).

4   Energy and Performance Results

4.1   Experimental Framework

We have performed a cycle-accurate simulation of an SMT implementation of an ARMv7 architecture-compliant processor using the EEMBC benchmark suite [16]. We have used 24 benchmarks from the EEMBC benchmark suite covering a wide range of embedded applications including consumer, automotive, telecommunications and DSP. We run all possible dual-thread permutations of these benchmarks (i.e. 576 runs). A dual-thread simulation run completes when the HP thread finishes its execution, and then we collect statistics such as total IPC, degree of LP thread progress, HP thread speedup and etc. We present the average of these statistics over all runs in the figures.

The simulated processor model is a dual-issue in-order superscalar dual-thread SMT processor core with 4-way 1KB Icache, 4-way 8KB Dcache, and 8-way 16KB L2 cache. The hit latency is 1 cycle for L1 caches and 8 cycles for the L2 cache, the memory latency is 60 cycles and the cache line size is 64B for all caches. There is a 4096-entry global branch predictor with a shared branch history buffer and a replicated global branch history register for each thread, 2-way set associative 512-entry branch target buffer, and 8-entry replicated return address stack for each thread. The ICache delivers 2 32-bit instructions to the core per instruction fetch request. We used two thread fetch select policies: *Fetch-around* and *HPFirst*. *HPFirst* is the baseline fetch policy in which only one thread can fetch at a time, and the priority is always given to the HP thread first. There are two decoders in the decode stage that can decode up to instructions, and the HP thread has the priority over the LP thread to use the two decoders. If the HP thread instruction fetch queue is empty, then the LP thread instructions, if any, are decoded. Similarly, the HP thread has the priority to use the two issue slots. If it can issue only 1 instruction or cannot issue at all, then the LP thread is able to issue 1 or 2 instructions.

Most of the EEMBC benchmarks can fit into 2-to-8KB instruction cache. Thus, we deliberately select a very small instruction cache size (i.e. 1KB) to measure the effect of instruction cache stress. The L2 line size is 512 bits and the L1 instruction fetch width is 64 bits. From L2 to L1 ICache, a line size of 512 bits (i.e. 8 64 bits) are allocated on an ICache miss. ICache contains 4 banks or ways, and each bank consists of 2 sub-banks of 64 bits, so 8 sub-banks of 64 bits comprise a line of 512 bits. When an ICache linefill is performed, all sub-banks tag and data banks are written. We model both ICache and L2 cache as serial access caches meaning that the selected data bank is sense-amplified only after a tag match.

4.2   Thread Performance

We have measured 2 metrics to compare these fetch policies:

1. Slowdown in terms of execution time of the highest priority thread relative to itself running on the single-threaded processor,
2. Slowdown in terms of CPI of the lowest priority thread. As the HP thread has the priority to use all processor resources,

Sharing resources with other LP threads lengthens the HP thread execution time, and therefore we need to measure how the HP thread execution time in the SMT mode compares against its single-threaded run. In the single-threaded run, the execution time of the HP thread running alone is measured. Ideally, we would like not to degrade the performance of the HP thread but at the same time we would like to improve the performance of the LP thread. Thus, we measure the slowdown in LP thread CPI under SMT for each configuration with respect to their single-threaded CPI. The CPI of the LP thread is measured when it runs alone.

Table 1 shows the percentage slowdown in HP thread execution time relative to its single-threaded execution time. Although the ICache is not shared among threads in *Fetch-around*, the slowdown in the HP thread by about 10% occurs due to inter-thread interferences in data cache, L2 cache, branch prediction tables and execution units. On the other hand, the HP thread slowdown is about 13% in *HPFirst*. Since *Fetch-around* is the only fetch policy that does not allow the LP thread to use the ICache, the HP thread has the freedom to use the entire ICache and does not encounter any inter-thread interference.

Table 1 also shows the progress of the LP thread under the shadow of the HP thread measured in CPI. The progress of the LP thread is the slowest in *Fetch-around* as expected because the LP thread fetches instructions from L2, which is 8-cycles away from the core. *HPFirst* has better LP thread performance as LP

Table 1. Percentage slowdown in HP thread, and the progress of the LP thread

	Single-thread	HPFirst	Fetch-around
Percentage slowdown in HP	N/A	12.7%	9.5%
The LP CPI	1.6	3.8	5.1

thread instructions are being fetched from the ICache in a single cycle access. However, this benefit comes at the price of evicting HP thread instructions from the ICache due to interthread interference and increasing the HP thread runtime.

4.3   Area Efficiency of the Fetch-Around Policy

We take a further step by increasing the ICache size from 1KB to 2KB and 4KB for *HPFirst* and compare its performance to *Fetch-around* using only a 1KB instruction cache. Table 2 shows that *Fetch-around* using only a 1KB instruction cache still outperforms the other policies having 2 and 4KB ICache sizes. In addition to *Fetch-around* and *HPFirst* fetch policies, we also include the round-robin (RR) fetch policy for illustration purposes where the threads are fetched in a round-robin fashion even though it may not be an appropriate fetch technique for a real-time SMT processor. Although some improvement in HP thread slowdown (i.e. drop in percentage) is observed in these 2 policies when the ICache size is doubled from 1KB to 2KB, and quadrupled to 4KB, it is still far from being close to 9.5% in *Fetch-around* using 1KB ICache. Thus, these policies suffer a considerable amount of inter-thread interference in the ICache even when the ICache size is quadrupled. Table 3 supports this argument by showing the HP thread instruction cache hit rates. As the ICache is only used by the HP thread in *Fetch-around*, its hit rate is exactly the same as the hit rate of the single-thread model running only the HP thread. On the other hand, the hit rates in *HPFirst* and *RR* are lower than *Fetch-around* because both policies observe the LP thread interfering and evicting the HP thread cache lines. These results suggest that *Fetch-around* is much more area-efficient than the other fetch policies.

Table 2. Comparing the HP thread slowdown of *Fetch-around* using only 1KB instruction cache to *HPFirst* and *RR* policies using 2KB and 4KB instruction caches

Fetch-around 1K	HPFirst 2K	HPFirst 4K	RR 2K	RR 4K
9.5%	12.3%	11.7%	17.7%	17.2%

Table 3. HP Thread ICache hit rates

HPFirst	Fetch-around	RR
98.6%	97.6%	95.4%

4.4 Iside Dynamic Cache Energy Consumption

For each fetch policy, the dynamic energy spent in the Iside of the L1 and L2 caches is calculated during instruction fetch activities. We call this *Iside dynamic cache energy*. We measure the Iside dynamic cache energy increase in each fetch policy relative to the Iside dynamic energy consumed when the HP thread runs alone. We use Artisan 90nm SRAM [17] library to model tag and data RAM read and write energies for L1I and L2 caches.

Table 4. Percentage of Iside cache energy increase with respect to the HP thread running in single-threaded mode for 1KB instruction cache

HPFirst	Fetch-around	RR
75.2%	47%	75%

Table 4 shows the percentage energy increase in the Iside dynamic cache energy relative to the energy consumed when the HP thread runs alone. Although accessing the L2 consumes more power than the L1 due to looking up more ways and reading a wider data width (i.e. 512 bits), *Fetch-around* consumes less L2 energy than normal L2 I-side read operations by reading only 64-bits (i.e. instruction fetch width) for the LP threads. *Fetch-around* also reduces the L2 energy to some degree as the LP thread does not thrash the HP thread in the ICache, reducing the HP thread miss rate compared to *HPFirst*. This smaller miss rate translates to less L2 accesses from the HP thread, and a reduction in L2 energy. Besides, *Fetch-around* also eliminates ICache tag comparisons and dataRAM read energy for the LP thread. And further saves ICache line allocation energy by bypassing the ICache allocation for the LP thread. *Fetch-around* consumes the least amount of energy among all fetch policies at the expense of executing fewer LP thread instructions. This fact can be observed more clearly if the individual energy consumption per instruction of each thread is presented.

Table 5. Energy per Instruction (uJ)

uJ/Inst	HPFirst	Fetch-around	RR
HP Thread	34.3	28.8	34.3
LP Thread	55.3	72.6	47.8

Table 5 presents the energy consumption per HP and LP threads separately. *Fetch-around* consumes the least amount of energy per HP thread instruction even though the execution of an LP thread instruction is the most energy-hungry among all fetch policies. As the number of HP thread instructions dominate the number of LP thread instructions, having very low energy-per-HP-instruction causes the *Fetch-around* policy to obtain the lowest overall Iside cache energy consumption levels. *HPFirst* and *RR* have about the same energy-per-HP-instruction while *RR* has lower energy-per-LP-instruction than *HPFirst*. *RR* retires more LP thread instructions than *HPFirst*, and this behavior (i.e. *RR* retiring a high number of low-energy LP thread instructions and *HPFirst* retiring a low number of high-energy LP thread instructions) brings the total Iside cache energy consumption of both fetch policies to the same level.

4.5 Energy Efficiency of the Fetch-Around Policy

The best fetch policy can be determined as the one that gives higher performance (i.e. low HP thread slowdown and low LP thread CPI) and lower Iside cache energy consumption, and should minimize the product of the thread performance and Iside cache energy consumption overheads. The thread performance overhead is calculated as the weighted mean of the normalized HP Execution Time and LP Thread CPI as these two metrics contribute at different importance weights or degrees of importance into the overall performance of the real-time SMT processor. Thus, we introduce two new qualitative parameters called *HP thread degree of importance* and *LP thread degree of importance*, which can take any real number. When these two weights are equal, this means that the performance of both threads is equally important. If the HP thread degree of importance is higher than the LP thread degree of importance, the LP thread performance is sacrificed in favor of attaining higher HP thread performance. For a real-time SMT system, the HP thread degree of importance should be much greater than the LP thread degree of importance. HP Execution Time, LP Thread CPI, and Iside Cache Energy are normalized by dividing each term obtained in SMT mode by the equivalent statistic obtained when the relevant thread runs alone. The Iside Cache Energy is normalized to the Iside cache energy consumption value when the HP thread runs alone. These normalized values are always greater than 1 and represent performance and energy overhead relative to the single-thread version.

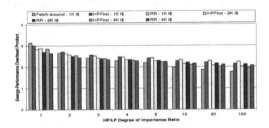

Fig. 2. Comparison of the energy-performance overhead products

Figure 2 presents the energy-performance overhead products for all fetch policies using 1KB instruction cache. The x-axis represents the ratio of the HP thread degree of importance to the LP thread degree of importance. In addition to this, the figure shows the overhead product values for *HPFirst* and *RR* policies using 2KB and 4KB instruction caches. When the ratio is 1, both threads are equally important, and there is no real advantage of using *Fetch-around* as it has the highest energy-performance overhead product. When the ratio becomes about 3, *Fetch-around* has lower overhead product than the other two policies using the same size ICache. In fact, it is even slightly better than *HPFirst* using 2KB ICache. When the ratio is 5 and above, not only *Fetch-around* is more energy-efficient than *HPFirst* and *RR* using the same ICache size but also better than *HPFirst* and *RR* using 2KB and 4KB ICaches. When it becomes 10, *Fetch-around* is 13% and 15% more efficient than *HPFirst* and *RR* for the same ICache size. When the ratio ramps up towards 100, the energy-efficiency of *Fetch-around* increases significantly. For instance, it becomes from 10% to 21% more efficient that the other two policies with equal and larger ICaches when the ratio is 100.

5 Conclusion

We propose a new SMT thread fetching policy to be used in the context of systems that have priorities associated with threads, i.e. soft real-time applications like real audio/video and tele/video conferencing. The proposed solution, *Fetch-around*, has high priority threads access the ICache while requiring low priority threads to directly access the L2 cache. This prevents the low priority threads from thrashing the ICache and degrading the performance of the high priority thread. It also allows the threads to simultaneously fetch instructions, improving the aggregate performance of the system. When considering the energy performance of the system, the *Fetch-around* policy does 13% better than the next best policy with the same cache sizes when the priority of the high performance thread is 10x that of the low priority thread. Alternatively, it achieves the same performance while requiring only a quarter to half of the instruction cache space.

References

1. Tullsen, D., Eggers, S.J., Levy, H.M.: Simultaneous multithreading: Maximizing on-chip parallelism. In: Proceedings of the 22nd Annual Intl. Symposium on Computer Architecture (June 1995)
2. Brandt, S., Nutt, G., Berk, T., Humphrey, M.: Soft real-time application execution with dynamic quality of service assurance. In: Proceedings of the 6th IEEE/IFIP International Workshop on Quality of Service (May 1998)
3. Raasch, S.E., Reinhardt, S.K.: Applications of thread prioritization in smt processors. In: Proceedings of Multithreaded Execution, Architecture and Compilation Workshop (January 1999)
4. Dorai, G.K., Yeung, D.: Transparent threads: Resource sharing in smt processors for high single-thread performance. In: Proceedings of the 2002 International Conference on Parallel Architectures and Compilation Techniques (2002)
5. Yamasaki, N.: Responsive multithreaded processor for distributed real-time processing. Journal of Robotics and Mechatronics, 44–56 (2006)
6. Falcón, A., Ramirez, A., Valero, M.: A low-complexity, high-performance fetch unit for simultaneous multithreading processors. In: Proceedings of the 10th Intl. Conference on High Performance Computer Architecture (February 2004)

7. Klauser, A., Grunwald, D.: Instruction fetch mechanisms for multipath execution processors. In: Proceedings of the 32nd Annual ACM/IEEE International Symposium on Microarchitecture (November 1999)
8. Burns, J., Gaudiot, J.L.: Quantifying the smt layout overhead, does smt pull its weight? In: Proc. Sixth Int'l Symp. High Performance Computer Architecture (HPCA) (January 2000)
9. Suh, G., Devadas, S., Rudolph, L.: Dynamic cache partitioning for simultaneous multithreading systems. In: The 13th International Conference on Parallel and Distributed Computing System (PDCS) (August 2001)
10. Tullsen, D.M., Eggers, S.J., Emer, J.S., Levy, H.M., Lo, J.L., Stamm, R.L.: Exploiting choice: instruction fetch and issue on an implementable simultaneous multithreading processor. In: Proceedings of the 23rd Annual International Symposium on Computer Architecture (ISCA) (May 1996)
11. El-Moursy, A., Albonesi, D.H.: Front-end policies for improved issue efficiency in smt processors. In: Proceedings of the 9th International Symposium on High-Performance Computer Architecture (HPCA) (February 2003)
12. Cazorla, F.J., Knijnenburg, P.M., Sakellariou, R., Fernández, E., Ramirez, A., Valero, M.: Predictable performance in smt processors. In: Proceedings of the 1st Conference on Computing Frontiers (April 2004)
13. Yamasaki, N., Magaki, I., Itou, T.: Prioritized smt architecture with ipc control method for real-time processing. In: 13th IEEE Real Time and Embedded Technology and Applications Symposium (RTAS 2007), pp. 12–21 (2007)
14. Jain, R., Hughes, C.J., Adve, S.V.: Soft real-time scheduling on simultaneous multithreaded processors. In: Proceedings of the 23rd IEEE Real-Time Systems Symposium (December 2002)
15. El-Haj-Mahmoud, A., AL-Zawawi, A.S., Anantaraman, A., Rotenberg, E.: Virtual multiprocessor: An analyzable, high-performance microarchitecture for real-time computing. In: Proceedings of the 2005 International Conference on Compilers, Architecture, and Synthesis for Embedded Systems (CASES 2005) (September 2005)
16. EEMBC, http://www.eembc.com
17. Artisan, http://www.arm.com/products/physicalip/productsservices.html

Impact of Software Bypassing on Instruction Level Parallelism and Register File Traffic

Vladimír Guzma, Pekka Jääskeläinen, Pertti Kellomäki, and Jarmo Takala

Tampere University of Technology, Department of Computer Systems
P.O. Box 527, FI-33720 Tampere, Finland
{vladimir.guzma,pekka.jaaskelainen,pertti.kellomaki,jarmo.takala}@tut.fi

Abstract. Software bypassing is a technique that allows programmer-controlled direct transfer of results of computations to the operands of data dependent operations, possibly removing the need to store some values in general purpose registers, while reducing the number of reads from the register file. Software bypassing also improves instruction level parallelism by reducing the number of false dependencies between operations caused by the reuse of registers. In this work we show how software bypassing affects cycle count and reduces register file reads and writes. We analyze previous register file bypassing methods and compare them with our improved software bypassing implementation. In addition, we propose heuristics when not to apply software bypassing to retain scheduling freedom when selecting function units for operations. The results show that we get at best 27% improvement to cycle count, as well as up to 48% less register reads and 45% less register writes with the use of bypassing.

1 Introduction

Instruction level parallelism (ILP) requires large numbers of function units (FU) and registers, which increases the size of the bypassing network used by the processor hardware to shortcut values from producer operations to consumer operations, producing architectures with high energy demands. While increase in explorable ILP allows to retain performance on lower clock speed, energy efficiency can also be improved by limiting the number of registers and register file (RF) reads and writes [1]. Therefore, approaches aiming to reduce register pressure and RF traffic by bypassing the RF and transporting results of computation from one operation to another directly provide cost savings in RF read. Some results may not need to be written to registers at all, resulting in additional savings. Allowing values to stay in FUs reduces further the need to access a general purpose RF, while keeping FUs occupied as a storage for values, thus introducing a tradeoff between the number of registers needed and number of FUs.

Programs often reuse GPRs for storing different variables. This leads to economical utilization of registers, but it also introduces artificial serialization constraints, so called "false dependencies". Some of these dependencies can be avoided in case all uses of a variable can be bypassed. Such a variable does not need to be stored in a GPR at all, thus avoiding false dependencies with

M. Berekovic, N. Dimopoulos, and S. Wong (Eds.): SAMOS 2008, LNCS 5114, pp. 23–32, 2008.

other variables sharing the same GPR. In this paper we present several improvements to the earlier RF bypassing implementations. The main improvements are listed below.

- In our work we attempt to bypass also variables with several uses in different cycles, even if not all the uses could be successfully bypassed.
- We allow variables to stay in FU result registers longer, and thus allow bypassing at later cycles, or early transports into operand register before other operands of same operation are ready. This increases the scheduling freedom of the compiler and allows for further decrease in RF traffic.
- We use a parameter we call "the look back distance" to control the aggressiveness of the software bypassing algorithm. The parameter defines the maximum distance between the producer of a value and the consumer in the scheduled code that is considered for bypassing.

2   Related Work

Effective use of RF bypassing is dependent on the architecture's division of work between the software and the hardware. In order to bypass the RF, the compiler or hardware logic must be able to determine what are the consumers of the bypassed value, effectively requiring data flow information, and how the direct operand transfer can be performed in hardware.

While hardware implementations of RF bypassing may be transparent to programmer, they also require additional logic and wiring in the processor and can only analyze a limited instruction window for the required data flow information. Hardware implementations of bypassing cannot get the benefit of reduced register pressure since the registers are already allocated to the variables when the program is executing. However, the benefits from reduced number of RF accesses are achieved. Register renaming [2] also produces the increase in available ILP from removal of false dependencies. Dynamic Strands presented in [3] are an example of an alternative hardware implementation of RF bypassing. Strands are dynamically detected atomic units of execution where registers can be replaced by direct data transports between operations. In EDGE architectures [4], operations are statically assigned to execution units, but they are scheduled dynamically in dataflow fashion. Instructions are organized in blocks, and each block specifies its register and memory inputs and outputs. Execution units are arranged in a matrix, and each unit in the matrix is assigned a sequence of operations from the block to be executed. Each operation is annotated with the address of the execution unit to which the result should be sent. Intermediate results are thus transported directly to their destinations.

Static Strands in [5] follows earlier work [3] to decrease hardware costs. Strands are found statically during compilation, and annotated to pass the information to hardware. As a result, the number of required registers is reduced already in compile time. This method was however applied only to transient operands with a single definition and single use, effectively up to 72% of dynamic integer operands, bypassing about half of them [5]. Dataflow Mini-Graphs [6] are treated

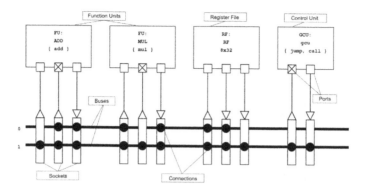

Fig. 1. Example of TTA concept

```
                  r2 -> add.t; r1 -> add.o;
                  add.r -> r3; r4 -> add.o;      r2 -> add.t; r1 -> add.o;
add r3,r1,r2      r3 -> mul.o; r3 -> add.t;      add.r -> mul.o; r4 -> add.o;
add r5,r4,r3      add.r -> r5; ...;              add.r -> add.t; ...;
mul r1,r3,r5      ...; r5 -> mul.t;              ...; add.r -> mul.t;
    (a)           mul.r -> r1; ...;              mul.r -> r1; ...;
                   (b) Without bypassing (.o and  (c) Register r3 bypassed twice and
                  .t denoting inputs and .r result)          r5 once
```

Fig. 2. Example of schedule for two *add* and one *mul* operations for Risc like architecture (a) and TTA architecture (b)(c) from Fig. 1

as atomic units by a processor. They have the interface of a single instruction, with intermediate variables alive only in the bypass network.

Architecturally visible "virtual registers" are used to reduce register pressure through bypassing in [7]. In this method, a virtual register is only a tag marking a data dependence between operations without having physical storage location in the RF. Software implementations of bypassing analyze code during compile time and pass to the processor the exact information about the sources and the destinations of bypassed data transports, thus avoiding any additional bypassing and analyzing logic in the hardware. This requires an architecture with an exposed bypass network that allows such direct programming, like the *Transport Triggered Architectures (TTA)* [8], *Synchronous Transfer Architecture (STA)* [9] or *FlexCore* [10]. The assignment of destination addresses in an EDGE architecture corresponds to software bypassing in a transport triggered setting. Software only bypassing was previously implemented for TTA architecture using the experimental MOVE framework [11] [12]. TTAs are a special type of VLIW architectures as shown on Fig. 1. They allow programs to define explicitly the operations executed in each FU, as well as to define how (with position in instruction defining bus) and when data is transferred (*moved*) to each particular port of each unit, as shown on Fig. 2(b)(c). A commercial application of the paradigm is the Maxim MAXQ general purpose microcontroller family [13].

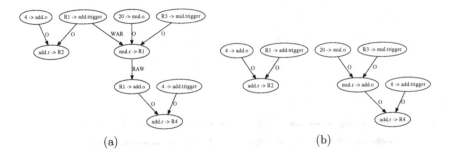

Fig. 3. DDG: a) without bypassing b) with bypassing and dead result move elimination

With the option of having registers in input and output ports of FUs, TTA allows the scheduler to move operands to FUs in different cycles and reading results several cycles after they are computed. Therefore the limiting factor for bypassing is the availability of connections between source FU and destination FUs. The MOVE compiler did not actively software bypass, but performed it only if the "opportunity arose".

3   Software Bypassing

Instruction level parallelism (ILP) is a measure of how many operations in a program can be performed simultaneously. Architectural factors that prevent achieving the maximum ILP available in a program include the number of buses, the number of FUs, as well as the size of and the number of read and write ports in RFs. Software bypassing helps to avoid some of these factors. Figure 3(a) shows a fragment of a Data Dependence Graph (DDG). In the example, $R1$ is used as an operand of the first *add*, and also as a store for the result of the *mul*, subsequently read as an operand of the second *add* ("read after write" dependence, RAW). This reuse of $R1$ creates a "write after read" dependence between read and write of $R1$, labeled WAR. When the result of the *mul* operation is bypassed directly into the *add* operation, as shown in Fig. 3(b), the WAR dependence induced by the shared register $R1$ disappears. Since the DDG fragments are now independent of each other, the scheduler has more freedom in scheduling them. Careless use of software bypassing by the instruction scheduling algorithm can also decrease performance. One of the limiting factors of ILP is the number of available FUs to perform the operations in parallel. Using the input and result registers of an FU as temporary storage renders the unit unavailable for other operations. We have identified a parameter, *look back distance*, for controlling the tradeoff. The parameter defines the distance between a move that writes a value into the RF, and a subsequent move that reads an operand from the same register. The larger the distance, the larger number of register accesses can be omitted. However, the FUs will be occupied for longer, which may increase

```
 1: function SCHEDULEOPERATION(inputs, outputs, lookBack)
 2:     success := false
 3:     cycle := 0
 4:     while not success do
 5:         ScheduleASAP(cycle, inputs)
 6:         TryBypassOperands(lookBack, inputs)
 7:         success := ScheduleASAP(cycle, outputs)
 8:         if success then
 9:             RemoveDeadResults(inputs)
10:         else
11:             Unschedule(inputs)
12:             Unschedule(outputs)
13:             cycle := cycle + 1
14:         end if
15:     end while
16: end function
```

Fig. 4. Schedule and bypass an operation

the cycle count. Conversely, smaller distance leads to smaller number of register reads and writes removed, but more efficient use of FUs.

Multiported RFs are expensive, so architects try to keep the number of register ports low. However, this can limit the achievable ILP, as register accesses may need to be spread over several cycles. Software bypassing reduces RF port requirements in two ways. A write into a RF can be completely omitted, if all the uses of the value can be bypassed to the consumer FUs (*dead result move elimination* [14]).

Reducing the number of times the result value of a FU is read from a register also reduces pressure on register ports. With less simultaneous RF reads there is need for less read ports. This reduction applies even when dead result move elimination cannot be applied because of uses of value still later in code. The additional scheduling freedom gained by eliminating false dependencies also contributes to reduction of required RF ports. The data transports which still require register reads or writes have less restrictions and could be scheduled earlier or later, thus reducing the bottleneck of limited RF ports available in single cycle.

Our instruction scheduler uses operation-based top-down list scheduling on a data dependence graph, where an operation becomes available for scheduling once all producers of its operands have been scheduled [15]. Figure 4 outlines the algorithm to schedule operands and results of a single operation. Once all the operands are ready, all input moves of operation are scheduled (Fig. 4, line 5). Afterwards, bypassing is attempted for each of the input operands that reads register, guided by the look back distance parameter (line 6). After all the input moves have been scheduled, the result moves of operation are scheduled (line 7). After an operation has been successfully scheduled, the algorithm removes writes into register that will not be read (line 9). If scheduling of result moves fails,

```
 1: function TRYBYPASSOPERANDS(inputs, lookBack)
 2:     for each candidate in inputs do
 3:         if candidate reads constant then
 4:             continue
 5:         end if
 6:         producer = producer of value read by candidate
 7:         limitCycle = producer.cycle + lookBack
 8:         if limitCycle < candidate.cycle then
 9:             continue                        ▷ Producer move too far away
10:         end if
11:         Unschedule(candidate)
12:         mergedMove := Merge(producer, candidate)
13:         success := ScheduleASAP(mergedMove)
14:         if not success then
15:             Restore producer and consumer
16:         end if
17:     end for
18:     return true
19: end function
```

Fig. 5. Software bypassing algorithm

possibly due to writer after read or write after write dependency on other already scheduled moves, all of the scheduled moves of operation are unscheduled and scheduling restarts with higher starting cycle (lines 11 to 13).

Figure 5 shows the outline of our bypassing algorithm. When considering bypassing of register, algorithm computes the distance between the producers result write into the RF and the read of a register, scheduled previously (Fig. 4, line 5). If this distance is larger than specified (Fig. 5, line 8), bypassing is not performed. Otherwise, the candidate moves is unscheduled and a new move is created with the producer's FU result port as the source and consumer's FU operand port as the destination. Such a merged move is then scheduled to as early as possible cycle with respect to data dependencies and restrictions of the resources induced by the already scheduled code. If scheduling fails, the original producer and the costumer are restored and algorithm continues with the next input operand. Figure 2 shows scheduled code without bypassing(b) and with bypassing(c).

4   Experimental Setup

In order to implement a purely software solution to RF bypassing, we based our experimental setup on the TTA architecture template. For comparing the effect of software bypassing on the number of RF reads, writes, and on ILP, we varied the look back distance used by the algorithm. We explored the effectiveness of software bypassing with limited RF port resources by defining two TTA processors with different RF resources, as described in Table 1(a). The machine

Table 1. Resources of architectures (a) and benchmark applications (b) used in our experimental setup

(a)

Machine name	"big"	"small"	"wide"
Registers in RF	128	128	128
RF read ports	10	5	5
RF write ports	5	1	1
Count of FUs	7 (11)	7 (11)	14 (22)
$\sum$ of FUs inputs	14 (27)	14 (27)	28 (54)
$\sum$ of FUs results	7 (12)	7 (12)	14 (24)
Count of buses	10	10	10

(b)

adpcm	ADPCM routine test
fft	In-place radix-4 DIT FFT
jpeg	JPEG decoding
mpeg4	Mpeg4 decoding (192x192)
Tremor	Ogg Vorbis decoding (40KB)

Table 2. Number of dynamic register reads and writes and ratio reads/writes (r/w) for small machine: a) without bypassing, b) with best bypassing

(a)

	reads	writes	r/w
adpcm	203053	172103	1.17
fft	84493	37143	2.27
jpeg	11401300	7628810	1.49
mpeg4	311915000	190901000	1.63
Tremor	301137000	207185000	1.45

(b)

	reads	writes	r/w
adpcm	122266	114219	1.07
fft	62728	27927	2.24
jpeg	5877870	4182930	1.40
mpeg4	175806000	125165000	1.40
Tremor	180258000	129774000	1.38

we refer to as "big" allowed us to see to what extent a large enough number of ports in the RF defeats the benefits of software bypassing. The machine named "small" is identical to "big" except for the much reduced number of ports in the RF. This machine should show how much the proposed software bypassing algorithm is able to reduce the need for additional RF ports while maintaining the performance. We also explored the effect of software bypassing with different number of FUs. The machine referred to as "wide" has identical number of registers and RF read and write ports as "small", but double the number of FUs as in the "small" machine. This allowed us to investigate tradeoffs in storing results longer in FUs by varying look back distance values. The benchmarks are listed in Table 1(b).

5   Results

Figure 6(a) shows the comparison for a small machine with look back distances of one to fifteen, against a schedule without software bypassing. The results show that for most of the benchmarks, the performance for different look back distances varies, with a general tendency for better results with smaller look back distance. Improvements in the cycle count for the best look back distance ranges from 27% to 16%.

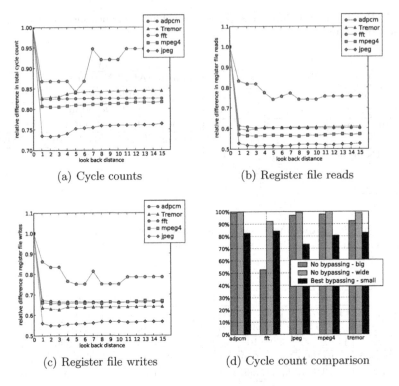

(a) Cycle counts   (b) Register file reads

(c) Register file writes   (d) Cycle count comparison

Fig. 6. Relative comparison: (a), (b), (c) small machine with different look back distances and (d) small, big and wide machines vs. small machine without bypassing (100%)

Figures 6(b) and 6(c) compare RF reads and writes for a small machine with look back distances 1–15, against a schedule without bypassing, with the *jpeg* benchmark having the highest decrease in RF reads of 48%, and RF writes of 45%, and *fft* having a smallest decrease of 25% for reads and writes. The best performing look back distance in terms of cycle count does not correspond with best results in decrease of the number of RF reads and writes. This supports our claim from Section 3, that too aggressive use of bypassing may lead to FUs being occupied for too long time, forcing the scheduler to delay other operations on the same FU, while on the other hand, saving more of the register reads and possibly writes.

Table 2(a) shows the ratio between register reads and writes without bypassing, ranging from 1.17 to 2.27. Table 2(b) shows the same ratio with best bypassing for reducing register accesses, ranging from 1.07 to 2.24. This decrease indicates that more register reads than writes were bypassed, thus not only transient variables were bypassed, but also variables with multiple reads.

Figure 6(d) takes the cycle counts of the small machine without software bypassing, and compares them with the big machine without software bypassing, the wide machine without software bypassing, and with bypassing using the best performing look back distance for the small machine for each of the benchmarks (see Fig. 6(a)). The limited number of RF read and write ports in the small machine causes an increase in cycle counts for the small machine without software bypassing due to serialization of RF accesses. In addition, added FUs in the wide machine allowed the compiler to exploit ILP better, also providing a better cycle count than the small machine.

With software bypassing, however, the cycle counts on the small machine are in most cases smaller than on the big machine and the wide machine, with *jpeg* having the highest decrease of 24% compared to the big machine. The loop-oriented *fft* benchmark is an exception. This is due to the current bypassing algorithm being unable to handle variable uses crossing loop boundaries. There-fore, the RF bottleneck could be avoided poorly in this case due to the need to fill the FUs at the beginning of the loop and read the results to GPRs at the end of the loop. However, the presented software bypassing algorithm decreased cycle count for *fft* by 16%, narrowing the gap between the big and the small machines from 48%, without bypassing, to 32% with bypassing.

6   Conclusions

This work explored some of the benefits that software bypassing offers to improve performance and reduce the cost of embedded applications implemented using TTA processors. In particular, we explored the effect of the bypassing look back distance on performance, and showed that using software bypassing, an archi-tecture with a limited number of RF ports can outperform an architecture with more RF ports or additional FUs without software bypassing. We also showed that while small look back distance leads to higher savings in cycle counts, larger distance leads to saving more register reads and writes.

In the future we plan to explore the possibilities of software bypassing in global instruction scheduling and cyclic scheduling, bypassing whole subgraphs of data dependence graph atomically. We predict that software bypassing is most beneficial when done before or during register allocation, which will be verified by experiments. In addition, we plan to evaluate the effect of reduced number of RF reads and writes on energy savings.

This work was supported by the Academy of Finland, project 205743.

References

1. Hoogerbrugge, J., Corporaal, H.: Register file port requirements of Transport Trig-gered Architectures. In: MICRO 27: Proceedings of the 27th annual international symposium on Microarchitecture, pp. 191–195. ACM Press, New York (1994)
2. Patterson, D.A., Hennessy, J.L.: Computer Organization and Design: The Hard-ware/Software Interface. Morgan Kaufmann, San Francisco (1998)
3. Sassone, P.G., Wills, D.S.: Dynamic strands: Collapsing speculative dependence chains for reducing pipeline communication. In: Proc. IEEE/ACM Int. Symp. Mi-croarchitecture, pp. 7–17. IEEE Computer Society, Washington (2004)

4. Burger, D., Keckler, S.W., McKinley, K.S., Dahlin, M., John, L.K., Lin, C., Moore, C.R., Burrill, J., McDonald, R.G., Yoder, W.: The TRIPS Team: Scaling to the end of silicon with EDGE architectures. Computer 37(7), 44–55 (2004)

5. Sassone, P.G., Wills, D.S., Loh, G.H.: Static strands: Safely exposing dependence chains for increasing embedded power efficiency. Trans. on Embedded Computing Sys. 6(4), 24 (2007)

6. Bracy, A., Prahlad, P., Roth, A.: Dataflow mini-graphs: Amplifying superscalar capacity and bandwidth. In: MICRO 37: Proceedings of the 37th annual IEEE/ACM International Symposium on Microarchitecture, pp. 18–29. IEEE Computer Society, Washington (2004)

7. Yan, J., Zhang, W.: Virtual registers: Reducing register pressure without enlarging the register file. In: De Bosschere, K., Kaeli, D., Stenström, P., Whalley, D., Ungerer, T. (eds.) HiPEAC 2007. LNCS, vol. 4367, pp. 57–70. Springer, Heidelberg (2007)

8. Corporaal, H.: Microprocessor Architectures: from VLIW to TTA. John Wiley & Sons, Chichester (1997)

9. Cichon, G., Robelly, P., Seidel, H., Bronzel, M., Fettweis, G.: Compiler scheduling for STA-processors. In: PARELEC 2004: Proceedings of the international conference on Parallel Computing in Electrical Engineering, pp. 45–60. IEEE Computer Society, Washington (2004)

10. Thuresson, M., Sjalander, M., Bjork, M., Svensson, L., Larsson-Edefors, P., Stenstrom, P.: Flexcore: Utilizing exposed datapath control for efficient computing. In: Proc. Int. Conf. on Embedded Computer Systems: Architectures, Modeling and Simulation, Samos, Greece, pp. 18–25 (2007)

11. Corporaal, H., Mulder, H.J.: Move: a framework for high-performance processor design. In: Proc. ACM/IEEE Conf. Supercomputing, Albuquerque, NM, pp. 692–701 (1991)

12. Janssen, J., Corporaal, H.: Partitioned register file for TTAs. In: Proc. 28th Annual Workshop on Microprogramming (MICRO-28), pp. 303–312 (1996)

13. Maxim Corporation: MAXQ microcontroller home page (2007), http://www.maxim-ic.com/products/microcontrollers/maxq.cfm

14. Corporaal, H., Hoogerbrugge, J.: Code generation for Transport Triggered Architectures. In: Code Generation for Embedded Processors, pp. 240–259. Springer, Heidelberg (1995)

15. Aho, A.V., Sethi, R., Ullman, J.D.: Compilers: Principles, Techniques, and Tools. Addison-Wesley Longman Publishing Co., Amsterdam (1986)

Scalable Architecture for Prefix Preserving Anonymization of IP Addresses

Anthony Blake and Richard Nelson

University of Waikato
School of Computing and Mathematical Sciences
Hamilton, New Zealand
{amb33,richardn}@cs.waikato.ac.nz

Abstract. This paper describes a highly scalable architecture based on field-programmable gate-array (FPGA) technology for prefix-preserving anonymization of IP addresses at increasingly high network line rates. The Crypto-PAn technique, with the Advanced Encryption Standard (AES) as the underlying pseudo-random function, is fully mapped into reconfigurable hardware. A 32 Gb/s fully-pipelined AES engine was developed and used to prototype the Crypto-PAn architecture. The prototype was implemented on a Xilinx Virtex-4 device achieving a worst-case Ethernet throughput of 8 Gb/s using 141 block RAM's and 4262 logic cells. This is considerably faster than software implementations which generally achieve much less than 100 Mb/s throughput. A technology-independent analysis is presented to explore the scalability of the architecture to higher multi-gigabit line-rates.

1 Introduction

The availability of real-world Internet traffic traces is essential for network research such as performance analysis, protocol development and traffic characterization. The development or confirmation of most advances in this field are only possible with the use of actual network data made available to the research community. Unfortunately, network operators are often reluctant to make traces publicly available because of privacy and legal concerns. In particular, information about the sender and receiver present in the packet headers may reveal confidential information about commercial organisations, or private information about individuals. Furthermore, local, state or national laws may restrict network monitoring and access to network records[1].

When network operators release traces to the public, several steps are usually taken to increase compliance with the law and to minimize the risk of privacy intrusions. The packets are usually truncated soon after the transport layer, as the actual payload isn't required in many cases, and can contain sensitive or private information. Additionally, the IP addresses in the packet headers are usually anonymized before the traces are released[2]. A simple approach is to use a random one-to-one mapping, however this approach loses information encoded in the prefixes. A common prefix of any two IP addresses is important

M. Berekovic, N. Dimopoulos, and S. Wong (Eds.): SAMOS 2008, LNCS 5114, pp. 33–42, 2008.
© Springer-Verlag Berlin Heidelberg 2008

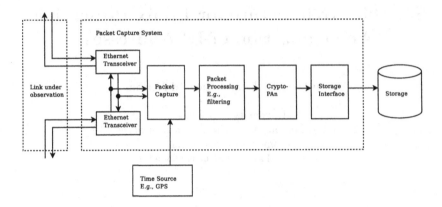

Fig. 1. Network traffic monitoring system with Crypto-PAn anonymization module

in several areas of research, such as routing performance analysis or clustering of end systems[3]. Thus the use of such schemes has been largely deprecated in favour of prefix preserving schemes, such as Crypto-PAn[4].

Crypto-PAn provides a one-to-one mapping between the original IP address and the anonymized IP address, while preserving the prefix. That is, if two original IP addresses share a k-bit prefix, then their anonymized mappings also share a k-bit prefix. Additionally, Crypto-PAn enables consistency to be maintained across traces. The same original IP addresses in different traces are mapped to the same anonymized IP address if the same secret key is used, and thus distributed and parallel anonymization is possible. These properties have made Crypto-PAn the most desirable scheme to use, however Crypto-PAn is computationally expensive due to the computation of one AES 128-bit block cipher for every bit of the IP address.

Existing implementations of Crypto-PAn are software-based. The original implementation of Crypto-PAn was able to process 10 Kp/s (thousands of packets per second) on an 800 MHz Intel Pentium III[4], and an implementation included with the libtrace[5] trace processing library obtains a throughput of 211 Kp/s running on a AMD Opteron 250, with pre-computation of prefixes. Assuming worst-case Ethernet conditions, the throughput falls short of 100 Mb/s line-rates, which has a packet throughput of 312.5 Kp/s. Thus, software implementations performing anonymization on-line must drop packets when throughput exceeds capabilities, and off-line implementations pose a security or legal risk storing raw traces for a period of time.

A hardware implementation of a prefix-preserving anonymization scheme has been reported[6], however this scheme does not guarantee a one-to-one mapping between original IP addresses and the anonymized IP addresses. Some IP addresses may overlap, however this scheme has the benefits of relatively low computational requirements.

The aim of this paper is to provide a scalable hardware-based Crypto-PAn architecture capable of anonymizing current and future network throughput's at line-rate. The architecture is designed to be compatible with existing software Crypto-PAn implementations, so that highly distributed network monitoring is possible using a mix of hardware monitors for high-speed links, and software monitors for low-speed links, while maintaining consistency across the entire system.

The contributions of this paper are as follows:

- a hardware architecture is presented (Section 2);
- a technology independent model of the system is provided, so that performance or area required can be predicted (Section 3);
- a 32 Gb/s fully pipelined AES core is presented (Section 4);
- a prototype of the architecture, using two 32 Gb/s AES engines is discussed (Section 4);
- performance results are presented (Section 5).

2   Architecture

The Crypto-PAn module is designed to be integrated into a network traffic monitoring system. These systems typically consist of a passive link tap, a packet capture device such as an Endace Measurement Systems DAG card[7], and a storage system (Figure 1). For the purposes of research, network traffic monitors generally only store truncated packet headers[8,9,10], or aggregated flow records[11,12]. In such systems, the proposed Crypto-PAn module can be integrated into the datapath of the packet capture device, performing anonymization in real-time before the records are exported to the storage system, eliminating the need for off-line processing.

2.1   Crypto-PAn Scheme

The Crypto-PAn function, $F(a)$, is defined as follows[4]:

$$F(a) = \mathcal{L}(\mathcal{R}(\mathcal{P}(a), \kappa)) \oplus a \qquad (1)$$

where $a = a_1 a_2 \ldots a_{32}$ is the original IPv4 address and $\mathcal{L}$ returns the least significant bit (LSB). $\mathcal{R}$ is the pseudo-random function, in this case AES, with secret key κ. $\mathcal{P}$ is a padding function that expands $a_1 a_2 \ldots a_{32}$ into a 128-bit string in order to match the block size of the AES cipher. The exclusive-or operation is represented by the $\oplus$ symbol.

For a more detailed treatment of the algorithm, including proofs, see [4].

2.2   Hardware Architecture

Figure 2 is a block diagram of the Crypto-PAn architecture, showing the primary components. The module must first be initialized with a 256-bit secret key; 128-bits are used for key-expansion by the AES engines, while the remaining 128-bits are encrypted with an AES engine, and the encrypted block used as the pad.

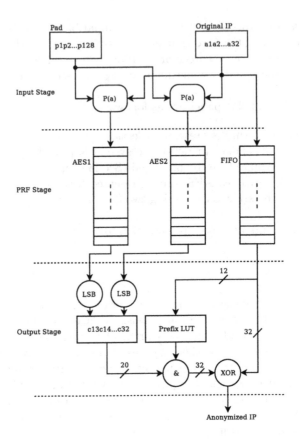

Fig. 2. Hardware Architecture of Crypto-PAn module

Our design divides the Crypto-PAn module into three stages: input stage, pseudo-random function, and output stage. The design reduces the heavy AES computation by pre-computing a number of bits and storing them in a look-up table, in order to reduce the hardware requirements.

In the input stage, original IP addresses are first loaded into a register. For each bit n which has not been pre-computed, the bits $a_1a_2\ldots a_n$ are padded out to 128-bits with the pre-determined pad, and passed to an AES engine. Because there is no data dependence between the computation for each bit of the anonymized IP address, AES engines operating in parallel can be utilised to increase throughput.

The AES engines contained in the pseudo-random function stage may be multi-cycle or fully pipelined. In the case that the AES engines are multi-cycle, a register is used to pass the original IP address through to the output stage. The latency of fully pipelined AES engines could be up to 30 cycles or more, in which case it could be possible that multiple original IP addresses are in-flight simultaneously in the AES pipeline during a given cycle. In this case, a FIFO may be required to pass the original IP addresses along with the prefixes being encrypted.

There are two constraints on the number of AES engines that may be utilised in parallel. Firstly, the sum of the number of AES engines and the number of prefix bits pre-computed should not exceed the length of the IP address, in this case, 32. If more parallelism is needed, multiple Crypto-PAn modules should be instantiated in parallel. Secondly, if the number of IP address bits divided by the number of AES engines in parallel is not a whole number, this would result in "bubbles" in the pseudo-random function stage, unless extra hardware is added at the input and output stages to process two IP addresses in the same cycle. Both of these cases should be avoided.

The output stage combines the appropriate bits of the AES engine results into a register until all the bits necessary have been obtained. Only the least significant bit of the AES engine result is used, and multiplexers are used to select AES engine outputs into the correct bit register. A number of bits from the original IP address are used to look-up an anonymized prefix from a table of pre-computed results. The pre-computed portion of the IP address and the remaining part that required pseudo-random function computation are combined and the exclusive-or operation is performed with the original IP address. The result is the anonymized IP address with the prefix preserved.

A change in secret key would require all the data in the pre-computed prefix look-up table be re-loaded, the AES engines would require key-expansion to be performed, and the pad would need to be encrypted. The computation of prefixes for the look-up table, key-expansion for the AES engines, and the calculation of the pad can be performed on a work-station off-line, and the data loaded into the Crypto-PAn module via a control bus, or through partial re-configuration.

3   Technology-Independent Analysis

We quantify the maximum throughput of the Crypto-PAn architecture T_{max}, in IP addresses per second, by providing technology independent algebraic expressions. The equations may be used to estimate the resource usage given a target throughput, or to predict the maximum throughput of a given device. T_{max} is expressed as a function of T_{aes}, the throughput of an AES engine (in bits per second), and N_{aes}, the number of AES engines utilised in parallel. The number of pre-computed bits, $N_{precomp}$, is also used to determine T_{max}. Equation 2 expresses T_{max} in terms of IPv4 addresses per second:

$$T_{max} = \frac{T_{aes}N_{aes}}{128(32 - N_{precomp})}, \quad \text{for } 1 \le N_{aes} \le 32 - N_{precomp} \qquad (2)$$

where T_{aes} is expressed in bits per second. The throughput of an AES engine instance is divided by the block size, 128 bits, as one block cipher is required for every bit of the IP address. The AES throughput is further divided by the number of IP address bits remaining after accounting for the prefix bits that have been pre-computed. Finally, the total throughput is multiplied by the number of AES instances operating in parallel, N_{aes}. The number of AES engines operating in parallel must be less than or equal to the number of IP address bits remaining after prefix pre-computation. If $(32 - N_{precomp}) \div N_{aes} \notin \mathbb{W}$, then additional circuitry is required to process two IP addresses in the same cycle. Otherwise, AES engines will be under utilised.

To determine the maximum number of AES engines that may be instantiated in parallel, we assume that the modules shown in Figure 2, with the exception of the AES engines, use a constant number of logic cells, L_{const}. This is used to determine one maximum value for the number of AES engines based on the logic resources available on a particular device:

$$N_{aes-max-logic} = \left\lfloor \frac{L_{total} - L_{const}}{L_{aes}} \right\rfloor \tag{3}$$

where L_{aes} is the logic required for a single instance of the AES engine, and L_{total} is the total logic available on the device. Another possible value for the maximum number of AES instances, $N_{aes-max-bram}$, is derived from the availability of block RAM's on the target device:

$$N_{bram-avail} = N_{total-bram} - N_{const-bram} - N_{precomp-bram} \tag{4}$$

$$N_{aes-max-bram} = \left\lfloor \frac{N_{bram-avail}}{N_{aes-bram}} \right\rfloor \tag{5}$$

where $N_{aes-bram}$ is the number of block RAM's required to instantiate a single AES engine, $N_{total-bram}$ is the total number of block RAM's available on the device, and $N_{const-bram}$ is the constant number of block RAM's used by modules other than the pre-computation module and the AES engines. The calculation of $N_{aes-max-bram}$ also depends on the number of block RAM's used by the pre-computation module, $N_{precomp-bram}$, which is defined as follows:

$$N_{precomp-bram} = \left\lceil \frac{N_{precomp-bits} \times 2^{N_{precomp-bits}}}{D_{bram}} \right\rceil \tag{6}$$

where $N_{precomp-bits}$ is defined as the number of bits of the prefix to be pre-computed, and D_{bram} is the density of an individual block RAM on the target device. Thus, $N_{precomp-bram}$ is the number of block RAM's needed to pre-compute $N_{precomp-bits}$.

We determine the maximum number of AES engines possible with the constraints placed on logic and block memory resources, with Equations 3 and 4, as follows:

$$N_{aes-max} = \min\left(N_{aes-max-logic}, N_{aes-max-bram}\right) \tag{7}$$

The throughput of the Crypto-PAn engine T_{max}, in IPv4 addresses per second, can be related to the Ethernet link speed, T_{eth}. The minimum sized Ethernet frame is defined to be 64 bytes, with eight bytes of preamble and start of frame delimiter, and eight bytes of inter-frame gap. Thus, in the worst case, a packet is received every 80 bytes. The relationship between T_{max} and T_{eth} is as follows:

$$T_{eth} = \frac{80 \times 8 \times T_{max}}{2 \times 2} \tag{8}$$

where T_{eth} is expressed in bits per second. As there are two IPv4 addresses in a packet to be anonymized, and a link is assumed to be a full-duplex link with two directions, T_{max} is divided by four.

In Section 5, these equations are utilized to estimate the throughput and area of the Crypto-PAn module with two fully pipelined implementations of AES, on a Xilinx Virtex-4 XC4VFX60-10 device.

4   Device-Specific Mapping

We developed a prototype for the proposed architecture using a development board populated with a Xilinx Virtex-4 XC4VFX60-10 FPGA and two gigabit Ethernet transceivers. A fully-pipelined 32 Gb/s encryption only AES engine was developed for the prototype.

4.1   AES Engine

The Advanced Encryption Standard (AES) was standardised by the US Federal Institute of Processing Standards (FIPS) in 2001[13]. The algorithm is a symmetric block cipher, processing data in blocks of 128 bits. The AES standard supports cipher keys of sizes 128, 192 and 256 bits. Since the introduction of the standard, many implementations in reconfigurable logic have been documented, some focusing on high-throughput[14,15], while others were optimized for minimum area.

Our AES design is fully-pipelined and highly parametrized. It supports the following parameters:

- All the key sizes specified for the standard: 128, 192 and 256-bit;
- Encryption and/or decryption;
- Substitution boxes can be implemented with either logic or dual-ported block RAM's;
- Key-expansion performed in hardware, or off-line on an embedded microprocessor or workstation.

The AES datapath consists of ten rounds, each of which contains three pipeline cuts, designed to reach a clock rate of 250 MHz on the target device. Thus the AES engine has a latency of 31 cycles. The datapath is the width of a 128-bit AES block, and thus at 250 MHz, has a throughput of 32 Gb/s.

The primary difference between our design and others[14,15,16,17] is the implementation of substitution boxes (S-Boxes). We instantiate dual-ported block RAM's by hand so that each block RAM implements two S-Boxes, where as other designs don't appear to utilize both ports available on some devices block RAM's.

4.2   Crypto-PAn Implementation

The Crypto-PAn design was prototyped with two 32 Gb/s AES-128 encryption only engines, and a twelve bit pre-computed prefix look-up table. Key expansion for the AES engine, encryption of the secret pad, and the pre-computation of the prefix look-up table was performed offline on a workstation.

The number of block RAM's required for the pre-computation look-up table can be determined with Equation 6. With the Xilinx XC4VFX60-10, $D_{bram} =$ 18kbit, and thus the look-up table requires three block RAM's.

The design was synthesized with Synplicity Synplify Pro and Xilinx ISE 8.2, with a hardware test-bench and an integrated logic analyzer (Xilinx Chipscope). Verification was performed with a test-bench consisting of a test vector generator, checker and error counter. The test vectors used were those distributed with Jinliang Fan's software implementation of Crypto-PAn. Furthermore, the output of the Crypto-PAn unit was observed with the integrated logic analyzer.

The prototype design, including the test-bench, used 4308 logic cells and 143 block RAM's. 138 block RAM's were used by the two AES engines, two block RAM's were used by the test-bench, and three block RAM's were used by the look-up table. The Crypto-PAn module required 4262 logic cells, 4124 of which (96%) were used by the AES engines. On the Xilinx XC4VFX60-10 device, the Crypto-PAn module requires 8% of the available logic cells, and 61% of the block RAM resources.

5   Performance Results

The resulting maximum throughput of the Crypto-PAn module, in terms of IPv4 addresses per second, can be computed using Equation 2. Using $N_{aes} = 2$, $T_{aes} = 32 \times 10^9$, and $N_{precomp} = 12$, the maximum throughput is determined to be 25×10^6 IP addresses/second. The maximum worst case Ethernet line-rate able to be processed can then be determined using Equation 8. With $T_{max} = 25 \times 10^6$, $T_{eth} = 4 \times 10^9$ b/s, enabling four gigabit Ethernet links (8 Gb/s total throughput) to be monitored while guaranteeing no packet loss.

6   Conclusion

We have described how prefix-preserving anonymization can be used in traffic monitoring systems to increase compliance with the law and to reduce the risk of private or confidential information being inferred from the headers of IP packet traces. Having found that current software-based solutions of Crypto-PAn lack the ability to process traffic at even 100 Mb/s line-rates, we provide a scalable hardware architecture capable of supporting multi-gigabit line-rates and beyond.

A 32 Gb/s fully pipelined AES engine was described, and in conjunction with partial pre-computation of prefixes, was used to develop a prototype capable of sanitizing four 1 Gb/s Ethernet links at line-rate. The prototype was synthesized for a Xilinx XC4VFX60-10 FPGA, and used 4262 logic cells and 141 block RAM's.

Future work includes extending the work to support 128-bit IPv6 addresses. The technology independent analysis also showed that smaller multi-cycle AES engines operating in parallel with logic/block RAM ratios closer to that of the target device would utilize resources better and maximise throughput.

References

1. Sicker, D., Ohm, P., Grunwald, D.: Legal issues surrounding monitoring during network research. In: Proceedings of the 7th ACM SIGCOMM conference on Internet measurement, pp. 141–148 (2007)
2. University of Waikato: Waikato Internet Traffic Storage
3. Krishnamurthy, B., Wang, J.: On network-aware clustering of Web clients. In: Proceedings of the conference on Applications, Technologies, Architectures, and Protocols for Computer Communication, pp. 97–110 (2000)
4. Fan, J., Xu, J., Ammar, M., Moon, S.: Prefix-preserving IP address anonymization: measurement-based security evaluation and a new cryptography-based scheme. Computer Networks 46(2), 253–272 (2004)
5. WAND Network Research Group: libtrace
6. Ubik, S., Zejdl, P., Halak, J.: Real-time anonymization in passive network monitoring. In: Proceedings of the Third International Conference on Networking and Services (2007)
7. Cleary, J., Donnelly, S., Graham, I., McGregor, A., Pearson, M.: Design principles for accurate passive measurement. In: Proceedings of Passive and Active Measurement Workshop (2000)
8. Nelson, R., Lawson, D., Lorier, P.: Analysis of long duration traces. ACM SIGCOMM Computer Communication Review 35(1), 45–52 (2005)
9. Fraleigh, C., Moon, S., Lyles, B., Cotton, C., Khan, M., Moll, D., Rockell, R., Seely, T., Diot, S.: Packet-level traffic measurements from the Sprint IP backbone. Network, IEEE 17(6), 6–16 (2003)
10. Iannaccone, G., Bhattacharyya, S., Taft, N., Diot, C.: Always-on monitoring of IP backbones: Requirements and design challenges. Sprint ATL Research Report RR03-ATL-071821, Sprint ATL (2003)
11. Schuehler, D., Lockwood, J.: TCP-Splitter: A TCP/IP flow monitor in reconfigurable hardware. In: Proceedings. 10th Symposium on High Performance Interconnects, pp. 127–131 (2002)
12. Yusuf, S., Luk, W., Sloman, M., Dulay, N., Lupu, E., Brown, G.: Reconfigurable Architecture for Network Flow Analysis. IEEE Transactions on Very Large Scale Integration (VLSI) Systems 16(1), 57–65 (2008)
13. FIPS, P.: 197. Advanced Encryption Standard (AES) 26 (2001)
14. Hodjat, A., Verbauwhede, I.: A 21.54 Gbits/s fully pipelined AES processor on FPGA. In: 12th Annual IEEE Symposium on Field-Programmable Custom Computing Machines. FCCM 2004, (2004), pp. 308–309 (2004)
15. Saggese, G., Mazzeo, A., Mazzocca, N., Strollo, A.: An FPGA-based performance analysis of the unrolling, tiling, and pipelining of the AES algorithm. In: Y. K. Cheung, P., Constantinides, G.A. (eds.) FPL 2003. LNCS, vol. 2778, pp. 292–302. Springer, Heidelberg (2003)

16. Standaert, F., Rouvroy, G., Quisquater, J., Legat, J.: Efficient Implementation of Rijndael Encryption in Reconfigurable Hardware: Improvements and Design Trade-offs. In: D.Walter, C., Koç, Ç.K., Paar, C. (eds.) CHES 2003. LNCS, vol. 2779, pp. 334–350. Springer, Heidelberg (2003)
17. McLoone, M., McCanny, J.: High Performance Single-Chip FPGA Rijndael Algorithm Implementations. In: Koç, Ç.K., Naccache, D., Paar, C. (eds.) CHES 2001. LNCS, vol. 2162, pp. 65–76. Springer, Heidelberg (2001)

Arithmetic Design on Quantum-Dot Cellular Automata Nanotechnology

Ismo Hänninen and Jarmo Takala

Tampere University of Technology,
Department of Computer Systems
PO BOX 553, FI-33101 Tampere, Finland
{ismo.hanninen,jarmo.takala}@tut.fi
http://www.tkt.cs.tut.fi/index-english.html

Abstract. Quantum-dot cellular automata nanotechnology promises molecular digital circuits with ultra-high clock frequencies, to replace the traditional approaches reaching their physical limits. Although large scale utilization requires still several breakthroughs, there has been serious effort in digital design on this sunrise technology. This review describes the basic concepts of the nanotechnology and the most important existing designs, providing new research directions for the digital community.

Keywords: Nanotechnology, digital design, arithmetic.

1 Introduction

Quantum-dot cellular automata (QCA) is a promising nanotechnology, which offers ways to reach molecular circuit densities and clock frequencies surpassing traditional digital technologies by several orders of magnitude. The concept was introduced in early 1990s [1, 2] and has been demonstrated in laboratory environment with small proof-of-concept systems [3, 4, 5], but large scale utilization requires several breakthroughs in the manufacturing and design methods. The revolutionary operating principle of QCA promises outstanding energy efficiency and performance, which has evoked considerable interest in the digital community and resulted in early effort to design logic circuits, showing the potential gains and challenges, although the implementation technologies do not yet exist.

This paper presents a review of digital design on QCA, concentrating on the state-of-the-art computer arithmetic, and is organized as follows: Section 2 summarizes the background of the nanotechnology, and Section 3 describes the existing design proposals and some prospective research directions. Section 4 concludes the paper with discussion of the general challenges of nanotechnology design work.

2 Background of QCA Nanotechnology

The intuitive QCA concept is based on bistable cellular automata, where the information storage and transport utilizes the local position of charged particles

M. Berekovic, N. Dimopoulos, and S. Wong (Eds.): SAMOS 2008, LNCS 5114, pp. 43–52, 2008.
© Springer-Verlag Berlin Heidelberg 2008

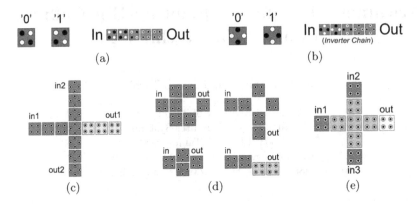

Fig. 1. QCA primitives: a) type 1 cell and wire, b) type 2 cell and wire, c) coplanar wire crossing, d) inverters, and e) three-input majority gate

inside a small section of the circuit (there is no electrical particle current at all). This QCA cell has a limited number of quantum-dots, which the particles can occupy, and these dots are arranged such that the cell can have only two polarizations (two degenerate quantum mechanical ground states), representing binary value zero or one. A cell can switch between the two states by letting the charged particles tunnel between the dots quantum mechanically.

The cells exchange information by classical Coulombic interaction. An input cell forced to a polarization drives the next cell into the same polarization, since this combination of states has minimum energy in the electric field between the charged particles in neighboring cells. Information is copied and propagated in a wire consisting of the cell automata. Figures 1(a) and 1(b) show the available two cell types and the corresponding wires, which can be positioned to have minimal interaction with each other. This enables a *coplanar wire crossing* shown in Fig. 1(c), where the crossing wires are on the same fabrication layer. Also a traditional *multi-layer crossing* can be constructed, but it requires an implementation technology with many active QCA layers on top of each other.

The QCA cells can form the primitive logic gates shown in Figs. 1(d) and 1(e). The inverter is usually formed by placing the cells with only their corners touching, effectively inverting the electrostatic interaction, since the quantum-dots of different polarizations are misaligned between the cells. Other gates are usually based on a three-input majority gate, settling into minimum energy between the input and output cells: the gate performs the two-input AND-operation when the third input is fixed at logical zero, and the two-input OR-operation when the third input is fixed at logical one. Together with the inverter this forms a universal logic set, capable of implementing any combinatorial computation. [1].

A clocking mechanism determines via an electric field when the cells are unpolarized, latch their input values, and start driving other cells. It is used both for designing sequential circuits and forcing the circuit to stay in the quantum mechanical ground state, which represents the correct computation result

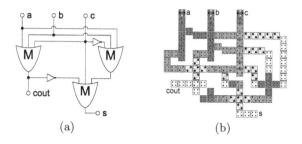

Fig. 2. Full adder: a) optimal majority logic structure [7] and b) QCA layout [9] (Copyright IEEE)

and successful signal propagation. The active phase of the clock is applied to a small section of the circuit at each instant, with two possible approaches: *zone clocking*, where the cell array is divided into discrete zones controlled by several clocks, different clock phases for adjacent zones [2], and *wave clocking*, where an inhomogeneous, smoothly graded electric field is propagated over the QCA plane [6]. Clocking leads to digital circuits, which are inherently pipelined on very fine-grained level, and provides also energy for true signal gain.

3   Design Proposals

There has been a considerable amount of research into circuits on QCA nanotechnology, aiming to solve the challenges of general digital design.

3.1   Basic Components

Full Adder. The papers introducing the QCA concept contained already sketches of a combinatorial full adder unit [1], followed by a more feasible clocked design in [2], consisting of five majority gates and three inverters. An optimal majority logic full adder, shown in Fig. 2(a), consists of only three majority gates and two inverters, producing the sum s and the carry c_{out} as follows [7]:

$$s = M[\overline{c_{out}}, c_{in}, M(a, b, \overline{c_{in}})] ; \tag{1}$$
$$c_{out} = M(a, b, c_{in}) ; \tag{2}$$
$$M(a, b, c) = (a \wedge b) \vee (b \wedge c) \vee (a \wedge c) \tag{3}$$

where a and b are the input operands, c_{in} is the input carry, and $M()$ is the majority function with $\wedge$ and $\vee$ denoting the logical AND and OR operations. A general three-variable majority logic optimization was developed in [8].

The QCA designs are pipelined on the sub-gate level, since reliable operation requires that only a small section of the circuit is switching at one time. The zone clocked full adder layout shown in Fig. 2(b) forms a two-stage pipeline, which can compute with two different operands in parallel. The total latency of the sum is two full QCA clock cycles (each consisting of four clock fractions), while the carry is computed in one clock cycle. This is beneficial for designing larger arithmetic units, since the propagating carries usually limit the performance. [9].

Register. The nanotechnology prevents the construction of pure combinatorial logic, but on the other hand, the implementation of registers is very straightforward: a wire of QCA cells placed on several clocking zones acts as a D-type flip-flop, or a shift register, separating and delaying the bits with the pipeline stages. Other latch and flip-flop types can be similarly constructed, based on the inherent self-latching of the technology, with some additional logic gates. [10].

State Machine. The basic construct of all sequential logic, the state machine, has not been much utilized in current QCA designs. Small units are easily constructed, but for larger designs with the traditional Mealy or Moore approach, the nanotechnology presents a considerable challenge: the logic computing the next state and the feedback wiring cause always a significant delay, before the new state can be stored back into the register bank. This delay, caused by the layout translating directly into timing requirements, slows down the update speed of the state transitions, wasting a growing number of clock cycles, proportional to the number of states. More research effort is needed here, possibly coming up with a beneficial distributed state machine scheme. [11, 10].

3.2   Multi Bit Adders

Serial And Ripple Carry Adder. Multi bit addition on QCA nanotechnology was first sketched with a standard bit-serial adder [12, 13] and a ripple carry adder (RCA) [7, 14], directly based on the full adder component, with the logical structures shown in Figs. 3(a) and 3(c). Radius-of-effect induced noise coupling was first considered in the designs proposed in [15], and we presented more cost-efficient QCA layouts shown in Figs. 3(b) and 3(d) [9].

The performance of the basic n-bit adders was compared in [16], showing that the QCA serial and the ripple carry adder have exactly the same latency, which is linearly proportional to the operand word length. This is due to the pipelined operation of the full adder units in both structures. However, the throughput is very different, since the serial adder computes a single addition, while the pipelined ripple carry adder computes several additions in parallel, completing a result on every clock cycle. The circuit area of the serial adder is constant, while the pipelined RCA unit grows *quadratically*, in proportion to the operand length. [9].

Carry Lookahead Adder And Condition Sum Adder. The carry lookahead adder (CLA) and the condition sum adder (CSA, a case of the carry-select approach), were adapted to QCA and analyzed in detail in [17]. These designs with reduced carry rippling were shown to have also reduced latency, but due to the pipelined operation, the throughput is the same as the simple ripple carry

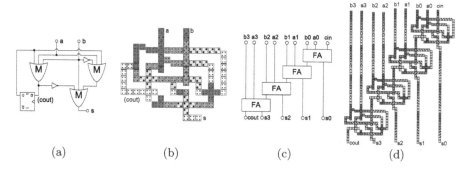

Fig. 3. Serial adder: a) logical structure and b) QCA layout (Copyright IEEE), and ripple carry adder (4-bit case): c) logical structure and d) QCA layout (Copyright IEEE)

adder has. An interesting result was to show that a CLA unit with block size of four bits can actually have a smaller circuit area than a corresponding RCA unit (on traditional technologies, the CLA is usually much larger than the RCA). Both the CLA and CSA structures suffer from considerable layout complexity, and very long wires spanning across the design.

Advanced Structures. The studied adder structures do not quite match the characteristics of QCA nanotechnology, one reason being the wiring overhead costing heavily in circuit area. Parallel prefix adders might have the beneficial properties, since they can be laid out in a regular systolic array and compute in a highly parallel manner, and there are other approaches that have not been tried: divergent number systems and redundancy schemes might match the technology well, and sequential control might offer adaptive tolerance against circuit faults.

3.3 Multipliers

Binary multiplication on QCA nanotechnology has been based on the direct paper-and-pencil algorithm, with n-bit input operands $A = (a_{n-1}, \ldots, a_1, a_0)$ and $B = (b_{n-1}, \ldots, b_1, b_0)$, resulting in a $2n$-bit output $M = (m_{2n-1}, \ldots, m_1, m_0)$, where $a_0, b_0,$ and m_0 are the least significant bits, respectively:

$$
\begin{array}{r}
a_{n-1} \quad \cdots \quad a_1 \quad a_0 \\
\times \quad\quad\quad b_{n-1} \quad \cdots \quad b_1 \quad b_0 \\
\hline
a_{n-1}b_0 \quad \cdots \quad a_1b_0 \;\; a_0b_0 \\
a_{n-1}b_1 \quad \cdots \quad a_1b_1 \;\; a_0b_1 \quad 0 \\
\vdots \quad\quad\quad 0 \quad 0 \\
+ \; a_{n-1}b_{n-1} \cdots a_1b_{n-1} \;\; a_0b_{n-1} \quad 0 \quad 0 \quad 0 \\
\hline
m_{2n-1} \quad \cdots \quad\quad \cdots \quad\quad \cdots \quad\quad \cdots \quad m_1 \quad m_0
\end{array}
$$

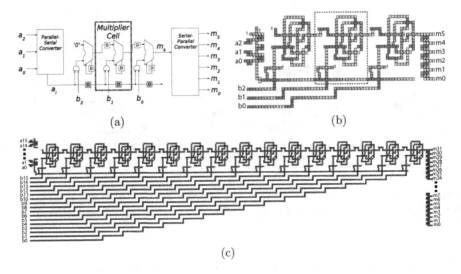

Fig. 4. Serial-parallel multiplier: a) logical structure, b) 3-bit QCA layout, and c) 16-bit QCA layout

Each single bit multiplication $a_i b_j$ is computed with an AND-gate, forming a *summand* s_k, and each row of the summands corresponds to a *partial product*. Two approaches for multiplexing the actual hardware and fixing the amount of parallel computations have been proposed (see comparison in Table 1).

Serial-Parallel Multiplier. The first multiplier proposal for QCA processes one of the operand words in bit-serial format and the other as a parallel word, accumulating each partial product with the chain of the time-multiplexed basic cells, shown in Fig. 4(a). Since distance translates into timing on QCA, the serial operand a_i cannot reach every multiplier cell on the same clock cycle, and it has to be fed through a shifting pipeline, effectively spreading the computation both in space and time. The final result is available in bit-serial format on the output m_k on the right, on consecutive clock cycles, the latency growing linearly with the operand word length, while the throughput has inverse dependence. [12, 19, 18]

A QCA layout of the design is shown in Figs. 4(b) and 4(c), where the register components have been absorbed into the clocking zones of the serial adders. The active circuit area is linearly proportional to the operand word length, but the

Table 1. Asymptotic comparison of the n-bit QCA multipliers

Design	Latency	Throughput	Area
Serial-Parallel Multiplier [12, 18], optimized in [19]	$3n + 2$ $2n$	$1/(2n)$	n^2
Array Multiplier [18]	$4n - 1$	1	$40n^2$

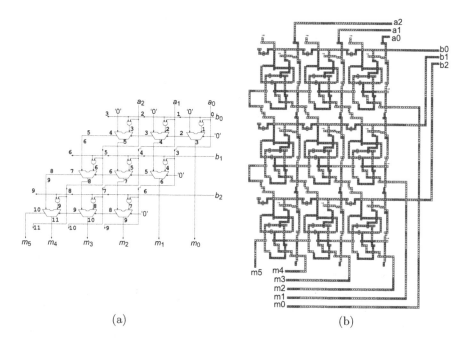

Fig. 5. Array multiplier: a) logical structure and b) 3-bit QCA layout

wiring necessary for distributing the parallel operand, originating from a compact bus, is actually quadratical (shown on the bottom-left). This wiring overhead makes also the total area of the practical design to depend quadratically on the word length, contrary to the original expectations of reaching a linear area. [18].

Array Multiplier. Our multiplier proposal maps the paper-and-pencil algorithm on a pipelined lattice of identical functional cells, shown in Figs. 5(a). Both of the operands and the result are in parallel format, and the structure has one cell for each summand, but due to the self-latching of the technology, the partial products are computed on consequent clock cycles and consequent rows. The computation proceeds from top-right to bottom-left corner, the diagonal critical path latency growing linearly with the operand word length, while the throughput of the unit is constant, one result completed each clock cycle.

A QCA layout of the design is shown in Fig. 5(b). The circuit area in the active core array grows quadratically in proportion to the operand word length, and there is also a quadratical wiring overhead on the outer edges, since the operand bits have to be delayed according to the computation order between different rows and columns. The array multiplier reaches top performance, due to maximally parallel computation, but it is up to 40 times as large as the previous structure; however, this ratio will not be exceeded, since on QCA, *both* of the designs have quadratical area (as opposed to traditional technologies). [18].

Advanced Structures. The proposed units represent opposite extremities in the design space of variable parallelism, where one might find other approaches that form a more beneficial compromise between performance and cost. The adaptation of sophisticated algorithms has not been explored, one of the reasons being the lack of an efficient state machine to enable complex sequential control. The logical next step is to implement multiplier recoding (at first, the Booth algorithm) on QCA, followed by advanced number systems including redundancy to achieve carry-free computation and improved reliability.

3.4   Other Designs

Arithmetic proposals for QCA include a binary shifter [14] and a bit-stream pattern matcher [20], which offers a starting point for developing a full capability cross correlator. A decoder, full adder, and parity checker were presented in [21], using a tile-based approach aiming at modular low-level design and redundancy against manufacturing defects, while small sequential circuits and a re-timing approach for delay matching were presented in [10] (gray code counter, traffic light controller, ISCAS89 S27 benchmark) and [22] (semaphore, lock).

A globally asynchronous, locally synchronous (GALS) paradigm was developed in [23] to ease the timing requirements of QCA design and demonstrated with a null convention logic (NCL) full adder unit, and a multiplexer, decoder, full adder and flip-flop with a two-dimensional clocking scheme were presented in [24], to achieve systolic placing with reduced wire lengths.

4   Discussion

The existing design proposals for QCA are well justified by the benefits of mastering the new technology quickly, and guiding the development of the physical implementations at their early stage; additional research effort in the directions pointed out in this paper is most welcome, since the most suitable approaches are still to be found. However, there are some general challenges requiring the attention of digital designers and computer architects, described shortly here.

The technologies-to-be are predicted to have very high defect rates in the manufacturing process, and various dynamic faults occurring also during the runtime operation. Circuit primitives (logic gates, wires, and registers) function with unideal stochastic characteristics, and the probability of failure grows with design size. The primitives cannot be made robust enough, to enable a straight-forward composition into robust circuits, which makes the fabrication of large components extremely challenging. The reliability problem is not yet adequately solved on QCA: The existing reliability improvements are aimed at certain design levels, but used separately, they are not strong enough to overcome the enormous amount of predicted failures. This raises the reliability as the highest design priority, requiring a multi-level redundancy scheme to be developed.

An epoch-making reduction in the power dissipation of digital circuits can be achieved with QCA. The nanotechnology completely avoids the major dissipation present in traditional technologies, since the signal energy needed to overcome the thermal noise floor does not have to be repeatedly dissipated. Most of the energy can be transferred from cell to cell and re-used, making the thermodynamical irreversibility dissipation a significant factor [25]. The Landauer's principle (bit erasure requires always dissipation) [26] will limit the operating frequency of irreversible circuits, if they are implemented with the very much sought-for molecular QCA [18]. The only way to reach smaller power densities and higher clock frequencies is to adopt reversible computing principles into the designs [27], with the various approaches offered by QCA technology: reversible components on several design levels and tailored clocking [28].

Systems design has to cope with abundance of new technology characteristics, in addition to the growing importance of reliability and power issues, affecting everything from the physical layout to high architectural level. The design challenges call for novel architectural solutions, modeling abstractions, and computer tools for the nanotechnology.

References

1. Lent, C., Tougaw, P., Porod, W.: Quantum cellular automata: the physics of computing with arrays of quantum dot molecules. In: Proc. Workshop Physics and Compution, Dallas, TX, November 17–20, pp. 5–13 (1994)
2. Lent, C., Tougaw, P.: A device architecture for computing with quantum dots. Proc. IEEE 85(4), 541–557 (1997)
3. Snider, G., Orlov, A., Amlani, I., Bernstein, G., Lent, C., Merz, J., Porod, W.: Quantum-dot cellular automata. In: Dig. Papers of Microprocesses and Nanotechnology Conf., Yokohama, Japan, July 6–8, pp. 90–91 (1999)
4. Orlov, A., Kummamuru, R., Ramasubramaniam, R., Lent, C., Bernstein, G., Snider, G.: Clocked quantum-dot cellular automata devices: experimental studies. In: Proc. IEEE Conf. Nanotechnology, Maui, HI, October 28–30, pp. 425–430 (2001)
5. Kummamuru, R., Orlov, A., Ramasubramaniam, R., Lent, C., Bernstein, G., Snider, G.: Operation of a quantum-dot cellular automata (QCA) shift register and analysis of errors. IEEE Trans. Electron Devices 50(9), 1906–1913 (2003)
6. Blair, E., Lent, C.: Quantum-dot cellular automata: an architecture for molecular computing. In: Proc. Int. Conf. Simulation of Semiconductor Processes and Devices, Boston, MA, September 3–5, pp. 14–18 (2003)
7. Wang, W., Walus, K., Jullien, G.: Quantum-dot cellular automata adders. In: Proc. IEEE Conf. Nanotechnology, San Francisco, CA, August 11–14, pp. 461–464 (2003)
8. Zhang, R., Walus, K., Wang, W., Jullien, G.: A method of majority logic reduction for quantum cellular automata. IEEE Trans. Nanotechnol. 3(4), 443–450 (2004)
9. Hänninen, I., Takala, J.: Robust adders based on quantum-dot cellular automata. In: Proc. IEEE Int. Conf. Application-Specific Systems, Architectures and Processors, Montréal, QC, Canada, July 8–11, pp. 391–396 (2007)
10. Huang, J., Momenzadeh, M., Lombardi, F.: Design of sequential circuits by quantum-dot cellular automata. Microelectr. J. 38(4–5), 525–537 (2007)
11. Niemier, M., Kogge, P.: Exploring and exploiting wire-level pipelining in emerging technologies. In: Proc. Annu. Int. Symp. Computer Architecture, Göteborg, Sweden, June 30–July 4, pp. 166–177 (2001)

12. Walus, K., Jullien, G., Dimitrow, V.: Computer arithmetic structures for quantum cellular automata. In: Conf. Rec. 37th Asilomar Conf. Signals, Systems and Computers, Pacific Grove, CA, November 9–12, pp. 1435–1439 (2003)
13. Fijany, A., Toomarian, N., Modarress, K., Spotnitz, M.: Bit-serial adder based on quantum dots. Technical Report NPO-20869, NASA's Jet Propulsion Laboratory, Pasadena, CA (2003)
14. Vetteth, A., Walus, K., Dimitrov, V., Jullien, G.: Quantum-dot cellular automata carry-look-ahead adder and barrel shifter. In: Proc. IEEE Conf. Emerging Telecommunications Technologies, Dallas, TX, September 23–24 (2002)
15. Kim, K., Wu, K., Karri, R.: The robust QCA adder designs using composable QCA building blocks. IEEE Trans. Computer-Aided Design Integr. Circuits Syst. 26(1), 176–183 (2007)
16. Zhang, R., Walus, K., Wang, W., Jullien, G.: Performance comparison of quantum-dot cellular automata adders. In: IEEE Int. Symp. Circuits and Systems, Kobe, Japan, May 23–26, pp. 2522–2526 (2005)
17. Cho, H., Swartzlander, E.: Adder designs and analyses for qauntum-dot cellular automata. IEEE Trans. Nanotechnol. 6(3), 374–383 (2007)
18. Hänninen, I., Takala, J.: Binary multipliers on quantum-dot cellular automata. Facta Universitatis 20(3), 541–560 (2007)
19. Cho, H., Swartzlander, E.: Serial parallel multiplier design in quantum-dot cellular automata. In: Proc. IEEE Symp. Computer Arithmetic, Montepellier, France, June 25–27, pp. 7–15 (2007)
20. Janulis, J., Tougaw, P., Henderson, S., Johnson, E.: Serial bit-stream analysis using quantum-dot cellular automata. IEEE Trans. Nanotechnol. 3(1), 158–164 (2004)
21. Huang, J., Momenzadeh, M., Schiano, L., Ottavi, M., Lombardi, F.: Tile-based QCA design using majority-like logic primitives. ACM J. Emerging Technologies in Computing Systems 1(3), 163–185 (2005)
22. Huang, J., Momenzadeh, M., Lombardi, F.: Analysis of missing and additional cell defects in sequential quantum-dot cellular automata. Integration, the VLSI Journal 40(4), 503–515 (2007)
23. Choi, M., Patitz, Z., Jin, B., Tao, F., Park, N., Choi, M.: Designing layout-timing independent quantum-dot cellular automata (QCA) circuits by global asynchrony. J. System Architecture 53(9), 551–567 (2007)
24. Vankamamidi, V., Ottavi, M., Lombardi, F.: Dimensional schemes for clocking/timing of QCA circuits. T. IEEE Trans. Computer-Aided Design Integr. Circuits Syst. 27(1), 34–44 (2008)
25. Timler, J., Lent, C.: Maxwell's demon and quantum-dot cellular automata. J. Appl. Phys. 94, 1050–1060 (2003)
26. Landauer, R.: Irreversibility and heat generation in the computing process. IBM J. Res. Dev. 5, 183–191 (1961)
27. Bennett, C.: Logical reversibility of computation. IBM J. Res. Dev. 17, 525–532 (1973)
28. Frost-Murphy, S., Ottavi, M., Frank, M., DeBenedictis, E.: On the design of reversible qdca systems. Tech. Report SAND2006-5990, Sandia Nat. Lab, Albuquerque, NM, and Livermore, CA (2006)

Preliminary Analysis of the Cell BE Processor Limitations for Sequence Alignment Applications

Sebastian Isaza[1], Friman Sánchez[2], Georgi Gaydadjiev[1], Alex Ramirez[2,3], and Mateo Valero[2,3]

[1] Delft University of Technology, Computer Engineering Lab, The Netherlands
{sisaza,georgi}@ce.et.tudelft.nl
[2] Technical University of Catalonia, Computer Architecture Department, Spain
fsanchez@ac.upc.edu
[3] Barcelona Supercomputing Center-CNS, Spain
{mateo.valero,alex.ramirez}@bsc.es

Abstract. The fast growth of bioinformatics field has attracted the attention of computer scientists in the last few years. At the same time the increasing database sizes require greater efforts to improve the computational performance. From a computer architecture point of view, we intend to investigate how bioinformatics applications can benefit from future multi-core processors. In this paper we present a preliminary study of the Cell BE processor limitations when executing two representative sequence alignment applications (Ssearch and ClustalW). The inherent large parallelism of the targeted algorithms makes them ideal for architectures supporting multiple dimensions of parallelism (TLP and DLP). However, in the case of Cell BE we identified several architectural limitations that need a careful study and quantification.

1 Introduction

Currently, bioinformatics is considered as one of the fields of computing technology with fastest growth and development [4]. This is a vast field composed of a variety of tasks, each with different computational requirements, algorithms, data, and so on. One of the most important tasks is the comparison and alignment of biological sequences (DNA, proteins, RNA), which is basically the problem of finding an approximate pattern matching between two or more sequences.

At the algorithmic level, researchers have developed various approaches for sequence comparison that fall into two categories: *global alignment* and *local alignment*. In the first case, the goal is to find the best possible alignment that span the entire length of the sequences. In contrast, the local alignment goal is to identify some regions of the sequences where similarity between them exists. Several algorithms using dynamic programming techniques (DP) for the two approaches have been proposed. Among them, the Smith-Waterman (SW) [17] and the Needleman-Wunsch (NW) [9] algorithms are widely recognized as the best optimal methods for local and global alignment, respectively [15].

M. Berekovic, N. Dimopoulos, and S. Wong (Eds.): SAMOS 2008, LNCS 5114, pp. 53–64, 2008.
© Springer-Verlag Berlin Heidelberg 2008

Regardless of the method used, sequence comparison using DP techniques is computationally demanding. In addition, the scenario becomes more challenging when it is required to study the similarity between one sequence and hundreds of thousands of sequences stored in a database; or when it is required to compare complete genomes of several organisms. The computational complexity of these algorithms depends on the sequences length, for example, for two sequences of length n and m, both algorithms have a complexity of $O(nm)$. Efficient implementations of the targeted algorithms are available in the Ssearch [10] and ClustalW [7] applications. They are widely recognized applications to perform sequence comparison and are representative of the field. Ssearch performs pairwise sequence alignment using the SW algorithm while ClustalW performs multiple sequences alignment using a slightly modified NW version. It is important to note that sequence alignment is a typical operation in many other bioinformatics algorithms, making our analysis applicable to a wider range of applications.

The traditional general-purpose processors do not provide a sufficient solution for bioinformatics. In addition, processor designers are lately moving away from the old superscalar approach toward multi-core systems. This is also the case with the Cell Broadband Engine processor [8] developed jointly by IBM, Sony and Toshiba, whose original target was the game box market. However, several researchers have shown that due to its characteristics, this processor is able to achieve impressive performance in other application domains such as signal processing, encryption, scientific applications and more [11]. The Cell BE architecture has a PowerPC Processing Unit (PPU) connected to 8 128-bit SIMD cores called Synergistic Processing Units (SPUs). Each SPU has a 256KB scratch pad memory called Local Store (LS) and the nine cores are connected through the Element Interconnect Bus (EIB). The EIB is a circular bus made of two channels in opposite directions each. It is also connected to the L2 cache and the memory controller.

The main contributions of this paper are:

- mapping and optimization alternatives for Ssearch and ClustalW applications while targeting Cell BE;
- qualitative analysis of the architectural limitations identified during the mapping process and their impact on performance;
- some architectural guidelines for future multi-core systems aiming at improved performance for bioinformatics workloads.

This paper is organized as follows: Section 2 provides a brief overview of recent works related to bioinformatics applications implementations on different platforms. Section 3 describes our experimental methodology. Section 4 outlines Ssearch and ClustalW applications and their implementations on the Cell BE. Section 5 analyzes the limitations we found when porting the applications to Cell BE. Finally, section 6 summarizes the paper and describes some future work directions.

2   Related Work

Various implementations of bioinformatics applications on different platforms have been reported in the literature. Some of them are based on Single-Instruction Multiple-Data (SIMD) augmented general purpose processors [12,14] to exploit the fine-grained parallelism present in the sequence alignment applications. In the past, the SIMD processing has proven its efficiency in other application domains such as multimedia. However, due to the permanent and almost exponential growth of the amount of biological data, it becomes clear that this solution alone does not satisfy the performance demands imposed by this field.

On the other hand, many studies about bioinformatics workloads target parallel machines combining the SIMD approach with multiple processing nodes. This in order to additionally distribute the job among the different nodes. Most of these studies focus on performance evaluation and parallelization on large high-performance supercomputers [16]. These alternatives, however, are expensive and exhibit severe limitations especially in terms of power consumption.

The use of heterogeneous multi-core architectures on a single chip, e.g. the Cell BE, combines the parallelism benefits of multiprocessor systems, with the lower power consumption and higher speed interconnects of the systems on a chip. However, these alternatives have not been completely studied as a solution for bioinformatics applications. Sachdeva et. al [13] present some results on the viability of Cell BE for bioinformatics applications (ClustalW, Ssearch and Hmmer), all performing sequence alignment. In the case of Ssearch, a preliminary evaluation is reported that uses the SPUs for a pairwise alignment of only 8 sequence pairs that fit entirely in the LS memories. We believe that in order to get valid conclusions and given the different programming strategies and models that Cell BE offers, it is important to analyze the architecture behavior under the most demanding conditions, such as using large, realistic databases containing many sequences with various sizes.

Vandierendonck et al. [18], describe their ClustalW parallelization experience for the Cell BE. Their work is mainly focused on various programming optimizations while our interest is on discovering architectural limitations for a wider range of bioinformatics applications.

3   Experimental Methodology

As starting point of our study, we selected Altivec-SIMD implementations of Ssearch [2] and ClustalW [1]. We ported them to the Cell BE ISA and used an IBM BladeCenter featuring two 3.2 GHz SMT-enabled Cell BE processors each with 512 MB of RAM to gain realistic performance results.

For the Ssearch inputs we use several protein query sequences against the SwissProt database [3]. These queries represent a range of well characterized protein families used in other works to evaluate different alignment approaches [12]. The SwissProt database contains 333,445 sequence entries. We used the *blosum62* amino-acid substitution score matrix [6]. For ClustalW, the default application parameters were used and the inputs are taken from *BioPerf* benchmark suite [5]. Here we show results for data set C, which is the most challenging case containing 318 sequences of average length 1043. The applications are implemented in C. The code segments running on the PPU were compiled with ppu-gcc 4.1.1 with -O3 -maltivec options. The code in the SPU side was compiled using spu-gcc with -O3 option.

4   Applications Description and Implementation on Cell BE

This section introduces Ssearch and ClustalW workloads and discusses specific issues related with their Cell BE implementations. It is important to recall that our intention is not the development of highly optimized Cell BE specific versions of the targeted applications. Our main focus is on the analysis of the limitations that Cell BE presents at several levels in order to guide the architecture design of future multi-core systems for bioinformatics applications.

4.1   Ssearch

The Ssearch execution scenario is as follows: a query sequence is compared against all sequences of the SwissProt database. Each comparison uses the SW algorithm to compute the similarity score between sequences. During this process, scores or weights are assigned to each character-to-character comparison: positive for exact matches/substitutions, negative for insertions/deletions. As described in the SW algorithm [17], the optimal score is computed recursively. This recursion has data dependencies as shown in figure 1, where computation of the matrix cell (i, j) depends on previous results $(i-1, j)$, $(i, j-1)$ and $(i-1, j-1)$. Note that the computation of cells across the anti-diagonals are independent and the final score is reached when all the symbols have been compared.

4.2   SIMD and Cell BE Implementation of the Ssearch

As previously mentioned, the SW algorithm is the main kernel of Ssearch. It takes about 90% of the execution time of the entire application, making it the target for optimizations. For our study, we use the following implementations:

* Ssearch Altivec SIMD version:
This version uses the Altivec SIMD extension of PowerPC architecture with 128-bit wide registers to extract data-level parallelism by calculating temporal vector of scores of cells parallel to the anti-diagonals, as it is shown in figure 2. The process starts at the upper left moving from left to right and from top to bottom. Every time a vector anti-diagonal is computed, some temporal results have to be stored in memory because they will be used in the computation of a vector in the next row. In previous works [14], advantages and limitations of this approach were discussed extensively. In this work, we concentrate on the analysis of Cell BE implementations.

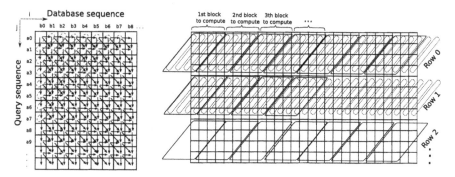

Fig. 1. Data dependencies in SW   **Fig. 2.** Proccess by blocks of SW

* *Ssearch version using one SPU:*

Porting the SW implementation of Ssearch to Cell BE ISA has relevant details that impact the performance. They are described in section 5. In this implementation, we perform the same methodology that was commented in the previous paragraph for the Altivec SIMD version. In this case, the processing sometimes requires that temporal computations of a row (the border between rows) have to be stored back in memory instead of the SPUs LS. This is because the amount of computed temporal data of a row (that depends on the sequence sizes) does not always fit entirely into the LS. As a result of this, not only the traffic gets increased between memory and the LS, but also the processing of data has to wait for the DMA transfers completion. However, the impact of this limitation can be diminished by using multi-buffering to overlap the SPU processing with DMA transfers of the next data. The important decision here is the choice of appropriate block sizes of data to be computed and transferred using DMA. Figure 2 shows an example where the block size equals to 4.

* *Parallel Ssearch version 1 using multiple SPUs:*

In addition to the SIMD version above, a multi-SPU implementation was developed. The main idea was to use all available SPUs to perform the comparison between a query against the database sequences. This approach is shown in figure 3a, where every SPU is responsible for the comparison between the query and a group of database sequences, using the same scheme as in the previous paragraph. There are two important issues to consider: the efficiency of data transfers between the main memory and the LSs and the scalability. The former is related to the cases when all SPUs are communicating to the PPU simultaneously and saturating the Element Interconnect Bus. The latter is important when a higher number of SPUs are used for the parallelization.

* *Parallel Ssearch version 2 using multiple SPUs:*

Another parallel alternative is shown in figure 3b. In this case the available SPUs perform the comparison between the query and a single database sequence. In this case, the computation of each matrix is distributed between the SPUs, that is, each SPU is responsible for computing several rows of the matrix. For example,

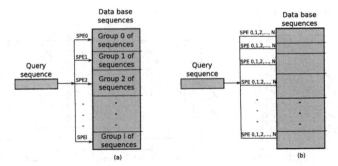

Fig. 3. Multi-SPU parallel options: (a) One SPU processes groups of sequences and (b) available SPUs process each sequence

when 8 SPUs are used, SPU0 computes row 0, row 8, row 16, etc; SPU1 computes row 1, row 9, row 17, and so on. There are some possible advantages of this alternative and the following issues are important: better bandwidth utilization and scalability than the previous approach. Improved bandwidth utilization can be achieved since not all the temporal results are written to main memory (the SPUs exchange data in a streaming fashion). This approach seems more scalable with increasing sequence sizes because each SPU is holding smaller pieces of data in its LS as compared to version 1 above. This alternative, however, requires additional synchronization between SPUs that can potentially degrade the performance.

4.3 ClustalW

Unlike pairwise sequence alignment, multiple sequence alignment (MSA) applications like ClustalW, align a set of sequences altogether, that are expected to have some evolutionary relationships. While for pairwise alignments it is still computationally feasible to produce optimal alignments with DP algorithms, for MSA is prohibitive and heuristics must be applied to avoid time and space complexity explosion. In particular, the time complexity of ClustalW is $O(n^4 + l^2)$, where n is the number of sequences and l their length. Using a technique called *progressive alignment* [7], ClustalW performs the multiple alignment in three main steps: 1) All-to-all pairwise alignment, 2) Creation of a phylogenetic tree, 3) Use of the phylogenetic tree to carry out a multiple alignment.

According to profiling results of the original code, the function that performs the alignments in the first step, i.e. *forward_pass*, consumes about 70% of the total execution time. This function calculates a similarity score among two sequences implementing a modified version of NW, following an approach similar to the one shown in figure 1. It is called $n(n-1)/2$ times to perform the multiple alignment of n sequences (all-to-all). As opposed to the first step, the final alignment step performs only $n-1$ alignments.

It is important to mention that *forward_pass* iterations are data independent making parallelization very appealing. Furthermore, the interior of the function can be at least partially vectorized to explore data-level parallelism.

4.4   Cell BE Implementation of the ClustalW

We ported *forward_pass* function to the SPU ISA and implemented a number of optimizations. DMA transfers are used to exchange data between main memory and the SPUs LS. Saturated addition and maximum instructions were emulated with 9 and 2 SPU instructions respectively. The first optimization uses 16-bit vector elements instead of 32-bit. This theoretically allows doubling the throughput but requires the implementation of an overflow check in software.

Inside the inner loop of the kernel there are instructions responsible for loading the sequence elements to be compared and using them to index a matrix that provides the comparison score. This is a random scalar memory access that is performed within a loop also containing a complex branch for checking boundary conditions. This type of operations are very inefficient in the SPUs. We have unrolled this loop and manually evaluated the boundary conditions outside the inner loop. Section 5 discusses the impact of these optimizations.

In the case of the multi-SPU versions of ClustalW, the PPU distributes pairs of sequences for each SPU to process independently. A first such a version was implemented using a simple round-robin strategy for load distribution. This version is not really efficient and is not further discussed. A second strategy uses a table of flags that SPUs can raise to indicate idleness. This way the PPU can take better decisions on where to allocate the tasks. As explained in the previous section, the parallelization of *forward_pass* in multiple threads is easy so there is no need to optimize much the load balancing nor the communication efficiency. Section 5 shows the scalability of our strategy.

5   Analysis of Cell BE Limitations and Results

Experiments performed included a number of optimizations that increase performance. We have looked mostly at parallel execution issues due to the inherent parallelism existing in the applications and some relevant Cell BE ISA aspects that impact the performance.

5.1   Performance Results

Figure 4 shows the execution of Ssearch on different platforms. As expected, scalar executions are less efficient than the remaining alternatives. The G5 platform contains a powerful out-of-order superscalar PowerPC970 that runs scalar code very efficiently while the PPU has limited capabilities (less functional units and registers, in-order execution, etc). Similar observation is done for the *Altivec G5* and *AltivecPPU* alternatives. The *Cell1SPU* version is 1.07× slower than the *AltivecPPU* version. We have found two main reasons for this: 1) the non existing support for some instructions in the SPU ISA (discussed in the next section) and 2) the need of transferring data between LS and memory. We are currently working on further code optimizations to reduce the data reorganization overhead and the traffic between main memory and the LSs.

Figure 6 shows the execution time of Ssearch to compare a query sequence of length 553 and the whole SwissProt database. Results correspond to the parallel version 1. Each group of bars represents execution using a different number of SPUs. And each bar of the group corresponds to a different block size (in bytes) that is transfered between LS and memory as it was described in section 4.2. These results show that the strategy of computing several vector anti-diagonals of the same row before sending results to main memory is an important source of speedup (Using 1 SPU: 2,33× faster between 32 bytes and 512 bytes bars. Using 8 SPUs: 2,13× faster between 32 and 512 bytes bars). Other interesting observation is related to performance scalability across the number of SPUs used. Figure 5 shows how the performance scale almost linearly with the number of SPUs. However, part of our current work is to investigate this trend with greater number of SPUs.

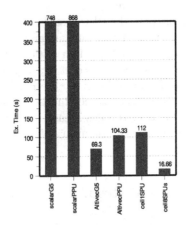

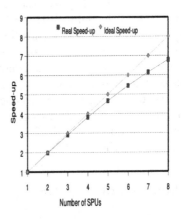

Fig. 4. Ssearch execution on different platforms

Fig. 5. Speedup across SPUs (using 512-byte block size)

Figure 7 shows a comparison of ClustalW running on various single-core platforms as compared to different versions using a single SPU. Since the clock frequency of the G5 is more than twice as low as the Cell, it is clear that in terms of cycles it outperforms any Cell 1SPU version. The fourth bar shows the straightforward SPU implementation of ClustalW, where only thread creation, DMA transfers and mailboxes are implemented for basic operation and no attention is given to optimizing the kernel code. The fifth bar shows a significant speedup (1.7×) when using 16-bit data type. This double vector parallelism is most of the time achievable but the program should always check for overflow and go back to the 32-bit version if needed. Since the SPUs do not provide any support for overflow check (unlike the PPU), this had to be implemented in software and consequently affecting the performance. The next two bars show results for unrolling a small loop located within the inner loop of the kernel allowing us to achieve accumulative 2.6× speedup. And the last two versions went

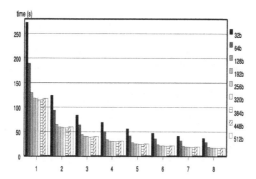

Fig. 6. Time vs SPUs for different block sizes in Ssearch

further into optimizing this small loop by removing the boundary conditions involved in a scalar branch and handling them explicitly outside the loop. This final (accumulative) optimization provided about 4.2× speedup with respect to the initial version.

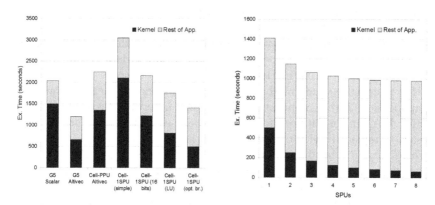

Fig. 7. ClustalW performance for different platforms and optimizations

Fig. 8. ClsutalW speedup using multiple
SPUs

Figure 8 shows the scalability of ClustalW kernel when using multiple SPUs. The black part of the bars reveals a perfect scalability (8× for 8 SPUs). This is due to the relatively low amount of data transfered and the independence between every instance of the kernel. In future experiments, it will be interesting to see how far will this perfect scalability continue.

After the successful reduction of the execution time for *forward_pass*, significant application speedups are only possible by accelerating other parts of the program. The progressive alignment phase is now the portion consuming most of the time. This issue is currently being studied.

5.2   Analysis of Limitations

Here we list and discuss some limitations we found at both architecture- and micro-architecture levels. Although experiments have given us an insight about the individual contribution to performance degradation, an on-going quantitative study will tell us the real impact of every limitation.

* *Unaligned data accesses:* The lack of hardware support for unaligned data accesses is one of the issues that can limit the performance the most. When the application needs to do unaligned loads or stores, the compiler must introduce extra code that contains additional memory accesses plus some shift instructions for data reorganization. If this sort of situation appears in critical parts of the code (as is the case in ClustalW), the performance will be dramatically affected.

* *Scalar operations:* Given the SIMD-only nature of the SPUs ISA and the lack of unaligned access support, scalar instructions may cause performance degradation too. Since there are only vector instructions, scalar operations must be performed employing vectors with only one useful element. Apart from power inefficiency issues, this works well only if the scalars are in the appropriate position within the vector. If not, the compiler has to introduce some extra instructions to make the scalar operands aligned and perform the instruction. This limitation is responsible for a significant efficiency reduction.

* *Saturated arithmetics:* These frequently executed operations are present in Altivec but not in the SPU ISA. They are used to compute partial scores avoiding that they are zeroed when overflow occurs with unsigned addition. This limitation may become expensive depending on the data types. For *signed short*, 9 additional SPU instructions are needed.

* *Max instruction:* One of the most important and frequent operations in both applications is the computation of a maximum between two or more values. The SPU ISA, unlike Altivec, does not provide such an instruction. It is then necessary to replace it with two SPU instructions.

* *Overflow flag:* This flag is easily accessible in Altivec in case the application needs a wider data type to compute. In the SPU this is not available and it has to be implemented in software adding overhead.

* *Branch prediction:* The SPUs do not handle efficiently branches and the penalty of a mispredicted branch is about 18 cycles. The SPU will always predict branches as non-taken unless a software branch hint explicitly says the opposite. Although some control-dependencies (branches) can be converted in data dependencies (using select instruction) some others cannot and branches will remain. The kernel of ClustalW has several branches that, when mispredicted, reduce the application execution speed.

* *Local Store size:* As was mentioned in section 4.2, the size of SPUs LS is relevant because it is not always possible to ensure that each database sequence, query sequence and temporal computations fit in the LS. Our SW implementation takes this into account by partitioning the work in blocks, as explained before. Other optimizations are being currently developed to dynamically identify whether space in main memory is required or not. This will help to reduce data transfer between LS and memory.

It is important to say that there are other commercial processors (apart from PowerPC) that support the missing features we found in Cell BE. For instance, TriMedia processor supports unaligned memory accesses, Intel SSE has saturating arithmetic instructions, etc. However, not all these features can be found on a single product.

6 Conclusions and Future Work

In this paper we described the mapping and some optimization alternatives of two representative bioinformatics applications targeting Cell BE. We have also presented a qualitative analysis of the architectural shortcomings identified during this process. Our study revealed various architectural aspects that negatively impact Cell BE performance for bioinformatics workloads. More precisely, the missing HW support for unaligned memory accesses, the limited memory bandwidth and LS sizes appear to be the most critical. However, additional experiments are being performed in order to measure bandwidth usage, load balancing, LS usage, functional units usage, stall rates and communication patterns. In addition, our future work involves the usage of architecture simulation techniques in order to evaluate possible solutions to the identified limitations. We are using this research as guidance for the architecture design of future multi-core systems targeting bioinformatics. We intend to widen our study to other applications of the same field.

This work is our first step towards future multi-core architectures incorporating domain specific bio-accelerators. We believe that heterogeneous multi-core architectures able to exploit multiple dimensions of parallelism are a valid option that will play an important role in the future of bioinformatics.

Acknowledgements

This work was partially sponsored by the European Commission in the context of the SARC Integrated Project #27648 (FP6), the HiPEAC Network of Excellence, the FEDER funds under contract TIN2007-60625 and by the Spanish Ministry of Science. The authors would like to thank the Barcelona Supercomputing Center for the access to the Cell BE blades.

References

1. Altivec enabled clustalw1.83, http://powerdev.osuosl.org/node/49
2. Fasta web site, http://wrpmg5c.bioch.virginia.edu/fasta_www2/
3. Swissprot, universal protein database, http://www.expasy.org/sprot/
4. Bioinformatics market study for washington technology center (June 2003), http://www.altabiomedical.com
5. Bader, D.A., Li, Y., Li, T., Sachdeva, V.: Bioperf: A benchmark suite to evaluate high-performance computer architecture on bioinformatics applications. In: IEEE International Symposium on Workload Characterization (IISWC), pp. 1–8 (October 2005)

6. Henikoff, J., Henikoff, S., Pietrokovski, S.: Blocks+: a non-redundant database of protein alignment blocks derived from multiple compilations. Bioinformatics 15 (1999)
7. Higgins, D., Thompson, J., Gibson, T., Thompson, J.: Clustal w: improving the sensitivity of progressive multiple sequence alignment through sequence weighting, position-specific gap penalties and weight matrix choice. Nucleic Acids Research 22, 4673–4680 (1994)
8. Kahle, J.A., Day, M.N., Hofstee, H.P., Johns, C.R., Shippy, D.: Introduction to the cell multiprocessor. IBM Systems Journal 49(4/5), 589–604 (2005)
9. Needleman, S., Wunsch, C.: A general method applicable to the search for similarities in the amino acid sequence of two proteins. Journal of Molecular Biology 48, 443–453 (1970)
10. Pearson, W.R.: Searching protein sequence libraries: comparison of the sensitivity and selectivity of the smith-waterman and FASTA algorithms. Genomics 11, 635–650 (1991)
11. Petrini, F., Fossum, G., Fernandez, J., Varbanescu, A.L., Kistler, M., Perrone, M.: Multicore surprises: Lessons learned from optimizing sweep3d on the cellbe. In: IEEE International Parallel and Distributed Processing Symposium, IPDPS, pp. 1–10 (2007)
12. Rognes, T.: Rapid and sensitive methods for protein sequence comparison and database searching. PhD thesis, Institue of Medical Microbiology, University of Oslo (2000)
13. Sachdeva, V., Kistler, M., Speight, E., Tzeng, T.H.K.: Exploring the viability of the cell broadband engine for bioinformatics applications. In: Proceedings of the 6th Workshop on High Performance Computational Biology, pp. 1–8 (2007)
14. Sanchez, F., Salami, E., Ramirez, A., Valero, M.: Performance analysis of sequence alignment applications. In: Proceedings of the IEEE International Symposium on Workload Characterization (IISWC), pp. 51–60 (2006)
15. Shpaer, E., Robinson, M., Yee, D., Candlin, J., Mines, R., Hunkapiller, T.: Sensitivity and selectivity in protein similarity searches: A comparison of smith-waterman in hardware to blast and fasta. Genomics 38, 179–191 (1996)
16. Smith, S., Frenzel, J.: Bioinformatics application of a scalable supercomputer-on-chip architecture. Proceedings of the International Conference on Parallel and Distributed Processing Techniques 1, 385–391 (2003)
17. Smith, T.F., Waterman, M.S.: Identification of common molecular subsequences. Journal of Molecular Biology 147, 195–197 (1981)
18. Vandierendonck, H., Rul, S., Questier, M., Bosschere, K.D.: Experiences with parallelizing a bio-informatics program on the cell be. In: Stenström, P., et al. (eds.) Third International Conference, HiPEAC. LNCS, vol. 4917, pp. 161–175. Springer, Heidelberg (2008)

802.15.3 Transmitter: A Fast Design Cycle Using OFDM Framework in Bluespec

Teemu Pitkänen[1], Vesa-Matti Hartikainen[1], Nirav Dave[2], and Gopal Raghavan[3]

[1] Tampere University of Technology, P.O. Box 553, FIN-33101 Tampere, Finland
{teemu.pitkanen, vesa-matti.hartikainen}@tut.fi
[2] Massachusetts Institute of Technology, Cambridge, USA
ndave@csail.mit.edu
[3] Nokia Research Center Cambridge
Nokia Corporation
gopal.raghavan@nokia.com

Abstract. Orthogonal Frequency-Division Multiplexing (OFDM) has become the preferred modulation scheme for both broadband and high bitrate digital wireless protocols because of its spectral efficiency and robustness against multipath interference. Although the components and overall structure of different OFDM protocols are functionally similar, the characteristics of the environment for which a wireless protocol is designed often result in different instantiations of various components. In this paper we present a new baseband processing transmitter case, namely 802.15.3 (WUSB), to existing OFDM framework which consists highly parametrized code in Bluespec for two different wireless baseband processing cases, namely 802.11a (WiFi) and 802.16 (WiMAX). The design cycle for transmitter of WUSB took only six week's for two designers which were not familiar with Bluespec, WUSB protocol or the OFDM framework.

1 Introduction

Wireless systems are experiencing rapid development as more applications call for mobile and distributed use. To effectively meet the vastly varying application requirements (*e.g.,* power, bitrate, and flexibility) a variety of different wireless protocols have been designed. In recent years, Orthogonal Frequency-Division Multiplexing (OFDM) has become preferred modulation scheme for both broadband and high bitrate digital wireless protocols because of its spectral efficiency and robustness against multipath interference. These protocols are sufficiently similar that many of the component blocks in transceivers across protocols could be described using the same parametric module with different parameters in the various forms including bitsizes, default values, pipelining strategies and combinational functions.

Despite the capability for sharing and the significant time pressure on designers to ship designs quickly, in practice engineers still write each design from scratch ignoring possible reuse between designs. Much of this is due to the fact that while most hardware description languages (HDLs) like Verilog and VHDL provide the ability for parameterization, only very low-level parameterization is supported (*e.g.,* values and bit-sizes) leaving many important parameterizations very hard to describe.

M. Berekovic, N. Dimopoulos, and S. Wong (Eds.): SAMOS 2008, LNCS 5114, pp. 65–74, 2008.
© Springer-Verlag Berlin Heidelberg 2008

Recently, Ng et. al. developed a parameterized suite for quickly generating OFDM baseband transceivers [1] in Bluespec SystemVerilog (BSV), a high-level hardware description language which can be compiled mechanically in to efficient high-quality RTL code [2]. This suite consists of a number of highly parameterized OFDM component blocks which can be reused across multiple designs. These parametric designs cause no additional hardware overhead, as the Bluespec compiler can remove all static parameterization during design elaboration.

The OFDM framework provides specific baseband implementations for both the 802.11a (WiFi) and 802.16 (WiMAX) protocols. Using this as a starting point we add the design of a 802.15.3 (WUSB) transmitter. This work took very little time, taking only six weeks for two designer unfamiliar with both BSV and OFDM protocols to complete.

2   OFDM Framework

The OFDM Framework used has been developed as part of the ARMO project by Nokia Research Center and Massachusetts Institute of Technology [3]. The project started out focusing on studying the cost-area tradeoffs possible in the RTL design of a 802.11a transmitter [5]. As the project progressed it became clear that many of the key blocks in both the transmitter and reciever, the receiver size, it then became clear that many of the key blocks, while complex, were reusable across multiple OFDM-based protocols. This framework has been released to the public under the MIT license [4].

The structure of OFDM implementations described in this framework is shown in Figure 1. To aid comprehension, we briefly discuss the high-level functionality of each blocks:

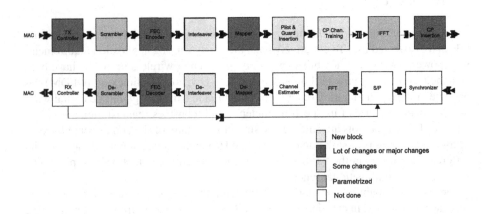

Fig. 1. Structure of the OFDM Framework and changes made

2.1 Transmitter

TX Controller: Receives information from the MAC. Adds header data before actual payload and generates control for all the subsequent blocks.

Scrambler: Randomizes the data stream to remove repeated patterns.

FEC Encoder: Encodes and adds some redundancy to data making it possible for the receiver to detect and correct errors. The encoded data is punctured to reduce the transmitted number of bits.

Interleaver: Interleaves bit stream to provide robustness against burst errors.

Mapper: Passes interleaved data through a serial to parallel converter, mapping groups of bits to separate carriers, and encoding each bit group by frequency, amplitude, and phase. The output of the Mapper contains the values of data subcarriers for an OFDM symbol.

Pilot/Guard Insertion: Adds the values for pilot and guard subcarriers to OFDM symbols.

IFFT: Converts OFDM symbols from the frequency domain to the time domain.

CP Insertion: Copies some samples from the end of the symbol to the front to add some redundancy to the symbols to avoid Inter-Symbol Interference. The block also adds a preamble before the first transmitted symbol.

After CP insertion, OFDM symbols are outputted to a DAC, which converts them to analog signals which can them be transmitted.

2.2 Receiver

The receiver roughly applies the transmitter transformations in reverse. However, it requires some additional feedback to help synchronize to to the expected phase.

Synchronizer: Detects the starting position of an incoming packet based on preambles.

Serial to Parallel (S/P): Removes the cyclic prefix (CP) and then aggregates samples into symbols before passing them to the FFT. It also propagates the control information from the RX Controller to subsequent blocks.

FFT: Converts OFDM symbols from the time domain into the frequency domain.

Channel Estimator: Compensates for frequency-dependent signal degradation based on pilots and corrects the errors caused by multi-path interference.

Demapper: Demodulates data and converts samples to encoded bits.

Deinterleaver: Reverses the interleaving and restores the original arrangement of bits.

FEC Decoder: Uses the redundant information to detect and correct errors occurred during transmission.

Descrambler: Reverses the scrambling.

RX Controller: Based on the decoded data, the RX Controller generates the control feedback to S/P block.

3   The WUSB Transmitter

The OFDM Framework provided a very good starting point for WUSB implementation. It included almost all of the functionality needed, and most changes were just changes to parameters of the framework. Only few bigger changes to the framework were needed. Figure 1 illustrates the structure of OFDM Framework and changes necessary for WUSB. In this chapter we discuss some of the specific changes and how they were represented.

3.1   Parameterization

Many of the modifications needed in the WUSB design are captured by the component module parameterization. Table 1 lists some of the parameter settings of each protocol.

Convolutional Encoder: One of the simplest examples of parameterization we encountered was in the convolutional encoder. In this design, we needed to generate a 3-bit output for each 1-bit input using a moving history of 8 input bits. To represent this change the input and output sizes to match the expected rates (8 and 24 respectively) and pass in three values representing the individual polynomial for each output bit. The computation necessary for each output bit can be described by a single polynomial in $\mathbb{Z}_2$. These are represented as $8 - bit$ values. Thus we need to pass in 3 8-bit values to the parameterized module.

Due to a restriction in the current Bluespec compiler, to generate a separate Verilog module for this block, the Bluespec module be non-parameterized. This requires us to add a small wrapper module to restrict the type and provides the modules arguments to make the module self-contained.

```
typedef 8 ConvEncoderInDataSz;
typedef TMul#(3,ConvEncoderInDataSz) ConvEncoderOutDataSz;
module mkConvEncoderInstance(ConvEncoder#(TXGlobalCtrl,
                                          ConvEncoderInDataSz,
                                          ConvEncoderOutDataSz));
   ConvEncoder#(TXGlobalCtrl, ConvEncoderInDataSz
                    , ConvEncoderOutDataSz) convEncoder
         <- mkConvEncoder(convEncoderG1, convEncoderG2,convEncoderG3);
   return convEncoder;
endmodule
```

Puncturer: A slightly more interesting parameterization can be found in the puncturer. Puncturing is a feature of the FEC encoder which allows the transmitter to reduce the number of bits being sent. For higher transmission rate, in low-noise channels, the encoded data is punctured by deleting bits before transmission and replacing them with fixed values on reception. This reduces the number of bits to be carried over the channel as we can depend on the error correction in the receiver to correctly reconstruct the data.

The WUSB protocol specifies 7 separate puncturing modes, of which 5 are already described the previous framework. To add a new puncturing mode, we define the new functions puncturerHalf which takes 3 bits and returns 2 bits and puncturerEleven-ThirtySecond which takes 33 bits and returns 32 bits.

```
function Bit#(2) puncturerHalf (Bit#(3) x);
   return {x[2], x[0]};
endfunction
function Bit#(32) puncturerElevenThirtySecond (Bit#(33) x);
   return x[31:0];
endfunction
```

Each function is then extended to the apply to the input size using the `parFunc` function. These new functions, along with the other functions corresponding to the other modes along with a function which determines which function corresponds to which mode (`puncturerMapCtrl`).

```
puncturer <- mkPuncturer(puncturerMapCtrl,
                 parFunc(f0_sz,puncturerHalf),
                 parFunc(f1_sz,puncturerTwoThird),
                 ...,
                 parFunc(f6_sz,puncturerFiveEigth) );
```

Using functions as parameters is possible because functions are considered first-order objects in Bluespec.

Table 1. Algorithmic settings for WiFi, WiMAX and WUSB

Blocks	Parameters	WiFi	WiMAX	WUSB
Scrambler	Generator Polynomial	$X^7 + X^4 + 1$	$X^{15} + X^{14} + 1$	$X^{15} + X^{14} + 1$
Convolutional	Generator Polynomials	133oct & 171oct	133oct & 171oct	133oct, 165oct & 171oct
Interleaver	Coding Rate	1/2, 2/3, 3/4	1/2, 2/3, 3/4, 5/6	1/2, 11/32, 5/8, 3/4
	No. Stages	2	2	3
Mapper	Modulation Schemes	BPSK, QPSK, 16-QAM, 64-QAM	BPSK, QPSK, 16-QAM, 64-QAM	QPSK
Pilot & Guard Insertion	No. Pilot Subcarriers	4	8	12
	No. Guard Subcarriers	12	56	10
FFT/IFFT	Size	64	256	128
Cyclic Prefix Insertion	Size	1/4	1/32, 1/16, 1/8, 1/4	N/A

3.2   Further Changes

Since the frame header is protocol specific, the transmission controller also needs to be changed. Figure 2 illustrates the WUSB frame format. While, this format is similar to both the WiFi and WiMAX protocols, these differences are not well-suited to parameterization, since the description complexity required to express the controller in a parametric way is worth the cost of writing a new module.

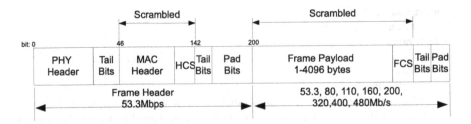

Fig. 2. PLCP Frame Format for WUSB

The biggest change in the controller was the addition of a side scrambler. In WiFi all header data is scrambled. In WiMAX all header data is sent unscrambled. In WUSB we had to change scrambling of the headers, since a combination of the MAC header and header checksum (HCS) needed to be scrambled and the PHY header should not be scrambled. Since the scrambled parts of the header do not fit the byte alignment, we either needed to change the scrambler to support non-byte aligned scrambling, add a new module to the main pipeline for adding tail bits after the PHY header or add a side scrambler that is used only for encoding scrambled part of the header. We choose to implement the later two options. The two options we considered are illustrated in Figure 3 We decided to use a separate side scrambler. This allows use the library scrambler implementation more easily. The side scrambler is only used for headers; the payload is still scrambled by the main scrambler instance in the pipeline.

Interleaver: In WiFi and WiMAX the data interleaving is done only inside symbol. In WUSB, the interleaver must support interleaving of data across symbol triplets. This change did not require changing the parameteric interleaver, only a new interleaving function using three symbols as an input, not one.

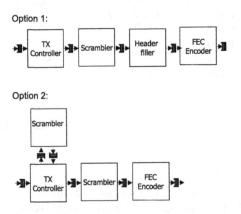

Fig. 3. Implementation Options for Header Scrambling. Option 1 adds a "header filler" module to add tail bits. Option 2 uses a separate side-scrambler for side scrambling.

Preamble Generation: In WUSB, there are 4 different preambles added to symbols in both the time and frequency. The choice for these is not specified. As a result we only implemented the first choice. Augmenting the system to add the other preambles can be easily done.

Previous OFDM transmitters did not need to support frequency-domain preambles. To add this functionality, we need to add a new block into our pipeline: the CP Channel Training Block. This block adds 6 prefixed sequences to the input of the IFFT separately. The system sends this frequency preamble before sending the symbol header and payload.

Mapping Values: In WiFi and WiMAX the mapping always remains the same in WUSB there are two different mappings. At data rates below 110 Mbps we encode 100 input bits to 50 complex numbers and calculate complex conjugate of the numbers and append it to end to form a single OFDM Symbol. At faster rates this redundancy is removed and an OFDM symbol is formed directly of 200 input bits. Other change is contents of the guard bits at the edges of frequency. WiFi and WiMAX uses zeros as contents of guard bits. Instead in WUSB we replicate outermost data bits and use them as content of the guard bits.

The Mapper for WUSB only needs to support QPSK-modulation, and therefore input and output sizes are less constrained than other schemes where other modulation schemes more restrict the choices, meaning the provided parameterized mapper did not cover all cases for the protocol. To generate a WUSB mapper we had to manually strip modulation and generate a specialized mapper. A more parameterized mapper must be designed to capture this implementation as well.

4   Implementation Results

In the following section we describe the result of synthesis of the WUSB transmitter and evaluate the value of the OFDM framework.

4.1   Technical Results

The WUSB transmitter is synthesized with Synopsys Design Compiler to 130 nm technology with 1.5 V operating voltage and power dissipation is acquired through gate-level simulation at 100 MHz.

The results of the synthesis are presented in the Table 2. Most of the area and power are consumed by the 128-point IFFT block. We compare our designs to two comparable FFT implementations compatible with our design.

To meet the frequency requirements of the protocol, we must be able to complete an IFFT in 312.5 ns. We use a folded pipeline design using the same Bluespec pipelining framework [5]. Thus it is easy to quickly change the area/performance tradeoff. Our final IFFT design uses 32 radix-2 butterflies and requires 14 cycles of computation per input.

To match the performance requirements for our IFFT block needs to run at 44.8 MHz. In fact, the critical path 9.5 ns which allows the block to be clocked at 105 MHz.

Other FFT implementations in the literature have similar results. Mathew et. al [6], use a pseudo parallel datapath structure to calculate a 128-point FFT in 10 cycles that

Table 2. Area and Power Dissipation of WUSB Transmitter

Component	# of Gates (K)	Power (mW)	Component	# of Gates (K)	Power (mW)
TX Controller	2.8	1.18	Scrambler	0.5	0.085
FEC Encoder	7.5	2.31	Interleaver	15.9	4.81
Pilot & Guard Insertion	47.5	14.4	CP Channel Training	46.2	10.2
IFFT	718.2	36.2	CP Insertion	23.6	0.45
Mapper	57.8	11.3	Total	920	92.3

can be clocked at 275 MHz. The architecture used 3 butterfly stages, and with each butterfly stage containing 8 separate datapaths. Power figures for this design are measured using a clock speed of 33.3 MHz.

Chen et. al [7] present a different 128-point FFT core, with four radix-2^2 and four radix-$2^2/2$ butterflies. The first two and last two stages each use a separate sets of butterflies requiring 32 cycles to compute one input. The design also used six eight-bank single ported RAMs, two coefficient ROMs, and two address generators. While the authors were only able to run the system at 66 MHz, scaling down the technology would give comparable results to ours.

The comparison FFT presented here is shown in Table 3. Area and power consumption numbers is normalized to 130 nm technology to give a fair comparison between designs. the maximum clock describes how fast each design can run, required clock describes how fast the design must run to achieve the performance requirement. The parameterized BSV code requires approximately 50% more area and slightly more power compared to [6], and 3.5 times more area compared [7]. From experience much of this area overhead is due to our choices of using radix-2 butterflies as the base block in our design. Larger radices would improve the design, though they would require the FFT either be partitioned into two parts, or the inputs changed so that the 2^7 size input is naturally factor by the radix size.

5   Development Experience

The WUSB design was done by two engineers as a six-week project. Only one had any previous hardware design experience (i.e. VHDL). The pair spent approximately two weeks learning the language, the OFDM framework, and the WUSB specification before starting on the design. The remaining four weeks to complete the transmitter design and the much of the receiver design. We estimate that it would take another 1-2 weeks to complete the receiver design.

One of the keys points which makes the OFDM framework so effective is the rich parameterization properties of Bluespec. Bluespec's rich type structure, parameterized types, and higher-order functions, made expressing much of the parameterized designs natural. Functions do not need to be represented as bit-vectors to be a parameter. Most

Table 3. Comparison between FFT architectures

Name	Butter-flies	Radix of Butterflies	# of Gates (K)	Power (mW)	Tech	max.clk (MHz)	req. clk (MHz)
BSV	32	2	718.2	36.2	130 nm	105	44.8
[6]	24	8, 2	968	60.6	180 nm	275	31.7
		normalized	504.9	31.6			
[7]	8	4, 2,	$5.85mm^2$	n/a	250 nm	66	102.3
		approx.	760.3				
		normalized	205.6				

of the work involved in using the library was simply understanding what block was desired.

The OFDM systems modular decomposition also proved to be highly valuable. because all modules were expected to be latency insensitive and have FIFO buffering, adding new stages to the pipeline and setting up complete testbenches were both easy. One can handle each input or output to a module separately.

Other Bluespec language features also proved to be helpful in a number of minor ways. Bluespec's static elaboration allowed the design to be expressed recursively; the system elaborates the description into non-recursive description automatically. Type provisos which represent the assumptions needed to use a function of module provided both useful documentation as well guarantees that designs are being parameterized in legal ways.

6   Conclusions

The primary goal of this work was not to see how much time and effort was needed in generating a new protocol; it was to see how effectively high-level design language ideas could be leveraged by engineers not already steeped in the language. In our views, this work has been a stunning success. The OFDM framework, though well structured, represents a fairly sophisticated system with significant parameterization. For inexperienced engineers to be able to understand, use, and even augment the system in so short a time argues for how natural the system is represented.

Our experience suggests that in the hands of experienced designers, our findings will be even more magnified, leading to greater focus on much larger design choices and hopefully leading to better implementation results.

References

1. Ng, M.C., Vijayaraghavan, M., Dave, N., Arvind, Raghavan, G., Hicks, J.: From WiFi to WiMAX: Techniques for high-level ip reuse across different OFDM protocols. In: Proc. IEEE MEMOCODE, Nice, France, pp. 71–80 (2007)
2. Arvind, Nikhil, R.S., Rosenband, D.L., Dave, N.: High-level Synthesis: An Essential Ingredient for Designing Complex ASICs. In: Proceedings of ICCAD 2004, San Jose, CA (2004)
3. http://www.research.nokia.com/projects/armo

4. http://opensource.nokia.com/projects/armo-open-source-hardware/index.html
5. Dave, N., Pellauer, M., Gerding, S., Arvind: 802.11a Transmitter: A Case Study in Microarchitectural Exploration. In: Proceedings of Formal Methods and Models for Codesign (MEMOCODE), Napa, CA (2006)
6. Mathew, J., Maharatna, K., Pradhan, D., Vinod, A.P.: Exploration of power optimal implementation technique of 128-pt fft/ifft for wpan using pseudo-parallel datapath structure. In: Proc. IEEE ICCS, Singapore, pp. 1–5 (2006)
7. Chen, S., Yu, Y., Chen, B., Lai, S., Zeng, Y., Zhang, Y., Wang, C.: Design of a 128-point fourier transform chip for uwb applications. In: Proc. IEEE ICSICT, Shanghai, China, pp. 1957–1959 (2006)
8. IEEE: 802.15 High Rate Alternative PHY Task Group (tg3a) for Wireless Personal Area Networks, Multi-band OFDM physical layer proposal for IEEE 802.15 Task Group 3a, IEEE P802.15-03

A Real-Time Programming Model for Heterogeneous MPSoCs

Torsten Limberg, Bastian Ristau, and Gerhard Fettweis

Technische Universität Dresden
Vodafone Chair Mobile Communications Systems
01062 Dresden, Germany
{limberg,ristau,fettweis}@ifn.et.tu-dresden.de

Abstract. Modern multi-core processors suffer from the lack of a programming model which allows efficient utilization of the available hardware. Massive software overhead is required to handle task scheduling and synchronization, resulting in power inefficiencies. In this paper we present a C++ based, real-time enabled task level programming model, which allows efficient hardware utilization. Task scheduling and synchronization is performed by a hardware unit at run-time. The automated scheduler unit is guided by offline information extracted from source code by a specialized compiler

1 Introduction

Heterogeneous MPSoC will be the preferred topology for high performance, low power signal processing systems of the future [1]. These systems will be set up from established, highly optimized components such as RISC processors, DSPs, ASIPs and ASICs. MPSoCs can deliver unlimited processing power to the programmer. Unfortunately programming such systems is not trivial [2]. Understandable programming models which utilize hardware effectively are required, in order to get the maximum benefit out of parallel systems.

Besides the programming model, MPSoCs impose other problems which could easily dilute the benefits drawn out of the parallelism. Two of the most profound problems are overheads introduced by context switches and hardware/software interfacing [3]. It is common practice to add specialized accelerators to signal processing systems in order to improve performance and power efficiency. However, the interface between hardware accelerators is usually interrupt based. This causes scheduling overhead for processing interrupt requests, drawing off compute power from the application and reducing the energy efficiency.

Another problem is the increasing number of applications running concurrently on modern signal processing systems such as mobile phones. Many of these applications are required to fulfill real-time requirements. This causes an increase of scheduling overhead which forces the hardware designers to put more powerful hardware into the system, causing further degradation of power efficiency. Future systems will have to cope with even more concurrent and dynamically changing applications. Unfortunately most existing programming models

M. Berekovic, N. Dimopoulos, and S. Wong (Eds.): SAMOS 2008, LNCS 5114, pp. 75–84, 2008.
© Springer-Verlag Berlin Heidelberg 2008

are totally unsuitable for handling dynamics. This is mainly, because the user is required to perform resource allocation statically at compile time. With the increasing number of applications which are candidate to be run in parallel in a real-time environment, this is getting impractical. Therefore, dynamic resource allocation at run-time is required from our point of view.

We are addressing all of these challenges with our platform concept. To solve the problem of resource allocation and task synchronization we pick up the idea of having a task level programming model along with a dedicated hardware unit named CoreManager [4]. The CoreManager is absorbing a good portion of the operating system scheduler work and removes interrupts for accelerator synchronization completely. We extend [4] by adding real-time capabilities to the programming model and the CoreManager. According to [4], we call our real-time enabled CoreManager version Real-Time-CoreManager (RT-CoreManager). Offline information which is needed by the RT-CoreManager to perform task prioritization is added automatically by a specialized compiler.

In this paper we are focusing on the real-time programming model (section 4) and its required compiler (section 5). Nevertheless, a short introduction into hardware architecture is given in section 3. Section 6 gives some first results obtained from the compiler. A conclusion and an overview over future work can be found in section 7.

2   Related Work

In [5] recommendations for the development and evaluation of future "manycore" processors are given. MPSoCs are proposed to provide adequate processing capabilities at low power consumption. In order to program such architectures, more human centric, and efficient parallel programming models are claimed. Existing parallel programming models such as OpenMP [6], NVidias CUDA [7], Cilk [8] or μTC [9] are targeted shared memory architectures. They extend the C language in order to allow the programmer to specify parallelism explicitly. However, these programming models exploit fine grain parallelism and heterogeneity is not supported. MPSoCs for application tailored signal processors require a programming model exploiting coarse grain parallelism, since fine grain instruction and data parallelism is already utilized by the single processing elements (e.g. with very long instruction words and single instruction multiple data processing).

Sequoia [10] is a programming model explicitly requiring an abstract description of the processor memory hierarchy. Programs are architecture independent and therefore portable to new targets. However, static mapping of tasks to resources is required.

A hardware concept for heterogeneous MPSoCs along with an appropriate C-based programming model is proposed by Seidel [4]. CellSs [11], which was developed to utilize the parallelism of the Cell BE [12], is closely related to this approach. Both propose a runtime scheduler which dynamically distributes tasks to processing elements. However, CellSs performs scheduling in software, while Seidels approach uses a dedicated hardware unit called CoreManager. We extend

Seidels work by adding real-time capabilities to the programming model and the hardware unit. When writing about real-time in this paper, we always refer to soft or semi-hard real-time constraints, since these are the types of constraints typically appearing in multimedia and communication systems.

3   MPSoC Platform Overview

A basic schematic of our MPSoC platform is depicted in Fig. 1. The software part is required in order to compile programs for the underlying hardware architecture. This will be detailed in section 5. In this section we will give a short overview over the hardware required to execute our real-time programs.

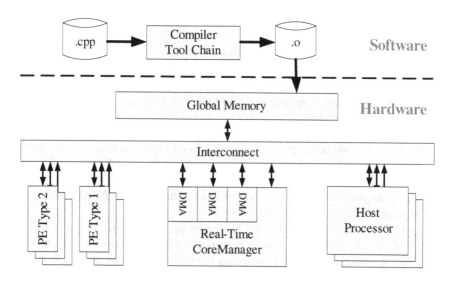

Fig. 1. Architecture schematic

Host Processor. The system may have one or multiple host processors (HP) which are typically RISC processors. They are used to run the operating system and control code. The host processors share the global memory. Whenever a task is instantiated from control code, the HP sends a task description containing all relevant information for task execution to the RT-CoreManager.

Processing Elements. A processing element (PE) can be any kind of hardware. This includes general purpose, domain and application specific processors as well as application specific fixed logic blocks or components for external interfacing. PEs are used to execute computational kernels. Each PE has its own local memory which is managed by the RT-CoreManager. PEs do not have direct access to external resources. In order to allow a wide range of existing components to be used, we do not expect PEs to be able to support context switching in hardware.

Real-Time CoreManager. The RT-CoreManager is the key component of the system. It is responsible for mapping tasks to the processing elements and handles task prioritization and dependency checking. Furthermore it performs local memory management for the PEs and controls data transfers from and to them. The real-time extension prioritizes tasks based on the remaining time (slack) until the tasks latest possible start time weighted with the static priority of the thread. Scheduling is performed by a list scheduler which handles highest priority tasks first. In average 60 clock cycles are required to schedule one task.

Interfacing between RT-CoreManager and host processor is done without any interrupts. The HP sends task descriptions and receives status information over memory mapped registers.

4 Programming Model

The programming model is a crucial component of a MPSoC platform, since it influences the acceptance among programmers. Languages such as C, C++ or Java are popular and therefore more likely to be accepted than other languages. We use C++ as the base language in order to implement our programming model in the most convenient way.

Our real-time programs basically consist of two components: tasks and real-time threads. A task is an atomic computational kernel which is executed on a processing element. Tasks consume and produce chunks of data. They come in two different flavors: either a task is a program running on some kind of programmable processor or it is an algorithm executed on an ASIC. We assume tasks to have a run-time of at least a few hundred cycles.

Real-time threads are threads with an execution time limit. They live as normal threads in the real-time operating system and are executed interleaved on the host processor. Tasks are instantiated from the sequential thread code and are executed concurrently on the available processing elements. When a task was instantiated, the threads continues execution immediately. Thread execution only has to be stopped, if the task queue of the RT-CoreManager is full or if control code depends on data which is computed by one of the PEs. Synchronization statements to wait for data to be ready are generated automatically by our compiler. Synchronization between threads can be implemented using any mechanism provided by the used threading model.

Threads and Tasks have to be identified explicitly by the programmer. But in contrast to other approaches, the decision which kind of PE or even which concrete PE is used is not done at compile-time. Instead of this the programmer simply defines one or more types of PEs a task can be executed on and leaves the selection of the appropriate PE to the RT-CoreManager. For automatic extraction of task deadlines, the programmer annotates the maximum execution time of a task on each PE. The RT-CoreManager performs dependency checking between tasks at run-time and schedules a task not before all its dependencies are resolved. Thus, tasks are reordered at run-time. This is similar to instruction scheduling in superscalar processors.

4.1   Real-Time Support

Each thread has a static priority which reflects the importance of meeting its deadline. As an example threads of media applications will typically have less priority over communication applications in mobile phones. Static priorities and deadlines are assigned by the programmer.

In a real-time system only threads have an explicit deadline but task do not. To allow dynamic prioritization of tasks by the CoreManager, each tasks deadline in a thread must be annotated. Since this would be a cumbersome and error prone task for the programmer, we compute task deadlines using a specialized compiler. All information gathered by the compiler are annotated in the so called Thread Description Graph which is linked into program and guides the RT-CoreManager scheduling.

The Thread Description Graph (TDG) is a directed acyclic graph consisting of nodes representing task instances and edges representing possible control flow paths in the thread. Edges have annotated the probability of the control flow path to be taken. Tasks have annotated different parameters:

Program memory locations: For each possible implementation on a processing element, the CoreManager needs a pointer to the location of program code for this task. If the PE is an ASIC which does not require program memory, a unique dummy pointer is used. This is required since program memory pointers are used to track the path of execution in the RT-CoreManager. Starting from an initial root node provided with the start of a thread, the RT-CoreManager checks which path of execution is taken, whenever a new task arrives. The tracking mechanism compares the program memory pointers of the new task with the pointers annotated in the TDG to find out witch path was taken.

The **best case latest possible start time** (BCLPST) represents the latest start time of a task on a machine with unlimited PEs and DMA controllers under the assumption, that always the shortest control flow path is taken. The BCLPST is annotated in time units relative to the thread deadline. If a task is not able to meet its BCLPST, the corresponding thread is guaranteed to miss its deadline, too.

The **worst case latest possible start time** (WCLPST) is similar to the BCLPST but the longest control flow path is assumed for its calculation. Thus, when a task meets this deadline, it is guaranteed, that all succeeding tasks are also able to meet their deadline, too. However, if the WCLPST is missed, it is still possible to meet the thread deadline if a more optimistic case than that one assumed for WCLPST computation occurs. Therefore, we use the WCLPST for dynamic prioritization in the RT-CoreManager and the BCLPST as the cancellation criterion of a thread.

Loop information: When task calls are found in of loop bodies, special loop nodes are generated. Loop nodes denote start or end of a loop body. They have annotated their iteration count, the maximum execution time of the loop body as well as the deadline for the final iteration.

4.2 C++ Implementation

A thread is modeled by a class derived from `RtThread_t`. This base class has a pure virtual function `_Execute` which must be implemented by the programmer. `_Execute` contains the threads functionality. It must never be called directly from user code but is invoked implicitly when the threads `Start` function is called.

The `RtThread_t` base class encapsulates implementation details such as the threading model of the target operating system. Furthermore `RtThread_t` hides the details of communication with the RT-CoreManager from the programmer. Thus, user code does not need to contain any hardware or operating system specific information. Execution of code on another operating system or a new hardware with modified RT-CoreManager interface can easily be accomplished by simply replacing the `RtThread_t` base class.

Tasks are functions with a number of pointer arguments. They may be static class members or global non-member functions. Data is passed as pointer to its global memory location. Tasks are declared in the same way as normal C/C++ functions, but the definition is enclosed in some pragmas. These pragmas determine the entry point of the task and the processor types it may be executed on.

Listing 1.1 gives an example of a very basic real-time thread containing two task calls. For convenience the macros `TASK`, `IN` and `OUT` are available. `TASK` encapsulates a complete task call. The first parameter is the task name to be executed, the following parameters are the input and output data, which are passed to the task using the `IN` and `OUT` macros. Their arguments determine data location and the size of the data block.

Note that all extensions are implemented using standard C++ features, allowing compilation of the applications with any C++ compiler. Therefore, the program code can be used as reference as well as multi-core implementation without any changes. This allows functional verification to take place without any simulation runs on MPSoC simulators.

5   Compiler Tool Chain

For compilation, the C++ sources are passing a fully automated compiler tool chain. The complete chain is depicted in Fig. 2. In the first step, task and control code are separated by the TaskSplitter. Task code is compiled by the PE C/C++ compilers. The Thread Description Graph Compiler (TDGC) generates a C++ representation of the TDG for each thread in the application. The application source code along with the TDGs is compiled with the HP compiler. Finally the PE objects are linked as data blocks into the HP object code.

The TDG generated by the TDGC is fully annotated. Thus, no user modification is required. For TDGC implementation we extended the GCC source code in order support the special features of our programming model. Graph generation is performed in four successive steps. At first, control flow analysis is performed, followed by memory alias analysis. From the results of the first two steps, TDGC computes the BCLPST and WCLPST as well as all data dependencies and annotates them in the graph. Finally the graph is transformed to reduce memory consumption.

During control flow analysis, a tree representation of the compiled thread is generated. In order to remove back-edges, we add loop-start and loop-end-nodes at the source and the destination of back-edges in the control flow graph. These loop-nodes contain the loop information and are required to make the graph acyclic.

```cpp
// Task that can be executed on ASIP or DSP
#pragma TASK_BEGIN    FFT                 // start task declaration
#pragma TASK_TARGET   FFT-ASIP,    410    // target, execution time
#pragma TASK_TARGET   StandardDSP, 2050   // target, execution time

// this is the task entry point
void FFT ( void *i1, void *i2, void *o ) {
  // function implementation goes here, even sub-function are allowed ...
}

#pragma TASK_END                          // finish task declaration

// A very basic real-time thread class declaration
class MyThread_t :
  public RtThread_t {                     // thread base-class

private:
  void _Execute ( );                      // thread entry point function

  int   _mode;                            // internal variables
  int*  _a, _b, _c;                       // internal variables
  // further functions and variables ...
};

// Implementation of the thread functionality
void MyThread_t::_Execute ( ) {
  if ( _mode == 1 )                       // if in the one mode, perform FFT ...
    TASK ( FFT, IN ( _a, 1024 * sizeof ( int ) ),
               IN ( _b, 512  * sizeof ( int ) ),
               OUT( _c, 1024 * sizeof ( int ) ) );
  else                                    // ... otherwise perform IFFT
    TASK ( IFFT, IN ( _a, 1024 * sizeof ( int ) ),
               IN ( _b, 512  * sizeof ( int ) ),
               OUT( _c, 1024 * sizeof ( int ) ) );
}

// main function implementation
int main ( ) {
  MyThread_t instance1;      // Create thread instances (but don't execute)

  // Start execution of the thread
  instance1 . Start ( 4, 10000 );        // priority=4, deadline in 10000 cycles

  // Start other threads here ...

  return 0;
}
```

Listing 1.1. C++ Implementation of a Real-Time Thread (The base class is RtThread_t, the thread entry function is _Execute)

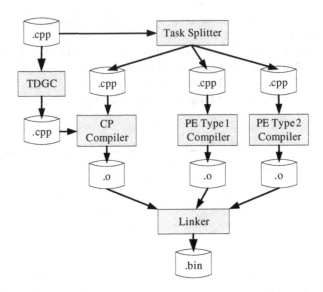

Fig. 2. The Compiler Tool Chain

During the memory alias analysis phase, task dependencies are analyzed. In order to do that, the compiler searches each control flow path separately for memory aliases [13]. A dependency is considered as present if at least one of the following conditions holds (assuming task B is issued after task A):

- One or more outputs of task A are aliased with one or more inputs of task B (read after write dependency).
- One or more outputs of task A are aliased with one or more outputs of task B (write after write dependency).
- One or more inputs of task A are aliased with one or more output of task B (write after read dependency).

If none of the above is true and the aliasing of inputs and output of two tasks is uncertain, the dependency between two tasks is annotated as uncertain. If no certain or uncertain dependency is found, two task are treated as independent.

The third compilation step computes the latest possible start times for each task node. For LPST computation we assume unlimited availability of PEs and DMA controllers. Network traffic is modeled according to the characteristics of the interconnection network. An "as late as possible" (ALAP) schedule is computed for this kind of machine, providing the start times for each thread in the TDG. The assumption of unlimited resources ensures, that the obtained deadlines are suitable for architectures with arbitrary parallelism, thus making the TDG only dependent on the kind of used PEs on an MPSoC but not on their count.

The last step tries to reduce memory consumption of the graph by merging nodes of equal tasks existing in different execution paths. In principle this could be done for any nodes of equal tasks in the graph but we have to take care that BCLPST and WCLPST, do not diverge so much because of merging. In practice a restriction has to be placed on merging which limits this divergence.

6   Results

At the current development stage, the compiler is able to cope with arbitrary programs without loops. First tests on 802.11a WLAN C++ code resulted in 100% of correctly detected dependencies. Further tests with hand written test-cases resulted in 10% of uncertain task dependencies.

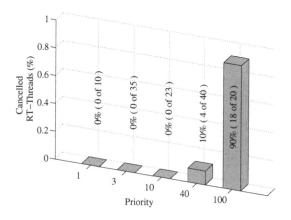

Fig. 3. Canceled tasks in an overloaded system

Figure 3 shows the cancellation rates of threads with different priorities which are executed in a heavily overloaded system. As it can be seen, only low prior-ity threads (higher priority numbers denote less priority) are canceled due to the overload situation. The TDG for these threads has been generated with the TDGC. Results have been obtained by simulation on a transaction level simu-lator with 8 processors.

7   Conclusions and Future Work

In this paper we stated, that existing programming models and hardware archi-tectures are not able to cope with future application requirements. We presented an alternative approach solving the problem of task synchronization and reduc-ing scheduling overhead caused by hardware/software interfacing. Furthermore a real-time enabled programming model was suggested which makes concurrent real-time programming quite straightforward. Our first experiments showed, that a run-time scheduling is feasible under real-time constraints. Furthermore, it has been shown, that the compiler can deliver results of the quality required for annotation of reasonable real time constraints.

Currently data flow analysis within loops is under development for the TDGC. Different real application benchmarks from the wireless communications and the multimedia domain are under development in order to prove the applicability of our approach to real time applications. Furthermore, we are aiming to allocate and manage communication resources in order to improve predictability of data transfer behavior.

References

1. Horowitz, M., Dally, W.: How scaling will change processor architecture. In: Proceedings of the IEEE Solid-State Circuits Conference, 2004, Digest of Technical Papers, ISSCC, pp. 132–133 (February 2004)
2. Lee, E.A.: The problem with threads. IEEE Computer 39(5), 33–42 (2006)
3. Silven, O., Jyrkkä, K.: Observations on power-efficiency trends in mobile communication devices. EURASIP Journal on Embedded Systems 2007, 10 pages (2007), Article ID 56976, doi:10.1155/2007/56976
4. Seidel, H.: A Task-level Programmable Processor, WiKu, Duisburg (October 2006)
5. Asanovic, K., Bodik, R., Catanzaro, B.C., Gebis, J.J., Husbands, P., Keutzer, K., Patterson, D.A., Plishker, W.L., Shalf, J., Williams, S.W., Yelick, K.A.: The landscape of parallel computing research: A view from berkeley. Technical Report UCB/EECS-2006-183, EECS Department, University of California, Berkeley (December 2006)
6. Dagum, L., Menon, R.: Openmp: An industry-standard api for shared-memory programming. IEEE Computational Science and Engineering 05(1), 46–55 (1998)
7. Ghuloum, A., Sprangle, E., Fang, J.: NVidia: CUDA Programming Guide 1.1 (November 2007), http://www.nvidia.com/object/cuda_develop.html
8. Blumofe, R.D., Joerg, C.F., Kuszmaul, B.C., Leiserson, C.E., Randall, K.H., Zhou, Y.: Cilk: an efficient multithreaded runtime system. SIGPLAN Not. 30(8), 207–216 (1995)
9. Bernard, T., Bousias, K., Geus, B.d., Lankamp, M., Zhang, L., Pimentel, A., Knijnenburg, P., Jesshope, C.: A microthreaded architecture and its compiler (2006)
10. Fatahalian, K., Knight, T.J., Houston, M., Erez, M., Horn, D.R., Leem, L., Park, J.Y., Ren, M., Aiken, A., Dally, W.J., Hanrahan, P.: Sequoia: Programming the memory hierarchy. In: Proceedings of the 2006 ACM/IEEE Conference on Supercomputing (2006)
11. Bellens, P., Perez, J.M., Rosa, M., Badia, Labarta, J.: CellSs: a programming model for the cell be architecture. In: Proceedings of the ACM/IEEE Supercomputing 2006 Conference (November 2006)
12. Pham, D., Asano, S., Bolliger, M., Day, M., Hofstee, H., Johns, C., Kahle, J., Kameyama, A., Keaty, J., Masubuchi, Y., Riley, M., Shippy, D., Stasiak, D., Suzuoki, M., Wang, M., Warnock, J., Weitzel, S., Wendel, D., Yamazaki, T., Yazawa, K.: The design and implementation of a first-generation cell processor. In: Solid-State Circuits Conference 2005. Digest of Technical Papers ISSCC 2005, IEEE International, vol. 1, pp. 184–592 (February 2005)
13. Muchnick, S.S.: Advanced Compiler Design & Implementation. Morgan Kaufman Publishers, San Francisco (1997)

A Multi-objective and Hierarchical Exploration Tool for SoC Performance Estimation

Alexis Vander Biest, Alienor Richard, Dragomir Milojevic, and Frederic Robert

Université Libre de Bruxelles, BEAMS Department
Av. F. D. Roosevelt 50, 1050 Brussels, Belgium
{avdbiest, arichard, dmilojevic, frrobert}@ulb.ac.be

Abstract. In this paper we present a flexible performance estimation tool called Nessie developed to provide system-on-chip designers with automated multi-objective design space exploration and its related tool called Yeti building and executing reusable closed-formed models. After reviewing the existing closed-formed expressions based and application/platform mapping performance estimation tools, we propose an hybrid tool to cope with their limitations. We present a brief summary of the functionalities of Yeti and describe Nessie, our hierarchical application/platform performance estimation mapping tool which banalizes all the degrees of freedom for in-depth design space exploration and introduces multi-objective modeling. Through this paper, we explain how the combination of these tools provides the designer with innovative and powerful functionalities for performance prediction at the earlier stages of the design flow.

1 Introduction and Context

What makes design of embedded systems (especially SoCs) highly challenging is the fact that besides presenting a complex functionality, these systems have to comply with ever more severe non-functional constraints in various dimensions (power consumption, silicon area, cost, etc). Moreover, the SoC architectural complexity (number of primitives) and heterogeneity (variety of primitives) increase with time, which puts even more pressure on the design process.

To face this complexity, evolved design flows have emerged, that can be viewed as a series of steps, each of these steps consisting in taking decisions about the structure of the system, in order to move progressively from a pencil-and-paper system description to the real device meeting the specifications. In this process, multi-level abstraction both at software and hardware level is mandatory to limit the number of degrees of freedom considered simultaneously and simplify the automated design tools task.

Design iterations, in which a decision taken previously at a higher abstraction level has to be reconsidered when reaching lower abstraction levels (where implementation costs are better known), are the enemy of designers and industry, simply because they cost time. That's why the development and use of models allowing the designer to predict as early as possible in the design flow the impact of a design decision on performances is crucial.

M. Berekovic, N. Dimopoulos, and S. Wong (Eds.): SAMOS 2008, LNCS 5114, pp. 85–95, 2008.

Reconfigurable systems can be viewed as a target of choice for such an analysis since reconfigurability can be defined as keeping, at runtime, some degrees of freedom about the structure (hardware or software) of the system. Hence reconfigurability is viewed here as the final steps, acting at runtime, of a more general design process.

In this paper, we review different tools focusing on performance prediction and discuss their current limitations in Sec.2. Based on this related work, we present our own tools and explain the benefits that we could gain over classical solutions: Yeti is a closed-formed flexible modeling tool (Sec.3) and Nessie, our second tool, enables platform/applicaiton hierarchical representation and multi-objective performance estimation (Sec.4). Finally Sec.5 ends with some conclusions and future work.

2   Related Work

Across the literature, the most common and wide-accepted definition of System-level performance models is the following: "System-level performance models can be defined as first order models that attempt to capture the majority of relevant system design issues in order to provide useful predictions or early feedback to designers."[1] How useful it can be to give the general idea about the models involved in this activity, this definition has the main drawback of including a too large part of the computer science related literature.

In the scope of this paper we define the system as the combination of an application and a platform enabling its execution. To classify the different system-level modeling tools that have been produced, we can separate them into two different categories:

- Tools that explicitly describe the application and the platform in a structured way to measure the performances resulting of their mapping. We will call them *HW/SW mapping performance estimation tools*[1].
- Tools that compute the performances by using compact closed-formed capturing the information of both the application and the platform. We will call the *closed-formed based performances estimation tools*.

2.1   HW/SW Mapping Performance Estimation Tools

In the past years many tools have been proposed both in the industrial and academic field to model the software/hardware interaction and its impact on performances. Rather then reviewing them all in details, we chose the most relevant and developed frameworks based on worthy and comparable criteria (Table1): the SW/HW description language (SWD, HWD), the care for multi-objective performance modeling (MO), the tool automatic exploration capabilities (AE),

---

[1] In the rest of this paper, the application will be referred to as Software (SW) and the platform as Hardware (HW) whatever the considered abstraction level.

the possibility of building hierarchical modeling both for HW and SW (HM) and the synthesis capability (Synth.).

Looking in this table we can notice a few interesting things:

1. Most of the reviewed tools often focus only on timing (latency, computation time) while other aspects are somewhat left behind. Only Metropolis allows the designer to model the different performance metrics he's interested in.
2. Few of them offer automatic design space exploration and when it's the case, this exploration is only limited to the architecture (number of processors, communication architecture etc.) and hidden inside the tool.
3. Many of them operate at the highest abstraction level of the design flow but don't offer the possibility to describe lower abstraction levels. This is especially an issue when it comes to take into account technological related parameters and measure their impact on performances.

Table 1. Table of the state-of-the-art HW/SW mapping performance tools

Tool	SWD	HWD	MO	AE	HM	Synth.
SESAME[2]	KPN	XML based	No	No	Yes	No
Koski[3]	UML	UML	No	Yes	No	No
Design trotter[4]	HCDFG	XMl based	Yes	Yes	No	No
Metropolis [5]	meta-model	meta-model	Yes	No	Yes	Yes
Cofluent[6]	SystemC	SystemC	No	Yes	No	Yes
Chinook[7]	Verilog	Verilog	No	No	No	No

2.2   Closed-Formed Based Performances Estimation Tools

A large part of the literature focuses on proposing closed-formed models targeting fast modeling for the estimation of some performance variable whatever the considered abstraction level. To cut down on the related state-of-the-art, we only consider complete *modeling systems* that encompass models enabling high-level variables performance estimation (throughput, instruction-per-cycle for a microprocessor unit, total chip power consumption) based on low abstraction level information (technology, CAD tool routing efficiency etc.).

Performance prediction tools of first generation were mainly focused on clock cycle for (multi-)processor architectures (RIPE[8], SUSPENS[9], Codrescu model[10]). Progressively they gained in functionality by introducing a modeling hierarchy with GENESYS[11] and by enabling multiple-objective modeling with BACPAC[12] (timing related metrics, power consumption, silicon area etc.).

The state-of-the-art tool named GTX[13] has been developed to provide the user with a platform to incorporate existing models found throughout the literature with its own. This effort to avoid the redundant development of modeling tools and to make previously hard-coded models explicit unfortunately never got the success it deserved and its further implementation has been abandoned. Furthermore some limitations prevent the user from using GTX as efficiently as he should:

- No scripting functionality is available; large campaign simulations where successive models need to be built, loaded and executed for a given set of inputs require the constant intervention of the user.
- GTX is a GUI-based tool; no interfacing with another tool is possible
- The underlying grammar to specify models is too permissive and lacks some restrictions about the model specification and variable name uniqueness verification.
- Input sensitivity analysis (which consists in studying the impact of the input variations on the model output values) is supported at the expense of performing numerous model evaluations while sweeping the input values around their nominal values to measure the output variation.

2.3 Towards an Hybrid Tool for Performance Estimation

Comparing closed-formed based and HW/SW mapping performance estimation tools , we can draw two interesting conclusions:

- While closed-formed based tools mostly focus on platform details (technology node, interconnect, micro-archiecture parameters etc.), it does barely care about application related parameters (degree of parallelism, instruction mix etc.). On the contrary, HW/SW mapping tools describe in details the application but don't consider as much low-level technology information as the previous type of tool does.
- Closed-formed based tools allow the designer to simultaneously take information from all the design process abstraction levels and encompass them into closed-formed relations while HW/SW mapping tools focus in details on one abstraction level with precise information about both the platform and application structure.

From the above statements, it is clear that an hybrid performance prediction tool could combine the best of the two worlds by providing detailed and structured information about the HW/SW couple where accurate modeling is needed combined with simplified closed-formed models to bridge the abstraction levels gap. This paper addresses this issue by presenting two different tools of our own whose combination precisely leads to that kind of hybrid tool:

- *Yeti* is a C++ library that allows the user to build and estimate models extracted from a repository of models described in XML. It has powerful scripting possibilities, offer special support for input sensitivity analysis and can also work as a standalone tool if desired.
- *Nessie* is a framework enabling hierarchical description of the application and its platform (again in XML). It provides multi-objective HW/SW mapping performance estimation based on a customizable policy mapping algorithm.

3 Yeti

Yeti[14] is a flexible framework for the building and evaluation of closed-formed based performance prediction models. It can either be used as a C++ library or as a standalone tool. The functionalities of Yeti are the following:

- *Specification and reuse of models* thanks to an XML schema based grammar. Models are defined in XML files and can be chained[2] to form larger and more complex models.
- *Output sensitivity study.* In the case of closed-formed models, Yeti uses a mechanism that enables fast model output sensitivity estimation based on input value bounds. Closed-formed expressions are represented as trees composed out of basic operations (addition, logarithm, division etc.); for each of them, we can easily compute the bounds starting from the leaves of the tree and then propagate the result to the top of the tree until we get the output bounds. This method is a lot faster than sweeping the input values to find the extrema since it only requires one sole closed-formed expression evaluation.
- *Model sensitivity study.* Since models are read from XML files and built at run-time, it is easy to swap a model for another and measure the impact on the predicted output parameter. Furthermore this procedure can easily be automated by the use of our XML based scripts.
- *Evaluation and plot.* Results are stored in an XML file that can be processed by Yeti afterwards to extract the data to transmit them to a plotting program (Matlab for instance).

More information and results about Yeti can be found in [14] where we compared several interconnect models and successfully performed interconnect delay sensitivity analysis to process variations.

4   Nessie

Nessie is a framework providing the user with flexible, multi-objective and hierarchical representation of the application/platform couple. The purpose of this tool is to extend the features and generality of the existing systems reviewed in Sec.2.1 and offer an interface for automatic design space exploration.

4.1   Criteria and Degrees of Freedom

Before beginning to explore the design space, the designer has to determine two different things: the criteria and the degrees of freedom (DoFs).

Criteria are measurable variables of the design quality that can be used to fairly compare different design options (for instance silicon area, fault tolerance rating, power consumption, execution time, heat density etc.). If each criteria of a solution 1 is better than the corresponding one of a solution 2, the latter solution will be discarded and inversely. There is no restriction on the definition and number of criteria; from one design to another, the constraints may be different so that it makes no sense to fix a list of criteria. It's up to the designer to:

---

[2] Model chaining means that we use models output predictions to feed other model inputs creating a tree structure of model.

1. Choose the criteria[3] and tell Nessie how they evolve over time and how to compute them
2. Define the explicit constraints (i.e. a minimum and/or maximum value for each criterion).

Degrees of freedom are the design variables that we have to fix during the design flow implementation process: they include information about the application, the material support and the mapping tools. Fixing all the DoFs leads to one design solution: the complete set of solutions can be generated by combining all the possible DoFs values.

4.2 Hierarchical Modeling

Nessie models both the platform and application in a hierarchical way. Each abstraction level is thus composed of different SW/HW primitives (called *SW/HW types*) that can be instantiated at will to form a more complex *SW/HW structure*. Different SW/HW structures may be added to one single SW/HW type so that it defines possible degrees of freedom for the SW/HW structures. This mechanism allows the user to swap an algorithm for another at design-time or choose from different SW implementations at run-time in the case of dynamically reconfigurable systems (in the case of SW blocks), test different platform topologies (HW blocks) but even more important to evaluate how well a particular application matches a certain platform.

Since we have defined a hierarchical structure, we need a flexible mechanism to support the estimation of the criteria. Fig.1 illustrates the different possibilities that we have when we want to compute the criteria resulting from the execution of $SW_{L,j}$ on $HW_{L,i}$[4]:

1. To have a direct estimation of the criteria, we can use a Yeti model: each SW block and HW block description therefore comes with a set of parameters (defining new degrees of freedom) that are used as inputs for the Yeti model.
2. To get a more detailed estimation of the performances (at the expense of a greater estimation time), we can explore the structure deeper. We move on to the lower SW/HW abstraction level $L+1$ using a mapping algorithm that will perform the scheduling of the SW_{L+1} blocks and map them on the HW_{L+1} blocks to compute the criteria. To obtain the criteria $SW_{L+1,k}$ and $HW_{L,m}$, we proceed recursively by using a Yeti model or exploring deeper the hierarchy.

By combining Nessie and Yeti, we are thus able to provide the user with different compromises between modeling accuracy and modeling estimation time. As Nessie automatically performs exploration, the user can define an exploration policy (explore as deep as possible, explore until abstraction level L etc.).

---

[3] Time is the only mandatory criteria since it is needed for scheduling.

[4] $SW_{L,j}$ is an instance of SW type j defined at abstraction level L.

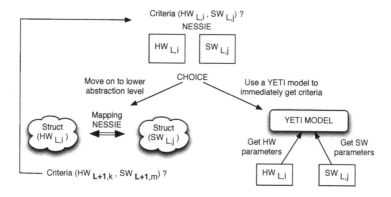

Fig. 1. Exploration of the HW/SW hierarchy for criteria estimation

4.3 Application Description

A software can be described in many different ways: depending on its characteristics (control- or data-dominated, synchronous or not, sequential or parallel etc.) there is likely one model of computation[5] that will offer good support for its description. Among all these MoC's we have chosen to implement Petri Nets since they are able to represent data and control dependency as well concurrency and parallelism[6].

Fig.2 illustrates a very simple example of Petri Net in the case of a basic operation $a = b + c * d$. The petri network is composed out of places and transitions. *Places* represent operations to perform: once a place is triggered, it generates a token after a certain time (i.e. the time required for the operation to complete). *Transitions* represent the conditions that need to fulfilled for the next place to be triggered. If the required number of tokens is present in the places linked to the transition incoming edges, the transition is valid, tokens are consumed and a request is asked to the outgoing edges linked places to generate a token. We can notice on the figure that tokens actually represent the data amount (in bits in our case) that flows between the different places[7].

4.4 Platform Description

Nessie represents the hardware using a netlist of HW blocks elements. It is important to understand that not only computing units are part of the HW

---

[5] The term *Model of computation* (or *MoC*) has been introduced within the framework Ptolemy[15]. It refers to executable models capturing the behaviour of an application that can be classified in different categories[16] (state-oriented, activity-oriented, data flow graphs, process-oriented etc.).

[6] Our implementation is however sufficiently flexible to implement other MoC's and to make them automatically interoperate without any additional effort.

[7] In the case of control flows, the data size associated to the token equals zero: no data exchange need to be performed between the concerned places.

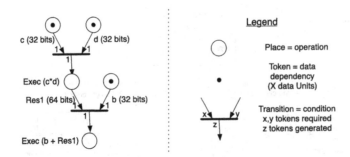

Fig. 2. Petri Net representation for the $a = b + c * d$ operation

blocks: memory and interconnect also fall into that category and are explicitly modeled.

Hardware blocks have several properties:

- *Compatibility*: since hardware can be seen as the material support for the demands of the software, each HW block comes with a list of compatible SW blocks of the same abstraction level. For instance a hardware multiplier is only compatible with the multiply operation while an ALU will likely be able to execute multiply, addition, shifting operations.
- *Costs*: Hardware blocks enable software execution at the expense of some costs. Taking back our ALU/multiplier example, it is obvious that an ALU pays the price for flexibility by consuming more power, occupying more surface and being likely slower than a single hardware multiplier.
- *State*: The dynamic nature of HW blocks behaviour is represented by the use of states: a HW block is either idle, in sleep mode to save energy, computing (one of the compatible SW blocks), memorizing or transmitting data's. To switch from one state to another, we have implemented a transitional time table that takes into account any possible dead time that the HW block may experience (for example a microprocessor recovering from sleeping mode).

To exchange data, HW blocks instantiate one or more communication ports connected through logical links[8]. Fig.3 illustrates two examples of HW structures. The left part of the figure shows two computing nodes connected by a shared interconnect medium to a memory while the right part shows a 4-tile regular mesh with its interconnect network.

Our HW structure representation provides an ideal support for reconfigurable platforms: we are able to represent the effects of a platform run-time reconfiguration by changing the costs, the SW compatibility list (since the new block probably supports other operations) and by adding a *reconfiguration state* to account for the reconfiguration time overhead.

---

[8] Logical must not be mistaken for interconnect: contrarily to the latter, they don't add any cost and are used to connect any block whatever its type (memory, computation or interconnect).

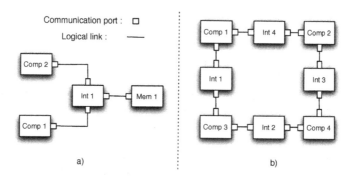

Fig. 3. Examples of HW structures: a) two computing nodes connected by a shared interconnect medium to a memory and b) 4-tile regular mesh with its interconnect network

4.5   Mapping

Now that we have defined general structures for the representation of software and hardware, we have to evaluate the criteria that will result from their mapping. We have define an algorithm that combines allocation, scheduling and routing while preserving a high level of generality. The main steps are the following:

- priority scheduling: the SW block with the highest priority is selected among a ready-to-execute SW queue. The priority is defined by a sum of several variables (the time that the SW block spent waiting in the ready-to-execute queue, the number of dependent SW blocks that will be triggered after current SW block execution etc.) and is part of the mapping algorithm degrees of freedom[9].
- routing/allocation: among the compatible HW types, we select the one with the smallest global routing cost reaching it starting from the HW blocks producing the required data to consume (using a Dijkstra routing algorithm). Again the routing cost calculation is a degree of freedom (it can include information about power consumption, timing, network congestion etc.).

4.6   Example: Communication Network Optimization

To illustrate Nessie functionalities, we have chosen an example focusing on the optimization of communication networks where we try to evaluate the impact of the communication network choice on performances and show its dependence with the application. From a simple shared bus to networks-on-chips, there are many different available choices for interconnect: while the first has the advantage of being very simple and easy to set up, it offers no communication parallelism at

---

[9] The priority is computed using a Yeti model so that we can easily change it at run-time.

all between the different interconnected processing nodes. Networks-on-chips, on the contrary, require more silicon area (multiple wires, routers, network interfaces and so on) but provide the platform with flexible and parallel communication capabilities. Furthermore the choice of the network highly relies on the application: small tasks exchanging numerous information will take advantage of more parallel communication networks than a few computation-centric tasks would do.

Nessie is therefore able to represent the interaction between the communication network and the application and compare the performances for different performance criteria defined by the user (total execution time, power consumption, silicon area, etc.). Therefore we define different architectural choices (HW structures) and different applications descriptions (SW structures) as input and let Nessie explore the different solutions using a fixed allocation/schaduling policy: this results for each possible combination in the performance criteria and allows the designer to choose the best combination.

5   Conclusions and Future Work

Through this paper we have presented how our tools can help the user to capture all the relevant aspects of the chip he has to design. Thanks to our definition of criteria enabling multi-objective optimization, design space exploration can be performed based on all the defined degrees of freedom (HW/SW structure, algorithm weights and costs functions, HW/SW parameters and exploration policy). With such an interface of criteria/degrees of freedom, it is easy to apply more clever exploration methods like metaheuristics that we plan to integrate on top of the Nessie framework. Currently Nessie is in final stages of implementation and we plan to demonstrate very soon its capabilities on some basic HW/SW examples. In the long term, we will try to use Nessie and Yeti on real design flows to evaluate its benefits over classical design methods.

References

1. Sylvester, D., Hu, C.: Analytical modeling and characterization of deep-submicrometer interconnect. In: IEEE (ed.) Proc. IEEE, vol. 89, pp. 634–664 (2001)
2. Polstra, S.: A systematic approach to exploring embedded system architectures at multiple abstraction levels. IEEE Trans. Comput. 55(2), 99–112 (2006); Member-Andy D. Pimentel and Student Member-Cagkan Erbas
3. Kangas, T., Kukkala, P., Orsila, H., Salminen, E., Hännikäinen, M., Hämäläinen, T.D., Riihimäki, J., Kuusilinna, K.: Uml-based multiprocessor soc design framework. Trans. on Embedded Computing Sys. 5(2), 281–320 (2006)
4. Moullec, Y.L., Diguet, J.P., Philippe, J.L.: Design-trotter: a multimedia embedded systems design space exploration tool. In: IEEE Workshop on Multimedia Signal Processing, pp. 448–451 (2002)
5. Balarin, F., Watanabe, Y., Hsieh, H., Lavagno, L., Passerone, C., Sangiovanni-Vincentelli, A.: Metropolis: An integrated electronic system design environment. Computer 36(4), 45–52 (2003)

6. Calvez, J.P., Pasquier, O.: Performance assessment of embedded hw/sw systems. In: ICCD 1995: Proceedings of the 1995 International Conference on Computer Design, pp. 52–57. IEEE Computer Society, Washington (1995)

7. Chou, P.H., Ortega, R.B., Borriello, G.: The chinook hardware/software co-synthesis system. In: ISSS 1995: Proceedings of the 8th international symposium on System synthesis, pp. 22–27. ACM Press, New York (1995)

8. Mangaser, R., Rose, K.: Facilitating interconnect-based vlsi design. In: MSE 1997: Proceedings of the 1997 International Conference on Microelectronics Systems Education (MSE 1997), p. 139. IEEE Computer Society, Washington (1997)

9. Takahashi, S., Edahiro, M., Hayashi, Y.: A new lsi performance prediction model for interconnection analysis of future lsis. In: ASP-DAC, pp. 51–56 (1998)

10. Codrescu, L., Pant, M.D., Taha, T.M., Eble, J., Wills, D.S., Meindl, J.D.: Exploring microprocessor architectures for gigascale integration. In: ARVLSI, pp. 242–255 (1999)

11. Eble, J.C., De, V.K., Wills, D.S., Meindl, J.D.: A generic system simulator (genesys) for asic technology and architecture beyond 2001. In: ASIC Conference and Exhibit proceedings, pp. 193–196 (1996)

12. Sylvester, D., Keutzer, K.: System-level performance modeling with bacpac – berkeley advanced chip performance calculator (1999)

13. Caldwell, A.E., Cao, Y., Kahng, A.B., Koushanfar, F., Lu, H., Markov, I.L., Oliver, M., Stroobandt, D., Sylvester, D.: GTX: the MARCO GSRC technology extrapolation system. In: Design Automation Conference, pp. 693–698 (2000)

14. Vander Biest, A., Richard, A., Milojevic, D., Robert, F.: A framework introducing model reversibility in soc design space exploration. In: Vassiliadis, S., Bereković, M., Hämäläinen, T.D. (eds.) SAMOS 2007. LNCS, vol. 4599, pp. 211–221. Springer, Heidelberg (2007)

15. Davis, J.: Ptolemy ii - heterogeneous concurrent modeling and design in java (2000)

16. Panagopoulos, I.: Models, specification languages and their interrelationship models, specification languages and their interrelationship for system level design. Technical report, HPCL,The George Washington University (2002)

A Novel Non-exclusive Dual-Mode Architecture for MPSoCs-Oriented Network on Chip Designs

Francesca Palumbo, Simone Secchi, Danilo Pani, and Luigi Raffo

University of Cagliari, DIEE - Dept. of Electrical and Electronic Engineering
Piazza D'Armi, 09123 Cagliari, Italy
{francesca.palumbo,simone.secchi,pani,luigi}@diee.unica.it

Abstract. Multi-Processor Systems-on-Chip (MPSoCs) are the most recent challenge of the VLSI technologies and Networks on Chip represent a high performance alternative to the traditional bus architectures. In this paper, a novel approach to the design of a dual-mode router, based on the idea of supporting both circuit and packet switching in a non-exclusive way, is presented and evaluated. This feature makes the proposed architecture suitable for MPSoCs which have to deal with heterogeneous traffic characteristics especially in terms of data size, such as the Massively Parallel Processors. Non-exclusivity enables packets latency reduction, which in turn implies lower task completion times, and also it increases throughput.

Keywords: Networks on Chip, Dual-mode switching, Non-exclusive switching, Circuit switching.

1   Introduction

Nowadays it is a widely shared opinion that Multi-Processor Systems on Chip (MPSoCs) are the most recent challenge of VLSI technologies. Due to the increased on-die integration capacity, system complexity can be considered one of the two main hot topics dealing with MPSoCs. The other one is instead related to the wiring issues in the high gate count designs [1]. A feasible solution for both problems seems to be provided by tile-based architectures. These architectures are composed of several elements, namely the tiles, all identical and formed by Intellectual Properties (IPs). Typically in the tile-based architectures, interconnection networks replace ad-hoc global wiring structures.

Complexity does not mean only integration density but also an efficient support for complex applications, which could require heavy concurrency to be handled and wide thread parallelism to be exploited [1]. A very promising solution to withstand this kind of applications is provided by Massively Parallel Processors (MPPs). MPPs are tiled architectures composed of a large number of processors regularly interconnected to form a multiprocessor environment on a single chip [2]. The interconnection medium for MPSoCs and, even more, for MPPs is a non-trivial design concern: large bandwidth and efficient support for the parallelism have to be enabled. Traditional interconnection networks such

M. Berekovic, N. Dimopoulos, and S. Wong (Eds.): SAMOS 2008, LNCS 5114, pp. 96–105, 2008.

as busses, even if small are not capable of providing parallel access to the interconnected resources, present poor scalability and wiring optimization. All the limitations experienced by busses are points of strength of the Networks on Chip (NoCs), widely used for this reason in MPSoCs and MPPs design [3].

In this paper, a novel NoC architecture including all the abovementioned features but also flexible in terms of traffic to be supported is presented and evaluated. The possibility of providing guaranteed throughput service and best effort service together, at the price of having a router which embeds two crossbars, has been explored. Motivations reside mainly in the fact that, in real applications, continuous and discontinuous traffic coexist. Moreover particular applications are very likely to run different threads in parallel on different tiles, but with the need of exchanging scalar data vectors or even threads, which are intrinsically very different.

The rest of the paper is dedicated to a brief panoramic of the state of the art of related topics (Section 2), to point out the architectural issues this approach wants to address (Section 3), to a detailed description of the implemented solution (Section 4) and its validation (Section 5) and finally, in Section 6, conclusions and future works are presented.

2   Related Works

There are many different ways to classify a NoC. From the point of view of the kind of switching it is possible to highlight two categories: packed switched networks and circuit switched networks [4].

The circuit switching technique is the method by which a dedicated path, or circuit, is established prior the sending of the sensitive data. This characteristic makes circuit switched networks suitable for guaranteed throughput applications, especially in case of real time communications.

In packet switching methodologies the intermediate routers are responsible for routing the individual packets through the network, neither following a predefined nor a reserved path. Since this technique does not require reserving any resource in advance, it is suitable for best-effort services or for soft-timing constrained communications.

In this scenario, some NoC architectures claim to be dual-mode, being able to support both types of switching. The benefits of these hybrid networks consist in a better usage of the available bandwidth and the increasing of the overall throughput, at the price of a more complex hardware implementation.

This issue has been firstly addressed by Shin at al. [5]: combining two different types of packet switching (virtual cut-through and wormhole routing) they were able to guarantee a higher throughput (with respect to pure wormhole) and to reduce buffering demand (with respect to pure virtual cut-through). Philips Research Lab [6,7] pushed these improvements even further, implementing a dual-mode switch which provides both guaranteed and best-effort services. Similar results have been obtained also by Hsu et al. [8] and by Ahmad et. al [9]. The abovementioned works [6,7,8,9] mainly differ on the type of implementation and supported application (e.g. the architecture of Hsu et al. is conceived for AMBA-based IPs).

The novelty of the presented approach mainly resides in the possibility of having circuit switching and packet switching in parallel and contemporary.

3   Architectural Requirements

MPP architectures are conceived to efficiently implement the Thread Level Parallelism (TLP), a common characteristic of the MPSoCs. Each IP in an MPP has to execute a particular instructions flow, known as *thread*, in a completely self-sufficient manner and to be able to communicate with other IPs, in order to exchange data shared among different threads. The demand of parallelism required by MPPs and MPSoCs implies the design of an efficient communication layer able to sustain it. This means that the interconnection medium has to be scalable, to allow multiple accesses of the different IPs to the shared resources and to be optimized in terms of wiring.

The choice of a particular interconnection structure, among all the available ones in literature, is highly dependent on the type of traffic to be routed. In MPSoCs, such as the MPPs, it is necessary to provide a quick resolution of the interdependencies among different threads, single scalar data or even vectors, which are responsible for the suspension of a thread from its execution, thus delaying its completion time. Moreover, in MPP architectures, load balancing techniques to avoid hot spots and to efficiently exploit all the IPs available on-chip are usually required. Threads migrations between IPs generates a regular and continuous traffic, made up of long streams of data. Thus long streams of data, vectors and single data have to be efficiently served.

4   Proposed Dual-Mode Router Micro-architecture

In this paper a novel NoC architecture able to combine the benefits of the circuit switching and the packet switching techniques is proposed. The key idea is to make them feasible at the same time, avoiding packet switching communications stalls for long time intervals due to circuit switched communications. This allows to solve data interdependencies quickly, which otherwise could stay un-solved for all the time necessary to migrate a task [7,9]. The price to pay is to split a wider link such as a 32 bit one, into two different parallel links (16+18 bits) driven by two different crossbars.

This novel architecture is also able to provide all the typical services a NoC has to guarantee [10]: data integrity, deadlock free communications, lossless data delivery, in-order data delivery, throughput and latency. Deadlock free communications are ensured by the adoption of a fair arbitration scheme in case of contentions and of the X-Y routing scheme (deadlock free by construction). Lossless data delivery and in-order data delivery are guaranteed by the control flow (credit-based) and the switching (wormhole) implemented policies. Finally, throughput and latency depend merely on the transaction to be initiated: circuit switching or packet switching is appropriately selected at the transport layer, in an ISO-OSI like description [3] of the NoC.

A generic NoC architecture is composed by several different instances of three elements: the link, the Network Interface (NI) and the router. Links, from our point of view, are simple wires which connect each NI with an IP on one side and with a router on the other, and also routers among themselves. NIs are responsible to translate the end-to-end communication protocol into the network protocol and vice versa, moreover in this particular architecture NIs are responsible to set up the appropriate kind of transaction to be initiated (circuit/packet). Nevertheless, due to the fact that this paper is mainly related to the NoC itself, a description of the internal details of the NI is meaningless, because too much related to the IP which is connected to.

4.1   Dual-Mode Router

A key feature of the proposed router architecture is that packet switching and circuit switching are not implemented in an exclusive fashion, such as all the other routers in literature [6,7,8,9]. The general view of a typical packet switching router [4] has been enriched by the presence of a circuit handling section, thus the upper part of the block diagram in Figure 1 is hereafter named *Packet Handling* (PH) section and the lower one *Circuit Handling* (CH) section. This fact does not mean that each router is composed of two separated couples of datapath and control path serving separately packets and circuits. The two aforementioned sections cooperate and exchange control signals in order to allow the establishment of the circuits and the packets flow (PH section) and the communication over the reserved circuits (CH section).

Keeping in mind that this architecture has been designed to be suitable for MPSoCs and MPPs, we have decided to adopt a 2-D mesh topology, mainly for two reasons: normally MPPs are organized in grid structures and moreover a 2-D mesh is easily traceable on a 2-D layout. Each node of our network is connected with 4 neighbours and with one NI.

The PH section is standard [4], with respect to packets management. Packets are routed according to the wormhole switching technique and the flits are stored, along the path to destination, into output buffers. Input buffering has not been implemented, even though each incoming flit is stored in a register prior to be sent to the proper virtual output channel, in order to avoid any loss in case of congested FIFO. Moreover, in order to provide two levels of priorities, the output channels are organized into two different virtual output channels multiplexed on the same physical output link. Priorities are assigned by the source NI and reside in the header flit of each packet, together with all other control information. Packets with priority 0 are used to set up a circuit, whereas priority 1 is meant for sending single data. The implemented control flow technique is credit based and if more than one input channel ask for the same virtual output channel, contentions are solved in a round robin fashion.

The only difference with respect to a standard packet switched router resides in the control of the input channel when a set up packet for the circuit

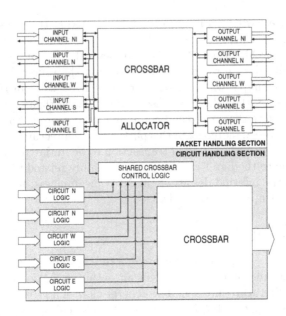

Fig. 1. High-level router architectural overview. Shaded area represents the structure of the Circuit Handling (CH) Section, brighter one the Packet Handling (PH) Section.

is received. A first level of adaptability has been introduced in the system by allowing to change the X-Y routing scheme into Y-X (and vice versa if necessary), if the originally requested output link in the CH section has been already reserved for another circuit (either is just reserved or already in use). Each input channel exchanges control signals with the shared crossbar control logic in the CH section, to check if the requested link can be reserved or not. If not, it tries the complementary routing scheme and, if even in this case the link is already booked, the set up packet will be turned in a nack packet and sent back to the source. This mechanism does not lead to any form of deadlock because the module responsible to select the proper virtual output channel, placed in each input channel, does not allow a set up packet to be routed back to the source. It simply compares the destination coordinates, stored in the header of the set up packet, with respect to the local coordinates of the intermediate routers the packet has reached: switching from X-Y to Y-X is allowed only if the link on the X direction has already been reserved and if at the same time, following the Y direction, the distance beetween the local and the destination tiles will be reduced (defininig the distance as $|X\text{DEST} - X\text{LOC}| - |Y\text{DEST} - Y\text{LOC}|$). Obviously the dual case is also admitted. The worst case that can appear is that from source to destination the routing scheme has to switch from X-Y to Y-X (and vice versa) at each intermediate router due to traffic congestion leading to a stepwise reserved path for the circuit.

The CH section has its own 18 bits crossbar: 16 for the data, 1 validity bit and 1 release bit (to manage the tear down of the circuit). In the dual-mode exclusive routers in literature, circuit switching has been handled mainly using time division multiplexing [7,9], but those solutions imply to exploit recording tables [8], slot tables [6], or routing tables [9]. In order to save area, we decided to get rid of any sort of table adopting a simple shared 5 bits register, accessible by all the input channels that need to check for the availability of a certain output port of the CH section, with a round robin based arbitration in order to avoid collisions and write hazards. This register is initialized to zero by default. It is synchronously written and asynchronously read. When an input channel receives a set up packet and evaluates which output link has to be reserved, the correspondent bit of the register is accessed. If the link is already reserved, the evaluated bit will be found to be one and the input channel requesting it can not be served. If the link is free, it means that the correspondent bit of the register is zero, the input channel can reserve it and the bit is turned to one. At the end of the communication over the established circuit, the source NI raises a release signal which follows blindly the circuit and is used to tear it down by switching back to zero the proper bit in the shared 5 bits register.

When a set up packet cannot go further, due to the fact that both the link in the X-Y and the one in the Y-X directions are already reserved, the control logic of the input channel turns the set up packet in a nack packet and sends it back to the source NI. The source NI is responsible to retry the sending.

5   Performance Exploration

The testing environment, shown in Figure 2, has been implemented in SystemC at Register Transfer Level (RTL) to allow cycle accurate simulations. SystemC is a C++ library that, compared to the other HDLs, is less effective for the automatic synthesis but is more expressive in terms of high level debugging features. Moreover SystemC is suitable in the perspective of performing hardware-software co-design, a typical step of MPSoC development [1].

An 8x8 2-D mesh has been explored. Each node of the mesh represents a Tile and is connected to a Traffic Generator and to all the neighbouring Tiles. Each Tile embeds the NoC building blocks (NI and router), a DMA and two memories. Traffic injection [11] into the network is governed by 3 different distributions, namely Gaussian (G), uniform (U) and Poisson (P). Moreover it has been decided that 10% of the initiated transaction ask for communication over circuit, whether the rest are simple data that can traverse the NoC over the PH section. Transaction length is obviously fixed for single data transactions (32 bits), whereas the length of the communication over circuit varies between 50 and 500 32 bits data according to a uniform distribution. All of the above mentioned traffic characteristics are mainly temporal and define the degree of regularity and burstiness of the transactions. In addition the traffic has been characterized also from a spatial point of view. 7 different tasks are going to be executed on the tiles on different sub-mesh sections, known as *clusters*, in a non-overlapping fashion. Each cluster is composed of a number of nodes correspondent to the number of threads constituting the associated task; the number of threads per task is

$N_{Th} = (8, 5, 6, 14, 10, 8)$. Threads allocation on the grid has been performed according to three different allocation strategies: a non contiguous scheme, known as Leapfrog Allocation Algorithm (L) [12]; a contiguous scheme, known as Multiple Buddy Strategy Algorithm (B) [13], which reserves rectangular areas even if not all the allocated tiles will be actually used, and finally a custom nature-inspired contiguous algorithm (C) which actually exploits all the allocated tiles [14]. The total number of transactions on the network is approximately 5000, meaning that on average each node initiates 79 communications.

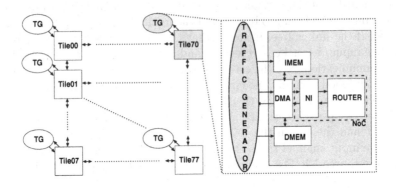

Fig. 2. View of the 2-D mesh, focusing on the single tile building blocks

Combining together the three distributions with the three allocation schemes, 9 different traffic characteristics have been generated, which are summarized in Table 1. Moreover, as Table 1 shows, the proposed approach has been compared with an exclusive state of the art-like architecture [6,7,8,9].

Table 1. Injected traffic specifications

Architecture	Exclusive Dual-Mode	Non-Exclusive Dual-Mode
Traffic Injection	{G,U,P}	{G,U,P}
Allocation Scheme	{B,L,C}	{B,L,C}
Number of 32 bits transactions	1 (PS) 50-500 (CS)	1 (PS) 50-500 (CS)
Combinations	9	9

5.1 Simulations Results

The main objective of an interconnection network is to deliver all the data from source to destination without any loss and as quickly as possible, to reduce the overall task completion time. According with this assumption the Latency relative to packets delivery, i.e. the time spent by each packet along the path linking source and destination tiles, has been evaluated. In order to minimize task completion time, which is the key requirement in a multithreaded environment from the side of the interconnection network, latency should be minimized. For this reason the first step in the validation process is to demonstrate that non-exclusivity is able to guarantee better results in terms of latency compared to exclusive solutions. Table 2 summarizes the obtained results for the aforementioned configurations of clusters and traffic. Table 2 highlights how the non-exclusive approach is able to guarantee lower average latency values, while exclusive architecture performs on average from 2 to 5 times worst. Since in the exclusive model packets latency is highly affected by the contemporary presence of a circuit on the same link, standard deviations and maximum values are noticeably higher than the non-exclusive case, even though the minimum values are quite similar, behaving the two architectures in the same way in absence of established circuits. Latencies also depend on the kind of arrival time statistical distributions: in fact in uniform traffic configurations the difference between exclusive and non-exclusive cases is definitely lower compared to the Poisson distribution configuration. The reason resides in the fact that Poisson distribution implies a higher probability of having injected packets and established circuits in smaller time intervals, hence generating longer stalls of packets inside queues.

Table 2. Latency evaluation for both exclusive and non-exclusive architectures: average values (*Avg*), standard deviations (*Std*), maximum and minimum values (*Max* and *Min*) and statistical median (*Med*). All the data are expressed in clock ticks.

	Avg		Std		Max		Min		Med	
	Excl.	N-Ex.	Excl.	N-Ex.	Excl.	N-Ex.	Excl.	N-Ex.	Excl.	N-Ex.
BU	48.4	21.1	67.5	6.4	511.0	60.0	11.6	12.0	25.0	19.0
LU	55.3	20.1	98.2	6.9	848.0	75.0	11.6	11.4	22.5	18.0
CU	61.6	21.6	103.4	7.6	751.0	93.0	11.8	11.8	26.0	19.0
BG	96.9	22.8	155.2	9.5	1339.0	152.0	12.1	12.0	29.0	19.5
LG	69.6	21.0	108.3	10.0	1004.0	228	11.5	11.5	27.0	18.0
CG	83.5	22.3	137.8	9.0	987.0	179.0	12.0	11.8	26.0	19.5
BP	119.6	25.1	252.1	14.1	2540.0	200.0	12.0	12.0	36.5	21.0
LP	101.1	23.3	144.0	13.1	917.0	301.0	11.5	11.4	33.0	19.5
CP	101.0	23.5	137.2	10.1	1040.0	137.0	11.8	11.8	30.0	20.0

Figure 3 depicts an example of latencies distribution in both the exclusive and non-exclusive cases, with regard to the Leapfrog allocation algorithm with a Poisson traffic distribution. It is clear that latency values for the exclusive case (on the left) are more spread compared to those of the non exclusive one (on the right). This affects the average value and even more the standard deviation. The median is not so affected as the other two metrics since the population has a considerably high peak for low latency values in both cases. The distribution of the latency values in the exclusive case does not show any gap but reaches its maximum in a continuous way: this is likely due to the fact that the more the

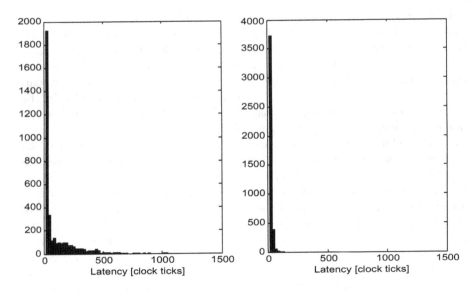

Fig. 3. Latencies histograms for the exclusive (*left side*) and not-exclusive (*right side*) architectures, with Poisson traffic distribution and Leapfrog Allocation Algorithm

circuits overlap in time the more is the congestion of the NoC, so that packets have to wait more time on intermediate queues.

6   Conclusions

In this paper, a novel non-exclusive dual-mode interconnection network has been proposed and the achieved simulation results in terms of latency values have been deeply investigated. The proposed approach has been motivated by the key idea that in a multithreaded environment, such as the one supported by MPPs, it is very likely to have the coexistence of different traffic characteristics. An efficient support for tasks migration, generating regular and long continuous streams of data, has to be efficiently served along with data interdependencies exchanges (vectors or scalar data). A non-exclusive approach is able to guarantee that on average, no matter of the injected traffic, the latency is always lower that the achievable one with an exclusive solution. The next step in this research work is to deal with other common metrics in the NoC field, such as the congestion of the network and the link workload. Nevertheless congestion is strongly related with latency, because the more is the latency of a packet the more is the time spent by that packet inside queues. The link workload will be meaningful instead to highlight the possibility of better usage of the bandwidth to solve data interdependencies among tasks more quickly, and is correlated to the latency because better workload exploitation can provide smaller latencies.

Acknowledgments. This work is partially supported by the projects CYBER-SAR (MUR-PON 2000-06) and SHAPES (IST-FET-26285).

References

1. Jerraya, A.A., Wolf, W.: The what, why and how of MPSoC. The Morgan Kaufmann Series in Systems on Silicon, pp. 1–18 (2005)
2. Sohi, G.S., Breach, S.E., Vijaykumar, T.: Multiscalar processors. In: Proc. 22nd Annu. Int. Symp. Computer Architecture, pp. 414–425 (June 1995)
3. Benini, L., Micheli, G.D.: Networks on Chips: A New Paradigm for Component-Based MPSoC Design. The Morgan Kaufmann Series in Systems on Silicon, pp. 49–80 (2005)
4. Dally, W., Towles, B.: Principles and Practices of Interconnection Network. Morgan Kaufmann, San Francisco (2004)
5. Shin, K.G., Daniel, S.: Analysis and implementation of hybrid switching. IEEE Transaction on Computers, 211–219 (1996)
6. Rijpkema, E., Goossens, K., Radulescu, A., Dielissen, J., Meerbergen, J.V., Wielage, P., Waterlander, E.: Trade-offs in the design of a router with both guaranteed and best-effort services for network on chip. In: Proc. of the conference on Design, Automation and Test in Europe, vol. 1, pp. 294–302 (2003)
7. Goossens, K., Meerbergen, J.V., Peeters, A., Wielage, P.: Network on silicon: Combining best-effort and guaranteed services. In: Proc. of the Design, Automation and Test in Europe Conference and Exhibition, DATE (2002)
8. Hsu, S.H., Lin, Y.X., Jou, J.M.: Design of a dual-mode NoC router integrated with network interface for AMBA-based IPs. In: Proc. IEEE Asian Solid-State Circuits Conference, pp. 211–214 (2006)
9. Ahamad, B., Erdogan, A.T., Khawarm, S.: Architecture of a dynamically reconfigurable NoC for adaptive reconfigurable MPSoC. In: Proceedings of the first NASA/ESA Conference on Adaptive Hardware and Systems (AHS 2006) (2006)
10. Radulescu, A., Goossens, K.: Communication services for networks on silicon. Domain-Specific Processors: Systems, Architectures, Modelling, and Simulation 275–299 (2004)
11. Lahiri, K., Raghunathan, A., Dey, S.: Evaluation of the traffic-performance characteristics of system-on-chip communication architectures. In: Proc. of the 14th International Conference on VLSI Design, pp. 29–35 (2000)
12. Lo, V., Windisch, K., Liu, W., Nitzberg, B.: Noncontiguous processor allocation algorithms for mesh-connectedmulticomputers. IEEE Transactions on Parallel and Distributed Systems 8(7), 712–726 (1997)
13. Wu, F., Hsu, C., Chou, L.: Processor allocation in the mesh multiprocessors using the leapfrog method. IEEE Transactions on Parallel and Distributed Systems, 273–289 (2003)
14. Palumbo, F., Pani, D., Raffo, L., Secchi, S.: A surface tension and coalescence model for dynamic distributed resources allocation in massively parallel processors on-chip. In: Proc. International Workshop on Nature Inspired Cooperative Strategies for Optimization - NICSO 2007, Acireale, Italy (November 2007)

Energy and Performance Evaluation of an FPGA-Based SoC Platform with AES and PRESENT Coprocessors

Xu Guo, Zhimin Chen, and Patrick Schaumont

Virginia Tech, Blacksburg VA 24061, USA
{xuguo,chenzm,schaum}@vt.edu

Abstract. Hardware implementations of block ciphers have been intensively evaluated for years. The hardware profile, including the performance, area and power of a block cipher, only considers the block cipher as a standalone component, and does not consider it as a coprocessor in a system design. In this paper we consider system integration of AES and PRESENT crypto coprocessors, and analyze the system profile in a co-simulation environment and then on an actual FPGA-based SoC platform. Energy, performance and implementation results for both the AES- and PRESENT-based systems are presented. Our research emphasizes the need to consider energy efficiency and performance at system-level when evaluating a block cipher for real embedded systems. Simulation results reveal that the hardware/software interfaces, as the communication bottleneck, have major impact on the system performance. Experimental results further demonstrate that the PRESENT, a power-efficient lightweight block cipher with lower security level, becomes less energy-efficient than AES when system-integration overhead is included.

1 Introduction

In recent years, Field Programmable Logic Arrays (FPGAs) have had major impact on hardware/software codesign. Compared to the early frequent use as devices for rapid prototyping, FPGAs are now used for final products, thanks to their reduced time-to-market and the cost advantages of standard devices. Due to the importance of reconfigurable devices, numerous FPGA AES implementations have been published, most of which focus on high throughput rates [1, 2]. In [3], an AES design achieves a throughput of 25 Gb/s on a Xilinx Spartan-3 FPGA. This number only reflects the raw processing ability of the hardware to encrypt bits. However, FPGAs are now becoming a preferred platform for System-on-Chip (SoC). By providing hard and soft embedded processors on FPGAs, they enable on-chip integration of co-processors and processors. If we re-examine the above high throughput designs in the context of a SoC system, the communication bandwidth between system components becomes a critical design factor. Fox example, If we only consider an AES coprocessor that runs at 100 MHz and requires 11 clock cycles per encryption round, each round requires a 128-bit key, 128-bit plaintext and 128-bit cryptotext, then we need an

M. Berekovic, N. Dimopoulos, and S. Wong (Eds.): SAMOS 2008, LNCS 5114, pp. 106–115, 2008.

input/output bandwidth of about 3.5Gb/s. Dedicated communication hardware (e.g. direct-memory-access (DMA) chips on fixed-latency buses) may achieve this bandwidth. In many cases however, this bandwidth needs to be provided directly through the software. The bandwidth of 3.5Gb/s indeed is outside the capability of most embedded processors [4].

This shows the most optimal hardware design (in terms of performance) may not always be the most optimal solution at system level. In fact, not only the performance, but also the power or energy efficiency should be re-considered at system-level. In this paper, we consider AES and PRESENT for hardware acceleration, and using hardware/software interfaces provided with StrongARM and Microblaze processors. The results for StrongARM are estimated using cosimulation [5]. The results for Microblaze have been implemented on an FPGA board and measured using a hardware timer. In addition, power estimation was performed at system level using Xilinx XPower.

The contribution of this article is two-fold: (1) to present a system-level design flow, covering simulation up to FPGA implementation, that evaluates the performance and power consumption of a crypto coprocessor integrated in a complete system; (2) to point out that a lightweight and power-efficient cipher (PRESENT) integrated in a SoC environment may actually be less energy-efficient than a standard block cipher (AES).

The paper is organized as follows. Section 2 briefly presents the background of PRESENT block cipher. Section 3 explains the system-level design flow used in the paper and performs some analysis on the performance and power consumption under co-simulation environment. Section 4 describes the FPGA-based SoC design and illustrates the experimental results. Section 5 concludes the paper.

2   PRESENT Block Cipher

Although Rijndael has been selected by the American National Institute of Standards and Technology (NIST) as the Advanced Encryption Standard (AES) after a critical assessment, which included extensive benchmarking on a variety of platforms ranging from smart cards [6] to high end parallel machines [7], still many new block ciphers were proposed with special implementation properties, such as TEA, IDEA, Hight, Clefia, DESXL, and PRESENT [8]. In this paper, we are especially interested in comparing the AES with the newly published PRESENT block cipher, which was designed with area and power constraints uppermost in mind.

PRESENT is an SPN-based (substitution permutation network) block cipher with 31 rounds, a block size of 64-bit, and a key size of 80- or 128-bit. Fig. 1 shows the top level algorithmic description and hardware structure of PRESENT. It comprises three stages: a key-mixing step, a substitution layer, and a permutation layer. For the key mixing, simply a XOR is used. The key schedule consists essentially of a 61-bit rotation together with an S-box and a round counter (Present-80 uses a single Sbox, whereas Present-128 requires two S-boxes). The substitution layer comprises 16 S-boxes with 4-bit inputs and 4-bit outputs.

Similar S-boxes are used in both the data path and the key scheduling. The permutation layer is a simple bit transposition and can be realized by simple wiring [9].

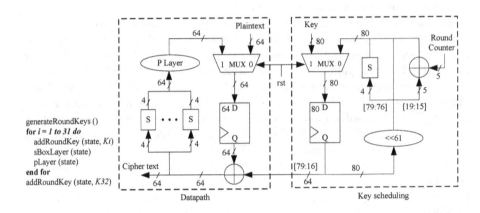

Fig. 1. Algorithmic description and hardware structure of PRESENT-80

3   System-Level Design and Analysis Using GEZEL

In order to narrow the gap between performance and flexibility, reduce the time required to complete a design and reduce the risk of errors that might result from translating a high-level prototype (e.g. C model) into HDLs, we use GEZEL to perform system-level design.

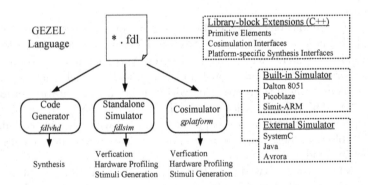

Fig. 2. Overview of GEZEL cosimulation environment

The GEZEL cosimulation environment creates a platform simulator by combining a hardware simulation kernel with one or more instruction-set simulators. The hardware part of the platform is programmed in GEZEL, a deterministic, cycle-true and implementation-oriented hardware description language. After cycle-accurate simulation, the GEZEL description of hardware can be converted into synthesizable VHDL [10].

3.1   Hardware/Software Interfaces

There are three commonly available hardware/software interfaces: direct connection busses (e.g. Fast Simplex Link), processor local busses and general-purpose system busses (e.g. On-chip Peripheral Bus). Direct-connection buses and processor local busses are processor specific, while system busses are generic. In this research, we will only discuss the design using OPB system bus.

The OPB interface is a traditional memory-mapped interface for peripheral components. The OPB bus is a shared, variable latency bus which is part of IBM's CoreConnect specification. It is also used to interconnect soft- and hard-core processors in a Xilinx FPGA. The hardware side of an OPB interface consists of a decoder for a memory-read or memory-write cycle on a selected address in the memory range mapped to the OPB. The decoded memory cycle is translated to a read-from or a write-into a register in the coprocessor. A memory-mapped interface is an easy and popular interface technique, in particular because it works with standard C on any core that has a system bus. The drawback of this interface is the low-speed connection between hardware and software. Even on an embedded core, a simple round-trip communication between software and hardware can run into several tens of CPU clock cycles [4].

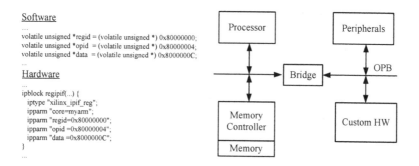

Fig. 3. Hardware/Software interface OPB

3.2   Cosimulation Based on StrongARM

Under the GEZEL simulation environment we first implement the AES and PRESENT in GEZEL based on based on Finite State Machine with Datapath (FSMD) model. A standalone simulation is then used to verify the correctness of the AES and PRESENT encryption core. Next, the AES and PRESENT cores are integrated into a coprocessor shell as follows. Three memory-mapped registers have been added: a data-input port, a data-output port, and control port. Since the maximum data width supported by the OPB bus is 32-bit and the AES-128 and PRESENT-80 used in this paper have 128-bit, 80-bit and 64-bit ports, additional registers should be added to perform serial-to-parallel and parallel-to-serial conversions. The control shell also contains a dedicated controller that controls the operations of the hardware/software interface, which is OPB interface in our design. This controller implements the 'instruction-set' for the coprocessor, and decodes the commands sent from the software driver to the coprocessor. The final step is to write a software driver to perform a series of memory reads and writes.

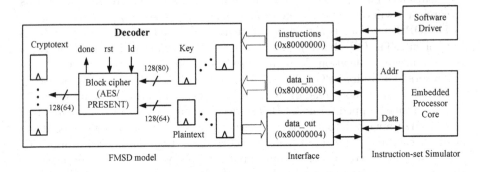

Fig. 4. Cosimulation based on instruction-set simulators

The simulation results for the AES and PRESENT under GEZEL environment are illustrated in Table 1.

Table 1. Cosimulation performance results (100 encryptions for each block cipher)

	SW cycle counts	HW cycle counts	HW/SW cycle counts	HW speedup	HW/SW speedup
AES-128	217,603	1,200	134,599	181.3	1.6
PRESENT-80	1,924,547	3,300	85,306	583.2	22.6

Note that the AES-128 hardware implementation is based on the core developed by Rudolf Usselman, available from OpenCores, and the software version is a 32-bit AES derived from the SSH open source package; the PRESENT-80 hardware design is based on the structure depicted in Fig. 1, and the software version was provided by one of the PRESENT authors. Both the hardware and software versions are basic implementations without specific optimization goals, and here the designs consider the encryption only with each plaintext assigned an initial key. 100 iterations for the AES and PRESENT algorithms (which transmit the plaintext and key to the cipher for each iteration) result in the above performance numbers.

Table 2. Toggle counts (TC) of standalone simulation

	TC/cycle	TC/encryption	TC/(encryption * byte)
AES-128	3,798	45,576	2,849
PRESENT-80	2,746	90,618	11,327

From Table 1, it is obvious that if we only consider the hardware acceleration the design speedup is often dramatic, but, if we consider the system integration and take into account the communication overhead, the resulting speedup can be much lower.

The GEZEL simulation environment also provides technology-independent toggle counting at Register Transfer Level (RTL), which is useful to roughly estimate the dynamic power consumption of a design.

The toggle counts collected in Table 2 only includes the AES and PRESENT encryption core when doing standalone simulation. This data can be utilized to early estimate the power- and energy-efficiency of the hardware designs of AES and PRESENT. The first column of the table indicates that PRESENT-80 is more power efficient than AES, in terms of dynamic power consumption. However, since most light-weight block ciphers, like PRESENT, are specialized cryptographic implementations for tight cost constraint applications, such as RFID tags, the energy-efficiency instead of power-efficiency should be emphasized because most of these applications are battery powered. The second column of the table reflects the toggle counts per cycle multiplying the cycle counts for each encryption, the results of which can be approximately equivalent to the energy consumption per encryption. Further, we divide the toggle counts per encryption by the number of plaintext bytes in one encryption. The obtained values can be assumed to be the energy required for the block cipher to encrypt one byte plaintext. This indicates that the PRESENT-80 might be less energy-efficient than the AES in standalone encryption mode. Table 3 illustrates the power values (by using post-place and route simulation model in XPower, which will be discussed later) obtained in standalone simulation on Xilinx Spartan-3 XC3S1000 FPGA, which well support our assumption based on toggle counts. Moreover, it reflects the relative accuracy of GEZEL toggle counting when predicting the actual power consumption of designs. Note that both the quiescent and dynamic

Table 3. Power results of standalone FPGA implementations (10 encryptions for each block cipher working at 20MHz)

	Quiescent Power(mW)	Dynamic Power(mW)	Time (ms)	Energy (mJ)	Energy/byte (μJ/byte)
AES-128	51.51	40.75	6	0.55	3.46
PRESENT-80	44.06	3.49	16.5	0.78	9.81

power values are collected from Vccint, the FPGA core power supply voltage since we only consider the FPGA core power variation.

4 FPGA-Based Hardware/Software Co-design

Using the above GEZEL simulation environment we can translate the GEZEL description of the AES and PRESENT and control shells into synthesizable VHDL, which can be then added as coprocessors in the Xilinx Platform Studio (XPS) 9.1.02.

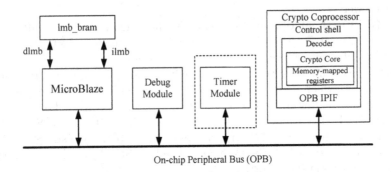

Fig. 5. FPGA-based SoC platform

The SoC system is built on a Xilinx Spartan-3E XC3S500EFG320 development board with both on- and off-chip memory. Since each on-chip memory read or write only takes 2 clock cycles compared to 22 and 23 clock cycles for off-chip memory read or write on our specific FPGA platform, we fully utilize the on-chip memory for our system design. Note that our research objective is trying to address some system integration issues or considerations for general SoC systems, and here the selection of Microblaze as the microprocessor and OPB as system bus is for detailed discussion.

A hardware timer module is added for measuring the speed of both crypto hardware coprocessor and the crypto software running on MicroBlaze. The timer will be removed when doing power estimation of the whole SoC system using XPower.

XPower is a commercial-off-the-shelf tool to estimate power consumption of Xilinx SRAM-based FPGAs. XPower utilizes either pre-routed or post-routed design data, and then makes a power model either for a unit or for the overall design. It considers resource usage, toggle rates, input/output power, and many other factors in estimation.

To get a good indication of the power consumed by the device using XPower, an accurate VCD file is needed. Here, we use a complete post-place-and-route, timing-accurate model built in XPS to generate the VCD file. Other system settings use the XPower default values.

Table 4. FPGA implementation areas (unit: slices)

	Crypto core	Coprocessor with wrapper
AES-128	1,877	2,097
PRESENT-80	271	460

The areas for AES and PRESENT coprocessors are presented in Table 4. The resources used for the other parts in both the systems are the same: 8Kb Block RAM, 8 slices for LMB wrapper, 99 slices for OPB wrapper, 749 slices for Microblaze and 65 slices for Debug module.

Table 5. FPGA system performance results (100 encryptions for each block cipher)

	SW cycle counts	HW cycle counts	HW/SW cycle counts	HW speedup	HW/SW speedup
AES-128	432,756	1,200	77,428	360.6	5.6
PRESENT-80	2,295,863	3,300	51,427	695.7	44.6

The numbers in Table 5 is for 100 iterations encryption for the AES and PRESENT, and each iteration transmits plaintext and key to the cipher. The performance improvement from using hardware/software co-design is satifying respect to software using C codes which were compiled with -O2 optimization. However, combined with the former co-simulation results in GEZEL we see that the overhead is substantial. Take AES-128 FPGA codesign for example, 100 iterations in hardware only should take 1200 clock cycles, while we have used 77,428. This overhead factor (65X) is due to the communication with the processor and implementation of various command sequences with the encapsulated hardware. Note that the big differences in cycle counts and speedup values between GEZEL co-simulation and FPGA SoC implementation are due to the different processors (StrongARM vs. MicroBlaze) and compilers (arm-linux-gcc vs. mb-gcc).

In the former relative power estimation using toggle counts, we deduced that the more power-efficient PRESENT block cipher is in fact less energy-efficient

Table 6. FPGA system power and energy simulation results (4 encryptions for each block cipher woking at 50MHz)

	Quiescent Power(mW)	Dynamic Power(mW)	Time (ms)	Energy (mJ)	Energy/byte (μJ/byte)
AES-128	31.25	19.97	62.08	3.18	49.68
PRESENT-80	31.25	19.61	41.2	2.10	65.48

than AES, in terms of toggles per encryption per byte together with the standalone FPGA simulation results. When we look at this problem again in an FPGA-based SoC platform, we can find that the system with PRESENT coprocessor consumes slightly less total power than that with the AES coprocessor. However, still we can find that the PRESENT-based system is less energy-efficient than the AES-based system.

5   Conclusions

Due to the encryption speed and ease of implementation, block ciphers have been widely used in various embedded applications. Much research effort has been put on the trade-off designs on hardware implementation of block ciphers, but, we think that the hardware profile is unable to predict the performance and energy (or power) in the context of a real embedded system.

Using our design flow we can not only get some early prediction of performance and dynamic power consumption under co-simulation environment, which can help designers to refine the design at an early stage, but also get accurate performance and energy values after on-board FPGA implementation, which can help designers select the crypto coprocessor best fitted to some specific platforms. The illustrated SoC designs with AES and PRESENT coprocessors identify the hardware/software interfaces design as an important system integration issue, and address the power- and energy-efficiency evaluation issue at the system level. Our future work may focus on different hardware/software interfaces' (e.g. FSL) impact on the performance and energy- or power-efficiency of a typical SoC system with different kinds of crypto coprocessors, and possible optimization methods.

Acknowledgments. We thank Axel Poschmann for providing the C programs of PRESENT. This work was supported in part by NSF Grant No 0644070.

References

1. Chodowiec, P., Khuon, P., Gaj, K.: Fast Implementations of Secret-Key Block Ciphers Using Mixed Inner- and Outer-Round Pipelining. In: FPGA 2001, pp. 94–102. ACM, New York (2001)
2. McLoone, M., McCanny, J.: High Performance Single Chip FPGA Rijndael Algorithm Implementations. In: Koç, Ç.K., Naccache, D., Paar, C. (eds.) CHES 2001. LNCS, vol. 2162, pp. 65–76. Springer, Heidelberg (2001)
3. Good, T., Benaissa, M.: AES from the fastest to the smallest. In: Rao, J.R., Sunar, B. (eds.) CHES 2005. LNCS, vol. 3659, pp. 427–440. Springer, Heidelberg (2005)
4. Schaumont, P., Verbauwhede, I.: Hardware/Software Codesign for Stream Ciphers. In: SASC (State of the Art of Stream Ciphers), Special workshop hosted by the ECRYPT Network of Excellence in Cryptology, Bochum, Germany (2007)
5. The GEZEL homepage, http://rijndael.ece.vt.edu/gezel2

6. Hachez, G., Koeune, F., Quisquater, J.-J.: cAESar results: Implementation of four AES candidates on two smart cards. In: 2nd AES Candidate Conference (AES2), Rome, Italy (1999)
7. Worley, J., Worley, B., Christian, T., Andworley, C.: AES Finalists on PA-RISC and IA-64: Implementations and Performance. In: 3rd AES Conference (AES3), NY, USA (2001)
8. Eisenbarth, T., Kumar, S., Paar, C., Poschmann, A., Uhsadel, L.: A Survey of Lightweight Cryptography Implementations. IEEE Design and Test of Computers – Special Issue on Secure ICs for Secure Embedded Computing 24, 522–533 (2007)
9. Bogdanov, A., et al.: PRESENT: An Ultra-Lightweight Block Cipher. In: Paillier, P., Verbauwhede, I. (eds.) CHES 2007. LNCS, vol. 4727, pp. 450–466. Springer, Heidelberg (2007)
10. Schaumont, P., Ching, D., Verbauwhede, I.: An Interactive Codesign Environment for Domain-specific Coprocessors. ACM Transactions on Design Automation of Electronic Systems 11(1), 70–87 (2006)

Area Reliability Trade-Off in Improved Reed Muller Coding

Costas Argyrides[2], Stephania Loizidou[1], and Dhiraj K. Pradhan[2]

[1] Department of Computer Science, Frederick University, Cyprus
[2] Department of Computer Science, University of Bristol, Bristol, UK
{Costas, Pradhan}@cs.bris.ac.uk,com.ls@fit.ac.cy

Abstract. Nanotechnology based fabrication, which relies on self-assembly of nanotubes or nanowires has been predicted to be an alternative to silicon technology since lithography based IC is approaching its limit in terms of feature size. However, such processes are expected to be less reliable, to have high defect density and to be handled with effective defect tolerant techniques. Thus, reliability is a major challenge in the future of IC design. To this end, different coding techniques have been proposed to improve reliability of future technologies. In this paper we analyze the trade-off between the area and the reliability added in each chip employing the Reed Muller coding as the coding technique. We estimate the reliability and area increase of different orders of the Reed Muller decoding and observed that while the area increases, the reliability decreases. Our approach is to define a framework and help designers in order to decide on the configuration of the Reed Muller to be used. Finally, we provide a guideline to optimize the architecture making an optimal trade off between the area and the reliability.

1 Introduction

The major challenges posed for future memory design is the problem of soft errors [1]–[4] and high power consumption [5]–[7]. As process technology scales to small nanometers, high-density, low cost, high performance integrated circuits, characterized by high operating frequencies, low voltage levels and small noise margins will be increasingly susceptible to temporary faults [8]. In very deep sub-micron technologies single-event upsets like atmospheric neutrons and alpha particles severely impact field-level product reliability, not only for memory, but for logic also. When these particles hit the silicon bulk, they create minority carriers which if collected by the source/drain diffusions, could change the voltage level of the node.

Transient faults are also a major concern in space applications, with potentially serious consequences for the spacecraft, including loss of information, functional failure or loss of control [9]. Although SEU is the major concern in space and terrestrial applications, multiple bit upsets (MBU) have also became important problems in designing memories because of the following: 1) The error rate of memories increased due to the continuing technology shrinkage [10,11]. Therefore the probability of having multiple errors increases. 2) MBUs can be induced by direct ionization or nuclear

M. Berekovic, N. Dimopoulos, and S. Wong (Eds.): SAMOS 2008, LNCS 5114, pp. 116–125, 2008.
© Springer-Verlag Berlin Heidelberg 2008

recoil after passing a high-energy ion [12]. 3) The experiments in memories under proton and heavy ions fluxes in [13,14] show that the probability of having multiple errors is increased when the size of memory is increased. Unfortunately, packaging and shielding cannot effectively be used to shield against SEUs and MBUs since they may be caused by neutrons which can be easily penetrate through packages [10, 15].

In order to maintain a good level of reliability, it is necessary to protect memory cells with protection codes. Hamming code and Odd Weight code are largely used to protect memories against SEU because of their efficient ability to correct single upsets with a reduced area and performance overhead [16]. However, multiple upsets cause by a single charged particle can provoke errors in the system protected by these single-error correcting codes. In the other hand, Reed-Muller is another error correcting code able to cope with multiple upsets. It has a wide range of digital applications including: storage systems, wireless or mobile communications and high-speed modems.

In this paper, we provide a guideline to optimize the architecture making an optimal trade off between the area and the reliability. Different configurations were described using the HDL language and results for power and area were obtained using Synopsys power tools. We have carried out different experiments for studying the power, performance and reliability tradeoffs and analytical models for estimation of reliability and Mean Time To Failure (MTTF) for different configurations are presented. The results show that while the area increases the reliability decreases. We introduced a metric for comparing the different configurations. The metric is based on dividing the MTTF of each of the configurations by the cost of the configuration implementation. Based on the experimental results, for different fault error rate different configuration is better than other configurations.

This paper is organized in as follows. Section 2 provides an overview of the Reed Muller's encoding and improved decoding followed by Section 3 that analyses the reliability and MTTF of the proposed configurations. In Section 4 the cost of embedding RMC into a memory is described and finally, section 5 illustrates some conclusions.

2 Reed Muller Codes (RMC)

Reed-Muller codes [17]–[19] are binary linear codes; that is, an RMC is a subspace of the vector space of all binary n-bit vectors. An RMC can be described in terms of a generator matrix, the linear combination of the rows of which over a field of two elements are the code words of RMC. The 0th order RMC of length 2^m has a single all ones row in the generator matrix. The ith order of $0 \leq i \leq m$, RMC is a linear code of length 2^m and is iteratively defined as below. The generator matrix of 1st order RMC is obtained by adding m more rows to the 0th order RMC generator matrix such as the columns of the generator matrix in the portion of the m rows now added are the 2^m binary m-tuples.

Definition: The rows of a generator matrix for linear codes are called the generators of the code.

Definition: The set of generators of a 1st order RMC excluding the generator of the 0th order RMC is denoted by S_1 and the generator for the 0th order RMC is denoted by S_0.

The generators of the ith order RMC are obtained by taking the union of S_0, S_1, S_2, ..., S_{i-1}, S_i, where $S_i = \{s1,1 \circ s1,2 \circ \ldots \circ s1j$: where $s1,k \in S1$, $1 \leq k \leq j$ and $s1,1 \circ s1,2 \circ \ldots \circ s1j$: is the vector obtained by taking the bit-by-bit AND of the elements of the j vectors$\}$ and $i \leq j \leq I$, up to no larger than m. It is known that the set of vectors $U_{j=0}^{i} S_j$ are linearly independent [18] and hence the number of generators for ith or-

der RMC is $\in \sum_{j=0}^{i} \binom{m}{j}$

$$G_{(2,3)} = \begin{bmatrix} S_0 = \{1 \ 1 \ 1 \ 1 \ 1 \ 1 \ 1 \ 1\} \\ S_1 = \begin{cases} 1 & 1 & 1 & 1 & 0 & 0 & 0 & 0 \\ 1 & 1 & 0 & 0 & 1 & 1 & 0 & 0 \\ 1 & 0 & 1 & 0 & 1 & 0 & 1 & 0 \end{cases} \\ S_2 = \{1 \ 0 \ 0 \ 0 \ 0 \ 0 \ 0 \ 0\} \end{bmatrix}$$

The generators of the 2nd order RMC of length 2^4 are $\{S_0 \cup S_1 \cup S_2\}$ and they are 11 in number.

It is known that the minimum Hamming distance between any two words of an ith order RMC $0 \leq i \leq m$ is equal to 2^{m-i}. Therefore an ith order RMC can be used to correct $\{(2^{m-i} - 1)/2\}$ errors and detect 2^{m-i-1} errors.

2.1 Reed Muller Encoding

If G is the generator matrix of a linear code with k rows and n columns, then a k-dimensional vector X can be encoded (i.e., the corresponding code word can be obtained) by computing X*G where * stands for matrix multiplication. Therefore any code word generated by G is a linear combination of the rows of the matrix. It is advantageous in implementation to derive the code word in what is known as a systematic form.

*Definition: A code generated by a matrix G is said to be systematic code if X*G=XP, where P is an (n-k) vector containing the check bits.*

2.2 Reed Muller Decoding

The essential idea behind this technique is that, for each row of the generator matrix, we attempt to determine through a majority vote whether or not that row was employed in the formation of the codeword corresponding to our message.

Definition: Let p be any monomial of degree d in RM with redundancy form p'. Then we form the set J of variables not in p' and their complements. The characteristic vectors of p are all vectors corresponding to monomials of degree m-d over variables of J. (*) Since v is a bijection and $v^{-1}(0)=0$, this implies that any monomial containing *both a variable and its complement is equivalent to the monomial of degree 0. Thus, without loss of generality we only consider monomials where the variables are distinct (i.e. no variable and its complement appears) [20, 21].*

(*) Note: Any monomial containing a variable and its complement corresponds to the 0 vector (through v: $v(x_1 x_1') = v(x_1)*v(x_1')=0$)

Example: Assume that we are working over RM(2,3). The characteristic vectors of x0x1 are the vectors corresponding to monomials $\{x_2, x_2'\}$. The characteristic vectors of x_0 are the vectors corresponding to the monomials $\{x_1 x_2, x_1 x_2', x_1' x_2, x_1' x_2'\}$.

Algorithm for RMC decoding technique

I.   Examine the rows with monomials of degree r.
II. Calculate the 2^{m-r} characteristic vectors for the row.
III. Take the dot product of each of these vectors with received message.
IV. If the majority of the dot products is 1 then set the position in our original message vector corresponding to this row to 1 else 0.
V.   When we finish with all monomials of degree r we take the vector of length $\binom{m}{r}$ and multiply it by the $\binom{m}{r}$ row used to calculate the vector.
VI. Add the result to the received message.
VII. Proceed to recursively on the rows corresponding to monomials of degree r-1.

2.2.1 Improved Reed Muller Decoding Circuit

The key to implementing the above algorithm is the majority voting. An improved decoding algorithm for 3 error correcting was proposed in [22]. The majority voting was traditionally done by using Wallace trees [23][24]. In general, Wallace Trees (Figure 1) (WT) based majority decoder is very hardware intensive and hence a new majority voting technique is required. We refer to this new voting (decoding) circuit as Improved Reed Muller Decoding Circuit (IRMD).

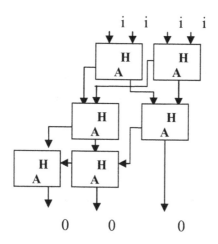

Fig. 1. 4 Bits Wallace Tree

For our analysis we will use the triple error correcting RMC with improved decoding and, instead of the traditional Wallace trees used for majority voting, we are using a set of OR and AND gates (shown in Figure 2). Note that the maximum number of errors is 3 so the maximum number of 1's or 0's is 3 in each case.

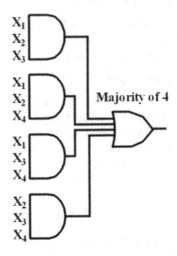

Fig. 2. IRMD circuit for 4 bits

In Table 1 we show the additional area in terms of 2 input AND gates and delay while incorporating in different configurations of RMC the IRMD decoder in a 256Mbits memory. The additional memory requirement for incorporating ECC is also given. It is clear that the currently proposed technique uses much less hardware for majority voting; it eventually reduces power consumption, area and delay.

Table 1. Additional Gates and Delay using IRMD

Coding Technique	Additional #Bits	Additional #Gates[*1]
RM(1,4)	220%	451
RM(2,5)	100%	1340
RM(3,6)	52.6%	5490

*1: Equivalent to 2 input AND gates

3 Reliability and MTTF

In order to improve reliability of a chip lets say memory, we have to add some reliability (redundant bits) in each codeword. The reliability of the chip is strongly dependent on the number of bits in each word. Hence, it is imperative to analyze the reliability of such an architecture technique to validate its applicability in real designs. In order to analyze the reliability of the proposed architecture we make the following assumptions [25]:

1. The probability of a number of faults occurring in a fixed period of time with a known average rate is independent of the time since the last event (Poisson distribution).
2. Bit failures are statistically independent.

The probability of having exactly i faulty bits in a word including check bits (w+c) can be given by:

$$P\{iF\} = \binom{w+c}{i} \cdot (1 - e^{-\lambda t})^i \cdot e^{-\lambda(w+c-i)t} \tag{1}$$

where λ is the fault rate of one bit and t is time parameter.

The reliability, r(t) of a word can be then expressed as:

$$r(t) = P\{NE\} + \sum_{i=1}^{N_d} P\{iF\} \tag{2}$$

where P{NE} denotes the probability that there is no error, and P{iF} indicates the probability of having i faults.

The reliability of memory is the product of the reliability of all its words and the integration of the reliability function gives the mean time to failure MTTF as,

$$MTTF = \int_0^\infty r^M(t)\,dt = \int_0^\infty R(t)\,dt \tag{3}$$

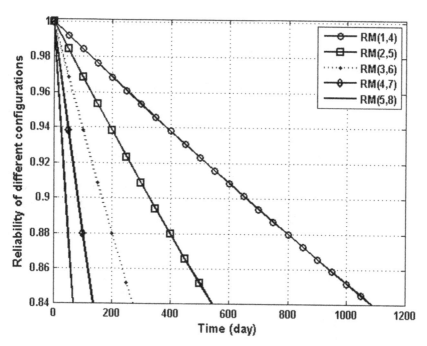

Fig. 3. Effect of time on the reliability of 256MBits memory ($\lambda = 10^{-5}$ upsets/bit per day)

Formulas (1)–(3) were described and solved using MATLAB for estimating the reliability and MTTFs of different organizations.

In Figure 3 one can see that reliability of the memory is improved dramatically using lower order RMC coding. While using first order decoding, RM(1,4) we can see that memory will fail after 1000 days while the memory will fail at less that 200 days using 4th and 5th order RMC. Memory using 3rd order RMC will fail at a stage just less than 300 days and using 2nd order just after 500 days which is less than half comparing to the most reliable configuration of the 1st order.

In Table 2 we are presenting the MTTF for a 256Mbits memory using different configurations of RMC in different fault rates. One can note that 1st order RMC wins out the other configurations. In high defect rates ($\lambda=10^{-2}$) the MTTF of the 1st order is almost 4X compared to the 5th order 4x while at lower defect rates the MTTF of 1st order is almost 10X. more than 5th order RMC.

Table 2. MTTF of 256Mbits memory in different fault rates using different configurations

	RMC (1,4)	RMC (2,5)	RMC (3,6)	RMC (4,7)	RMC (5,8)
$\lambda=10^{-5}$	3443	2495	1500	780.9	391.6
$\lambda=10^{-4}$	625.8	313	157.3	79.13	40.07
$\lambda=10^{-3}$	63.51	32.3	16.65	8.86	4.99
$\lambda=10^{-2}$	7.30	4.23	2.77	2.17	2.01

4   Cost Analysis

Reliability is not the only major issue in the design of future chips. The different organizations (orders) of Reed Muller Coding have been coded using HDL. The results reported here are for a 32X32 register file; however the design is generic in data path width. It should be mentioned that the design was simulated using *Modelsim[TM]* and was tested for functionality using various inputs.

The outputs from the VHDL coded architecture are validated against a standard MATLAB output. The architectures were synthesized using the Synopsys tools. *Synopsys design power[TM]* was used to estimate the power consumption. In Table 3 we can see the results while incorporating five orders of RMC in a 32x32 register file. As was expected while moving from one order to another (higher) the area and power overhead was decreased while reliability and MTTF is also decreased as shown in Figure 3 and Table 2.

Table 3. 32x32 register file RMC

	Area		Power	
	μm^2	%	Mw	%
Base	103658	100	93	100
RMC (1,4)	332949.5	321.2	292.20	314.2
RMC (2,5)	209596.5	202.2	193.81	208.4
RMC (3,6)	159011.4	153.40	144.43	155.3
RMC (4,7)	135076.7	130.31	127.70	137.31
RMC (5,8)	122223.1	117.91	110.68	119.01

In order to compare the efficiency of different configurations compared to their overhead and reliability (MTTF), we provide a metric that allow us to compare them in terms of efficiency of the MTTF improvement and cost overhead. Therefore, we define this metric as *MTTF Improvement Per Cost (MIC)* by

$$MIC = \frac{Mean\ Time\ To\ Fail}{Cost},\tag{4}$$

where *Cost* is defined by

$$Cost = Power \cdot Area \tag{5}$$

Designers like higher MTTF and cost to take high and low values, respectively. This lead that designs to have high value of the new metric *MTTF Improvement Per Cost (MIC)*.

Table 4. MIC for 256Mbits memory

	RMC (1,4)	RMC (2,5)	RMC (3,6)	RMC (4,7)	RMC (5,8)
$\lambda = 10^{-5}$	3.54	6.14	**6.53**	4.53	2.90
$\lambda = 10^{-4}$	6.43	**7.72**	6.85	4.59	2.96
$\lambda = 10^{-3}$	6.53	**7.94**	7.25	5.14	3.69
$\lambda = 10^{-2}$	7.50	10.41	12.06	12.58	**14.86**

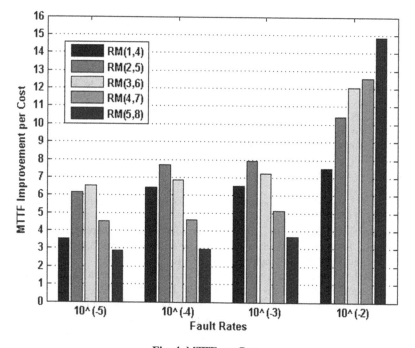

Fig. 4. MTTF per Cost

Table 4 and Figure 4 show the value of this two metric in different fault rates. We can observe that despite the MTTF showed that 1st order RMC wins out the other configurations and that the 5th order was the worst, suing this metric (Table 4, Figure 4) we can see that in higher fault rates ($\lambda=10^{-2}$) results in almost 2X compared to the most reliable 1st order RMC which is the worst in these fault rate compared to the other configurations. In the lower fault rates ($\lambda=10^{-5}$) the 3rd order RMC wins out. In fault rates of $\lambda=10^{-4}$ and $\lambda=10^{-3}$ the 2nd order of RMC wins out the other configurations.

Therefore, based on the results of Table 4 and Figure 4 in higher defect rates 5th order RMC is more valuable while 2nd and 3rd order RMC are better in the case of less fault rates.

5 Conclusions

In this paper, we have presented an analysis for different configurations (orders) of modified triple error RMC circuit. We have shown that using higher orders of RMC the area and thus power overhead of the circuit will be decreased significantly while the reliability and the MTTF will be decreased as well. On the other hand, we have significant improvements in the reliability and the MTTF when using RMC of lower orders like 1st, 2nd and even 3rd but the overhead penalty is also significant and thus we proposed a guideline how to construct circuits making an optimal trade-off between reliability and area overhead.

References

1. Bertozzi, D., et al.: Error control schemes for on-chip communication links: the energy-reliability tradeoff. IEEE Trans. on DAC 24(6) (June 2005)
2. Rossi, D., Metra, C.: Error correcting strategy for high speed and density reliable flash memories. IEEE J. Electronic Testing, Theory and applications 19(5), 511–521 (2003)
3. Nicolaidis, M.: Time Redundancy Based Soft-Error Tolerance to Rescue Nanometer Technologies. In: 17th IEEE VLSI Test Symposium, p. 86 (1999)
4. Mitra, S., et al.: Robust System Design with Built-In Soft-Error Resilience. IEEE computer society 38(2), 43–52 (2005)
5. Itoh, K.: Trends in megabit DRAM circuit design. IEEE J. Solid State Circuits 25, 778–789 (1990)
6. Itoh, K., et al.: Trends in low-power RAM circuit technologies. Proc. IEEE 83, 524–543 (1995)
7. Kimura, K., et al.: Power reduction in megabit DRAM's. IEEE Journal of Solid State Circuits SSC-21, 381–389 (1986)
8. International Technology Road map for Semiconductors (2002), http://public.itrs.net/
9. Barth, J.L., Dyer, C.S., Stassinopoulos, E.G.: Space, atmospheric, and terrestrial radiation environments. IEEE Trans. Nuclear Science 50, 466–482 (2003)
10. Hazucha, P., Svensson, C.: Impact of CMOS technology scaling on the atmospheric neutron soft error rate. IEEE Trans. Nucl. Sci. 47(6), 2586–2594 (2000)
11. Ferreyra, P.A., Marques, C.A., Ferreyra, R.T., Gaspar, J.P.: Failure map functions and accelerated mean time to failure tests: New approaches for improving the reliability estimation in systems exposed to single event upsets. IEEE Trans. Nucl. Sci. 52(1), 494–500 (2005)

12. Hentschke, R., Marques, R., Lima, F., Carro, L., Susin, A., Reis, R.: Analyzing Area and Performance Penalty of Protecting Different Digital Modules with Hamming Code and Triple Modular Redundancy. In: Symposium on Integrated Circuits and Systems Design, pp. 95–100 (2002)
13. Karlsson, J., Liden, P., Dahlgren, P., Johansson, R., Gunneflo, U.: Using Heavy-Ion Radiation to Validate Fault-Handling Mechanisms. IEEE Micro. 14, 8–23 (1994)
14. Reed, R.: Heavy Ion and Proton Induced Single Event Multiple Upsets. In: IEEE Nuclear and Space Radiation Effects Conference, pp. 2224–2229 (1997)
15. Seifert, N., Moyer, D., Leland, N., Hokinson, R.: Historical trend in alpha-particle induced soft error rates of the Alpha microprocessor. In: Proc. 39th Annu. IEEE Int. Reliab. Phys. Symp., pp. 259–265 (2001)
16. Hsiao, M.Y.: A class of Optimal Minimum Odd-Weight column SEC-DED codes. IBM J. of Research and Dev. (14), 395–401 (July 1970)
17. Prahdan, D.K., Reddy, S.M.: Error-Control Techniques for Logic Processors. IEEE Trans. on Comp. C-21(12) (December 1972)
18. Reed.: A class of multiple-error-correcting codes and the decoding scheme. IEEE Trans. on Information Theory 4(4), 38–49 (1954)
19. Assmus Jr., E.F., Key, J.D. (eds.): Designs and their Codes. Press Syndicate of the University of Cambridge, Cambridge (1992)
20. Roman, S.: Coding and information Theory. Graduate Texts in Mathematics (1992)
21. Rao, T.R.N., Fujiwara, E.: Error-Control Coding for Computer Systems. Prentice Hall, New Jersey (1989)
22. Argyrides, C., Pradhan, D.K.: Improved Decoding Algorithm for High Reliable Reed Muller Coding. In: 20th IEEE International System On Chip Conference (SOCC 2007) (September 2007)
23. Wallace, C.S.: A Suggestion for a Fast Multiplier. IEEE Trans. On Electronic Computer EC-14(1), 14–17 (1964)
24. Kinichiroh, T., et al.: New Decoding Algorithm for Reed-Muller Codes. IEEE Trans. on Infornation. Theory IT-28(5) (September 1982)
25. Argyrides, C., Zarandi, H., Pradhan, D.: Matrix Codes: Multiple Bit Upsets Tolerant Method for SRAM Memories. In: 22nd IEEE International Symposium on Defect and Fault Tolerance in VLSI Systems (DFT 2007) (September 2007)

Efficient Reed-Solomon Iterative Decoder Using Galois Field Instruction Set

Daniel Iancu[1], Mayan Moudgill[1], John Glossner[1], and Jarmo Takala[2]

[1] Sandbridge Technologies Inc., 120 White Plains Rd, Tarrytown, NY 10591, USA
{diancu,mmoudgill,jglossner}@sandbridge.com
[2] Tampere University of Technology, Korkeakoulunkatu 1, 33720 Tampere, Finland
jarmo.takala@tut.fi

Abstract. This paper presents a computationally efficient iterative Reed-Solomon (RS) decoder, which is suitable for software implementations on processors with instruction extensions for Galois field multiplication. Simulation models of proposed instructions were included into a processor simulator and performance of RS decoding was analyzed. The method has been validated for both Digital Video Broadcasting (DVB-T/H) and WiMAX and the method provides a total link budget improvement of up to 1 dB.

1 Introduction

Reed-Solomon (RS) codes are block-based error correcting codes with a wide range of applications in digital communications and storage. The code operates by oversampling a polynomial constructed from the data, thus redundant information is generated. This redundant information allows errors during transmission or storage to be corrected. The number and type of errors that can be corrected depends on the characteristics of the Reed-Solomon code.

The error correction capability of the RS code, i.e., the number of errors that can be corrected, t, is determined by the minimum distance $2t + 1$ of that specific code. There are many algorithms capable of correcting more than t errors as described in [1,2,3]. Exceeding the conventional errors correction capabilities requires significantly more computational complexity, reflected in additional silicon area and increased power consumption. Maximum-likelihood (ML) or near-to-ML decoding algorithms have prohibitive computational complexity for large alphabet RS codes [4]. Simplified VLSI implementations of the Koetter-Vardy algorithm are reported in the literature [5]. In [6], a soft input RS algorithm is described, which is based on an algebraic bounded distance decoder. The decoder iterates through several decoding attempts, with different numbers of erasures and compares the Euclidean distance between the candidate codeword and the received data with a threshold defined by an acceptance criterion. The iteration starts by assuming $2t$ erasures and each iteration decreases the expected number of erasures by two while in our case we start with two erasures and each iteration increases the expected number of erasures by two. Based on our end-to-end simulations of DVB-T/H and WiMAX, the total computational load is decreased by up to 15% using this approach.

M. Berekovic, N. Dimopoulos, and S. Wong (Eds.): SAMOS 2008, LNCS 5114, pp. 126–135, 2008.

Channel State Information (CSI) from the convolutional decoder is used to declare the erasures iteratively, as presented in [7] and in our previous work [8], such that the error correction capabilities of the RS decoder is maximized. Most of the erroneous data packets contain less than t errors per packet. In these cases, only the less computationally demanding Peterson-Gorenstein-Zierler RS decoding algorithm is used (see [4] for details). If there are more that t errors in a data packet, a more complex decoding algorithm is employed. We start with two erasures, based on the observation that erasure reliability information is inversely proportional to the number of erasures. Our decision to increase the number of erasures and start a new iteration is based on the degree of the error locator polynomial, as described in [8]. The rest of the paper is organized as follows: Section 2 describes the erasure iterative decoding algorithms. Section 3 describes the GF instruction set. The numerical simulations are given in Section 4 followed by conclusions in Section 5.

2 Erasure Iterative Decoding

The error and erasure decoding algorithm described in this section is applicable to any communication protocol utilizing RS $GF(2^m)$ fields. It also applies for any $GF(2^m)$ field for either full length or shortened codes. The total number of errors and erasures the algorithm can correct for is shown in Table 1. For most, if not all communication protocols, the link budget assumed in the standard is such that if the SNR at the receiver is in the bounds specified by the conformance testing, most of the time the RS packets have no errors at all. For example, based on our simulations for the DVB-T/H protocols, in the Quasi Error Free (QEF) transmission mode, on average only 0.02% of the packets have errors and the average number of erroneous symbols per packet is less than four. As the SNR further decreases, the number of packets with errors grows exponentially.

For an average of 99.98% of the time, there are no errors in the packets. For the remaining 0.02% of the time, if there are eight or less errors per packet, we use the Peterson-Gorenstein-Zierler [4] error-only correction algorithm. For low SNR, when more than eight erroneous symbols per packet are encountered, the error and erasure algorithm we developed, which is described below, becomes useful. In our previous

Table 1. Combinations of the number of errors and erasures

Errors (r)	Erasures (s)
8	0
7	2
6	4
5	6
4	8
3	10
2	12
1	14
0	16

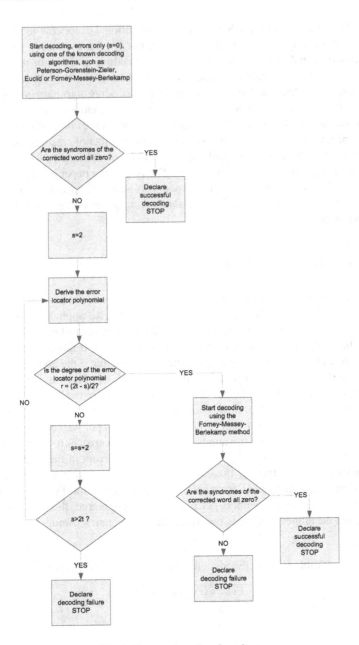

Fig. 1. Erasure decoding flowchart

work [8], we described the derivation of the CSI information and decoding algorithms only briefly touching the erasure decoding. For convenience, the decoding flowchart from [8] is illustrated in Fig. 1. The erasure decoding algorithm is described next. Throughout this section the following notations are used. Array $\mathbf{x} = (x_0, x_1, \ldots, x_{N-1})$

is a valid codeword and $\mathbf{r} = (r_0, r_1, \ldots, r_{N-1})$ is the received codeword. The generator polynomial $g(\cdot)$ is defined as

$$g(D) = \prod_{i=0}^{2t-1} (D - \alpha^{i+j}) \tag{1}$$

where α^j is the jth unity root, and $2t + 1$ is the code's minimum distance. Array $\mathbf{m} = (m_1, m_2, \ldots, m_t)$ is the error position vector and $\mathbf{e} = (e_{m_1}, e_{m_2}, \ldots, e_{m_t})$ is the error magnitude vector. The error polynomial, assuming that the decoder can decode t errors, reads as

$$e(D) = \sum_{i=0}^{t-1} e_{m_i} D^{m_i} . \tag{2}$$

The syndromes are denoted by $S_i, 0 \leq i \leq \delta - 2$ with $\delta = 2t + 1$, the minimum distance. The following formula can be written for the syndromes [4,9]

$$S_i = r(D)\Big|_{D=\varepsilon^{i+j}} = e(D)\Big|_{D=\alpha^{i+j}} = \sum_{p=1}^{t} e_{m_p}(\alpha^{i+j})^{m_p} . \tag{3}$$

The Fourier transform of the code word $\mathbf{x}$ in GF is

$$X_i = \sum_{k=0}^{N-1} x_k \alpha^{ik}, \ i = 0, \ldots, N - 1 \tag{4}$$

where $\alpha^N = 1$. This can be expressed in polynomial form as

$$X_i = \sum_{k=0}^{N-1} x_k D^k \Big|_{D=\alpha^i} . \tag{5}$$

In other words, the spectral coefficients are the evaluation of the polynomial at the roots α^j, $j = 0, \ldots, N - 1$. The inverse Fourier transform in GF is defined as:

$$x_k = \frac{1}{N'} X(D)\Big|_{D=\alpha^{-k}} . \tag{6}$$

where $N' = 1$ in $GF(2^m)$. Given the error locators $L_p = \alpha^{m_p}$, where $p = 1, \ldots, t$ the syndromes and the connection polynomial are

$$S_i = \sum_{p=1}^{t} e_{m_i} (L_p)^{i+j} \tag{7}$$

where $i = 0, \ldots, \delta - 2$ and respectively

$$B(D) = \prod_{i=1}^{t} (1 - L_p D) = 1 + B_1 D + \ldots + B_t D^t \tag{8}$$

where $B(D) = 0$ for $D = L_p$, $p = 0, \ldots, \delta - 2$.

Therefore, the inverse Fourier transform of the coefficients of the polynomial B will yield the $b_{m_p}b_m$ coefficients with nonzero values at the error locations. Since $b_m e_m = 0$ for $m = 0, \ldots, n-1$, the following convolution will be zero:

$$\sum_{p=0}^{n} B_p E_{i-p} = 0 . \tag{9}$$

Or, with $B_0 = 1$ and knowing that the maximum number of expected errors is t, the former expression becomes:

$$E_i = \sum_{p=1}^{t} B_p E_{i-p}, \ i = 0, \ldots, n-1 . \tag{10}$$

Since $E_i \equiv S_i$ it follows that:

$$S_i = \sum_{p=1}^{t} B_p S_{i-p} . \tag{11}$$

Any solution of the system equation (11) will lead to the error locators. In our approach, the error locations and magnitudes are determined using Peterson-Gorenstein-Zierler decoding described in [4].

After decoding, the syndromes are computed again and tested against zero. If all the syndromes are zero, the decoding process is successful and the next packet is passed to the decoder. If there are nonzero syndromes, the error and erasure decoding is enabled. The error and erasure decoding is described next. The interested reader can find a more detailed description in [4]. The error and erasure locators are $L_p = \alpha^{m_p}$ where $p = 1, \ldots, r$ and $Z_p = \alpha^{m_p}$, $p = 1, \ldots, s$, respectively, with r and s described in Table 1.

The decoding procedure is briefly introduced in the following. A more detailed description can be found, e.g., from [10,4].

1. Replace the symbols in the erasure positions with zero.
2. Compute the syndromes S_i, $0 \le i \le \delta - 2$. The syndromes will represent $\delta - 1$ successive entries in the GF Fourier Transform of the received sequence:

$$S_i = \sum_{p=1}^{r} e_{m_p} L_p^{i+j} - \sum_{p=1}^{s} x_{l_p} Z_p^{i+j}, \ i = 0, \ldots, \delta - 2$$

where l_p is the declared erasure position. The syndromes and the GF FT of the of the error and erasure pattern relationship is described as:

$$S_i = E_{i+j}, \ i = 0, \ldots, \delta - 2 .$$

The syndromes are located in the middle of the GF FT of the incoming word as:

$$E = \{E_0, E_1, \ldots \ldots, \underbrace{E_{i+j}, \ldots, E_{i+\delta-2}}_{S_i, \ldots, S_{i+j}}, \ldots \ldots, E_{N-1}\}$$

3. Define the erasure locator polynomial:

$$\Lambda(D) = \prod_{i=1}^{s}(D - Z_p) = \lambda_0 D^s + \ldots + \lambda_{s-1}D + \lambda_s .$$

4. Modify the original syndromes (Forney):

$$T_i = \sum_{p=0}^{s} \lambda_p S_{i+s-p}, \ i = 0,\ldots,\delta - s - 2$$

where T_i are the modified syndromes and contain the error and erasure information. It can be shown that the former expression is equivalent to:

$$T_i = -\sum_{p=1}^{r} B_p T_{i-p}, \ i = r, r+1,\ldots$$

5. Compute T_i coefficients. The error locator polynomial coefficients are obtained through the Massey shift register algorithm [11]. First, determine the $2t - s$ coefficients of T from:

$$T_i = \sum_{p=0}^{s} \lambda_p S_{i+s-p} .$$

For this step the syndrome and erasure locator polynomials have the following form:

$$S(D) = S_0 + S_1 D + \ldots + S_{2t-1}D^{2t-1}$$
$$\lambda(D) = \lambda_0 + \lambda_1 D + \ldots + \lambda_s D^s$$

6. Massey algorithm:
   (a) Initialize: $k = 0$, $B^{(0)}(x) = 1$, $L = 0$, and $T(x) = x$.
   (b) Loop $k = 1,\ldots, 2t - s$.
   (c) Compute the discrepancy

$$\Delta^{(k)} = T_k - \sum_{i=1}^{L} B_i^{(k-1)} T_{k-1} .$$

   (d) If $\Delta^{(k)} = 0$ then go to step (h).
   (e) Modify connection polynomial

$$B_i^{(k)}(x) = B_i^{(k-1)}(x) - \Delta^{(k)} T(x) .$$

   (f) If $2L \geq k$ then go to step (h).
   (g) $L = k - L$, $T(x) = B^{(k-1)}(x)\Delta^{(k)-1}$.
   (h) $T(x) = xT(x)$.
7. Compute the error locations by solving the $B(x)$. At this point, if the degree of the error locator polynomial is different from the assumed value r, the algorithm is reiterated for a different number of errors and erasures as illustrated in the flow chart.

8. Compute error magnitudes using Forney's algorithm [9]

$$\frac{L_k \Omega \left(L_k^{-1} \right)}{\Psi' \left(L_k^{-1} \right)}$$

where $\Omega(x) = B(x)[S(x) + 1]$, $\Psi'(D)$ is the formal derivative of $\Psi(D) = \Gamma(D)[S(D) + 1]$, and $\Gamma(D)$ is the erasure locator polynomial.

9. Compute the erasure magnitudes

$$\frac{Z_k \Omega \left(Z_k^{-1} \right)}{\Psi' \left(Z_k^{-1} \right)} \, .$$

10. Correct for errors and erasures.

3 GF Instructions

The instruction set extensions for GF arithmetic are depicted in Table 2. The definition of gfmul is designed to allow implementation of Galois field multiplication in the field $GF(2^M)$ when the lowest $16 - M$ bits are 0. In particular the results are undefined if the bits are not 0. The definition of gfnorm is designed to allow implementation of Galois field multiplication in the field $GF(2^M)$ when the lowest $16 - M$ bits are 0; parameter vt will hold the $2M - 1$ bits of the result of the un-normalized multiply, right-padded with $17 - 2M$ zeros. The parameter va will hold the M bits of the polynomial, right padded with $16 - M$ zeros. It is assumed that the MSB of the polynomial is a 1 and, therefore, does not need to be represented. Parameter N should be $M - 2$. In particular the results are undefined if the bits are other than 0. The instructions gfmul and gfnorm are described in Table 3.

Table 2. Galois field instructions (GF multiplier, multiplier add, normalize and multiply reduce). $\otimes$ denotes bitwise XOR, N is prime polynomial degree, acr is accumulator register.

Instruction	Operation
rgfmul (vt, va, vb)	$for(i = 0; i < 16; i++)$ $\quad vr[vt]_i \leftarrow gfmul(vr[va]_i, vr[vb]_i)$
rgfmac (vt, va, vb)	$for(i = 0; i < 16; i++)$ $\quad vr[vt]_i \leftarrow gfmul(vr[va]_i, vr[vb]_i) \otimes vr[vt]_i$
rgfnorm (vt, va, N)	$for(i = 0; i < 16; i++)$ $\quad vr[vt]_i \leftarrow gfnorm(vr[vt]_i, vr[va]_i)$
rgfmuldred (act, va, vb)	$t \leftarrow 0$ $for(i = 0; i < 16; i++)$ $\quad t \leftarrow gfmul(vr[va]_i, vr[vb]_i \otimes t$ $acr[act]_{31-0} \leftarrow (t \otimes acr[act]_{31-15}) \cdot 0^{15}$

Table 3. Definitions of instructions gfmul and gfnorm. $\wedge$ denotes bitwise AND.

gfmul (x,y): $N \geq 8$; $M_i \geq 8$	gfnorm (x,y):
$r \leftarrow 0$	$r \leftarrow x$
$for(i = 0; i < N; i++)$	$for(i = 0; i < N; i++)$
$\quad r \leftarrow r \otimes \left(\left(0^i \cdot x_{(15-M_i)} \cdot 0^{M_i - i} \right) \wedge y_{(15-i)}{}^{16} \right)$	$\quad \left(r \leftarrow r_{15-1} \cdot 0 \right) \otimes \left(c \wedge r_{15}{}^{16} \right)$
$return(r)$	$return(r)$

4 Performance Evaluation

In order to verify the applicability of the method and estimate the performance, experiments with Sandbridge Technologies SBX processor [12,13] were carried out. The SBX processor is a multithreaded processor with vector unit and the SBX development tools contain instruction set simulator allowing new instructions to be incorporated. We modeled the GF multiplication instructions from Tables 2 and 3 and included these special instructions to SBX simulation model. Next, software code for the iterative decoding algorithm described in this paper was written such that the code special Galois field instructions were exploited in the code.

As an example, in Table 4, it is illustrated the total number of GF instructions required to decode one RS(2004,188) packet for two distinct cases, first using only scalar and second using only vector instructions.

The total number of instructions required for decoding one RS packet is roughly 16 times higher in the scalar case then in the vector case. In the DVB-T case, for the highest bitrate of 31.67 Mbps, the decoder is called 21763 times per second. The total number of cycles spent by the processor in vector mode for the GF operations only is less then 18 MHz (a fraction of the SBX processor capabilities) compared to 277 MHz in scalar mode.

The iterative decoding algorithm was tested in the end-to-end DVB-T/H and WiMAX simulated systems, specified by ETSI EN 744 V1.4.1 (2001-01) and IEEE802.16d. The simulations were performed by using the SBX simulation tools. Using our GF instructions, the total number of cycles per second consumed in the SBX processor, for the highest bit rates specified in the standards and assuming that every packet has eight errors and eight erasures, are the following: 29 MHz for the 31.67 Mbps DVB-T, 9 MHz for the 4.4 Mbps DVB-H including the optional second RS decoder at

Table 4. Number of GF scalar and vector instructions required to decode one RS(204, 188) packet using the Peterson method

Scalar Instructions		Vector Instructions	
gfmul	$\rightarrow$ 3040	rgmul	$\rightarrow$ 190
gfmac	$\rightarrow$ 6656	rgfnorm	$\rightarrow$ 192
gfnorm	$\rightarrow$ 3072	rgfmulred	$\rightarrow$ 416
Total	**12768**	**Total**	**798**

the link layer, and 68 MHz for the WiMAX 73.19 Mbps. Based on Monte-Carlo analysis, for the end-to-end DVB-T/H and WiMAX system, our method provides a total link budget improvement of up to 1 dB.

The performed simulation experiments show the potential of the proposed method and effectiveness of the proposed special instructions. Although the GF instructions have been used in SBX processor, the described method and GF instructions are general-purpose. Significant improvement on software implementations for iterative decoding could be expected by extending GPP/ASIP platforms with the proposed GF instructions.

5   Conclusions

In this paper, a computationally efficient iterative RS decoder was proposed, which is suitable for software implementations on processors with instruction extensions for Galois Field multiplication. Our experiments showed that adding vector GF instructions to the SBX processor, the overall performance of the Reed Solomon decoding for both DVB-T/H and WiMAX was improved about 16 times. The significant speedup in the execution of cyclic codes decoding makes the iterative decoding possible, improving the total link budget with up to 1 dB, based on our end-to-end simulations. The total number of cycles per second consumed by the SBX processor were 29 MHz for the 31.67 Mbps DVB-T, 9 MHz for the 4.4 Mbps DVB-H and 68 MHz for the WiMAX 73.19 Mbps and these numbers prove the real time capabilities or the proposed approach.

References

1. Berlecamp, E.: Bounded distance+1 soft decision Reed-Solomon decoding. IEEE Trans. Inform. Theory 42(3), 704–720 (1996)
2. Forney, G.D.: Generalized minimum distance decoding. IEEE Trans. Inform. Theory 12(2), 125–131 (1966)
3. Taipale, D.J., Pursley, M.: An improvement to generalized minimum distance decoding. IEEE Trans. Inform. Theory 37(1), 167–172 (1991)
4. Wicker, S.B.: Error Control Systems for Digital Communication and Storage. Prentice Hall, Englewood Cliffs (1995)
5. Gross, W.J., Kschischang, F.R., Koetter, R., Gulak, P.G.: Towards a VLSI architecture for interpolation-based soft-decoding Reed-Solomon decoders. J. VLSI Sign. Proc. 39(1–2), 93–111 (2005)
6. Lamarca, M., Sala-Alvarez, J., Martinez, A.: Iterative decoding algorithm for RS-convolutional concatenated codes. In: Proc. 3rd Int. Symp. Turbo Codes and Related Topics, Brest, France, September 1–5, pp. 543–546 (2003)
7. Hagenauer, J., Hoeher, P., Viterbi, A.: Algorithm with soft decision outputs and its applications. In: Proc. IEEE GLOBECOM, Dallas, TX, November 27–30, pp. 1680–1686 (1989)
8. Iancu, D., Ye, H., Glossner, J., Schulte, M., Mamidi, S., Takala, J.: Improved spectral efficiency through iterative concatenated convolutional Reed-Solomon software decoding. In: Proc. Joint IST Workshop Sensor Network & Symp. Trends in Commun., Bratislava, Slovakia, June 24–26, pp. 1–5 (2006)
9. Forney, G.D.: On decoding BCH codes. IEEE Trans. Inform. Theory 11(4), 549–557 (1965)

10. Wilson, S.G.: Digital Modulation and Coding. Prentice-Hall, Englewood Cliffs (1996)
11. Massey, J.L.: Shift register synthesis and BCH decoding. IEEE Trans. Inform. Theory 15(1), 122–127 (1969)
12. Glossner, J., Moudgill, M., Iancu, D., Jintukar, S., Nacer, G., Schulte, M.J.: The Sandblaster SBX 2.0 architecture. In: Proc. Software Defined Radio Technical Conf., Denver, CO, November 5–9 (2007)
13. Mamidi, M., Iancu, D., Iancu, A., Schulte, M.J., Glossner, J.: Instruction set extensions for Reed-Solomon encoding and decoding. In: Proc. IEEE Int. Conf. Application-Specific Syst. Arch. Processors, Samos, Greece, July 23-25, pp. 231–237 (2005)

ASIP-eFPGA Architecture
for Multioperable GNSS Receivers

Thorsten von Sydow, Holger Blume, Götz Kappen, and Tobias G. Noll

Chair of Electrical Engineering and Computer Systems, RWTH Aachen University,
Schinkelstr. 2, 52062 Aachen, Germany
{sydow,blume,kappen,tgn}@eecs.rwth-aachen.de
http://www.eecs.rwth-aachen.de

Abstract. In this paper a novel flexible architecture exemplarily applied for multioperable GNSS receivers including an ASIP and an arithmetic oriented embedded FPGA is presented. The advent of next generation GNSS-systems as well as different demands in different system phases require high flexibility. The proposed architecture provides high energy and area efficiency compared to software-programmable processor while preserving flexibility. Exemplarily the mapping of the computational intensive base band processing of a Navstar GPS receiver to an ASIP-eFPGA architecture will be discussed. Results are based on a standard cell based design regarding the ASIP. A design method for physically optimized VLSI-macros has been applied for the implementation of the eFPGA. All results are acquired for a 90 nm-CMOS technology. It will be shown that the proposed heterogeneous architecture features an attractive position in the design space regarding area and energy efficiency as well as flexibility.

Keywords: ASIP, arithmetic oriented eFPGA, multioperable GNSS.

1   Introduction

Progresses of modern CMOS technology enables the integration of different architecture blocks in a so called heterogeneous System on Chip (SoC). These architecture blocks are programmable processors (general purpose, GPP; digital signal processing, DSP; application specific instruction set, ASIP) as well as reconfigurable processing units (RPUs) like embedded Field Programmable Gate Arrays (eFPGAs) and dedicated standard cell as well as physically optimized macros. One aspect of the design space describing energy and area efficiency for different discrete architecture blocks is shown in Fig. 5. Area and energy efficiency are increasing from programmable architectures (e.g. GPPs) to dedicated macros. However, flexibility is decreasing. The combination of different architecture blocks with different characteristics to an application specific architecture provides an attractive position in the design space. One interesting domain for such heterogeneous architectures are mobile handheld devices supporting global navigation satellite systems (GNSS). These systems are becoming more and more popular. Besides Navstar GPS there are a couple of systems which are currently

M. Berekovic, N. Dimopoulos, and S. Wong (Eds.): SAMOS 2008, LNCS 5114, pp. 136–145, 2008.

under development or in evaluation phase (e.g. Galileo, Compass, Glonass). Base band receiver architectures of these systems are comparable. The CDMA based systems (Navstar, Galileo, Compass) are differing e.g. concerning the spreading codes. Typically, base band processing tasks are mapped to dedicated macros. Therefore, adaptations to realize base band processing of other GNSS systems or required modifications caused by a change of specification are hardly realizable. One solution to gain flexibility is provided by realizing base band processing on a software-programmable processor [1]. Currently available solutions lack of either real time processing capabilities or reasonable power consumption acceptable for mobile handheld devices. The ASIP-eFPGA architecture proposed here provides on the one hand high flexibility and on the other hand higher energy as well as area efficiency compared to software-programmable processors.

The contribution is organized as follows: In section 2 architectures composed of a processor and an RPU are shortly sketched. The ASIP-eFPGA architecture is discussed in section 3. Afterwards the design flow of an ASIP-eFPGA architecture is presented in section 4. Section 5 provides a short description of a Navstar GPS receiver and the mapping to a ASIP-eFPGA architecture. Results and a discussion are given in section 6. The contribution is summarized with a short conclusion in section 7.

2 Processors Featuring a Reconfigurable Accelerator

Architectures including a programmable processor and a RPU are subject of several research projects (e.g. [2][3]). Devices based on such architectures are also employed in first commercial products (e.g. [4][5]). All these architectures typically include a RISC-based GPP and a general purpose RPU. RPUs can be classified into coarse and fine grain architectures. Coarse grain architectures are often based on ALU-like elementary processing elements while fine grain architectures like FPGAs are build on lookup-table-based (LUT) logic elements (LEs). These LEs are embedded in a flexible but costly interconnect structure. A detailed comparison of different Processor-RPU architectures is given e.g. in [6]. In the following the classification scheme of Processor-RPU architectures presented in [6] will be shortly sketched. This scheme classifies the coupling degree between RPU and processor into tight and loose coupling (see Fig. 1).

The integration of the RPU as reconfigurable functional unit (RFU) is the tightest coupling scheme. Data communication is realized by the central register file of the processor. The architecture of the processor has to be modified. The instruction set architecture (ISA) has to be enhanced by so called custom instructions (CIs). These CIs abstract the corresponding operations on the RPU. Furthermore, the corresponding control logic related to these CIs have to be realized. Dedicated functional units residing in the execute stage of the processor and the RPU usually have different maximum clock frequencies. Thus, a synchronisation mechanism has to be provided to guarantee coherency. Alltogether this coupling scheme results in a significant design effort.

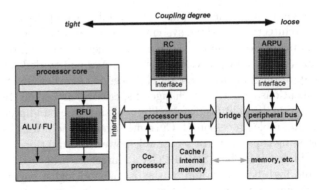

Fig. 1. Classification scheme according to the coupling degree of processor and RPU

The attachment of the RPU as reconfigurable coprocessor unit (RC) to the processor bus like e.g. an internal memory component is a more loose coupling scheme. The RPU can directly access the internal memory. Communication events between internal memory and RPU allocate the processor bus. So the processor can not access the internal memory meanwhile. This possibly restricts the computational parallelism of processor and RPU. The RPU can be mapped into the address space of the processor. Thus, the RPU can be controlled by the processor by means of memory load and write instructions.

The loosest coupling scheme is the integration of the RPU as so called attached reconfigurable processing unit (ARPU). Within this coupling mechanism the RPU is connected to a peripheral bus. The peripheral bus is connected with the processor bus via a bridge. Typically the peripheral bus is a bottleneck for high throughput communication events between processor and RPU. RPU and processor can be designed independently. The utilization of off-the-shelf IP-cores for the processor and the RPU reduces design complexity.

3   ASIP-eFPGA Architecture

Digital signal processing applications can usually be partioned into control and data flow oriented parts. Control oriented parts are most suited to be mapped on a programmable processor. Data flow oriented tasks are appropriate to be mapped on architecture blocks which provide the possibility to exploit concurrency. Dedicated macros or FPGA-like architecture blocks support concurrency of according data flow oriented tasks. The architecture presented in this contribution is composed of a programmable ASIP and an arithmetic oriented eFPGA. The programmability of the ASIP allows the realization of tasks in software. In order to increase the efficiency operations which are frequently occurring in a given application domain can be designed as special instructions. These special instructions are added to the ISA of the ASIP. The corresponding functional units of these instructions have to be realized. The ISA of the ASIP has to be specified before production of the overall architecture. The configurability of the eFPGA facilitates the mapping of variable datapaths also after production as so called eFPGA operators. Due to the overhead related to configurability the efficiency of mapped datapaths is worse than that of the implementation as dedicated macros. In order to increase efficiency the eFPGA architecture is tailored to an arithmetic oriented application domain (see also [7]). eFPGA operators are logically encapsulated by ASIP instructions provided in the ASIP ISA. Thus, complex data flow oriented operators are realized on the eFPGA and binded via inline assembler calls in the program code written in C.

3.1   ASIP

The ASIP core applied here is based on a Harvard architecture with an initial RISC-like ISA. The pipeline of the processor includes five stages (similar structure as the DLX-processor [8]). The ISA of the ASIP can be enhanced with instructions which realize operations frequently required in the given application domain. Exemplarily the effect of the insertion of a dedicated multiply instruction including the corresponding dedicated functional unit will be discussed in section 6. Furthermore, the ASIP ISA was enhanced with a CI activating operators which are configured on the eFPGA. The definition of the CI is independent of the functionality and the position of the eFPGA operators. The assembler syntax and binary coding of this CI includes the addresses of source and destination operands of the register file as well as an index field which is required to address a lookup table. This lookup table includes characteristics like position and delay of the eFPGA operators which are currently mapped on the eFPGA. The control logic related to the CI ensures data communication between ASIP and eFPGA as well as the synchronization on the ASIP side.

3.2   Arithmetic Oriented eFPGA

The eFPGA is based on a static reconfiguration concept and has been tailored to applications featuring basic arithmetic operators. The architecture consists of a two-dimensional alignment of identical cluster tiles. In Fig. 2 one cluster tile including a block diagram of an LE is depicted. Within a cluster tile a field of 16 LEs is included. This addresses the characteristics of arithmetic datapaths which are usually arranged in a two-dimensional way in so called bit and function slices. A function slice is composed of processing elements which all calculate the same elementary function on bit level, while bit slices represent all processing elements assigned to the same bit value. The LE is less complex than LEs residing in commercial general purpose FPGAs (e.g. [9]). An LE of the eFPGA includes three basic LUT2 components, two XOR-gates and a couple of configuration multiplexers. With these building blocks elementary arithmetic operators can be realized efficiently (e.g. two gated fulladditions within one LE). The interconnect architecture of the eFPGA is twofold. The global general purpose interconnect structure is based on an island style scheme including routing switches (RS) and connection boxes (CB) [10]. Besides the global interconnect the local interconnect directly connects inputs and outputs of neighboring LEs.

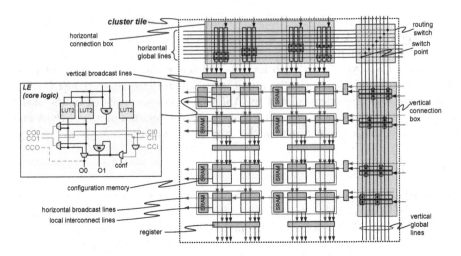

Fig. 2. Cluster tile and LE of the arithmetic oriented eFPGA

To support the mapping of arithmetic oriented datapaths broadcast lines assigned to the local interconnect are integrated. These broadcast lines allow the distribution of the same operands over a larger range of the eFPGA. Operand broadcasting is common in arithmetic datapaths. The local interconnect is not restricted by the boundaries of one cluster tile. In fact, broadcast lines and local LE connections are distributed across cluster boundaries, thus building a flat widespread two-dimensional array of interconnected LEs. Connection points between local and global interconnect is resided in the CBs. In the CBs local signals can be switched on the global general purpose interconnect and vice versa. Altogether the interconnect structure of the eFPGA is tailored to the mapping of arithmetic operations. The general purpose interconnect of the eFPGA which is typicalley critical concerning time and power consumption is much less complex for this optimized eFPGA than interconnect structures of commercial FPGAs.

3.3   ASIP-eFPGA Coupling

The coupling of eFPGA and ASIP has great impact on the overall efficiency and demands different mechanisms which are realized as dedicated control structure. For the ASIP-eFPGA architecture presented here a coupling scheme related to the RFU coupling class has been implemented. A simplified block diagram of the coupled ASIP-eFPGA architecture including the control structure is depicted in Fig. 3. The index field of the binary representation of the CI addresses a lookup table which includes the characteristics like number of delay cycles as well as the address on the eFPGA of the desired eFPGA operator. A component which generates a halt signal for the pipeline registers of the processor evaluates the entry of the delay field of the addressed line in the lookup table. The possibility to generate a halts signal is required if the delay of the eFPGA operator is longer than one ASIP clock cycle. Furthermore, the operator address entry is utilized to

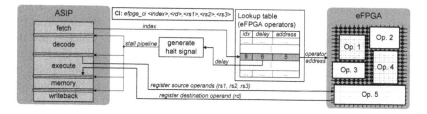

Fig. 3. ASIP-eFPGA architecture including the control structure required for coupling

select the corresponding eFPGA operator. The source operands are transferred from the pipeline register at the beginning of the execution of the execute stage to the eFPGA operator. Depending on the complexity of the operator the pipeline has to be stalled. After finishing the calculation the result is transferred back to the pipeline register between execute and memory stage. Whilst taking into account forwarding mechanisms which also have been implemented in the ASIP the result is written into the central register file in the writeback stage.

4   Design Flow

4.1   ASIP

The ASIP design flow is based on the *Processor Designer* environment provided by CoWare [11]. The *Processor Designer* enables the automatic generation of software development tools like compiler, assembler, linker and a cycle-accurate simulator from the the architecture description of the corresponding ASIP in LISA (language for instruction set architectures). The ASIP is derived from the *LT_RISC* processor template. The *LT_RISC* is a basic RISC-processor comparable to the DLX-processor of [8] and has been utilized as reference for comparison. The processor template also includes a basic compiler design description which is necessary to generate a corresponding C/C++ compiler semi-automatically. The realized LISA description of the ASIP is cycle-accurate and includes the implementation of the coupling control structures. Besides the software development tools the *Processor Designer* provides the generation of a synthesizable VHDL description of the ASIP including the coupling control structures all originating from the LISA description.

4.2   Arithmetic Oriented eFPGA

The realization of the arithmetic oriented eFPGA is based on a design approach utilizing an eFPGA architecture template which enables the possibility to prune the architecture of an eFPGA for an arithmetic oriented application domain [12]. The implementation of the layout is based on a design method utilized for the realization of physically optimized VLSI-macros. Therefore, the definition of all architecture parameters of the eFPGA according to the description of section 3.2 has been specified. In addition a couple of hand-crafted basic layout cells for structural components like LE, RS, CB, etc. have been implemented.

Currently, no automated place and route tool is available which translates a general netlist description of an eFPGA operator to a placed and routed architecture dependent netlist representation. Therefore, the realisation of applications is time consuming as the architecture dependend netlist has to be implemented manually. As most arithmetic datapaths are regular, manual mapping is viable. Power values related to eFPGA operators have been acquired by transistor netlist simulations based on the configuration information of the mapped datapaths.

4.3   Cycle Accurate ASIP-eFPGA Architecture Model

The cycle accurate model of the ASIP-eFPGA architecture has been assembled from the VHDL description generated from the LISA sources and a crafted behavioral VHDL description of the eFPGA. The LISA description incorporates the ASIP and the coupling control structures. The VHDL model of the eFPGA realizes the cycle accurate behavior of the addressed eFPGA operators at the interfaces between ASIP and eFPGA. Physical costs for the ASIP and the coupling control structures have been determined by means of a standard cell design flow. This design flow starts with the synthesis applying the *Design Compiler* environment from Synopsys. After generation of the standard cell netlist the design has been placed and routed utilizing *First Encounter* from Cadence. Area and power consumption values for the parts of the design which have been realized with LISA are based on a placed and routed standard cell design approach. To improve the results a couple of optimization steps like design flattening, uniquifying, clock gating, etc. have been performed. On the one hand the cycle accurate model of the ASIP-eFPGA architecture has been applied for the verification of the design. On the other hand the determination of the switching activity of each input, output and net of the design required the ASIP-eFPGA model. The switching activity has been used to acquire a detailed power profile.

5   Software GPS Correlator

The basic architecture of a typcial Navstar GPS receiver can be composed of three building blocks. The received signal is filtered, mixed to an intermediate frequency and subsequently digitized. The digital signal is processed in a following base band block. This block is typically composed of several correlator channels. The realization of one correlator channel used in this contribution is depicted in Fig. 4. Each channel is assigned to a satellite. The digital controlled oscillator (DCO) is used to generate the base band carrier frequency. The incoming signal is mixed by this frequency to in-phase and quadrature signals (I, Q). These signals are multiplied by satellite dependent pseudo random gold codes (EML, P). The length of the code is 1023 chips. Products are accumulated for a given period of time (1 ms) and saved in correlator registers. Their content is evaluated by the third building block (correlator control) which is in

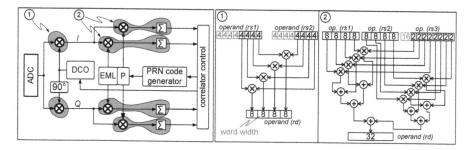

Fig. 4. Exemplary eFPGA operator (right) to realize a part of the correlator (left)

charge of controlling PRN code generation and the DCO. Beginning with a cold start of the receiver all visible satellites are determined in the acquisition phase. Therefore, a two-dimensinal search space spanned by carrier frequency and code phase variations have to be processed for each satellite. If a correlated value is greater than a threshold value, the corresponding satellite is visible. In the subsequent tracking phase the carrier frequency and code phases are permanently updated due to relative motion between satellite and receiver. Word widths of the processed signals within the correlator have great impact on the signal-to-noise ratio (SNR). In the following two scenarios incorporting different word widths are considered. The low-precision mode (LP) implies a digitized satellite signal and carrier frequency of 2 bit and a 4 bit signal at the output of the mixers. In the high-precision mode (HP) yielding a SNR gain of approx. 0.5 dB, word widths of the mixer inputs is 4 bit and 8 bit for the output respectively. At first, the corellator has been realized as ANSI-C software-implementation using integer arithmetic (*LT_RISC* reference values). As the *LT_RISC* allows no subword parallelism, the implementation of LP- and HP-mode is equal. Integration of the eFPGA provides advantageous exploitation of subword parallelism. Basic arithmetic operators have been replaced by two CIs representing the corresponding eFPGA operators (see 1 und 2 for HP mode in Fig. 4). The datapath of the ASIP and the registers of the register file have a word length of 32 bit. Thus, in HP mode four and in LP mode eight operations can be processed at once.

6   Results

Results have been acquired for a clock frequency constraint of 220 MHz. Delay and energy values have been determined each under worst case conditions for a 90 nm CMOS technology. Cost values for data and program memory (each 8 KB) have been included by applying memory models of *CACTI 5.0* [13]. Values depicted in Tab. 1 are related to the correlation for one combination of code phase and carrier frequency. Power consumption and chip area is dominated by program and data memory. For the *LT_RISC* with multiplier the memory area portion is 84 % of the overall area. This amount decreases for an ASIP-eFPGA with multiplier in HP-mode to 59 %, while eFPGA area contributes with 26 %.

Table 1. Area, energy and delay comparison for different architectures

	LT_RISC	LT_RISC with Multiplier.	ASIP-eFPGA		ASIP-eFPGA with Multiplier	
			LP	*HP*	*LP*	*HP*
Area [mm²]	0,633	0,655	0,803	0,914	0,829	0,939
Delay [μs]	9191	2545	237	413	184	322
Energy [μJ]	125.8	50.1	4.77	8.12	4.04	7.66

Implementation results for different architecture blocks including ASIP-eFPGA architectures and the *LT_RISC* are illustrated in Fig. 5. The diagram is based on implementation results of several typical digital signal processing applications [14]. Realizations utilizing the *LT_RISC* are less efficient than these of a state-of-the-art DSP (Texas Instruments, TMS320C642). Positions for implementations on the ASIP-eFPGA architecture are between the DSP and the FPGA domain. The efficiency gain achieved by integrating a dedicated multiplier unit for the *LT_RISC* is greater than for the ASIP-eFPGA architecture. This is caused by the fact that almost all multiply operations are relocated on the eFPGA. Only address operations take advantage of a dedicated multiplier. The realization of the operators depicted in Fig. 4 as dedicated macros would yield higher efficiency gains compared to the ASIP-eFPGA. However, such a solution would be fixed for these operators. Hence, there is no way to modify and adapt operators after production, while a flexible ASIP-eFPGA provides this opportunity. Mapping GNSS receivers to ASIP-eFPGA architectures is promising as computational intensive arithmetic operators can be executed advantegeously on the eFPGA. Furthermore, these operators can be easiliy adapted to meet changing requirments. Considering the discussed Navstar GPS receiver SNR could be traded for area and energy efficiency by changing the precision mode (LP, HP).

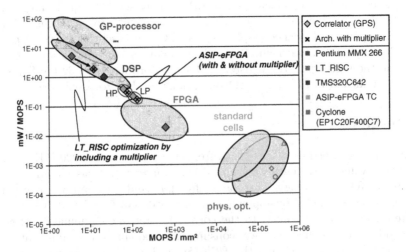

Fig. 5. Design space inlcuding ASIP-eFPGA-architectures [15]

7 Conclusion

Within this contribution a new architecture for GNSS receivers composed of an ASIP and an arithmetic oriented eFPGA has been introduced. In comparison to programmable processors ASIP-eFPGA architectures feature higher area and energy efficiency while retaining high flexibility. Both area and energy efficiency could be increased by more than one order of magnitude for the realization of a software Navstar GPS correlator compared to equivalent processor implementations. Physical costs for a 90 nm CMOS realization have been determined by means of a standard cell design regarding the ASIP and a transistor netlist based model related to the physically optimized design of the eFPGA component.

Acknowledgments. This work is funded by the Deutsche Forschungsgemeinschaft as part of the Priority Program 1148 - Reconfigurable Computing Systems.

References

1. Borre, K., Bertelsem, N., Jensen, S.H., Akos, D.M., Rinder, P.: A Software-Defined GPS and Galileo Receiver: A Single-Frequency Approach (Applied and Numerical Harmonic Analysis), 1st edn. Birkhäuser, Boston (2007)
2. Lodi, A., Toma, M., Campi, F., Cappelli, A., Canegallo, R., Guerrieri, R.: A VLIW processor with reconfigurable instruction set for embedded applications. IEEE Journal of Solid-State Circuits 38, 1876–1886 (2003)
3. Borgatti, M., Lertora, F., Foret, B., Cali, L.: A reconfigurable system featuring dynamically extensible embedded microprocessor, FPGA, and customizable I/O. IEEE Journal of Solid-State Circuits 38, 521–529 (2003)
4. PACT XPP Technologies: Smart Media Processor, http://www.pactxpp.com
5. Stretch Corporation: S5000, S6000, http://www.stretchinc.com
6. Enzler, R.: Architectural Trade-offs in Dynamically Reconfigurable Processors. PHD-thesis, ETH Zürich (2004)
7. von Sydow, T., Neumann, B., Blume, H., Noll, T.G.: Quantitative Analysis of Embedded FPGA-Architectures for Arithmetic. In: Proceedings of the International Conference on Application-specific Systems, Architectures and Processors (2006)
8. Hennessy, J., Patterson, D.A.: Computer Architecture: A Quantitative Approach, 4th edn. Morgan Kaufmann, San Francisco (2006)
9. Altera Corporation: Stratix III Device Handbook, vol. 1, http://www.altera.com
10. George, V., Rabaey, J.M.: Low-energy FPGAs: architecture and design. Kluwer Academic Publishers, Dordrecht (2001)
11. CoWare Corporation: LISA Language Reference Manual, http://www.coware.com
12. Neumann, B., von Sydow, T., Blume, H., Noll, T. G.: Design flow for embedded FPGAs based on a flexible architecture template. In: The conference on Design, automation and test in Europe (accepted for publication, 2008)
13. Hewlett-Packard Development Company: CACTI 5.0, http://www.hpl.hp.com
14. Blume, H., Feldkämper, H., Noll, T.G.: Model-Based Exploration of the Design Space for Heterogeneous Systems on Chip. Journal of VLSI Signal Processing Systems 40, 19–34 (2005)
15. Noll, T.G.: Application specific eFPGAs for SoC platforms. In: International Symposion on VLSI Design, Automation and Test (2005)

Introduction to System Level Design for Heterogeneous Systems

John McAllister*

Programmable Systems Laboratory
Institute of Electronics, Communication and Information Technology (ECIT)
Queens University Belfast
j.mcallister@ecit.qub.ac.uk

For the current generation of heterogeneous multi-core embedded processor, System-on-Chip and FPGA platforms, implementation and optimisation of Digital Signal and Image Processing applications is an exceptionally challenging task, with the widely accepted viewpoint being that moving towards high abstraction (system) level design principles is the only feasible option to increasing the productivity of application synthesis on such complex platforms. However, this movement, which has been widely touted for many years, has been slow to materialise due to the vast array of processing components, architectures and design methodologies at the disposal of any such system designer.

Despite the lack of standardisation in this area, it is apparent that design methodologies and portable application synthesis tools which exploit model-based design techniques are slowly becoming the norm and coming to the fore in both research and commercial contexts. The plethora of issues to be addressed by such synthesis methodologies is, however, expansive, incorporating partitioning, scheduling, synthesis of software, hardware, memory and interprocessor communication infrastructures, and optimisation of all of these physical and other real-time aspects such as throughput, latency and power. Significant advances must yet be made in all of these areas before any approach can be isolated as defacto-standard. This session brings together world leading academic and industrial experts in the areas of application modelling and transformation, synthesis methodologies and tools, implementation optimisation techniques and heterogeneous device architectures to present lessons thus far in the move towards system level design, and the potential presented by exploitation of such model-based design processes in the future.

---

* Special Session Chair.

M. Berekovic, N. Dimopoulos, and S. Wong (Eds.): SAMOS 2008, LNCS 5114, p. 146, 2008.
© Springer-Verlag Berlin Heidelberg 2008

Streaming Systems in FPGAs

Stephen Neuendorffer and Kees Vissers

Xilinx Research Labs
2100 Logic Dr., San Jose, CA, 95119, USA
{stephen.neuendorffer,kees.vissers}@xilinx.com
http://www.xilinx.com

Abstract. As FPGA devices have become larger and more capable, they have transitioned from being used primarily as flexible glue logic to being used as central data processing elements in many digital systems. Typically, these systems (including video processing, wired and wireless networking) rely on streaming architectures. These architectures differ significantly from traditional processor architectures and are able to offer unique challenges and benefits for system designers. In particular, streaming architectures in FPGAs are well suited for implementing upcoming digital convergence applications. We summarize how streaming architectures in FPGAs relate to other programmable platforms for embedded applications and focus on key problem areas related to the design tools and platform infrastructure that will drive these new applications.

Keywords: dataflow, FPGAs, digital convergence.

1 Introduction

Historically, FPGAs have been used primarily to implement small amounts of glue logic between other chips. In contrast with discrete logic gates, FPGAs and other programmable logic devices offered increased integration and flexibility in board-level design. Increasingly, however, FPGAs can be considered to be programmable platforms in their own right, and are capable of forming the central processing resource in a complex system with only a small number of additional parts.

However, there are significant barriers to using FPGAs as direct replacements for other programmable platforms. Despite the recent development of higher-level design tools for FPGAs, the bulk of FPGA systems are still coded largely in RTL. As a result, system designers must still overcome basic timing closure in order to meet throughput requirements. FPGAs have also become not only bigger, but also more complex and heterogeneous, including not only logic and routing resources, but also embedded memory blocks, specialized DSP elements, and complex external interface blocks for gigabit ethernet and PCI express. Effectively using such complex and diverse features can be time consuming, since they must not only be connected correctly to the datapath of a system but must also be integrated into the control logic.

M. Berekovic, N. Dimopoulos, and S. Wong (Eds.): SAMOS 2008, LNCS 5114, pp. 147–156, 2008.

We believe that overcoming these barriers is most likely to be found by re-thinking the programming models used to target FPGA design. On the programming model side, we argue that dataflow stream processing offers significant benefits for FPGA design. Dataflow neatly captures many processing-oriented FPGA applications, such as signal processing and networking, in a way that corresponds to how application designers conceptualize such problems. Dataflow models of computation also map well onto streaming architectures which can be directly implemented in FPGAs.

However, the data processing of most FPGA applications only provides a portion of the logic programmed into the FPGA. We seek not only programming models that are appropriate for specifying application kernels, such as FFTs or IPV4 packet processing, but also platforms for integrating those kernels into a system. This integration often requires a significant amount of logic which is not primarily application processing, such as physical interfaces for external memory controllers and processor busses. The complexity and real-time requirements of these components are not easily handled by dataflow design techniques. At the same time, most application designers are not interested or skilled in how to build such system-on-chip architectures.

As a result, we anticipate that tools for dataflow design in FPGA will become more commonplace making it easier for algorithmic designers to implement designs in FPGAs without HDL programming and explore a variety of architectural tradeoffs without significant source code changes. At the same time, these tools will assume more complete system-level infrastructure, such as complete working processor systems, avoiding the complexity of system-on-chip design.

2   Streaming Architectures in FPGA

FPGAs are unique among programmable platforms in that streaming architectures can be implemented with elements of varying granularity. This enables different actors in a dataflow specification to be easily implemented at matched data rates, despite differing computational loads. A flexible granularity, combined with memory elements distributed through the FPGA fabric, also enables elements to match the natural memory locality of actors in the specification. In contrast, multiprocessor architectures inevitably have fixed granularity elements. This requires actors with low computational load to be grouped together in order to use the processors efficiently, possibly incurring scheduling overhead and increasing latency. A fixed granularity architecture also requires actors with high computational load to be partitioned across multiple elements. Although in some cases these refactorings can be performed automatically by a compiler, such as StreamIT [1],

FPGA streaming architectures tend to be organized in systolic structures in which neighbors communicate directly through dedicated FIFOs. As a result, internal communication bandwidth can be very high while minimizing contention between elements. In contrast, multiprocessor architectures tend to be organized around shared communication networks. These networks typically provide a high aggregate communication bandwidth, but the bandwidth is shared between all or some communication elements, which can increase latency. If the communication latency is high enough, external shared memory may be necessary to provide efficient buffering. For applications where latency is not critical (such as video processing) this can be an effective streaming implementation, as in the Philips Trimedia Streaming Software Architecture. Some multiprocessor architectures do provide low-latency neighbor-neighbor interprocessor communication, such as Picochip, or the capability to support both neighbor-neighbor communication models and shared-memory communication such as the MIT RAW [2] architecture commercialized by Tilera.

In many embedded systems, data storage can be implemented entirely on chip in local buffers. Increasingly, however, external memory storage is necessary for some applications, such as multi-frame buffers in MPEG4-AVC decoding. Streaming FPGA systems typically include application-specific logic for external direct memory access (DMA). For example, the FlexWAFE framework [3] provides predefined memory interfaces for building such DMA logic. In contrast, high-performance multiprocessor architectures tend to rely either on processor-programmed DMA and explicitly managed scratchpad memories, or caches combined with prefetching.

Another example of such video processing architecture is shown in Figure 1. This diagram shows a streaming implementation of an MPEG 4 simple profile decoder. Most of the blocks are connected by object FIFOs, which are implemented out of memory blocks in the FPGA, and additionally provide the ability to randomly access the contents of the FIFO without removing data. This avoids the need to read data and store it in a separate memory location before being able to process it. The copy controller actor interacts with a memory controller implemented in the FPGA to keep a small window of the previous frame available for the motion compensation block while the bulk of the frame is stored in DRAM that is outside the FPGA. Using external DRAM enables scaling to frame sizes that exceed the internal memory of the FPGA. Conceptually, the copy controller, memory controller, and interface FIFO blocks combine to implement a large object FIFO, while taking into account the access patterns of a specific application to optimize memory performance.

Networking applications (such as the simplified router shown in Figure 2) are also commonly implemented using streaming architectures in the FPGA. Typically, the header and payload of the network packet are processed separately. In this case, the payload is stored in external DRAM, while a routing decision is made based on the contents of the header. In more complex applications, the payload may also be processed, such as in a network intrusion detection system. Note that some control information must be exchanged between the payload manager and IP lookup actors, since packets may be dropped due to high network traffic or completed out of order depending on the IP lookup algorithm used.

Although these examples are simplified representatives of todays FPGA applications, we believe that future applications will be dominated by streaming architectures. By decoupling components in a system, enabling them to be

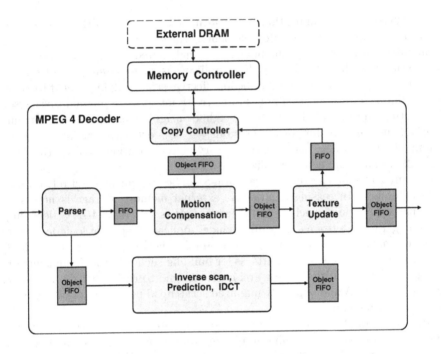

Fig. 1. Streaming FPGA architecture of an MPEG4 Simple Profile decoder

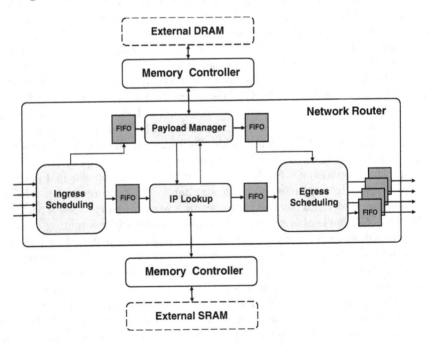

Fig. 2. Streaming FPGA architecture of a simplified network router

independently optimized and reused, large applications can be constructed. In particular, since they are suitable for both high-rate networking and video processing, streaming architectures will likely be central to the implementation of future digital convergence applications in FPGAs.

3   Design Tools

The most direct way to implement streaming architectures in FPGAs is using a design methodology based on dataflow process networks [4,5,6,7]. Dataflow models of computation allow the concurrency of an application to be expressed explicitly, since state accesses are localized, and components communicate only through deterministic channels. Additionally, the mapping into an FPGA implementation can be finely controlled, since each dataflow actor can be mapped independently to the FPGA, while being decoupled by queues. Conceptually, this leads to a globally asynchronous, locally synchronous (GALS) style model, even if the actual FPGA implementation is completely synchronous for efficiency purposes. By adding additional annotations, or through analysis by a compiler, the sizes of physical queues can be determined.

Although FPGA designers have been building streaming architectures for some time, it is only relatively recently that high-level design tools for supporting such a dataflow methodology have become available. Early versions of Xilinx System Generator provided a dataflow-like model by automatically instantiating logic to propagate when signals contain valid data [8]. In more recent versions, most signals are modeled as fixed rate data streams and data is assumed to always be valid. The small number of components that do not process data at fixed rates, such as the Viterbi decoder, include explicit data valid signals which must be connected to appropriate signals by a designer. A more general dataflow model, which uniformly represents not only when data is available in the implementation but also when it can be accepted is provided by the CAL tools [9].

The main downside of dataflow-oriented tools such as these is that many aspects of a system are not straightforward to describe in a strict dataflow model. For instance, control decisions must be coordinated between different actors as additional streams. Information arriving at irregular intervals compared to the primary data (such as user-initiated interaction) is difficult to model without allowing for 'peeking' at an input stream to see if data is available. However, this capability must be used carefully to avoid introducing unintended nondeterminism. A likely solution to these control operations is to make use of hierarchy, parameterization, and alternative models of computation in concert with dataflow, enabling the programming structure behind control decisions to be expressed more easily [10,11]. However, these techniques have not yet been widely adopted in tools.

A further downside of dataflow-oriented tools is that they typically require applications to be rewritten to explicitly use fine-grained streaming interfaces to achieve high performance. This makes it difficult for programmers accustomed to the sequential processing/unbounded memory model provided by most programming languages to transition to these tools. We believe that existing compiler technology, such as loop and memory dependence analysis, can solve this problem, enabling applications to be written using coarse grained domain-specific structures, such as packets in a networking application or macroblocks in a video application. Although these compiler transformations have not been used widely in general-purpose compilers, since they tend to scale to large programs poorly, we believe they can be successfully applied in this context, since individual dataflow actors exhibit a high degree of locality.

4   C-to-gates

The move towards advanced compiler technology is most easily seen in the changes in EDA tools based on C-to-gates. Many of these tools provide a dataflow-like design methodology where a programmer can use streaming APIs to express coarse-grained parallelism in a system. Whereas older tools often support a relatively simple mapping from C language constructs into RTL, newer tools in this area such as Synfora, a spinout of the HP Labs compiler team [12,13], employ a wider variety of algorithmic synthesis techniques. These techniques enable operator-level parallelism to be extracted from nested-loop code and for those operators to be scheduled onto FPGA resources, with automatic pipelining and resources sharing, if appropriate. Leveraging these compilation techniques within the context of a dataflow actor, and expressing the communication between actors using streaming interfaces results in a powerful design language for embedded systems. In particular, it allows designers to concentrate on interesting problems for meeting a desired throughput, such as eliminating unnecessary data dependencies and managing reference locality in external memory.

Although C-to-gates is a promising design methodology for streaming systems in FPGAs, many obstacles still remain. One disadvantage of adopting C as a design language for streaming systems is the widely varying usage models and compiler technology. Although C code is often valued for its portability, off-the-shelf C code must inevitably be rewritten to meet the constraints of a particular tool, achieve high-quality results, and (perhaps most importantly) explicitly express the streaming structure of the system. Even worse, due to variations in compiler technology and language requirements, the resulting code is unlikely to work well in another tool. The wide span of these tools is largely indicative of the lack of a good synthesizable standard in the area, as well as the high rate of innovation.

One key issue that any such standard will have to solve it is that it is often difficult to directly capture the richness of dataflow semantics in a sequential C simulation. For instance, dataflow actors can conceptually run forever, interacting through streams. In order to represent this, the actor behavior must be suspended and other actors executed. If feedback loops are present, this suspension might have to occur after every actor execution in order to avoid deadlock of the simulation. This can be dealt with conveniently by executing a multi-threaded simulation. SystemMOC [14] is a promising approach in this area, using SystemC for specification and simulation and as a front-end for simulation. Older modeling techniques such as YAPI [15] implemented similar simulation techniques without the benefit of SystemC abstractions.

Another important problem is the integration of generated components into a system, which might require communication of control and data information with a processor or external interfaces. For instance, Handel-C tools developed by Celoxica and now being marketed by Agility are bundled with board support packages targeting interfaces on many FPGA board (such as video input and output). ImpulseC provides integration with Xilinx EDK in order to implement processor accelerators in the FPGA fabric. Although these interfaces could be represented explicitly (as with HDL), it is preferable for a high-level tool flow to provide higher-level abstractions of such interfaces, in order to abstract the signal-level interfacing and timing issues. Abstracting these interfaces in standard platforms using standard APIs becomes crucial to enabling high-level design.

5   Memory Interfaces

One area where many of the issues in design tools combine is in memory interfaces. These interfaces contain many low-level timing details which are not handled well by high-level design tools, and hence the physical memory controller is typically treated as a black box with client-side streaming interfaces for providing addresses and exchanging data. However, from the perspective of high-level design tools, these client-side interfaces often have complex protocol requirements. For instance, memory controllers often support a variety of burst lengths, where consistency between the burst length specified and the number of data values read must be maintained. Programming errors may result in deadlock or misinterpretation of data. In other cases, timing requirement and inter-stream dependencies can be difficult to represent in a high-level design tool. For instance, a memory controller may require that all of the data is present before a write address is given. In other cases, because of the design of the memory technology, it may not be possible to stall a read transaction if data cannot be processed fast enough. Although additional buffering can be included in order to mitigate these problems, it can increase memory access latency and reduce the performance of the system. Simulation can also be a problem, since read/write and write/read dependencies within the memory controller are essentially tight dataflow feedback loops.

In order to solve these problems, we have begun investigating even higher-level programming APIs for memory interfaces. Our intention is that these APIs, combined with compiler-directed scheduling, can be a target-independent method of interfacing to memory. The intermediate requirements of a particular memory controller and/or memory technology can be handled explicitly in the library, likely using tool-specific pragmas or other techniques, and a library user can still obtain good performance. A first attempt in this direction is shown in Figure 3.

```
void write_word(u32 a, u32 d)
void write_line(u32 a, u32 d1, u32 d2, u32 d3, u32 d4)
void read_word(u32 a, u32 &d)
void read_line(u32 a, u32 &d1, u32 &d2, u32 &d3, u32 &d4)
```

Fig. 3. A memory interface API

This simple API is explicit about how data is aggregated into bursts, but not how the bursts are actually implemented in terms of stream transactions with a particular memory controller. A particular tool is likely to inline this API and schedule individual stream transactions with the memory controller across multiple cycles in order to achieve high throughput.

6   Implementation Platforms

To a large extent the platform infrastructure that supports these design tools can be generic, enabling the same underlying interfaces to be leveraged by many tools. One possibility is for these interfaces to be delivered as individual system components in a tool like Xilinx EDK. However, assembling such components, such as processor, memory interfaces, and networking interfaces, to construct a working system can be difficult. Particularly, when a control processor and operating system is involved, a large design space combined with complex system interactions and informal design constraints can make it difficult to get to a first working system.

Instead, we anticipate that the platform infrastructure to build streaming systems will be provided by partial designs preconfigured in the FPGA. An example of one such system is shown in Figure 4. This system encapsulates a basic working processor subsystem, along with a Linux operating system [16]. This subsystem can be preimplemented and verified without knowledge of the system that it will be coupled with. A user-defined streaming system can then be implemented in the remaining portion of the FPGA, without modifying the preconfigured design. This system can be implemented using the partial reconfiguration capabilities of Xilinx FPGAs.

The usage model of such a system is that the processor subsystem does not take part in the bulk of the data processing, but instead performs low-rate control processing which is not time-critical. However, the processor is capable of being involved in the configuration process of the FPGA, and providing a more programmer-friendly entry into the system. For instance, although the processor subsystem and operating system are initially loaded from the boot flash, the processor interacts with the internal configuration access port of the FPGA to configure the remaining portion with user-supplied logic. The operating system is also capable of providing robust libraries and process management, including memory protection, as the basis for building an application. Memory protection can also be provided on the fabric bridge between the FPGA and memory,

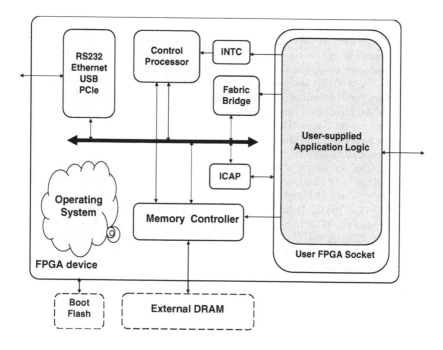

Fig. 4. A partially preconfigured FPGA system

coordinated with and managed by the processor, in order to protect the processor and other tasks using memory from programming errors in the FPGA.

7   Conclusion

Streaming architectures and dataflow design techniques are one of the great underlying approaches to addressing concurrent design. They have been used in FPGAs for some time, while being implemented in languages such as RTL HDL, with poor underlying support. Especially with the push towards multicore processors, it is likely that the general tool support for streaming programming models will improve greatly in this area. Fortunately, although the high-level abstractions may not yet be settled, the support for algorithmic programming of FPGAs from C means that FPGAs are likely well positioned to follow any trends that arrive. In contrast, FPGAs are significantly lacking in design libraries, since most FPGA IP is targetted towards system-on-chip design, rather than algorithmic design. We prefer to avoid the system-on-chip design problem by providing a combination of better design tools and better FPGA platforms. By combining these technologies in the right way, we believe it is possible to provide a 'user-space' design experience, where FPGA system designers will be comfortably abstracted from the bulk of the low-level programming detail. As a result, they can be enabled to build complex systems more quickly.

References

1. Gordon, M., Thies, W., Amarasinghe, S.: Exploiting coarse-grained task, data, and pipeline parallelism in stream programs. In: International Conference on Architectural Support for Programming Languages and Operating Systems (October 2006)
2. Taylor, M.B., et al.: Evaluation of the Raw microprocessor: An exposed-wire-delay architecture for ILP and streams. In: Proceedings of International Symposium on Computer Architecture (June 2004)
3. Heithecker, S., do Carmo Lucas, A., Ernst, R.: A high-end real-time digital film processing reconfigurable platform. EURASIP Journal on Embedded Systems 2007, 15 (2007) doi:10.1155/2007/85318
4. Kahn, G.: The semantics of a simple language for parallel programming. In: Proceedings of the IFIP Congress, International Federation for Information Processing, pp. 471–475. North-Holland, Amsterdam (1974)
5. Kahn, G., MacQueen, D.B.: Coroutines and networks of parallel processes. In: Proceedings of the IFIP Congress, pp. 993–998. North-Holland, Amsterdam (1977)
6. Stefanov, T., Zissulescu, C., Turjan, A., Kienhuis, B., Deprettere, E.: System design using kahn process networks: The compaan/laura approach. In: Proceedings of the Design Automation and Test in Europe (DATE) IEEE Computer Society, Los Alamitos (2004)
7. DeHon, A., et al.: Stream computations organized for reconfigurable execution. Journal of Microprocessors and Microsystems 30(6), 334–354 (2006)
8. Hwang, J., Milne, B., Shirazi, N., Stroomer, J.D.: System level tools for DSP in FPGAs. In: Brebner, G., Woods, R. (eds.) FPL 2001. LNCS, vol. 2147, pp. 534–543. Springer, Heidelberg (2001)
9. Eker, J., Janneck, J.: CAL language report: Specification of the CAL actor language. Technical Memorandum UCB/ERL 03/48, Electronics Research Lab, Department of Electrical Engineering and Computer Sciences, University of California Berkeley, CA 94720, USA (December 2003)
10. Bhattacharya, B., Bhattacharyya, S.S.: Parameterized dataflow modeling for DSP systems. IEEE Transactions on Signal Processing 49(10), 2408–2421 (2001)
11. Neuendorffer, S., Lee, E.A.: Hierarchical reconfiguration of dataflow models. In: Proceedings of the Conference on Methods and Models for Codesign (MEMOCODE) (June 2004)
12. Snider, G.: Performance-constrained pipelining of software loops onto reconfigurable hardware. In: Proceedings of the Symposium on Field-programmable Gate Arrays (FPGA), pp. 177–186 (2002)
13. Kathail, V., Aditya, S., Schreiber, R., Rau, B.R.B., Cronquist, D., Sivaraman, M.: PICO (Program In, Chip Out): Automatically Designing Custom Computers. IEEE Computer 35(9), 39–47 (2002)
14. Haubelt, C., Falk, J., Keinert, J., Schlichter, T., Streubühr, M., Deyhle, A., Hadert, A., Teich, J.: A SystemC-based Design Methodology for Digital Signal Processing Systems. EURASIP Journal on Embedded Systems, Special Issue on Embedded Digital Signal Processing Systems 2007, 22 (2007) doi:10.1155/2007/47580
15. de Kock, E., Essink, G., Smits, W., van der Wolf, P., Brunel, J., Kruijtzer, W., Lieverse, P., Vissers, K.: YAPI: Application modeling for signal processing systems. In: Proceedings of the Design Automation Conference (DAC), pp. 402–405 (June 2000)
16. Neuendorffer, S., Epifanio, C.: Generalizing partial reconfiguration designs. In: Proceedings of the Software Defined Radio Technical Conference (SDRForum) (November 2007)

Heterogeneous Design in Functional DIF

William Plishker, Nimish Sane, Mary Kiemb, and Shuvra S. Bhattacharyya

Department of Electrical and Computer Engineering, and Institute for Advanced
Computer Studies,
University of Maryland at College Park, USA
{plishker,nsane,kiemb,ssb}@umd.edu
http://www.ece.umd.edu/DSPCAD

Abstract. Dataflow formalisms have provided designers of digital signal processing systems with analysis and optimizations for many years.
As system complexity increases, designers are relying on more types of
dataflow models to describe applications while retaining these implementation benefits. The semantic range of DSP-oriented dataflow models has
expanded to cover heterogeneous models and dynamic applications, but
efficient design, simulation, and scheduling of such applications has not.
To facilitate implementing heterogeneous applications, we utilize a new
dataflow model of computation and show how actors designed in other
dataflow models are directly supported by this framework, allowing system designers to immediately compose and simulate actors from different
models. Using an example, we show how this approach can be applied
to quickly describe and functionally simulate a heterogeneous dataflow-
based application such that a designer may analyze and tune trade-offs
among different models and schedules for simulation time, memory consumption, and schedule size.

Keywords: Dataflow, Heterogeneous, Signal Processing.

1 Introduction

For a number of years, dataflow models have proven invaluable for application
areas such as digital signal processing. Their graph-based formalisms allow designers to describe applications in a natural yet semantically rigorous way. Such
a semantic foundation has permitted the development of a variety of analysis
tools, including determining buffer bounds and efficient scheduling [1]. As a result, dataflow languages are increasingly popular. Their diversity, portability,
and intuitive appeal have extended them to many application areas with a variety of targets (e.g., [2][3]).

As system complexity and the diversity of components in digital signal
processing platforms increases, designers are expressing more types of behavior in
dataflow languages to retain these implementation benefits. While the semantic
range of dataflow has expanded to cover quasi-static and dynamic interactions,
efficient functional simulation and the ability to experiment with more flexible

M. Berekovic, N. Dimopoulos, and S. Wong (Eds.): SAMOS 2008, LNCS 5114, pp. 157–166, 2008.
© Springer-Verlag Berlin Heidelberg 2008

scheduling techniques has not. Complexity in scheduling and modeling has impeded efforts of a functional simulation that matches the final implementation. Instead, designers are often forced to go all the way to implementation to verify that dynamic behavior and complex interaction with various domains are correct. Correcting functional behavior in the application creates a developmental bottleneck, slowing the time to implementation on a heterogeneous platform.

To understand complex interactions properly, designers should be able to describe their applications in a single environment. In the context of dataflow programming, this involves describing not only the top level connectivity and hierarchy of the application graph, but also the functionality of the graph actors (the functional modules that correspond to non-hierarchical graph vertices), preferably in a natural way that integrates with the semantics of the dataflow model they are embedded in. Once the application is captured, designers need to be able to evaluate static schedules (for high performance) alongside dynamic behavior without loosing semantic ground. With such a feature set, designers should arrive at heterogeneous implementations faster.

Leveraging our existing dataflow interchange format (DIF) package [4], we implement an extension to DIF based on a form of dataflow, called core function dataflow (CFDF), that facilitates the simulation of heterogeneous applications. This extension to DIF, called *functional DIF*, allows designers to verify the functionality of their application immediately. From this working application, designers may focus on efficient schedules and buffer sizing, and thus are able to arrive at quality implementations of heterogeneous systems quickly.

2   Background

2.1   Dataflow Modeling

Modeling DSP applications through coarse-grain dataflow graphs is widespread in the DSP design community, and a variety of dataflow models has been developed for dataflow-based design. A growing set of DSP design tools support such dataflow semantics [5][6][7]. Ideally, designers are able to find a match between their application and one of the well studied models, including cyclo-static dataflow (CSDF) [8], synchronous dataflow (SDF) [9], single-rate dataflow, homogeneous synchronous dataflow (HSDF), or a more complicated model such as boolean dataflow (BDF) [10].

Common to each of these modeling paradigms is the representation of computational behavior as a dataflow graph. A dataflow graph G is an ordered pair (V, E) , where V is a set of vertices (or nodes), and E is a set of directed edges. A directed edge $e = (v_1, v_2) \in E$ is an ordered pair of a source vertex $v_1 \in V$ and a sink vertex $v_2 \in V$. A *source function*, $src : E \rightarrow V$, maps edges to their source vertex, and a *sink function*, $snk : E \rightarrow V$ gives the sink vertex for an edge. Given a directed graph G and a vertex $v \in V$, the set of incoming edges of v is denoted as $in(v) = \{e \in E | snk(e) = v\}$, and similarly, the set of outgoing edges of v is denoted as $out(v) = \{e \in E | src(e) = v\}$.

2.2   Dataflow Interchange Format

To describe the dataflow applications for this wide range of dataflow models, application developers can use the dataflow interchange format (DIF) [4], a standard language founded in dataflow semantics and tailored for DSP system design. It provides an integrated set of syntactic and semantic features that can fully capture essential modeling information of DSP applications without over-specification. From a dataflow point of view, DIF is designed to describe mixed-grain graph topologies and hierarchies as well as to specify dataflow-related and actor-specific information. The dataflow semantic specification is based on dataflow modeling theory and independent of any design tool.

To utilize the DIF language, the DIF package has been built. Along with the ability to transform DIF descriptions into a manipulable internal representation, the DIF package contains graph utilities, optimization engines, algorithms that may prove useful properties of the application, and a C synthesis framework [11]. These facilities make the DIF package an effective environment for modeling dataflow applications, providing interoperability with other design environments, and developing new tools.

Beyond these features, DIF is also suitable as a design environment for implementing dataflow-based application representations. Describing an application graph is done by listing nodes and edges, and then annotating dataflow specific information. The DIF package also has an infrastructure for porting applications from other dataflow tools to DIF. What is lacking in the existing DIF package is the ability to simulate functional designs in the design environment. Such a feature would streamline the design process, allowing applications to be verified without having to go to implementation.

3   Related Work

A number of development environments utilize dataflow models to aid in the capture and optimization of functional application descriptions. Ptolemy II encompasses a diversity of dataflow-oriented and other kinds of models of computation [12]. To describe an application subsystem, developers employ a director that controls the communication and execution schedule of an associated application graph. If an application developer is able to write the functionality of an actor in a prescribed manner, it will be polymorphic with respect to other models of computation. To describe an application with multiple models of computation, developers can insert a "composite actor" that represents a subgraph operating with a different model of computation (and therefore its own director). In such hierarchical representations, directors manage the actors only at their associated levels, and directors of composite actors only invoke their actors when higher level directors execute the composite actors. This paradigm works well for developers who know a priori the modeling techniques with which they plan to represent their applications.

Other techniques employ SystemC to capture actors as composed of input ports, output ports, functionality, and an execution FSM, which determines the communication behavior of the actor [13]. Other languages specifically targeting actor descriptions such as CAL [14]. For complete functionality in Simulink [7], actors are described in the form of "S-functions." By describing them in a specific format, actors can be used in continuous, discrete-time, and hybrid systems. LABVIEW [6] even gives designers a way of programmatically describing graphical blocks for dataflow systems.

Semantically, perhaps the most related work is the Stream Based Function (SBF) model of computation [15]. In SBF, an actor is represented by a set of functions, a controller, state, and transition function. Each function is sequentially enabled by the controller, and uses on each invocation a blocking read for each input to consume a single token. Once a function is done executing, the transition function defines the next function in the set to be enabled.

Functional DIF differs from these related efforts in dataflow-based design in its integrated emphasis on minimally-restricted specification of actor functionality, and support for efficient prototyping of static, quasi-static, and dynamic scheduling techniques. Each may critical to prototyping overall dataflow graph functionality. Compared to models such as SBF, functional DIF allows a designer to describe actor functionality in an arbitrary set of fixed modes, instead of parceling out actor behavior as side-effect free functions, a controller, and a transition function. Functional DIF is also more general than SBF as it permits multi-token reads and can enable actors based on application state. As designers experiment with different dataflow representations with different levels of actor dynamics, they need corresponding capabilities to experiment with compatible scheduling techniques. This is a key motivation for the integrated actor- and scheduler-level prototyping considerations in functional DIF.

4   Semantic Foundation

For a formalism able to support this level of heterogeneity, we derive a special case of enable-invoke dataflow [16] that we refer to as core functional dataflow (CFDF), which ensures that the application is deterministic. In this formalism, each actor has a set of *modes* in which it can execute. Each mode, when executed, consumes and produces a fixed number of tokens. This set of modes can depend upon the type of dataflow model being employed or it may be user-defined. Given an actor $a \in V$ in a dataflow graph, the *enabling function* for a is defined as:

$$\varepsilon_a : (T_a \times M_a) \to B, \tag{1}$$

where $T_a = \aleph^{|in(a)|}$ is a tuple of the number of tokens on each of the input edges to actor a (here, $|in(a)|$ is the number of input edges to actor a); M_a is the set of modes associated with actor a; and $B = \{true, false\}$ is $true$ when an actor $a \in V$ has an appropriate number of tokens for mode $m \in M_a$ available on each input edge, and $false$ otherwise. An actor can be executed in a given mode at a given point in time if and only if the enabling function is true-valued.

The *invoking function* for an actor a is defined as:

$$\kappa_a : (I_a \times M_a) \to (O_a \times M_a), \tag{2}$$

where $I_a = X_1 \times X_2 \times \ldots \times X_{|in(a)|}$ is the set of all possible inputs to a, where X_i is the set of possible tokens on the edge on input port i of actor a. After a executes, it produces outputs $O_a = Y_1 \times Y_2 \times \ldots \times Y_{|out(a)|}$, where Y_i is the set of possible tokens on the edge connected to port i of actor a, where $|out(a)|$ is the number of output ports. Invoking an actor can in general change the mode of execution of the actor, so the invoking function also produces the next mode that is valid. This mode can then be subsequently checked by the enabling function, and if true for any mode, the actor may be invoked in that mode. If no mode is returned (i.e., an empty mode set is returned), the actor is forever disabled.

5   Translation to CFDF

Many common dataflow models may be directly translated to CFDF in an efficient and intuitive manner. In this section we show such constructions, demonstrating the expressibility of CFDF and how the burden of design is eased when starting from an existing dataflow model.

5.1   Static Dataflow

SDF, CSDF, and other static dataflow-actor behaviors can be translated into finite sequences of CFDF modes for equivalent operation. Consider, for example, CSDF, in which the production and consumption behavior of each actor a is divided into a finite sequence of periodic phases $P = (1, 2, ..., n_a)$. Each phase has a particular production and consumption behavior. The pattern of production and consumption across phases can captured by a function ϕ_a whose domain is P_a. Given a phase $i \in P_a$, $\phi_a(i) = (G_i, H_i)$, where G_i and H_i are vectors indexed by the input and output ports of a, respectively, that give the numbers of tokens produced and consumed on these edges for each port during the ith phase in the execution of actor a.

   To construct a CFDF actor from such a model, a mode is created for each phase, and we denote the set of all modes created in this way by M_a. Given a mode $m \in M_a$ corresponding to phase $p \in P_a$, the enable method for this mode checks the input edges of the actor for sufficient numbers of tokens based on what the phase requires in terms of the associated CSDF semantics. Thus, for each input port z of a, mode m checks for the availability of at least $G_p(z)$ tokens on that port, where $\phi(p) = (G_p, H_p)$. For the complementary invoke method, the consumption of input ports is fixed to G_p, the production of output ports is fixed to H_p. The next mode returned by the invoke method must be the mode corresponding to the next phase in the CSDF phase sequence. Since any SDF actor can be viewed as a single-phase CSDF actor, the CFDF construction process for SDF is a specialization of the CSDF-to-CFDF construction process described above in which there is only one mode created.

5.2 Boolean Dataflow

Boolean dataflow (BDF) adds dynamic behavior to dataflow. The two fundamental elements of BDF are Switch and Select. Switch routes a token from its
input to one of two outputs based on the Boolean value of a token on its control
input. The concept of a control input is also utilized for Select, in which the
value of the control token determines which input port will have a token read
and forwarded to its one output.

To construct a CFDF actor that implements BDF semantics, we create a
mode that is dedicated to reading that input value, which we call the control
mode. The result of this examination sends the actor into either a true mode
or a false mode that corresponds to that control port. In the case of Switch,
this implies three modes with behavior described in Table 1. Note that a single
invocation of a Switch in BDF corresponds to two modes being invoked in the
CFDF framework. For a strict construction of BDF, only the Switch and Select
actors are needed for implementation, but CFDF does permit more flexibility,
allowing designers to specify arbitrary behavior of true and false modes as long
as each mode has a fixed production and consumption behavior.

Table 1. The behavior of the switch actor modes in terms of tokens produced and
consumed

mode	consumes		produces	
	Control	Data	True	False
Control	1	0	0	0
True	0	1	1	0
False	0	1	0	1

6   Scheduling for a Heterogeneous Application

We use generalized schedule trees (GSTs) [17] to represent schedules generated
by schedulers in functional DIF. The GST representation is a generalization of
the (binary) schedule tree representation. The GST representation can be used
to represent dataflow graph schedules irrespective of the underlying dataflow
model or scheduling strategy being used. GSTs are ordered trees with leaf nodes
representing the actors of an associated dataflow graph. An internal node of the
GST represents the loop count of a schedule loop (an iteration construct to be
applied when executing the schedule) that is rooted at that internal node. The
GST representation allows us to exploit topological information and algorithms
for ordered trees in order to access and manipulate schedule elements. To functionally simulate an application, we need only to be able to generate a schedule
for the application, and then traverse the associated GST to iteratively enable
(and then execute, if appropriate) actors that correspond to the schedule tree
leaf nodes. Note that if actors are not enabled, the GST traversal simply skips
their invocation. Subsequent schedule rounds (and thus subsequent traversals of

the schedule tree) will generally revisit actors that were unable to execute in the current round.

We can always construct a *canonical schedule* for an application graph. This is the most trivial schedule that can be constructed from the application graph. The canonical schedule is a single appearance schedule (a schedule in which actors of the application graph appear once) which includes all actors in some order. In terms of the GST representation, a canonical schedule has a root node specifying the loop count of 1 with its child nodes forming leaves of the schedule tree. Each leaf node points to a unique actor in the application graph. The ordering of leaf nodes determines the order in which actors of the application graph are traversed. When the simulator traverses GST, each actor in the graph is fired, if it is enabled.

7 Design Example - Polynomial Evaluation

Polynomial evaluation is a commonly used primitive in various domains of signal processing, such as wireless communications and cryptography. Polynomial functions may change whenever senders transmit data to receivers. The kernel is the evaluation of a polynomial $P_i(x) = \sum_{k=0}^{n_i} c_k \times x^k$, where $c_1, c_2, \ldots, c_n$ are coefficients, x is the polynomial argument, and n_i is the degree of the polynomial. Since the coefficients may change at runtime, a programmable polynomial evaluation accelerator (PEA) is useful for accelerating the computation of multiple P_i's. To this end, we create a CSDF actor with two phases: reading the polynomial coefficients and then processing a block of x's to be evaluated.

To illustrate the problem of heterogeneous complexity, we suppose that a DSP application designer might use two PEA actors customized for different length polynomials. The overall PEA system is shown in Figure 1. Two PEA actors are in the same application and made them selectable by bracketing them with a Switch and a Select block. To manage the two PEA actors properly, this design requires control to select the *PEA1* or *PEA2* branch. In this system, the CSDF PEA actors consume a different number of polynomial coefficient tokens, so the control tokens driving the switch and select on the datapath must be able to create batches of 19 and 22 tokens, respectively for each path. If the designer is restricted to only Switch and Select for BDF functionality, the balloon with *CONTROLLER* shows how this can be done.

This design can certainly be captured with model oriented approach, pulling the proper actors into super-nodes with different models. But like many designs, this application has a natural functional hierarchy in it with the refinement of *CONTROLLER* and with *PEA1* and *PEA2*. We believe that competing design concerns of functional and model hierarchy will ultimately be distracting for a designer. With this work, we focus designers on efficient application representation and not model related issues.

Immediate simulation of the dual PEA application is possible to verify correctness by using the canonical schedule. We simulated the application with a random control source and a stream of integer data. A nontrivial schedule tree

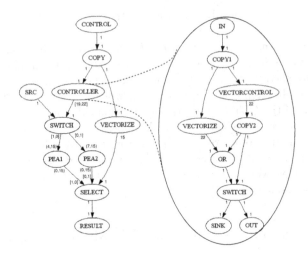

Fig. 1. A pictorial representation of the PEA application

can significantly improve upon the canonical performance. Given that the probability of a given PEA branch being selected is uniform, we can derive a single appearance schedule shown in Figure 2, where each leaf node is annotated with an actor and each interior node is annotated with a loop count. Leaf nodes are double ovals to indicate they are guarded by the enabling function. Figure 3 shows a manually designed multiple appearance schedule (a schedule in which actors may appear more than once) that attempts to process polynomial coefficients first, before queuing up data to be evaluated, to reduce buffering.

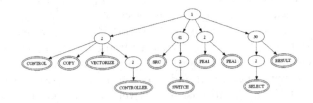

Fig. 2. Single appearance schedule for the dual PEA system

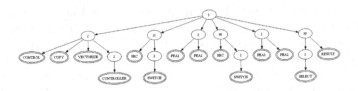

Fig. 3. Multiple appearance schedule for the dual PEA system

Table 2. Simulation times and max buffer sizes of the dual PEA design

Application style	Schedule	Simulation Time (s)	Max observed buffer size (tokens)
BDF Strict	Canonical	6.88	2,327,733
BDF Strict	Single appearance	1.72	1,729
BDF Strict	Multiple appearance	1.59	1,722
CFDF	Canonical	3.57	1,018,047
CFDF	Single appearance	0.95	1,791
CFDF	Multiple appearance	0.99	1,800

Results for these different styles of implementation with different schedules are summarized by Table 2. We simulated 10,000 evaluations running on a 1.7GHz Pentium with 1GB of physical memory. We measured the time it took to complete enough iterations to complete all of the evaluations and maximum total queue size. The manually designed schedules performed notably better than the canonical schedule. Such insight can be invaluable when considering the final implementation of the controller logic.

8   Conclusions and Future Work

In this work, we have presented a new dataflow approach to enable the description of heterogeneous applications that utilize multiple forms of dataflow. This is based on a new dataflow formalism, a construction scheme to translate from existing dataflow models to it, and a simulation framework that allows designers to model and verify interactions between those models. With this approach integrated into DIF package, we demonstrated it on the heterogeneous design of a dual polynomial evaluation accelerator. Such an approach allowed us to functionally simulate the design immediately and then to focus on experimenting on schedules and dataflow styles to improve performance.

We plan to build on this work in a number of ways. First, support for parameterized dataflow modeling will permit more natural description of certain kinds of dynamic behavior, without departing from strong dataflow formalisms. We are also interested in more general scheduling techniques that can automatically generate efficient schedules for such heterogeneous application. We believe the profiling results supplied by functional DIF could also provide valuable information for improving complex schedules automatically.

Acknowledgments

This research was sponsored in part by the U.S. National Science Foundation (Grant number 0720596), and the US Army Research Office (Contract number TCN07108, administered through Battelle-Scientific Services Program).

References

1. Lee, E.A., Messerschmitt, D.G.: Static scheduling of synchronous data flow programs for digital signal processing. IEEE Trans. Comput. 36(1), 24–35 (1987)
2. Shen, C., Plishker, W., Bhattacharyya, S.S., Goldsman, N.: An energy-driven design methodology for distributing DSP applications across wireless sensor networks. In: Proceedings of the IEEE Real-Time Systems Symposium, Tucson, Arizona, pp. 214–223 (December 2007)
3. Hemaraj, Y., Sen, M., Shekhar, R., Bhattacharyya, S.S.: Model-based mapping of image registration applications onto configurable hardware. In: Proceedings of the IEEE Asilomar Conference on Signals, Systems, and Computers, Pacific Grove, California, pp. 1453–1457 (October 2006) (invited paper)
4. Hsu, C., Corretjer, I., Ko., M., Plishker, W., Bhattacharyya, S.S.: Dataflow interchange format: Language reference for DIF language version 1.0, user's guide for DIF package version 1.0. Technical Report UMIACS-TR-2007-32, Institute for Advanced Computer Studies, University of Maryland at College Park (June 2007)
5. Flatscher, R.G.: Metamodeling in EIA/CDIF—meta-metamodel and metamodels. ACM Trans. Model. Comput. Simul. 12(4), 322–342 (2002)
6. Johnson, G.: LabVIEW Graphical Programming: Practical Applications in Instrumentation and Control. McGraw-Hill School Education Group (1997)
7. The MathWorks Inc.: Using Simulink. Version 3 edn. (January 1999)
8. Bilsen, G., Engels, M., Lauwereins, R., Peperstraete, J.A.: Cyclo-static data flow. In: Proceedings of ICASSP, pp. 3255–3258 (May 1995)
9. Lee, E.A., Messerschmitt, D.G.: Synchronous dataflow. Proceedings of the IEEE 75(9), 1235–1245 (1987)
10. Buck, J.T.: Scheduling dynamic dataflow graphs with bounded memory using the token flow model. PhD thesis, Chair-Edward A. Lee (1993)
11. Hsu, C., Ko, M., Bhattacharyya, S.S.: Software synthesis from the dataflow interchange format. In: Proceedings of the International Workshop on Software and Compilers for Embedded Systems, Dallas, Texas, pp. 37–49 (September 2005)
12. Eker, J., Janneck, J., Lee, E.A., Liu, J., Liu, X., Ludvig, J., Neuendorffer, S., Sachs, S.R., Xiong, Y.: Taming heterogeneity - the Ptolemy approach. Proceedings of the IEEE. Special Issue on Modeling and Design of Embedded Software 91(1), 127–144 (2003)
13. Haubelt, C., Falk, J., Keinert, J., Schlichter, T., Streubühr, M., Deyhle, A., Hadert, A., Teich, J.: A systemc-based design methodology for digital signal processing systems. EURASIP J. Embedded Syst. 2007(1), 15 (2007)
14. Eker, J., Janneck, J.: Caltrop—language report (draft). Technical memorandum, Electronics Research Lab, Department of Electrical Engineering and Computer Sciences, University of California at Berkeley, CA (2002)
15. Kienhuis, B., Deprettere, E.F.: Modeling stream-based applications using the sbf model of computation. J. VLSI Signal Process. Syst. 34(3), 291–300 (2003)
16. Plishker, W., Sane, N., Kiemb, M., Anand, K., Bhattacharyya, S.S.: Functional dif for rapid prototyping. In: Proceedings of International Symposium on Rapid System Prototyping, Monterey, California, USA (June 2008)
17. Ko, M., Zissulescu, C., Puthenpurayil, S., Bhattacharyya, S.S., Kienhuis, B., Deprettere, E.: Parameterized looped schedules for compact representation of execution sequences. In: Proceedings of the International Conference on Application Specific Systems, Architectures, and Processors, Steamboat Springs, Colorado, pp. 223–230 (September 2006)

Tool Integration and Interoperability Challenges of a System-Level Design Flow: A Case Study

Andy D. Pimentel[1], Todor Stefanov[2], Hristo Nikolov[2], Mark Thompson[1], Simon Polstra[1], and E.F. Deprettere[2]

[1] Computer Systems Architecture group
Informatics Institute, University of Amsterdam, The Netherlands
{andy,thompson,spolstra}@science.uva.nl
[2] Leiden Embedded Research Center, Leiden University, The Netherlands
{stefanov,nikolov,edd}@liacs.nl

Abstract. Daedalus is a system-level design flow for the design of multiprocessor system-on-chip (MP-SoC) based embedded multimedia systems. It offers a fully integrated tool-flow in which design exploration, system-level synthesis, application mapping, and system prototyping of MP-SoC architectures are highly automated. In this paper, we describe Daedalus from a software perspective, explaining its supporting software infrastructure and the way the various tools interoperate. Moreover, we discuss the lack of support for achieving tool interoperability that we have encountered during the development of Daedalus, and present several ideas of future research directions to address this issue. More specifically, we argue that a so-called Common Design Flow Infrastructure (CDFI) for system-level design flows is needed to improve and stimulate research and development in the area of system-level design methodology.

1 Introduction

The concept of system-level design of embedded systems, which raises the abstraction level of the design process to cope with design complexity, has been around for more than a decade now and has shown a lot of potential. Despite of this, system-level design still involves a substantial number of challenging design tasks. This is especially true for the design of MultiProcessor-SoC (MP-SoC) architectures, which become increasingly popular target platforms for modern embedded systems. For example, applications need to be decomposed into parallel specifications so that they can be mapped onto the multiple processing elements inside MP-SoC architectures [1]. Subsequently, applications need to be partitioned into HW and SW parts since MP-SoC architectures often are heterogeneous in nature. To this end, MP-SoC platform architectures need to be modeled and simulated to study system behavior and to evaluate a variety of different design options. Once a good candidate architecture has been found, it needs to be synthesized, which involves the synthesis of its architectural components as well as the mapping of applications onto the architecture. To accomplish all of these tasks, a range of different tools and tool-flows is often needed, potentially leaving designers with all kinds of interoperability problems. Moreover, there typically remains a large gap between the deployed system-level specifications (or models) and actual implementations of the system under study, known as the *implementation gap* [2]. Currently, there exist no mature

M. Berekovic, N. Dimopoulos, and S. Wong (Eds.): SAMOS 2008, LNCS 5114, pp. 167–176, 2008.
© Springer-Verlag Berlin Heidelberg 2008

methodologies, techniques, and tools to effectively and efficiently convert system-level system specifications to RTL specifications.

Recently, we presented our Daedalus system-level design framework which addresses the above design challenges [3,4,5]. Daedalus' main objective is to bridge the aforementioned implementation gap for the design of multimedia MP-SoCs. It does so by providing an integrated and highly-automated environment for system-level architectural exploration, system-level synthesis, programming and prototyping. The Daedalus design flow, starting from sequential application to an implemented MP-SoC system on an FPGA with a parallelized application mapped onto it, can be traversed in only a matter of hours. Evidently, this offers great potentials for quickly experimenting with different MP-SoCs and exploring design options during the early stages of design.

In this paper, we describe Daedalus from a software perspective, providing insight of how the different tools in the design flow interoperate and describing the supporting tool infrastructure that improves the actual deployment of the design flow. Moreover, we discuss the lessons that we have learned from the development of Daedalus, mostly recognizing the lack of support for achieving tool interoperability, and present several ideas of future research directions to address this issue. More specifically, we argue that a so-called Common Design Flow Infrastructure (CDFI) for system-level design flows is needed, which surpasses ongoing efforts in this direction, in order to improve and stimulate research and development in the area of system-level design methodology.

The next section provides a birds-eye, conceptual overview of the Daedalus design flow. Section 3 describes the software infrastructure of Daedalus, after which Section 4 discusses some of the lessons we have learned from Daedalus' development. In Section 5, we present several initial ideas about a Common Design Flow Infrastructure which aims at significantly improving the process of developing system-level design flows. Section 6 describes related work, and Section 7 concludes the paper.

2   The Daedalus Design Flow

In Figure 1, the conceptual design flow of the Daedalus framework is depicted. As mentioned before, Daedalus provides a single environment for rapid system-level architectural exploration, high-level synthesis, programming and prototyping of multimedia MP-SoC architectures. Here, a key assumption is that the MP-SoCs are constructed from a library of pre-determined and pre-verified IP components. These components include a variety of programmable and dedicated processors, memories and interconnects, thereby allowing the implementation of a wide range of MP-SoC platforms.

Starting from a sequential application specification in C, the KPNgen tool [6] allows for automatically converting the sequential application into a parallel Kahn Process Network (KPN) [7] specification. Here, the sequential input specifications are restricted to so-called static affine nested loop programs, which is an important class of programs in, e.g., the scientific and multimedia application domains. By means of automated source-level transformations [8], KPNgen is also capable of producing different input-output equivalent KPNs, in which for example the degree of parallelism can be varied. Such transformations enable application-level design space exploration.

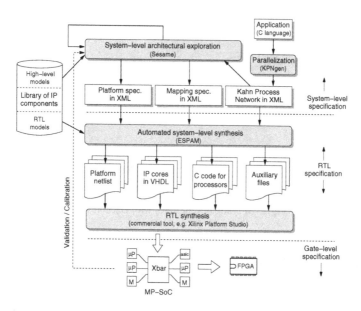

Fig. 1. The Daedalus design flow

The generated or handcrafted KPNs (the latter in the case that, e.g., the input specification did not entirely meet the requirements of the KPNgen tool) can subsequently be used by our Sesame modeling and simulation environment [9,10] to perform system-level architectural design space exploration. To this end, Sesame uses (high-level) architecture model components from the IP component library. Sesame allows for quickly evaluating the performance of different application to architecture mappings, HW/SW partitionings, and target platform architectures. Such exploration should result in a number of promising candidate system designs, of which their specifications (system-level platform description, application-architecture mapping description, and application description) act as input to the ESPAM tool [11,12]. This tool uses these system-level input specifications, together with RTL versions of the components from the IP library, to automatically generate synthesizable VHDL that implements the candidate MP-SoC platform architecture. In addition, it also generates the C code for those application processes that are mapped onto programmable cores. Using commercial synthesis tools and compilers, this implementation can be readily mapped onto an FPGA for prototyping. Such prototyping also allows for calibrating and validating Sesame's system-level models, and as a consequence, improving the trustworthiness of these models.

3   Daedalus' Software Infrastructure

Daedalus does not only consist of the three core tools KPNgen, Sesame and ESPAM, but also features several supporting tools to improve the user-friendliness, and therefore also the deployability, of the framework. This section provides an overview of Daedalus' software infrastructure.

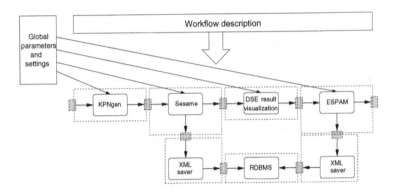

Fig. 2. Building design flows with Daedalus

Integrated RDBMS. In Daedalus, most design information (e.g., structural descriptions of the application, architecture, and the mapping of the former onto the latter) as well as experimental results are described using XML-based descriptions. Daedalus therefore contains the Oracle Berkeley DB XML relational database management system (RDBMS) to store all information (models, parameters and results) related to designs and experiments. Daedalus also features a graphical user interface (GUI) to this RDBMS, which provides the designer with a powerful tool to e.g. explore and visualize the large amounts of data generated by Daedalus' design space exploration. Moreover, it guarantees the reproducibility of experiments at all times.

Workflow control. The vision behind the Daedalus software infrastructure is that it should be open for integration of new tools as well as that it should allow for customization of the design flow. Therefore, the design flow (or tool flow) in Daedalus is composable and constructed from 'design flow blocks'. These design flow blocks, which are illustrated as the dashed boxes in Figure 2, are the tools that take part in the design flow together with their input- and output descriptions. The latter descriptions, illustrated by the gray boxes in Figure 2, provide information about what input/output data a tool consumes/produces and from/to where it reads/writes this data. This allows us to describe a design flow as a simple composition of the design flow blocks, specified in the *workflow description*. For example, Figure 2 shows a design flow which includes a visualization block to visualize Sesame's DSE results and which stores both the DSE and ESPAM's prototyping results in the RDBMS (using the so-called 'XML saver' tool). Evidently, this composability of the design flow allows for easily adding new design steps to a design flow, as well as to customize design flows for specific design domains.

Control and monitoring of MP-SoC prototypes on FPGAs. We have also developed control and monitoring software utilities to facilitate the process of setting up and executing experiments on the FPGA-based prototypes of MP-SoCs generated by Daedalus. Such utilities are necessary and very useful for: (i) conducting an effective and efficient design space exploration at implementation level of abstraction with 100% accuracy on a narrow design space defined by Sesame; (ii) measuring real performance and cost numbers used for calibration of the Daedalus' high-level architecture models [13]; (iii) preparing real HW/SW demonstrators. The control and monitoring utilities include a configuration manager, an execution control panel, and an on-line monitoring console, all supported by a GUI which allows users, unfamiliar with the FPGA prototyping board, to perform experiments with the MP-SoCs. The configuration manager is used to setup the prototyping FPGA board for a given experiment. The execution control panel allows to define and execute a sequence of instructions (e.g. initialize, start, stop, etc.) that control the interaction of the MP-SoC prototype with the surrounding environment (e.g. the user). The on-line monitoring console displays and stores the data streams that go in and out of the MP-SoC, the content of the status registers of the MP-SoC prototype, and the content of timers and counters that measure the real performance of the prototype.

The Open Source philosophy of Daedalus. The entire Daedalus framework has been developed as high-quality software distributed under Open Source licenses such as GPL or CPL (see `http://daedalus.liacs.nl/Site/Download.html`). This provides many advantages and opportunities (e.g., more easy take-up of the technology since no expensive licenses are required, possible world-wide contributions to the technology, etc.) but it also poses challenges related to software maintainability and tool interoperability. For example, regarding the maintainability, we have developed a configuration and installation utility for the whole Daedalus software framework. At a glance, this task seems to be trivial but our experience shows that it is not, especially when our goal is a fully automated installation process on all major Linux OS distributions. Daedalus consists of many tools that depend on other tools and libraries that have to be installed because they are not available on all or some of the Linux distributions. Identifying, documenting, and maintaining all these tool and library dependencies is a continuous process.

4 Lessons Learned: The Tool Interoperability Problem

A central problem for any design flow addressing the development of embedded systems is that it typically consists of a number of tools that need to inter-operate with each other for the design flow to be efficient and effective. From the experience with Daedalus, we found that tool interoperability is a major problem, which consumes an unnecessary amount of (software engineering) effort. In general, the lack of support for achieving interoperability between tools is becoming one of the big showstoppers for the much-needed productivity improvement in the embedded systems design area, which may seriously endanger the ability to cope with the rapidly growing design complexity. This lack of good tool-infrastructure is a problem that both concerns the embedded systems industry as well as academia. Many research groups develop algorithms and solutions for specific design problems and issues that are not (yet) addressed by commercial tool providers. But since commercial tool providers often refrain from publishing interfaces to their tools, research groups are typically left with the only option of building tool support for the whole design flow themselves, including very basic elements such as editors, graphical UI's, etc. Daedalus was no exception here. Also since there is no common well-defined notion of tool infrastructure, research groups find it often difficult to cooperate on tool research and development. The flow of ideas from academia to industry is also made more difficult, because it is difficult to deploy new algorithmic innovations into industrial design flows since the tools are not interoperable in any reasonable way.

Moreover, there do not exist good standard case studies and benchmarks for system-level design. We believe that this is due to the fact that (too) much effort is spent on the tool-building part of system-level design research projects instead. This tool development typically involves a significant (software) engineering effort, at the cost of the scientific content of such projects. With a tool infrastructure that fosters the re-use of design tools, this effort could be redirected to the development of good benchmarks and case studies. This would invigorate design flow research as it enables the comparison of research results. Currently, such a comparison of the various achievements in system-level research is not or hardly possible. Finally, we believe that good benchmarks and case studies will provide profit to the flow of ideas from academia to industry, because the design flow improvements can be demonstrated on industrially relevant examples, thus making them much more realistic.

5   Towards a Common Design Flow Infrastructure

To address the tool interoperability problem in system-level design flows, we argue that it is highly desirable to have a tool infrastructure that supports system-level design flows. This infrastructure, which should go beyond efforts such as OCP-IP [14] and SPIRIT's IP-XACT [15], would be a kind of meta-tool for developing system-level design flows, having design flow steps as "plug-ins". This requires the definition of standardized tool, model and data descriptions and file formats to allow the interchange of information between the framework and external tools (i.e., plug-ins). Moreover, the framework should also allow for explicitly defining design flows. This will make it possible to build pre-packaged standardized or customized design flows.

This Common Design Flow Infrastructure (CDFI), that should facilitate the construction and/or adaptation of complex system-level design flows, is conceptually shown in Figure 3. Central to the CDFI is a repository on which all participating tools operate and in which the key elements of system-level design flows (such as application specifications, application and architecture models in various models of computation and at various levels of abstraction, input/output data, simulation results, IP blocks, etc.) are stored in a structural manner. The tools that participate in the CDFI and operate on its repository could either directly belong to the implemented design flow, or have a more supporting role such as translators that, e.g., perform model refinement or translation between models specified in different models of computation.

For each tool that wishes to participate in the flow and thus operate on the CDFI repository, one needs to formally specify its preconditions and input requirements, its semantics, and its postconditions and output specification. To give a few examples, please consider Figure 3. Here, the input/output specification for a tool like KPNgen [6] could specify that it requires "sequential static affine nested loop programs" as input, and produces parallel specifications in the form of Kahn Process Networks (KPNs) [7]. Naturally, such specifications need to be formalized and should be based on a model

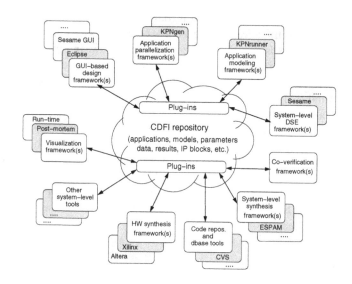

Fig. 3. The CDFI allows the interconnection of System-level Design tools

with clear denotational semantics. Subsequently, for a DSE tool like Sesame [9], it must be specified that it needs application models in the form of KPNs and generates a multitude of performance metrics for a range of architectural implementation instances. Finally, for a visualization tool it may be specified what performance metrics it needs in order to perform post-mortem or run-time visualization of these data. This also means that the output of tools as well as the input parameters must be structurally stored (i.e., described using meta-data) in the CDFI repository in order to allow other tools (such as visualizers) to relate these data, e.g., visualizing cycle-counts, component utilization, etc. for simulation runs with different input parameters. Moreover, we also need to formally relate the already existing models in the CDFI with the models used by any new tool. This specification will show if and how the new tool can be used in combination with other tools in a CDFI-based design flow.

To actually allow for interoperability between different plug-in tools, these tools must have a common understanding of the exact semantics of the CDFI repository elements (e.g., models, data, IP components) they use. This requires standardization with respect to the specification of these repository elements. For example, standardized model specifications (i.e. metamodels) should provide the means to formally relate models and to perform model translations (e.g., via a plug-in translator tool) when required. Essentially, we are looking for a type-system for the tools and their models, in which for example model translations can be seen as type casts. Clearly, developing methods for describing the semantic and input/output behavior of tools as well as for specifying the elements used by these tools (e.g., data, models, IP components) – all with the aim of tool interoperability in mind – is still a formidable research challenge. Evidently, for the actual implementation of the CDFI, existing software technology from e.g. the Model Driven Architecture (MDA) domain could be exploited.

So far, we have only described the CDFI from the perspective of individual tools. In addition, a coordination framework is needed that coordinates the control- and dataflow between the different tools that take part in the design flow. In other words, this co-ordination framework basically specifies a projection of the implemented design flow on top of the generic CDFI repository and associated tools. Because we explicitly separate the tools and tool specifications (semantic and input/output description) on one hand, and the coordination of the tools to form a specific design flow on the other hand, it should be fairly easy to construct new design flows by re-using tools, extend a design flow, and/or substitute certain tools in a design flow with other tools. Evidently, the development of such a coordination framework (accounting for the specification of control- and dataflow between the different tools in the flow in a generic and flexible manner) also requires substantial research, which could e.g. be inspired by the extensive research that has been performed on workflow frameworks in the domain of Grid Computing and eScience (e.g., [16]).

6   Related Work

Systematic and automated application-to-architecture mapping has been widely studied in the research community. The closest to our work is the Koski MP-SoC design flow [17]. Koski also provides a single infrastructure for modeling of applications, automatic architectural design space exploration, and automatic system-level synthesis, programming, and prototyping of selected MP-SoCs. But unlike Daedalus, Koski does not allow for parallelization of applications, nor design space exploration at application level. Koski requires applications to be specified by hand in UML. The Abhainn design framework [18] has similar objectives as Daedalus, but appears to lack automation for several design steps, such as automated parallelization of applications (applications are modeled using multidimensional arrayed synchronous dataflow specifications), automated design space exploration, and full-fledged MP-SoC synthesis. Other examples of related work can be found in [19,20,21,22]. However, these efforts are limited to processor-coprocesor architectures [19], only provide a limited degree of automation [20,21], or do not provide an automated step towards the register transfer level [22].

Companies such as Xilinx and Altera provide design tool chains attempting to generate efficient implementations starting from descriptions higher than (but still related to) the register transfer level of abstraction. The required input specifications are still so detailed that designing a single processor system is still error-prone and time consuming, let alone designing alternative multiprocessor systems. In contrast, Daedalus raises the design to an even higher level of abstraction allowing the exploration, design and programming of multiprocessor systems in a short amount of time.

With respect to our CDFI ideas, there are a number of related efforts. OCP-IP [14] is an industrial/academic initiative dedicated to proliferating a common standard for intellectual property (IP) core interfaces, or sockets, that facilitate "plug and play" System-on-Chip (SoC) design. Similarly, the SPIRIT consortium [15] aims at "Enabling Innovative IP Re-use and Design Automation". It has defined an XML schema (called IP-XACT) for meta-data that documents the characteristics of IP required for the automation of the configuration and integration of IP blocks as well as APIs to make this meta-data directly accessible to automation tools. Both the OCP-IP and SPIRIT initiatives focus on standardization with respect to IP blocks, while CDFI goes beyond that by targeting integration and standardization of not only IP blocks but also design tools and tool-flows that cover all aspects of the system design automation. The MoBIES initiative [23] studies model-driven approaches (or model-integrated approaches) to design flows. The goal is to develop new methods and tools that will increase the productivity of the designers. In a sense, the goal is the same as in the CDFI, but the means are different. The CDFI aims at increasing productivity by taking away the bottleneck caused by bad tool interoperability, whereas MoBIES tries to find new ways (i.e. methods) to build embedded systems. The CDFI approach is method neutral, it should increase the productivity of any method.

7   Conclusions

In this paper, we presented our Daedalus system-level design framework for multimedia MP-SoCs from a software perspective, describing how its tools interoperate and discussing the supporting tool infrastructure that improves the actual deployment of the design flow. We also discussed the lack of support for achieving tool interoperability that we have encountered during the development of Daedalus, and presented several initial ideas of future research directions to address this issue. More specifically, we argued that a so-called Common Design Flow Infrastructure (CDFI) for system-level design flows is needed, which surpasses ongoing efforts in this direction, in order to improve and stimulate research and development in the area of system-level design methodology. Such a CDFI would, among other things, heavily reduce the software engineering overheads in system-level design flow projects, enable the comparison of design methodologies/techniques between researchers, and enhance the knowledge transfer from research to industry.

Acknowledgements

We wish to acknowledge that the presented CDFI ideas were developed in cooperation with Timo D. Hämäläinen from Tampere University of Technology and Johan Lilius from Åbo Akademi University.

References

1. Martin, G.: Overview of the MPSoC Design Challenge. In: Proc. Design Automation Conference (DAC 2006), San Francisco, USA (2006)
2. Mihal, A., Keutzer, K.: Mapping concurrent applications onto architectural platforms. In: Networks on Chips, pp. 39–59. Kluwer Academic Publishers, Dordrecht (2003)
3. Thompson, M., Stefanov, T., Nikolov, H., Pimentel, A.D., Erbas, C., Polstra, S., Deprettere, E.F.: A framework for rapid system-level exploration, synthesis, and programming of multimedia MP-SoCs. In: Proc. of the Int. Conference on Hardware-Software Codesign and System Synthesis (CODES+ISSS 2007), pp. 9–14 (2007)

4. Nikolov, H., Thompson, M., Stefanov, T., Pimentel, A.D., Polstra, S., Bose, R., Zissulescu, C., Deprettere, E.F.: Daedalus: Toward composable multimedia MP-SoC design. In: Proc. of the Design Automation Conference (DAC 2008) (2008)
5. Daedalus system-level design, http://daedalus.liacs.nl/
6. Verdoolaege, S., Nikolov, H., Stefanov, T.: PN: a tool for improved derivation of process networks. EURASIP Journal on Embedded Systems (2007) doi:10.1155/2007/75947
7. Kahn, G.: The semantics of a simple language for parallel programming. In: Proc. of the IFIP Congress, vol. 74 (1974)
8. Stefanov, T., Kienhuis, B., Deprettere, E.F.: Algorithmic transformation techniques for efficient exploration of alternative application instances. In: Proc. of the Int. Symposium on Hardware/Software Codesign (CODES), pp. 7–12 (2002)
9. Pimentel, A.D., Erbas, C., Polstra, S.: A systematic approach to exploring embedded system architectures at multiple abstraction levels. IEEE Trans. on Computers 55, 99–112 (2006)
10. Erbas, C., Pimentel, A.D., Thompson, M., Polstra, S.: A framework for system-level modeling and simulation of embedded systems architectures. EURASIP Journal on Embedded Systems (2007) doi:10.1155/2007/82123
11. Nikolov, H., Stefanov, T., Deprettere, E.F.: Multi-processor system design with ESPAM. In: Proc. of the Int. Conf. on HW/SW Codesign and System Synthesis (CODES+ISSS 2006), pp. 211–216 (2006)
12. Nikolov, H., Stefanov, T., Deprettere, E.F.: Systematic and automated multi-processor system design, programming, and implementation. IEEE Transactions on Computer-Aided Design of Integrated Circuits and Systems (TCAD) 27, 542–555 (2008)
13. Pimentel, A.D., Thompson, M., Polstra, S., Erbas, C.: Calibration of abstract performance models for system-level design space exploration. Journal of Signal Processing Systems for Signal, Image, and Video Technology 50 (2008)
14. OCP-IP, http://www.ocpip.org/
15. SPIRIT, http://www.spiritconsortium.org/
16. Ludäscher, B., et al.: Scientific workflow management and the kepler system. Concurrency and Computation: Practice & Experience 18 (2006)
17. Kangas, T., et al.: UML-based multi-processor SoC design framework. ACM Trans. on Embedded Computing Systems 5, 281–320 (2006)
18. McAllister, J., Woods, R., Fischaber, S., Malins, E.: Rapid implementation and optimisation of DSP systems on FPGA-centric heterogeneous platforms. Journal of Systems Architecture 53, 511–523 (2007)
19. Stefanov, T., et al.: System design using Kahn process networks: The Compaan/Laura approach. In: Proc. of the Int. Conference on Design, Automation and Test in Europe (DATE), pp. 340–345 (2004)
20. Rutten, M.J., et al.: A Heterogeneous Multiprocessor Architecture for Flexible Media Processing. IEEE Design & Test of Computers 19 (2002)
21. Lyonnard, D., et al.: Automatic Generation of Application-Specific Architectures for Heterogeneous Multiprocessor System-on-Chip. In: Proc. of the Design Automation Conference (DAC 2001) (2001)
22. Gerstlauer, A., Gajski, D.: System-level abstraction semantics. In: Proc. 15th Int. Symposium on System Synthesis (ISSS 2002), pp. 231–236 (2002)
23. MoBIES, http://ptolemy.eecs.berkeley.edu/projects/mobies/

Evaluation of ASIPs Design with LISATek

Rashid Muhammad, Ludovic Apvrille, and Renaud Pacalet

System-on-Chip laboratory
LabSoC, GET/ENST
Sophia-Antipolis, France
muhamad.rashid@thomson.net,
{ludovic.apvrille,renaud.pacalet}telecom-paristech.fr,
http://www.comelec.enst.fr/recherche/labsoc.en

Abstract. This paper evaluates an ASIP design methodology based on the extension of an existing instruction set and architecture described with LISA 2.0 language. The objective is to accelerate the ASIPs design process by using partially predefined, configurable RISC-like embedded processor cores that can be quickly tuned to given applications by means of ISE (Instruction Set Extension) techniques. A case study demonstrates the methodological approach for the JPEG algorithm.

Keywords: LISATek, ASIPs, JPEG, Customized Instructions.

1 Introduction

An ASIP is an hardware architectural concept meant to fill the gap between ASICs (Application Specific Integrated Circuits) and DSPs (Digital Signal Processors). The formers are highly efficient but lack flexibility. On the other hand, software development on DSPs provide reusable and programmable solutions with less performance and energy inefficiency as compared to ASICs [1]. An ASIP is a microprocessor specialized for a given set of algorithms. By specialized, we mean that its instruction set is designed from scratch or extended from a known microprocessor. There may be two approaches to design ASIPs. The first approach is to design from scratch: an entirely new instruction set is specifically designed for the target application [10]. The second approach is to customize the instruction set of an existing general purpose partially predefined configurable processor [8] [14] [17]. In this paper, we have designed ASIPs by extending the instruction set of a 32-bit RISC processor. By partially sacrificing silicon efficiency, configurable processors make ASIPs design more incremental and less complex, since both the hardware architecture and software tools are partially predefined [15].

The main contribution of this paper is to evaluate the LISATek ASIP toolkit (from CoWare) [3] [4] [5]. We show that how LISATek assists an ASIP design process by automatically generating the software tool suite (compiler, assembler, linker, simulator) as well as the RTL (Register Transfer Level) description of the designed processor. As a starting point for model creation LISATek provides

M. Berekovic, N. Dimopoulos, and S. Wong (Eds.): SAMOS 2008, LNCS 5114, pp. 177–186, 2008.
© Springer-Verlag Berlin Heidelberg 2008

a library of sample models which contains processors for different architecture categories like VLIW (Very Large Instruction Word), SIMD (Single Instruction Multiple Data), RISC (Reduced Instruction Set Computer). We extend the instruction set of a 32-bit RISC processor. The reason of 32-bit RISC core selection is the observation that many ASIPs tend to have a RISC-like core architecture and ISA (Instruction Set Architecture) [8]. The well-known JPEG image compression standard serves as case study [12].

The rest of the paper is organized as follows: Section 2 introduces the evaluation methodology for LISATek design flow starting from the sample model. Section 3 describes ASIPs design for JPEG algorithm. Section 4 provides simulation and synthesis results. Section 5 comments on strengths and weaknesses of LISA-based design methodology. Section 6 describes related work and section 7 concludes the paper.

2   Evaluation Methodology for LISATek Design Flow

To evaluate LISATek, we propose the following ASIP design methodology:

- The design flow starts by writing the application specifications in a high level language like C.
- Application specifications written in C are profiled to identify critical parts of the application. Criticality refers to computational intensive parts of the application.
- Customized instructions are identified for critical parts of the application to increase computational performance. These customized instructions are application specific instructions with a higher complexity than generic instructions like ADD, SUB, etc. We further explain this identification step in the paper.
- Customized instructions are integrated into a LISATek predefined configurable processor template to speed up the application.
- Customized instructions are functionally verified and simulated using an adequate instruction set simulator (ISS) generated by LISATek [3] [5]. The simulation also makes it possible to calculate the application speedup in terms of cycle counts.
- After simulation, an RTL HDL model (VHDL or verilog) of target architecture is generated by LISATek from the corresponding LISA description. It triggers hardware synthesis process via standard logic synthesis tools. As a result, maximum clock rate and silicon area overhead is obtained for the selected CMOS target library.

2.1   Presentation of the Toolkit: Coware LISATek

The LISATek-based processor design flow [3] [5] covers all phases of the design process from algorithmic specification of the application down to implementation of the micro architecture. It improves flexibility of modeling target architectures and significantly reduces description efforts. It provides high level of flexibility to facilitate the description of various processors, such as SIMD, VLIW and RISC type architectures. To describe ASIPs, LISATek is based on a language called LISA 2.0. LISA offers two main features:

- The description of the ASIP structure: registers, pipeline structure, instruction set binary coding, instruction set syntax, etc.
- The description of the behavior of each instruction. This behavior is described with a pseudo C language.

Two main development phases of the LISA 2.0 based design flow are (1) architecture exploration phase and (2) architecture implementation phase. These phases are iterative and repeated until a best fit between selected architecture and target application is obtained. Every change to architecture specification requires a completely new set of software development tools. (i.e. C compiler, assembler, linker, simulator). This iterative exploration approach demands very flexible, retargetable software development tools to optimize computational performance, flexibility and silicon area.

2.2   Sample Architecture: 32-bit RISC Processor

LISATek provides a library of sample models for different architectural categories. Our case study relies on the LISATek 32-bit RISC processor. The sample architecture has following characteristics:

1. 32-bit instructions with five stage pipeline. (FE, DC, EX, MEM, WB)

    (a) FE: To fetch instructions from memory.
    (b) DC: To decode instructions for the next stages (EX, MEM, WB).
    (c) EX: To execute operations.
    (d) MEM: To store results in memory.
    (e) WB: To write results back into registers.

2. Sixteen 32-bit general purpose registers.
3. PC register, Status registers, Pipeline registers and Bypass registers.
4. Six functional units (ALU , Control, DSP, LDST, Shifter and Writeback).

    (a) ALU: To perform arithmetic and logical operations.
    (b) Control: To perform branching operations.
    (c) LDST: To perform load and store operations.
    (d) Shifter: To perform shift operations.
    (e) DSP: To perform DSP oriented operations.
    (f) Writeback: To perform write back operations.

The sample architecture has already a minimal instruction set. There are four types of instructions: Arithmetic and Logical instructions, Branch instructions, Compare instructions and Load/Store instructions.

3   Case Study: ASIP Design for JPEG Algorithm

To evaluate the strength of LISATek toolkit for ASIP designing, we have designed different ASIPs with different instructions set for the same JPEG algorithm. JPEG is a general purpose compression standard for still-image applications. The key functional blocks for JPEG compression are FDCT (Forward Discrete Cosine Transform), Quantization and Entropy Encoding while key functional blocks for JPEG Decompression are IDCT (Inverse Discrete Cosine Transform), Dequantization and Entropy Decoding.

3.1   Application Specification and Profiling Results

The starting point of our design process is a profile step. To perform that profiling, we consider an open source C implementation of the JPEG algorithm [9]. The application code is profiled using the *gprof* GNU profiler [7] on a Pentium machine. Profiling results show that FDCT and quantization are the most computational intensive parts for compression, while IDCT and dequantization are the most computational intensive parts for decompression. There are many algorithms to compute DCT and IDCT [18]. However, 1 D LLM algorithm [16] computes DCT and IDCT with minimum number of operations. The flow graph of the 1 D (8 point) LLM algorithm is shown in figure 1.

In figure 1, dots represent additions or subtractions. Hollow circles represent multiplication by a number. Rectangular boxes represent rotation and its computational cost is 4 multiplications and 2 additions. There are 4 stages in the LLM algorithm for DCT computation. Stage 1 consists of 8 additions/subtractions. In Stage 2, the algorithm splits into two parts. One part is for even coefficients (only additions and subtractions) and the second part is for odd coefficients (rotations). Stage 3 again splits into even and odd parts. The signal flow graph of LLM algorithm for forward and inverse DCTs are mirror images of each another.

3.2   Customization of Sample Model for JPEG

The LISATek RISC processor sample model is provided with an already-defined instruction set. We extend this instruction set by identifying and implementing customized instructions. These dedicated (customized) instructions are identified to accelerate the computational intensive parts of the application. However, an important challenge for these customized instructions is to accelerate the execution of computational intensive parts while being flexible enough to accommodate variations in the algorithm. There are large number of possible instruction set extensions and each set of extensions describes various levels of trade-offs between flexibility and efficiency. In this paper, we describe only one possible set of instruction set extension.

3.3   Data Memory Organization

To evaluate the efficiency of customized instructions, the following data memory organization is defined for each input image block.

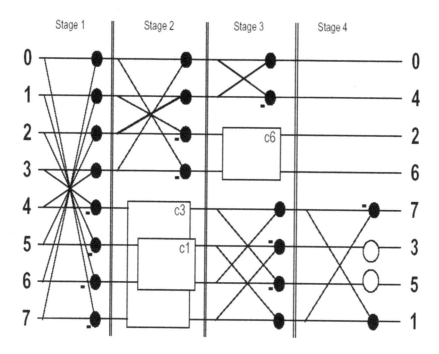

Fig. 1. LLM Algorithm Flow Graph for DCT Computations

TmpAddress is used to store partial DCT results and is calculated as:
TmpAddress = (BaseAddress + 64)
Quantization table address *Tabaddress* is calculated as:
TabAddress = (TmpAddress + 128)
CoefAddress shows the starting address of quantized DCT coefficients.
CoefAddress = (TabAddress + 128)

FDCT and Quantization is performed in two steps: First 8x8 block is loaded from memory, 1 D DCT is performed and temporary results are stored into memory. Then these temporary results are retrieved back from memory to compute 1 D DCT column wise, and quantize the results before storing them in memory and so on.

3.4 Customized Instructions

Stage 1 of the LLM algorithm shown in figure 1 loads 8-bit pixels from data memory. This stage outputs 16-bit data. All the subsequent stages (stage 2, stage 3, stage 4) work with 16-bit data input and output. On the basis of the LLM algorithm flow graph and selected memory organization, we have explored various possible instruction set extensions. One possible set of instruction set extension is presented hereafter.

- **DCT01ROW Rsrc1, Rsrc2** computes DCT stage 1 of the LLM algorithm. It computes 08 additions/subtractions. It takes two source operand registers (*Rsrc1, Rsrc2*) and returns results in the registers which are implicitly defined inside the definition of this instruction. The use of implicit registers is due to the 32-bit instruction set restriction.
- **DCT02 Rdst1, Rdst2, Rsrc1, Rsrc2** computes DCT stage 2 of the LLM algorithm. It takes input from two source registers (*Rsrc1, Rsrc2*) and returns results in two destination registers (*Rdst1, Rdst2*).
- **ADDEVEN Rdst1, Rdst2, Rsrc1, Rsrc2** computes upper part in stage 2 and lower parts in stage 3.
- **DCTEVEN Rdst, Rsrc** computes upper part in stage 3 of the LLM algorithm.
- **DCTODD Rdst, Rsrc1, Rsrc2, Rsrc3** computes DCT computations in stage 4.
- **QUANTIZE Rdst, Rsrc1, Rsrc2** computes quantization. First source register stores 2 DCT coefficients (16 bit data). Second source register stores 2 quantization factor (16 bit data). It takes DCT coefficient to be quantized from first register and takes quantization factor from second source register, performs the quantization and stores the result in *Rdst*.

3.5   Architecture Modifications

In order to implement customized instructions, LISA offers the possibility to either put the new instructions in a new *Functional Unit* or in (modified) existing *Functional Units*. In this paper, customized instructions are implemented by modifying existing *Functional Units*. The reason is that the sample architecture already contains some local registers in existing *Functional Units* that we can reuse for our purpose. Indeed, the creation of a new *Functional Unit* implies the creation of new local registers: already available local registers could not be reused. However, even in the existing *Functional Units*, some additional local registers are needed to implement the customized instructions. Thus, we have added nine 32-bit registers and fourteen 16-bit registers. In order to execute customized instructions in pipeline, additional pipeline registers are also needed. We have added ten 32-bit registers and four 8-bit registers to pass data between pipeline stages.

3.6   Generation of HDL Code

The LISATek *Processor Generator*[4] [3] tool allows the designer to automatically create an implementation model of the target architecture modelled in LISA 2.0 language. The output of the *Processor Generator* is *VHDL* or *VeriLog* code, which can be processed by standard synthesis tools.

4   Experimental Results

The following experiments have been performed to evaluate the relevance of the proposed LISA-based design flow.

4.1 Simulation Results with Native Instructions

To compute 2D DCT of one input block with only the native instructions of the sample model, 640 cycles are required. Similarly 128 cycles are needed to compute quantization for one input image block of size 8x8. In addition to this, some cycles are consumed in loading pixels from memory, loading quantization coefficient from memory, storing and loading partial results to and from memory respectively and storing quantized DCT coefficients in the memory. It has consumed additional 240 cycles for one input block. Hence total number of consumed cycles are **640+128+240 = 1008**. Computational cost for IDCT and dequantization is same as that of FDCT and quantization.

4.2 Simulation Results with Customized Instructions

To compute 2D DCT of one input block with our ASIP (i.e. customized instructions), 192 cycles are needed. 240 additional cycles are required to compute one input block. So total number of consumed cycles are **192+240 = 432**. Computational cost for IDCT and dequantization is same as that of FDCT and quantization.

The designed architecture is not specialized for this application only. The customized instructions are reusable even if we change the DCT algorithm. Also, some of the instructions could also be reused for other algorithm (For example FFT algorithm).

4.3 Summary of Simulation Results

- The speedup due to new instructions is: **Speedup = 1008/432 = 2.33**. The speedup is obtained at the cost of silicon area. The increase in area is due to the additional pipeline registers and local registers.
- 2.33 is not the maximum possible speedup. The computational efficiency of the designed architecture (Minimum cycle counts) can be increased at the cost of silicon area (additional registers) and flexibility (More specific towards a single application) demonstrating the trade-off between re-usability and efficiency.
- The entire design flow for the processor is performed beginning from the functional description of the application down to the hardware implementation within three man-weeks. This time also includes the creation of architecture simulators and production quality software development tools. This short development time demonstrates effectiveness of the design flow.

4.4 Synthesis Results

We have performed logic synthesis by means of Cadence Encounter RTL Compiler using a standard cell CMOS 0.13. The target frequency is 200MHz while external input and output delays are 2.5 ns.

The processor model instantiates three main subblocks: *PipeLine*, *RegisterFile* and *Memories*. The simulation memories are replaced with technology specific vendor memories.

Synthesis results for the entities *Pipeline* and *RegisterFile* are combined to get total area which is 42.5 k-gates at 160 MHz maximum frequency. For JPEG application, the minimum memory needs are:

- Program memory: The minimum size of program memory is the size of ASM code (assembly code) for the application.
- Data memory: The minimum size of required data memory depends on the size of stored image in memory.

5   LISATek Evaluation

5.1   Strengths of LISATek

- As a starting point of model creation LISATek provides a library of sample models which contains processors for different architecture categories. Taking such model as basis has a major advantage to directly have compiler support for the architecture due to the existence of an instruction set. This removes the entry barrier usually caused by new modeling languages and tools.
- It is quite easy to list a set of resources (memory, buses, registers). Operations are described in a hierarchical way, which facilitates reusability and modularity.
- Step by step simulation is quite useable.
- The toolkits *Processor Designer* and *Processor Debugger* [4] [5] creation have a good graphical user interface thus offering ways to design and debug the processor before the generation of its hardware description.

5.2   Weaknesses of LISATek

- Although toolkit *Processor Designer* and *Processor Debugger* has a good graphical user interface but design methodology still lacks the large degree of automation as compared to its counterpart like Tensilica [8] that has more automated approach.
- The LISA language analyzer is quite limited. It means that description errors may occur when compiling the simulation environment. In that case, we must understand gcc errors to correct the LISA description.
- Although VHDL code can be automatically generated from LISA source code by *Processor Generator* but generation process showed many errors in the generated *VHDL* code. So we have to modify the LISA code in order to remove those errors.
- LISATek profiler [6] provides detailed processor specific information. However, it is bound to specific architectures and not suitable for performance estimation in a general, target processor independent way. In [13], a tool has been propsed that estimates the cycles counts and memory profiles. However, it does not extract inherited spatial parallelism present in the application.
- Coarse grain reconfigurable architectures are getting more and more popular in the domain of embedded systems. Currently, LISATek based design methodology has no notion for modeling this class of architectures. The recent work in this regard is [2]. But it describes only fine grain reconfigurable architecture with static reconfiguration.

6 Related Work

The Xtensa [8] environment from Tensilica is built upon a choice between elements from a predefined set of hardware components which can be adapted to the user requirements. For this reason the design space exploration can be performed efficiently but the designer has not the flexibility of modeling arbitrary ASIPs. The PEAS-III [14] generates not only HDL (Hardware Description Language) descriptions but the target compiler and target assembler as well. However, it works with a set of predefined components which limits the resulting flexibility in modeling arbitrary processor architectures. The EXPRESSION[11] language allows the cycle-accurate processor description. It provides the mechanism for capturing the information needed to support ADL (Architecture Description Language) based design space exploration and software toolkit generation methodology. However, currently there is no information whether the implementation step can be done based on this language.

None of the introduced approaches provides the designer with efficient design exploration and implementation capabilities coupled with the required flexibility for the development of arbitrary ASIPs. In this paper, LISA 2.0 based design flow is evaluated to address these issues. We have used a manual approach where custom instructions are identified by the user after profiling. However, the readers are referred to a more automated approach in [17]. In this automated approach advanced profiling tools are used such that custom instructions are not identified by the user but generated automatically from the application code. For Customized instructions implementation, [17] relies on CorXpert (from Coware) tool. CorXpert is a graphical tool for capturing CI (Customized Instructions) of configurable processors.

7 Conclusions and Future Work

This paper evaluates LISA 2.0 based methodology to design ASIPs for multimedia applications. We have designed a processor architecture with an extended instruction set based on the profiling results. As far as area overhead and speedup are concerned, our solution is somewhere between pure software implementation and full custom designed ASIPs. Our case study has explored different types of ASIPs for JPEG algorithm.

A major disadvantage of our approach is the lack of automation in identifying the customized instructions. Design time can be significantly reduced to few hours by making this process automatic. Future work may be the modeling of further real world processor architectures while focusing on the evaluation of efficiency of both the generated RTL code and the efficiency of retargetable C compiler.

Acknowledgments. This work has been sponsored by Texas Instruments Inc.

References

1. Ienne, P., Leupers, R.: Customizable Embedded Processors: Design Technologies and Applications (Systems on Silicon). Morgan Kaufmann Publishers, San Francisco (2006)
2. Chattopadhyay, A., Ahmed, W., Karuri, K., Kammler, D., Leupers, R., Ascheid, G., Meyr, H.: Design space exploration of partially re-configurable embedded processors. In: Design, Automation & Test in Europe Conference & Exhibition, pp. 1–6 (2007)
3. CoWare. LISATek Creation Manual, product version v2005. 2.1 edn. (February 2006)
4. CoWare. LISATek Methodology Guidelines for the Processor Generator, product version v2005. 2.1 edn. (February 2006)
5. CoWare. LISATek Processor Designer Manual, product version v2005. 2.1 edn. (February 2006)
6. CoWare. LISATek Profiler, product version v2005.2.1 edn. (February 2006)
7. Fenlason, J., Stallman, R.: The GNU profiler
8. Gonzalez, R.E.: Xtensa: A configurable and extensible processor. IEEE Micro 20(2), 60–70 (2000)
9. I.J. group, www.ijg.org
10. Haddad, F., Apvrille, L., Pacalet, R.: Comparative Study of Toolkits for the fast Design of ASICs and ASIPs (September 2005)
11. Halambi, A., Grun, P., Ganesh, V., Khare, A., Dutt, N., Nicolau, A.: Expression: a language for architecture exploration through compiler/simulator retargetability. In: DATE 1999, New York, NY, USA, p. 100 (1999)
12. T. International Telegraphic and T.C. Committee. Information technology - digital compression and coding of continuous tone still images - requirements and guidelines. Recommendation T.81
13. Kempf, T., Karuri, K., Wallentowitz, S., Ascheid, G., Leupers, R., Meyr, H.: A sw performance estimation framework for early system-level-design using fine-grained instrumentation. In: DATE 2006, Belgium, pp. 468–473 (2006)
14. Kobayashi, S., Mita, K., Takeuchi, Y., Imai, M.: Rapid prototyping of jpeg encoding using the asip development system: PEAS-III. In: International Conference on Acoustics, Speech and Signal Processing, Hong Kong (April 2003)
15. Lee, J.-E., Choi, K., Dutt, N.D.: Instruction set synthesis with efficient instruction encoding for configurable processors. ACM Trans. Des. Autom. Electron. Syst. 12(1), 8 (2007)
16. Leoffler, C., Ligtenberg, A., Moschytz, G.: Practical fast id dct algorithms with 11 multiplications. In: Proc. IEEE ICASSP, pp. 988–991 (February 1989)
17. Leupers, R., Karuri, K., Kraemer, S., Pandey, M.: A design flow for configurable embedded processors based on optimized instruction set extension synthesis. In: DATE 2006, pp. 581–586 (2006)
18. Rao, K.R., Yip, P.: Discrete cosine transform algorithms, advantages and applications, pp. 90–93. Academic Press, San Diego (1990)

High Level Loop Transformations for Systematic Signal Processing Embedded Applications

Calin Glitia and Pierre Boulet

Laboratoire d'Informatique Fondamentale de Lille
Université des Sciences et Technologies de Lille
INRIA Lille - Nord Europe
59655 Villeneuve d'Ascq Cedex, France
{glitia.calin, pierre.boulet}@lifl.fr

Abstract. Array-OL specification model is a mixed graphical-textual language designed to model multidimensional intensive signal processing applications. Data and task parallelism are specified directly in the model. High level transformations are defined on this model, allowing the refactoring of an application and furthermore providing directions for optimization. The resemblances between with the wide-known and used *Loop transformations* lead us to try taking concepts and results from this domain and see how they fit in Array-OL context.

Keywords: Multidimensional Dataflow, optimizations, loop transformations.

1 Introduction

In the last years, the gap between the performances claimed by the constructors and the ones achieved with real code has drastically increased. This is caused mainly by the brutal increase in processor complexity which brought with it a drastic degradation of the code generated by the compilers. The three major directions for improving the performances are: (1) increasing the instruction parallelism while multiplying the mechanism to allow the simultaneous execution of instructions; (2) improving the speculative mechanisms that allow the prediction of programs local behavior; (3) the implementation of a complex memory hierarchy for exploiting as well as possible the time and space data locality.

For all these directions, the source-to-source transformations techniques have a determinant role. Most of these techniques are represented by transformations applied on "for" loops which are efficient in the case of code that contains extremely regular data treatment.

Array-OL (*Array Oriented Language*) is a modeling language designed in order to conform to the needs for specification, standardization and efficiency of the multidimensional systematic signal processing [2]. This application domain is characterized by systematic, regular, and massively data-parallel computations. Array-OL relies on a graphical formalism in which the signal processing appears as a graph of tasks. Each task reads and writes multidimensional arrays in an extremely regular pattern.

In this paper we try to make a comparison between loop transformations and the Array-OL transformations, identify the resemblances and directions for using results from loop transformations optimization techniques to Array-OL.

M. Berekovic, N. Dimopoulos, and S. Wong (Eds.): SAMOS 2008, LNCS 5114, pp. 187–196, 2008.

2 Loop Transformations

An important early system level technique, the loop transformation technique, is aiming at improving the data access regularity and locality. Hence it reduces the overall memory size requirement and the access frequency to big and slow memories. This is vital to area, power consumption, and performance. Improved data access regularity and locality shorten the lifetimes of data elements and increases the memory location reuse ratio since memory locations can be reused for data elements with non-overlapping life-times.

Methods are divided into two classes: global methods which deal with each loop as atomic computation unit and local methods which change the way loops are organized internally. Here is a list of some of the global transformations that are useful for optimization. Global methods:

- **Code moving** that changes the execution order between two loops in the program without modifying the loops.
- **Loop fusion** that groups several loops in a unique one, used to reduse the size of intermediate arrays.
- **Loop splitting** that represents the reverse of merging. It attempts to simplify a loop or eliminate dependencies by breaking it into multiple loops which iterate over different contiguous portions of the index range.

Local transformations explore more in depth the way loops are organized internally:

- **Loop tiling** acts on partitioning of large array into smaller blocks, thus fitting accessed array elements into cache size, enhancing cache reuse and reducing cache size requirements.
- **Loop pipelining** shifts some instructions from one to several iterations within the loop body. This is used to increase to data locality.
- **Loop collapsing** is the reverse of tiling.

These transformations usually are combined in order to achieve best performances. As an observation, these are just some of the existing loop transformations; the most common we could say.

2.1 Loop Optimization Techniques

Typically, applying a compiler optimization consists of three steps: decide upon a part of the program to optimize and the enchainment of transformations to be applied; verify the correctness of the optimization; and last, applying the transformations. As processor architectures become more and more complex, the number of dimensions in which optimizations are possible increase and this makes the decision process very complex.

The complexity of optimization algorithms is the reason why many compilers still use heuristics. This implies basically the use of the same chain of transformations, the one that proves to reach a relatively good result in most of the cases.

The complexity of the problem determined the need to introduce ways of representing the problem (constrains, transformations, cost function) using a more effective formalism and which could facilitate the manipulation of concepts like correctness, data dependencies, cost function. Some approached the problem using Linear Algebra [4], Polyhedral Abstraction [6], graph theory algorithms or Integer Linear Programming [5]. The introduction of formalism is extremely important for the decision part of the optimization. Correct and complex optimization algorithms need to be designed around such formalisms.

3 Array-OL Model of Specification

The initial goal of Array-OL is to give a mixed graphical-textual language to express multidimensional intensive signal processing applications. These applications work on multidimensional arrays and their complexity does not come from the elementary functions they combine, but from their combination of the ways they access the intermediate arrays. As these applications handle huge amounts of data under tight real-time constraints, the efficient use of the potential parallelism of the application on parallel hardware is mandatory.

3.1 Principles

Form these needs, we can state the basic principles that underly the language:

- Array-OL is a *data dependence expression* language. Only the true data dependencies are expressed in order to express the full parallelism of the application.
- Data access is done through sub arrays, called patterns.
- The language is *hierarchical* to allow descriptions at different granularity levels and to handle the complexity of the applications.
- All the potential parallelism in the application should be available in the specification, both *task parallelism* and *data parallelism*.
- It is a *single assignment* formalism.
- The spatial and temporal dimensions are treated equally in the arrays.
- The arrays are seen has tori.

The semantics of Array-OL is that of a first order functional language manipulating multidimensional arrays. It is not a data flow language but can be projected on such a language.

The usual model for dependence based algorithm description is the dependence graph where nodes represent statements and edges dependencies. In order to represent complex applications, a common extension of these graphs is the hierarchy. Array-OL builds upon such hierarchical dependence graphs and adds a special kind of node to represent the data-parallelism of the application: repetition nodes.

Formally, an Array-OL application is a set of *components* connected through *ports*. The components are equivalent to mathematical functions reading data on their input ports and writing data on their output ports. The components are of three kinds: *elementary*, *compound* and *repetition*. An *elementary* component is atomic (a black box). A *compound* is a dependence graph whose nodes are components connected via their ports. A *repetition* is a component expressing how a single sub-component is repeated.

All the data exchanged between the components are arrays. These arrays are multidimensional and are characterized by their *shape*, the number of elements on each of their dimension. Each port is thus characterized by the shape and the type of the elements of the array it reads from or writes to.

3.2   Tasks Parallelism

For a better understanding, in the rest of the study we will use to illustrate the Array-OL concepts on an application that scales an high definition TV signal down to a standard definition TV signal, called *downscaler*. Both signals are represented as a three dimensional array; the first two dimensions represent the frame resolutions (1920×1080 at the input and 720×480 at the output) while the third represents the flow of frames (in time). The application's task dependence is presented in *Figure 1*. The application is constituted from two filters, the horizontal and the vertical filter.

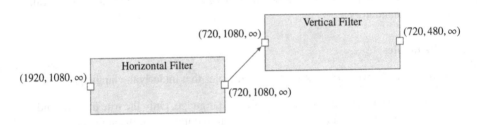

Fig. 1. Downscaler application – task dependence

Each execution of a task reads one full array on its inputs and writes the full output arrays. *The graph is a dependence graph, not a data flow graph.*

3.3   Data Parallelism

A data-parallel repetition of a task is specified in a repetition task. The basic hypothesis is that all the repetitions of this repeated task are independent. They can be scheduled in any order, even in parallel[1]. The second one is that each instance of the repeated task operates with sub-arrays of the inputs and outputs of the repetition. For a given input or output, all the sub-array instances have the same shape, are composed of regularly spaced elements and are regularly placed in the array. This hypothesis allows a compact representation of the repetition and is coherent with the application domain of Array-OL which describes very regular algorithms.

As these sub-arrays are conform, they are called *patterns*. In order to give all the information needed to create these patterns, a *tiler* is associated to each array (ie each edge). A tiler is able to build the patterns from an input array, or to store the patterns in an output array. It describes the coordinates of the elements of the tiles from the coordinates of the elements of the patterns. It contains the following information:

---

[1] This is why we talk of *repetitions* and not *iterations* which convey a sequential semantics.

- F: a *fitting* matrix.
- o: the *origin* of the *reference pattern* (for the *reference repetition*).
- P: a *paving* matrix.

The shapes of the arrays and patterns are, as in the compound description, noted on the ports. The *repetition space* indicating the number of repetitions is defined itself as an multidimensional array with a shape. Each dimension of this repetition space can be seen as a parallel loop and the shape of the repetition space gives the bounds of the loop indices of the nested parallel loops.

In the downscaler application, each of the two filters has a repetitive functionality, so this means we can represent them by using repetition components. Thus the complete representation is presented in *Figure 2*.

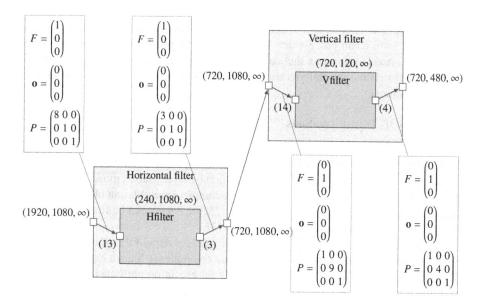

Each of the filter has a repetitive functionality that is described with the tilers. For example, the horizontal filter's elementary component takes a window of 13 elements that slides with 8 elements on each line of each image frame and produces 3 elements.

Fig. 2. Complete specification of the downscaler application

Returning now to the Array-OL specifications, for each repetition, one needs to design the reference elements of the input and output tiles and the elements of these tiles. The reference elements of the reference repetition are given by the *origin* vector, o, of each tiler. The reference elements of the other repetitions are built relatively to this one. Their coordinates are built as a linear combination of the vectors of the *paving* matrix as follows

$$\forall\, \mathbf{r}, 0 \le \mathbf{r} < s_{\text{repetition}}, \text{ref}_{\mathbf{r}} = \mathbf{o} + P \times \mathbf{r} \quad \text{mod } s_{\text{array}} \quad (1)$$

where $s_{repetition}$ is the shape of the repetition space, P the paving matrix and s_{array} the shape of the array. The elements of the tile of repetition r are built relatively to the reference element of this tile using a linear combination of the vectors of the *fitting* matrix as follows

$$\forall \mathbf{i}, 0 \leq \mathbf{i} < s_{pattern}, \mathbf{e_i} = ref_r + F \times \mathbf{i} \quad \bmod s_{array} \qquad (2)$$

where $s_{pattern}$ is the shape of the pattern.

3.4   Projection onto an Execution Model

It is a strength of Array-OL that the space-time mapping decision is separated from the functional specification. This allows to build functional component libraries for reuse and to carry out some architecture exploration with the least restrictions possible. Mapping compounds is not specially difficult. The problem comes when mapping repetitions. This problem is discussed in details in [1] where the authors study the projection of Array-OL onto Kahn process networks [7]. The key point is that some repetitions can be transformed to flows. In that case, the execution of the repetitions is sequentialized (or pipelined) and the patterns are read and written as a flow of tokens (each token carrying a pattern).

3.5   Array-OL Transformations

A set of Array-OL code transformations has been designed to allow to adapt the application to the execution, allowing to choose the granularity of the flows and a simple expression of the mapping by tagging each repetition by its execution mode: data-parallel or sequential. This paper is not meant to give a complete presentation of the Array-OL transformations; the topic is much too complex. More details can be found in the PhD thesis of Julien Soula [9] and Philippe Dumont [3].

A major problem for designing an execution model for Array-OL is introduced by the so called "synchronization barriers" between the components. Such a barrier is created by the data dependencies. A task cannot begin its execution until all its input arrays are entirely produced. A sequential execution is, by consequence, not appropriate; the presence of any intermediary array that contains an infinite dimension would cause the execution to be stalled in that point. A solution could be a pipelined execution by refactoring the application using the Array-OL transformations. Using the hierarchy, we intend to isolate the infinite dimensions at the top hierarchical level of the application (which will represent the data-flow), while in the lower levels we can choose a pipelined execution.

All the Array-OLtransformations are based on a mathematical formalism that ensures their correctness, but which will not be presented due to limited paper size. Details can be found in the bibliography.

Fusion This transformation basically takes two components that have at least one common array (the first component produces an array consumed by the second component) and these two components are merged into a single compound component containing the previous two. The result of fusion is the creation of a hierarchy level, with a common repetition and sub-repetitions on the lower level hierarchy. The components keep their functionality after the fusion but the difference is that the arrays that they work on are different (parts of the original arrays). The question is how the parts of the original arrays are chosen and why? In our implementation the fusion was designed is such a way that the created compound component takes the smallest possible patterns from the input arrays that can produce at least one element of each output arrays.

In *Figure 3* we can see the result of the fusion on the downscaler application. We can see that after the transformation the two initial filters are merged into a single component which contains the initial filters that now consume different arrays, the infinite dimension remaining at the top level.

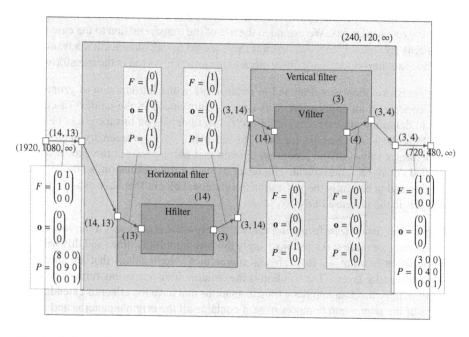

After the fusion, a hierarchy level was introduced in the application, the original filters were merged into a single compound component that passes now just parts of the initial arrays to the filters.

Fig. 3. Downscaler after fusion transformation

Change paving transformations can be used to change the granularity of the applications or of parts of the application by redistributing repetitions between hierarchy levels. As a direct consequence it can be used to reduce the redundant computations (called *recalculations*) generated in some cases by the fusion. This problem can appear after the fusion, if the first component before the fusion produced overlapping patterns. This will cause the first sub-component after the fusion to compute multiple times the same elements of the original arrays. What we can do is reducing the amount of re-calculations by extending the pattern of the compound component so it will include more. In the extreme case, if we extend to the maximum the pattern on all the paving vectors which cause re-calculations, we may even eliminate the phenomenon. Still, this is not possible in the case where the re-calculations are present on the infinite dimension without eliminating a major role of the fusion, that of isolating the infinite dimension on the top level of the hierarchy.

Change paving by adding dimensions, as its name indicates, extends the pattern by the use of an extra dimension, having the size of the change paving *level*. Parts of the repetition of the top level descend a level of hierarchy as new dimensions of the repetition spaces of sub-components. *Change paving by linear growth* transformation is designed specially to reduce the re-calculations and so it can be applied only on tasks that contain re-calculations. What this transformation does different than the previous is to calculate a surrounding pattern and in this way the transformation can be used to reduce the re-calculations. We extended the use of the transformation to the case where the patterns are "glued" together, even if there are no re-calculations. It's advantage is that it does not introduces extra dimensions to the arrays involved in the transformation.

Tiling transformation was designed in order to allow the introduction of *granularity degree* concept in an application. This concept, introduced in the context of control, allows to delimitate different *execution cycles*. More details on this topic can be found in the PhD thesis of Ouassila Labbani [8] (chapter 7.3). A *granularity degree* basically defines a subset of the repetition domain that corresponds at the execution to a controlled Array-OL component. The result of such a transformation is similar to the loop tiling and is basically the separation in functional blocks that have as an important characteristic the increased locality.

Collapse The fusion transformation can work only on two tasks at a time. In we want to fusion three or more tasks we must apply the fusion multiple times and this will lead to the creation of what we call "abyssal hierarchies", applications that are spread on multiple hierarchy layers. The solution is the collapse transformation, represented by a series of maximum change paving transformations that have the effect of extending the patterns of the compound component so it contains all the original patterns and in this way this component can be eliminated by replacing it with its sub-components, which will "climb" a level in the hierarchy.

By applying a certain number of transformations we can change the structure of an Array-OL application without modifying it's functionality. One can use these transformations to refactor the application to respect various constraints (timing, hardware mapping, memory optimization).

4 Array-OL vs. Loop Transformations

Loop transformations are most efficient on code that contains extremely regular data treatment (perfectly-nested loops) which is exactly the domain of Array-OL.

We start with some important observations on these transformations. First, Array-OL transformations have a major advantage over loop transformations that are usually local optimizations while the Array-OL ones can be applied at any level of the hierarchy thanks to the pattern based data accesses. The pattern based data accesses make the Array-OL access structure more visible and much easier to manipulate, differently from the complex formulas manipulating the loop indices. There are also disadvantages with Array-OL; the most important is introduced by the limitations of the language, one of them being the extreme regularity. This restrains the domain of applications that can be specified with Array-OL to a limited set.

We will not compare separately each pair of transformations, each Array-OL transformations resembles in functionality with it's homonym, but rather try to identify the role of each transformation and its possible usage. When passing to an execution model in Array-OL there are a set of key concepts that must be carefully analyzed. First, we must isolate as much as possible the infinite dimension but in the same time respect the internal constrains introduced by the data dependencies and avoid any blocking points in the execution. All these are done by the use of the fusion that has three major effects: it isolates the infinite dimension on the top hierarchy level, it minimizes the intermediate arrays and guaranties a non-blocking structure. As the loop fusion, they both have the role of merging two dependent entities (Array-OL components in the first case and loop-nest in the other) with the purpose of eliminating or at least reducing intermediate data size. An advantage of Array-OL fusion is that it automatically does the array resize, while the loop transformation needs other transformations in order to achieve this, like the scalar replacement or intra-array storage order optimization. The fusion in Array-OL can be used to reach a multi-level application structure where all the infinite dimensions are left on the top level that will represent the data-flow. The collapse transformation has an important role in connection with the fusion, for avoiding the apparition of "abyssal hierarchies" created by chaining fusions.

The change paving, resembles with the loop unrolling. They both act on redistributing the iterations between levels (hierarchy levels or nest levels). In the context of Array-OL we can use this type of transformation for example to restructurate the application so it respects the environment constrains.

The Array-OL tiling corresponds to the loop tiling or partitioning transformation; the first introduces a level of hierarchy while the second introduces a nesting level to the loop-nest. The both have the role of splitting the iteration space into functional blocks which has a positive influence on the data locality.

We must note that in the context of Array-OL optimizations we don't need to search to increase the parallelism of the application, the parallelism is evident, it was one of the starting point of Array-OL to produce a specification language where the parallelism is fully expressed in the specifications. What we are most interested in is memory optimizations (static and dynamic), but by respecting the application constrains. None the less, transformations change the structure of an application and this implies changes to the parallelism.

Algorithms based on loop transformations that can give the optimum solution for memory optimizations are not practical, due to complexity issues. Most of the times heuristics are used. In the context of Array-OL we can also use as a starting point a heuristic, the one that involved the transformation of an application to the multi-levels structure, which has proved extremely useful.

As said in the introduction, the Array-OL language presents some advantages. The application defined in Array-OL is extremely regular and this regularity is contained directly in the language; also the parallelism is evident so this is another thing that we don't have to worry about. Another advantage is brought by the ODT formalism, which guaranties the correctness of the transformations as regarding the data dependencies.

5   Conclusions

Array-OL transformations have a determinant role in the context of Array-OL. They can be used not only for optimization but also as a tool for refactoring the application. For now it is just an instrument in the hands of the designer but in the future, after the needed concepts will be introduced to Array-OL, optimization algorithms using the presented transformations will be designed and implemented. These optimizations also depend on the execution model chosen for the Array-OL model and they will evolve in parallel with the evolution of the execution models.

References

1. Amar, A., Boulet, P., Dumont, P.: Projection of the Array-OL specification language onto the Kahn process network computation model. In: International Symposium on Parallel Architectures, Algorithms, and Networks, Las Vegas, Nevada, USA (December 2005)
2. Demeure, A., Lafarge, A., Boutillon, E., Rozzonelli, D., Dufourd, J.-C., Marro, J.-L.: Array-OL: Proposition d'un formalisme tableau pourle traitement de signal multi-dimensionnel. In: Gretsi, Juan-Les-Pins, France (September 1995)
3. Dumont, P.: Spécification Multidimensionnelle pour le traitement du signal systématique. Phd thesis, Laboratoire d'informatique fondamentale de Lille (2005)
4. Feautrier, P.: Dataflow analysis of array and scalar references. International Journal of Parallel Programming 20(1), 23–53 (1991)
5. Fraboulet, A.: Optimisation de la mémoire et de la consommation des systémes multimédia embarque. Phd thesis, LIP (November 2001)
6. Girbal, S.: Optimisation dapplications - Composition de transformations de programme: model et outils. PhD thesis, University Paris 11, Orsay, France (September 2005)
7. Kahn, G., MacQueen, D.B.: Coroutines and networks of parallel processes. In: Gilchrist, B. (ed.) Information Processing 77: Proceedings of the IFIP Congress 77, pp. 993–998 (1977)
8. Labbani, O.: Modélisation à haut niveau du contrôle dans des applications de traitement systématique à parallélisme massif. Phd thesis, Laboratoire d'informatique fondamentale de Lille (2006).
9. Soula, J.: Principe de Compilation d'un Langage de Traitement de Signal. Phd thesis, Laboratoire d'informatique fondamentale de Lille (December 2001)

Memory-Centric Hardware Synthesis from Dataflow Models

Scott Fischaber, John McAllister, and Roger Woods

Programmable Systems Laboratory:
Institute for Electronic, Communication and Information Technology (ECIT)
Queen's University Belfast, Belfast, BT3 9DT, UK
{s.fischaber,j.mcallister,r.woods}@ecit.qub.ac.uk

Abstract. Generation of hardware architectures directly from dataflow representations is increasingly being considered as research moves toward system level design methodologies. Creation of networks of IP cores to implement actor functionality is a common approach to the problem, but often the memory sub-systems produced using these techniques are inefficiently utilised. This paper explores some of the issues in terms of memory organisation and accesses when developing systems from these high level representations. Using a template matching design study, challenges such as modelling memory reuse and minimising buffer requirements are examined, yielding results with significantly less memory requirements and costly off-chip memory accesses.

Keywords: dataflow, template matching, hardware synthesis.

1   Introduction

With system complexity and integration levels continuing to rise, there is a growing need for a high level comprehensive design flow. Modern signal processing applications are increasingly being implemented on heterogeneous multiprocessor platforms, particularly those including Field Programmable Gate Arrays (FPGAs), but the process of targeting these platforms is only now beginning to move from disparate techniques toward system level design. These tools are still in their infancy, and as each target domain has different requirements, many methods have arisen to assuage designer demands. In signal processing, because of the data dominated nature of the applications and parallel operation of many of the algorithms, dataflow based models of computation (MoC) are often employed, allowing concurrency to be visualised and exploited [1].

The point-to-point nature of these dataflow models has led to many of these system level design tools adopting a core network generation approach to implementing the hardware partition in these heterogeneous platforms [2][3][4]. They often employ simplistic memory interfaces that closely match the first-in first-out (FIFO) buffers seen in the dataflow models. The memory sub-system, however, can have a significant influence on the overall performance and energy consumption of an implementation [5], particularly when processing large tokens,

M. Berekovic, N. Dimopoulos, and S. Wong (Eds.): SAMOS 2008, LNCS 5114, pp. 197–206, 2008.
© Springer-Verlag Berlin Heidelberg 2008

for instance in image processing applications. The larger memory requirements often necessitate off-chip memory accesses, which will have longer access times and higher energy usage than on-chip, resulting in lower performance and higher overall power consumption [6]. One solution is the introduction of a layered memory architecture, using increasingly smaller buffers to store frequently accessed values. As the memory architecture can have a significant impact on the quality of the implementation, the ability to optimise and derive an efficient memory configuration from the system level becomes essential.

This paper will use the design study of a template matching algorithm to highlight various issues with implementing signal processing systems directly from high level representations, particularly in reference to memory organisation and utilisation. It proposes certain methods for refinement of these systems and addresses inefficiencies that arise when targeting these systems onto hardware partitions in FPGA-based heterogeneous platforms. Section 2 introduces some challenges in implementing the memory sub-system directly from the high level models currently in use. Section 3 describes the template matching study: firstly examining the algorithm, then modelling it, and lastly performing refinement.

2   Challenges Mapping from System-Level DFG to HW

Various DFG representations of the same algorithm can lead to significantly different resulting hardware systems. This means that refining the graph permits high-level modifications to be performed and allows system-level optimisations of the implementation. These can involve simply changing the graph parameters, modifying the graph to increase parallelism, or even changing the MoC.

Since the first iteration of a graph is often focused on ensuring the algorithm performs correctly, inefficiencies in a hardware design can be introduced by the system level model. Refining this algorithm to a more implementation specific version is a vital tool to create an efficient final implementation. Which refinements to perform will depend heavily on the application domain being targeted. For memory generation, [7] has demonstrated how manipulating the token sizes can have a significant impact on memory usage. Also [8] introduced exploiting data reuse using dataflow-based hardware design flows by changing the MoC. The next section examines refinement of a template matching application.

3   Template Matching

3.1   Template Matching Algorithm

Locating where (or if) a target object is in a given image is a computationally complex problem which can be performed by correlating the incoming images with a template representing the target object. To successfully perform this calculation, the target must be the same size and orientation in the image and the template, so in practical applications multiple kernels, representing various sizes and rotations are used. Here 32 kernel values are used and compared to

Fig. 1. Template matching block diagram

the incoming images. For large frames, converting the images and kernels into the frequency domain and multiplying them is more efficient, as a convolution in the spatial domain is equivalent to a multiplication in the frequency domain [9]. To compute the algorithm, the image is acquired from an external source and processed as shown in Fig. 1. To reduce the complexity, the 512x512 pixel images are divided into four 256x256 blocks and processed separately. The image is filtered using a 2-D convolution with a 3x3 pixel kernel and edge detection is performed as this yields a better result (another 2-D convolution).

Once pre-processed, the image is converted into the frequency domain in the feature extraction block using an FFT. This result is multipled by the 32 frequency kernels using an element-wise multiplication and all 32 images are converted back into the spatial domain using an IFFT. These results are examined in the classification block; if the pattern existed in the image, some of the results should contain a correlation peak at the location of the target object.

The 2-D convolution and FFT algorithms are both separable (given a separable kernel for the convolution), meaning that instead of performing a 2-D operation, two 1-D operations can instead be executed. This can be shown graphically in Fig. 2. Here the 3x3 kernel for the 2-D convolution is separated into two 3 pixel kernels, a row vector and a column vector. These can then be applied separately to the image. In this case, the row kernel is applied first, yielding the image i. The column kernel is then applied to i to give the 2-D convolved image. Since a 1-D convolution scans over an image, subsequent blocks will share pixels; Fig. 2 shows that the block for $h(k+1)$ will share two pixels with $h(k)$.

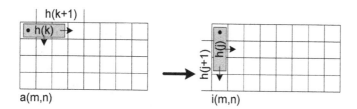

Fig. 2. Separable 2-D convolution algorithm

3.2 Template Matching Modelling

The block diagram representation can be converted into a dataflow graph for rapid implementation. The two convolution operations are modelled using

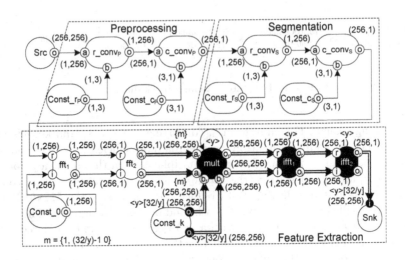

Fig. 3. Template matching dataflow graph

multi-dimensional dataflow (Fig. 3), where the dimensions of each token are represented in parenthesis, the first dimension representing the vertical direction and the second the horizontal. The number of tokens each actor consumes or produces in one firing (the threshold) is given by the value in square brackets (this value is omitted when equal to one to simplify the graph). Due to the 32 IFFTs that need to be performed for one image, using a single IFFT core cannot meet the real-time processing requirement (outside of the scope of this paper are the high level performance estimations which can be performed). To address this, an array of cores are used; multiple cores are used for the *mult* and *ifft* actors which can be modelled using multidimensional arrayed dataflow [11] as shown in Fig. 3. The filled actors or ports indicate an array with the size given in triangular braces (y) and the double lines show an array of arcs.

Since the 2-D convolutions are separable, they are replaced by two 1-D convolution actors. In the same way, the FFT/IFFT operations are converted into two 256-point FFT/IFFT actors. The filter values are produced by the $Const\_r_P/c_P$ and $Const\_r_S/c_S$ actors and the 32 kernel values are generated by $Const\_k$. Since the same FFT value is used for 32 kernel values, the input to the *mult* actor is cyclo-static, with a new data sample (i.e. a new FFT result) being consumed every $32/y$ firings. This is modelled using cyclo-static dataflow (CSDF), where the tokens thresholds are no longer static, but vary in a cyclic manner [10]. This is represented by a value in curly braces, in this case the *mult* actor consumes one token on A_r and A_i the first firing and then none for the next $(32/y)$-1 as indicated by the value of m. The multiplied images are then converted back into the spatial domain using the IFFT. In this case, two *mult* and *ifft* actors are sufficient for real-time processing ($y=2$).

Implementing this system directly from the model in Fig. 3 would require a 256x256 byte buffer between each actor (e.g. r_conv_P produces a row, but

c_conv_P requires a column, so all 256 row will need to be stored before c_conv_P can fire). Refining the graph from the algorithmic level will allow optimisations of the resulting memory subsystem to be performed. The template matching model will be further investigated, beginning with the 2-D convolution operation and then followed by the feature extraction block to examine these refinements.

3.3 2-D Convolution Model Refinement

Since the 1-D convolution cores do not consume an entire row or column at a time, the model will be altered to process one filter kernel at a time (one 3 pixel vector) and produce one pixel per firing. Two pixels between subsequent blocks are the same (as shown in Fig. 2), so an actor is inserted to store an entire frame, and produce the required 3 pixel values as shown in Fig. 4(a). Here the input image is consumed on the first firing of A and then stored using the self loop to produce all of the necessary row vectors for the image. Each of these are convolved with the kernel value and the output stored in an intermediate memory. In the same way, this data is kept over several firings of B, each time producing a new column vector. This is used with the column kernel to produce the final output value. A valid schedule for the DFG can be constructed by firing the Src actor, followed by A, $Const\_r$, and r_conv 67080 times (which complete one iteration of the cyclo-static schedule given for A, which uses the entire token produced by Src. This is followed by 66564 executions of B, $Const\_c$, and c_conv, which will produce the 66564 token needed for Snk to fire once. This schedule can be written as: $\{Src, 67080\{A,Const\_r, r\_conv\}, 66564\{B, Const\_c, c\_conv\}, Snk\}$, where the number outside of a bracket indicate the number of times the actors within fire. Using this schedule, the memory sizes and bandwidths required can be calculated. The necessary size of each buffer can be calculated by tracing the size of each memory during one execution of the schedule and taking the maximum value. The bandwidth is calculated using Eqn.(1), where β is the bandwidth, f is the number of firings of an actor, ρ_c is the number of bytes produces in one execution of a cyclo-static cycle (for static graphs, this is the bytes in one firing), L is the period of the that cycle (1 for static graphs), and fr is the frame rate.

$$\beta = f * \frac{\rho_C}{L} * fr \ . \tag{1}$$

Using the size and bandwidth calculations, the memory organisation graph in Fig. 4(b) can be determined. The minimum bandwidth between the image and r_conv should be 8.11 MB/s; this is calculated by taking the image size (260x260 pixels) and multiplying by the frame rate (4 images per frame at 30 fps). As the bandwidth required is 24.15MB/s, data is being read multiple times and it may be more efficient to implement the graph taking data reuse into account.

To model this reuse, an extension to CSDF to allow special channels is employed [12]. For a 1-D convolution, storing the two pixels reused between blocks reduces the necessary bandwidth to the larger frame memories by introducing closer, smaller memories to the hierarchy. This is accomplished by inserting special actors C and D into the graph as shown in Fig. 4(c) which break the link to the large memories and use the special channels nomenclature to reuse tokens between firings. This behaviour is characterised by three values on the actor ports. The *r* value defines the number of tokens an actor consumes on each firing, *p* indicates the number of tokens released, and the token dimensions are given in parenthesis.

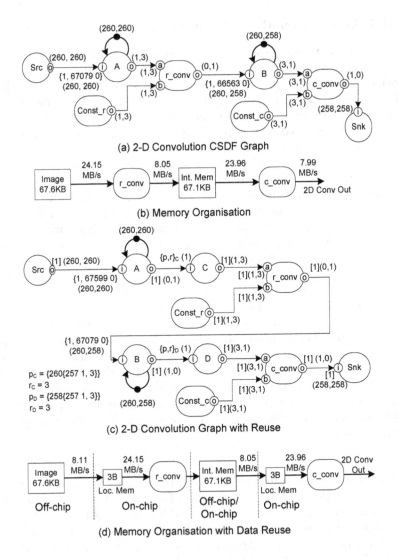

Fig. 4. 2-D convolution memory organisation

Here *r_conv* processes data in the horizontal direction; only one new pixel is required between firings as the other two are reused (up to an edge where three tokens are released). This pattern is given in Fig. 4(c) by the values of *r* and *p*.

Since $r_c=3$, r_conv will consume three tokens each time it fires, but p_c shows that for the first 257 times it will release one pixel, followed by 3 (when it reaches an image edge). To cover all of the rows, this is repeated 260. The convolution in the vertical direction, c_conv, proceeds after the row convolution. This time the data is scanned along the vertical axis, so that once again two pixel values can be reused between invocations, and the data is then output along the vertical direction. Scheduling this graph yields: $\{Src, 260\{2\{A\}, 258\{A,C,Const\_r,r\_conv\}\}, 258\{2\{B\},258\{B,D,Const\_c,c\_conv\}\}, Snk\}$. This can be used to determine the buffer requirements between actors along with the necessary bandwidths using Eqn.(1). As shown in Fig. 4(d) the bandwidth to the large memories is reduced to the minimum value previously calculated (8.11 MB/s). This is at the expense of a 3B local buffer to store the data for reuse between convolution calculations.

It can be noted that exploiting all possible reuse in an algorithm can actually hinder the memory efficiency of implementations. In the previous graph B required an entire frame before it could fire. This is a result of moving vertically down the intermediate image so that only a single pixel is required for each new block. Since the r_conv actor fills the intermediate image in the horizontal direction, the last row will be needed before B can process the first column. If this level of data reuse is not exploited and B proceeds in the horizontal direction, it could simply consume a (3,1) token as soon as one is available (this occurs after two rows and one pixel have been produced by r_conv). On each subsequent firing of r_conv a single pixel will be produced and since B has stored the two previous rows, it can fire again, consuming a single pixel and producing a (3,1) token. This means only 517 pixels (two 258 pixel rows and one pixel) need to be stored between the 1-D convolutions. The maximum amount of memory reuse is not exploited in this case, but since the memory requirements have been reduced such that the intermediate memory easily fits on chip, the number of memory accesses has a lesser effect on power or performance than if it was located off-chip. This is shown in Fig. 5(a), where the first convolution takes the image and stores it with A_p producing a token each time it fires. The r_conv_p actor consumes three of these tokens, but reuses two each time (up to the edge). It produces one token (moving across the horizontal) with the B_p actor consuming 517 of these on the first firing and one additional token on each subsequent firing in the schedule. Actor c_conv_p consumes a single (3,1) token each firing, allowing a new value to be written into the memory, so the intermediate buffer only needs to be 517 B. This means that the c_conv_p actor will not take advantage of the data reuse; as a result, the number of memory accesses will not be reduced, but it easily fits on-chip into a fast memory as shown in Fig. 5(b).

The output of the first convolution is a single token, moving across in the horizontal direction, which was the same as the output of the A_p actor. This implies that the segmentation block can use this data directly, removing the need for an entire image to be stored between them (hence no A_s actor exists). The r_conv_s actor can use this token directly, combining three of them into a (3,1) token and consuming it, reusing two tokens each time up to the edge. The B_s actor also needs two rows plus a single pixel, so 513 tokens need to be stored (the rows are 256 pixels at this point). This produces a (3,1) token which is finally convolved in the c_conv_s actor with the output of a single token moving across the graph in the horizontal direction being passed to the fft_1 actor.

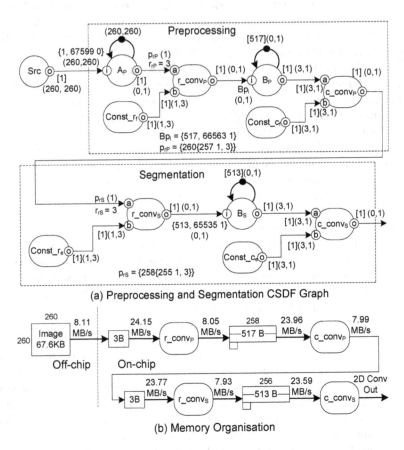

Fig. 5. Preprocessing and Segmentation Refined Model with Data Reuse

3.4   Feature Extraction Model Refinement

The FFT/IFFT cores operate on a single pixel at a time; they read in 256 pixels (over 256 cycles), process them for the next 256 cycles, and then write the results out for 256 cycles. The cores allow data to be written in while the core is processing and outputting data, so this is modelled using CSDF as shown in Fig.6(a). The memory sub-system for the feature extraction block can be examined, checking for any optimisations that could improve the memory utilisation. The memory architecture is outlined in Fig. 6(b). As the fft_2 actor requires an entire column of data, it has to wait until fft_1 has finished processing an image before beginning (after 66048 firings). This means that two entire 256x256 images (one real and one imaginary) will need to be stored between the fft_1 and fft_2

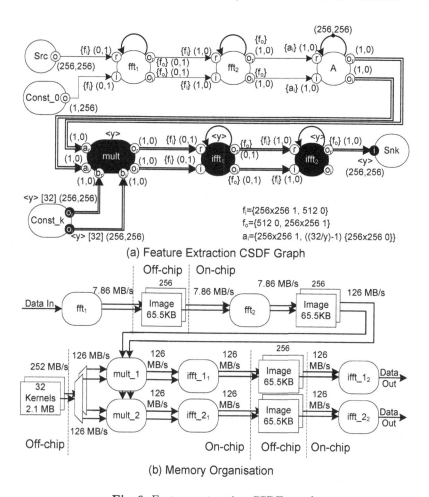

(a) Feature Extraction CSDF Graph

(b) Memory Organisation

Fig. 6. Feature extraction CSDF graph

actors (with the same for the IFFT). This will require a large, most likely off-chip memory, but as each pixel value will only need to be read once, there is little reason to try to introduce memory levels in this case. Calculating the memory bandwidth shows it is already at its minimum value as shown in Fig. 6(b).

Since the values from the FFT need to be multiplied by all 32 kernels, the A actor is used to store the data; it takes a complete image on the first execution, and then outputs the same image for the next $(32/y)$-1 firings (so for $y=2$ it reads in a new token every 16th firing). Looking at the memory organisation in Fig. 6(b), A translates into a memory to store the real and imaginary images; since this data is reused frequently, it is implemented in on-chip memory. The kernel values are stored off-chip and require 252MB/s on both the real and imaginary interfaces to process data in real-time with the bandwidth to each multiplier being 126 MB/s. The two IFFTs will also need an off-chip memory, so the total off-chip bandwidth can be calculated by summing the individual bandwidths, giving 1024 MB/s, which is possible with modern FPGAs.

4 Conclusion

Combining the above DFGs, gives a high-level description of the core functionality of the template matching algorithm and refining the graph from a purely algorithmic description into a implementation specific form has allowed the memory reuse inherent in the algorithm to be exploited, memory hierarchies to be introduced, and the size of the memory buffers required to be reduced. By modifying the graph to incorporate implementation specific characteristics, such as the platform being targeted and the cores being used, more optimal memory subsystems can be derived, and exploration of these systems allows the best memory architecture to be determined earlier in the design cycle, easing modification.

References

1. Bhattacharyya, S.S.: Hardware/Software Co-Synthesis of DSP Systems. In: Hu., Y.H. (ed.) Programmable Digital Signal Processors: Architecture, Programming, and Applications, pp. 333–378 (2002)
2. Ha, S., et al.: Hardware-Software Codesign of Multimedia Embedded Systems: the PeaCE Approach. In: 12th IEEE International Conference on Embedded and Real-Time Computing Systems and Applications. IEEE Comput. Soc., Sydney (2006)
3. Thompson, M., et al.: A Framework for Rapid System-level Exploration, Synthesis, and Programming of Multimedia MP-SoCs. In: Proc. of the 5th IEEE/ACM/IFIP International Conference on HW/SW Codesign of System Synthesis, Aus. (2007)
4. McAllister, J., Woods, R., Fischaber, S., Malins, E.: Rapid Implementation and Optimisation of DSP Systems on FPGA-Centric Heterogeneous Platforms. Journal of System Architecture 53(8), 511–523 (2007)
5. Wolf, W.: High Performance Embeddded Computing: Architectures, Applications, and Methodologies. Morgan Kaufmann, San Francisco (2006)
6. Al-Hashimi, B.: System-on-Chip: Next Generation Electronics. IET, London (2006)
7. Fischaber, S., McAllister, J., Woods, R., Malins, E.: Muir Hardware Synthesis for Multimedia Applications. IEEE/ACM/IFIP ESTIMedia, pp. 101–106 (2006)
8. Fischaber, S., Woods, R., McAllister, J.: SoC Memory Hierarchy Derivation from Dataflow Graphs. In: SIPS 2007, Shanghai, China (2007)
9. Smith, S.W.: The Scientist and Engineer's Guide to Digital Signal Processing. California Tecnical Pub., San Diego (1997)
10. Bilsend, G., et al.: Cyclo-Static Data Flow. In: International Conference on Acoustics, Speech, and Signal Processing, vol. 5, pp. 3255-3258 (1995)
11. McAllister, J., Woods, R., Walke, R., Reilly, D.: Multidimensional DSP Core Synthesis for FPGA. Journal of VLSI Signal Processing Systems for Signal, Image, and Video Technology 43(2), 207–221 (2006)
12. Denolf, K., et al.: Exploiting the Expressiveness of Cyclo-Static Dataflow to Model Multimedia Implementations. EURASIP Journal on Advances in Signal Processing (2007)

Introduction to Programming Multicores

Chris Jesshope*

Institute for Informatics
University of Amsterdam
jesshope@science.uva.nl

Already our technology is able to accommodate hundreds of cores on a single chip. The embedded market is already embracing this but the wider market is back-peddling. There is no doubt however that these markets will converge and that the processor will become the new building block of our chips and systems. The big problem problem however, will be in turning this technology into large complex systems. There are no lack of contenders for concurrent programming languages but the problem with most paradigms is that they mix algorithmic and concurrency engineering and do little to promote safe and composable parallel programs. The question that must be asked is whether there are programming models or combinations of models that are ubiquitous enough to form the basis for a co-ordinated solution to the problems of programming MPSOC. This special session has succeeded in bringing bringing together a number of key researchers working in the area of programming models for the next generation of complex systems based on multi- and many-core chips. Collectively they are developing models, languages and compilers to enable a paradigm shift in this important area. The scope of the contributions will cover deterministic approaches, such as functional languages and data-parallel languages as well as extracting concurrency from sequential code. In addition, a number of new co-ordination languages will be presented that range from static to dynamic mapping of components to resources. These are challenging problems but we are pleased to present some significant progress from invited and contributed papers in this session.

---

* Special Session Chair.

M. Berekovic, N. Dimopoulos, and S. Wong (Eds.): SAMOS 2008, LNCS 5114, p. 207, 2008.

Design Issues in Parallel Array Languages for Shared Memory*

James Brodman[1], Basilio B. Fraguela[2], María J. Garzarán[1], and David Padua[1]

[1] University of Illinois at Urbana-Champaign, Dept. of Computer Science
201 N. Goodwin Ave, Urbana, IL 61801 USA
{brodman2,garzaran,padua}@uiuc.edu
[2] Universidade da Coruña, Dept. de Electrónica y Sistemas
Campus de Elviña, s/n. 15071 A Coruña. Spain
basilio@udc.es

Abstract. The Hierarchically Tiled Array (HTA) is a data type that facilitates the definition and manipulation of arrays partitioned into tiles. The data type allows to exploit those tiles to attain both locality and parallelism. Parallel programs written with HTAs are based in data parallelism, and provide the programmer with a single-threaded view of the execution. In our experience, HTAs help to develop parallel codes in a much more productive way than other parallel programming approaches. While we have worked extensively with HTAs in distributed memory environments, only recently have we began to consider their adaption to shared memory environments such as those found in multicore systems. In this paper we review the design issues, opportunities and challenges that this migration raises.

Keywords: parallel programming, data parallelism, tiling, shared memory.

1 Introduction

Arrays are one of the most basic and useful data structures. The parallelism in the operations on their components, expressed as array operations and functions, has been exploited successfully since the days of the early array and vector processors [1]. The efforts to express the data parallelism in array operations have been often implemented as new languages or language extensions. The historical experience in the attempts to implant new languages with a focus on parallelism, coupled with the large base of existing legacy codes, makes us think that macros, and more in general, libraries, are a better vehicle to bring parallelism to mainstream computing. The advent of object oriented (OO) programming further supports our observation, as it enables to associate methods or tasks with sets

---

* This material is based upon work supported by the National Science Foundation under Awards CCF 0702260 and CNS 0509432. Basilio B. Fraguela was partially supported by the Ministry of Education and Science of Spain, FEDER funds of the European Union (Projects TIN2004-07797-C02-02 and TIN2007-67537-C03-02).

M. Berekovic, N. Dimopoulos, and S. Wong (Eds.): SAMOS 2008, LNCS 5114, pp. 208–217, 2008.

of data. In OO languages arrays can contain objects of any kind, and the operations on them need not be restricted to be the traditional simple mathematical operations as was the case for SIMD implementations. Rather, arbitrary tasks encapsulated as methods can be performed in parallel on the elements of the array. Integration of libraries and classes that express parallelism in OO languages is further facilitated by their polymorphic features and operator overloading, when available.

Tiling [2] is closely related to array processing. Tiles are used both to increase the locality of the accesses in sequential programs [3] and to describe data parallelism [4,5,6,7]. This led us to the development of the *Hierarchically Tiled Array* (HTA) data type [8]. HTAs represent arrays partitioned into tiles which can be further partitioned recursively. When parallelism is expressed using HTAs, programs have a single logical thread of execution. They express parallelism as array operations on HTAs, with the operations on the different tiles of an HTA taking place in parallel. This gives structure to parallel operations, which improves readability and maintainability over the SPMD (Single Program Multiple Data) approaches. The tiling allows to choose the granularity of the tasks with different purposes. For example, the number of tasks can be chosen so that the local working set fits in the memory of a node in a distributed memory environment. The tiles in an HTA can be recursively subtiled in order to subdivide the work to perform so that the data to process at each time fits in a given level of the memory hierarchy of the machine.

We have experimented with this data type for a number of years now [8,9] using both typical parallel benchmarks such as NAS [10] and serial codes that benefit from tiling. Our experience is that HTAs allow to write these codes in a much more productive way than traditional approaches while achieving good performance. Still, we have always worked on distributed memory environments, and it is for them that we have defined the semantics of our data type. Given the growing importance of multicore systems, and the conviction that most HPC systems in the future will have a hybrid memory model, the moment to define the HTA implementation options and semantics for these environments and build an HTA library for hybrid memory models has arrived.

The rest of this paper is organized as follows. Section 2 is a brief introduction to the HTA data type. Section 3 reviews the design issues that an HTA implementation for shared memory systems poses. Finally, we present our conclusions in Section 4.

2   The Hierarchical Tiled Array

The Hierarchically Tiled Array (HTA) [8] is an array data type which can be partitioned into tiles. Each tile can be either a conventional array or a lower level HTA. Tiles in an HTA can conceptually be mapped on to different levels of the memory hierarchy. At the top-most level, tiles can represent portions of the array that map to different nodes in a cluster. Each of those tiles could then carry additional levels of tiling that then map to the various levels of cache

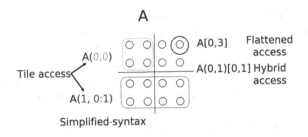

Fig. 1. HTA Indexing, () are used to index tiles, [] to index scalars

in a machine. One could then further partition the tiles to map the individual scalars to registers. Programmers see a single-threaded view of execution in HTA programs. Parallelism takes the form of concurrent operations across tiles. The tile size thus provides the granularity of parallel execution.

Figure 1 illustrates the three ways in which HTAs may be indexed. One can index HTAs at both the tile and scalar level and combine both indexing schemes. One can flatten the tiling structure to directly access the scalar elements of HTAs. A hybrid approach can also be used when the programmer wants to access one or more scalars found in one or more tiles. In the example, A(0,0) indexes the first tile in the first row. Likewise, A(1,0:1) indexes the entire second row of tiles. A[0,3] indexes the last scalar on the first row using the flattened notation. The same scalar can be indexed as A(0,1)[0,1] using the hybrid scheme.

HTAs support the three main constructs found in data-parallel computations:

- *Element-by-element operation*: A function is applied to each element of an array or corresponding elements of two or more conformable arrays.
- *Reductions*: These apply operations on an array to produce an array of lesser rank. For example, computing the sum of the elements of a one-dimensional array produces a scalar.
- *Scan*: A function computes a prefix operation across all the elements of an array.

These operations take the form of three methods in the HTA library: hmap (which implements element-by-element operations), reduce, and scan. The three constructs receive at least one argument, a function object that encapsulates the operation to be performed. In the case of hmap, the function may accept additional HTAs as parameters that must have the same tiling structure as the HTA instance on which the hmap is invoked. This effectively allows programmers to extend the library with new user-defined operations. A simple example of hmap can be seen in Figure 2. Here, two HTAs, X and Y, with ten tiles of ten elements are created. Function F is applied on them by hmap. In it, each tile in X assigns its elements the sum of their current values plus the values in the corresponding tiles of Y plus one, in parallel. HTAs overload the arithmetic operators (+,*,...) and also assignment so that these typical element-by-element operations can be expressed in a traditional array syntax instead of requiring the usage of hmap.

```
1  HTA X([10], [10])
2  HTA Y([10], [10])
3
4  ...
5
6  hmap(F(), X, Y)
7
8  F(HTA X, HTA Y) {
9    do i=1,10
10     X[i] = X[i] + Y[i] + 1
11 }
```

Fig. 2. hmap Example

Operations typical of array languages such as matrix multiplication, transposition, or stencil computations are also found in the library. All parallelism is explicit and takes the form of independent operations performed on tiles. Synchronization required by operations such as reductions is implicit and handled by the library.

The tiling structure of an HTA is normally specified at creation time. However, some problems are more naturally expressed in a dynamic or input-dependent fashion. The dynamic partitioning [9] feature enables the modification of the structure of an HTA after its creation by adding or removing partition lines, the abstract lines that separate the tiles in an HTA.

3 Design Issues for Multicore and Shared Memory Systems

As mentioned before, we have an implementation supporting HTAs that runs on distributed memory systems. An HTA program appears to the programmer as having a single thread of execution. Arrays are partitioned and distributed across a set of nodes and non-HTA data such as scalars and non-HTA arrays are replicated on all the nodes. When operating on an HTA each node works on its portion of the HTA. However, when operating on non-HTA data, our implementation uses the SPMD mode, and all the nodes execute the same code on its local copy of the non-HTA data. Synchronization is achieved implicitly, by the underlying send and receive messages used to communicate between the nodes.

When running an HTA program in a shared memory environment the situation changes quite a bit, and a wide space of design options can be explored, each of them resulting on different performance/productivity trade-offs. In this Section we discuss some of the issues that appear in this shared memory environment.

3.1 Dynamic Task Creation

In many parallel programs tasks can be identified before execution begins. In terms of HTAs, this means that HTAs can be created with a given partitioning suitable for the algorithm that is being parallelized and that this partitioning does not need to be modified later. In the HTA library, the parallel tasks are determined by the tiles. In distributed memory systems, the parallelism is also determined by the distribution of tiles to processors. In these systems, dynamic task creation or, in other words, repartitioning of an HTA, involves an expensive redistribution of the data. For this reason, we did not implement dynamic partitioning in our distributed memory implementation. Instead, we leave programmers to solve the problem.

In shared memory systems, however, the ability to create tasks dynamically, that is, to define and spawn parallel subtasks from a parallel task, can be useful and even necessary to obtain good performance. Dynamic task creation is good for two reasons: it allows programmers to more elegantly write their algorithms and can be used to improve load balance.

In HTA programs, tasks are created by hmap. hmap can be implemented by a parallel loop where each iteration corresponds to a tile. If the parallel loops are implemented using Intel's Threading Building Blocks [11], each processor is assigned a range of iterations and idle processors can steal part of the range of another processor, splitting one task into two. Dynamic task creation by the library, rather than by the program, could help improve load balance. These issues will be further discussed in Section 3.2.

Task creation can also be hierarchical as illustrated by the example in Figure 3, parallel merging of two sorted sequences (input1 and input2), where the partitioning is dependent on the input to be merged. A rough sketch of the algorithm states that one first splits the first input HTA in half. Next, the location of the first element greater than the midpoint element of the first input HTA is found in the second HTA and used to partition it. The output is partitioned such that its new tiles can fit the merged elements from the respective tiles of the input arrays. Finally, hmap recursively calls the Merge operation on the newly created left tiles of the two input arrays as well as the right tiles. Here, the Merge operation creates a tree of tasks during the course of its recursion.

Note that in this example, dynamic partitioning enables the implementation of merge in this elegant manner. In this case, dynamic task creation for both algorithmic elegance and load balancing can be combined. The programmer could change the number of partitions created in each invocation of Merge to improve load balance.

```
1  Merge(HTA output, HTA input1, HTA input2) {
2  ...
3     if (output.size() < THRESHOLD) {
4        SerialMerge(output, input1, input2)
5     }
6     else {
7        i = input1.size() / 2
8        input1.addPartition(i)
9
10       j = h2. location_first_gt (input1[i])
11       input2.addPartition(j)
12
13       k = i + j
14       output.addPartition(k)
15
16       output.hmap(Merge(), input1, input2)
17    }
18 ...
19 }
```

Fig. 3. Parallel Merge

3.2 Locality vs. Load Balancing

Conventional notation for task parallelism does not provide a convenient mechanism to express locality [12,13]. However, locality is very important to achieve good performance in multicore systems due to the existence of a hierarchy of private and shared caches, coupled with shared buses to memory systems which are much slower than the processors they feed. With HTAs we solved this problem in a very natural way for distributed systems. However, in shared memory, extensions are needed to achieve locality.

In shared memory we could promote locality by assigning tiles to processors when HTAs are created and maintaining this assignment throughout the program. This is similar to the way HTAs operate in distributed memory systems. However, the affinity between processors and tiles provided by this assignment would hinder load balancing.

To solve the problem of load imbalance a more dynamic strategy is necessary, and that could be to use task stealing. Task stealing provides a mechanism for dynamic task scheduling. With task stealing a processor places tasks into its own queue upon creation. Task queues could be implemented using parallel programming libraries like Intel's Threading Building Blocks [11] or written independently. Idle processors can then steal tasks and their associated tiles from the queue for execution. Task stealing has different implications for affinity depending on whether the parallelism resembles loops or whether it is hierarchical. The former case refers to common mathematical operations and hmaps. Here, in order to achieve locality, parallel operations performed on the same HTA should respect any prior affinity between processors and tiles, that is, execute operations on a given tile on the same processor that used it before. Task stealing should follow this approach when possible. However, task stealing can choose to change the affinity between tiles and processors when a load imbalance exists, trading better utilization for negative effects on locality.

The case of hierarchical task parallelism is shown in the Parallel Merge example in Figure 3. Here, the Merge function performs an operation on the input before partitioning. The new subtasks created by the subsequent invocation to hmap would ideally be placed in the queue of the processor that created the tasks because the data are in its cache. However, task stealing any of these dynamically created tasks can be necessary to balance the load, what would change the affinity of the tiles to processors. Care must be taken to properly address the consequences of affinity in our design.

In addition to the concerns about locality, load balancing could also have consequences on the correctness of HTA programs. Dynamic partitioning, as mentioned in the previous section, provides another alternative to load balancing in HTAs. When load imbalance is detected, a run-time element of the library could decide to dynamically split the tiles in an operation, creating additional tasks with smaller granularity. For that, the library would have to provide a new hmap or the programmer would have to annotate the operation passed to hmap to inform the library that such splitting is legal, that is, that the parallel operation defined would be legal if the size or shape of the tiles changed. The library could choose from several partitioning strategies such as split on the largest dimension, split on the smallest dimension, quarter, etc. The library would also need to know if it is safe to permanently alter the tiling structure of an HTA or if the original tiling structure must be restored at the end of the parallel operation.

Dynamic scheduling of tasks in the distributed memory implementation of HTA was not feasible. Consequently, it was up to the programmer to distribute tasks to processors in such a way as to distribute the load as evenly as possible. However, the lack of communication involved in dynamically moving tasks in order to improve load balance in shared memory has led us to explore this option for our implementation on these systems. We must handle affinity in a proper fashion whether our parallelism comes from hmap or from hierarchical dynamic task creation. We must also ensure that if the library is allowed to dynamically create tasks to improve that load balance that it does so in a correct manner.

3.3   Execution Models

In choosing the execution model for our shared memory implementation, we have two choices:

- *Master Thread*: A single master thread executes all serial portions of the program, and creates tasks for worker threads to run in the parallel portions. There is a single copy of shared non-HTA data.
- *Thread Private (SPMD)*: Every processor executes the whole program. However, each processor only executes operations on its own data during parallel operations. Shared data is replicated across all processors.

Different programming environments have chosen different answers to this problem, e.g., UPC [6] follows the SPMD model and OpenMP [13] follows the master thread model.

The master thread approach is conceptually the simpler of the two. One processor executes the sequential portions of the code and only one copy of shared data exists. When a parallel operation occurs, the master thread spawns tasks that the other processors execute. This approach requires synchronization at the beginning and the end of the parallel operations. One can imagine a parallel operation in this model as a parallel loop that iterates over all the tiles in an HTA, applying the operation to each tile. The loop itself would be executed only by the master thread, with the execution of the parallel body being assigned to different threads for different iterations. In the SPMD model each processor would execute all iterations of the loop, but the operations on each tile would be executed by only one processor. Another difference between the SMPD and the master thread approaches is that SPMD has a larger footprint due to the replication of the non HTA data. In either approach, threads do not explicitly communicate. Threads correspond to independent operations on tiles and no synchronization by the programmer is needed.

Figure 4 helps illustrate the differences between both models. In function B, we assign each tile the values of the previous tile. Using the master thread

```
                                          7   C() {
                                          8     do i = 1,10
                                          9       A[i] = i;
                                         10     hmap(F, H, A)
 1   int A[10]                            11   }
 2                                        12
 3   B() {                               13   F(HTA H, int[] A) {
 4     do i = 1,10                       14     do i=1,10
 5       H(i) = H(i−1)                    15       H[i] = H[i] + A[i]
 6   }                                    16   }
```

Fig. 4. Examples

approach, this occurs serially on only one processor. However, using SMPD, this loop will run in parallel, although the dependences will result in a serialization of the code. The reason is that processor that owns tile i has to wait for a signal from the processor that owns tile i-1 in order to perform its assignment. In shared memory, rather than using the *owner-computes* rule, SPMD can follow the more relaxed *Single Computation* rule. When an access to a tile of an HTA occurs, it is only performed once. Such an access could be handled by a single processor or even by multiple processors working on different sections if the tile is dynamically partitioned.

The handling of the shared data on these two execution models has implications on data locality. Remember that non-HTA data is shared in the master thread approach and replicated (and as result thread-private) in the SPMD model. For example, Function C in Figure 4 illustrates a shortcoming of the master thread approach. The master thread computes the values in array A, so when the processors perform function F on each tile of H, the non-HTA data, array A, is only in the cache of the processor that executed the serial portion of the code. However, in the SPMD model, array A is replicated across all processors. Thus, each processor assigns its own copy of the array A. This ensures non-HTA data will be in every processor's cache when hmap performs the parallel operation. Ultimately, performance should dictate which model we choose. We have not yet performed experiments to determine which model will provide better performance.

Finally, notice that under both execution models modifications of non-HTA data within hmap functions should not be allowed. The reason is that hmap is fully parallel. Thus, under the master thread model, synchronization would be necessary for correctness and this will result in hmap not being fully parallel. Under the SPMD model, such accesses will be a programming error, as different results could be obtained in different processors. Ideally, the library should disallow such accesses, but the languages in which the HTA library can be implemented do not provide the necessary mechanisms.

3.4   Reference/Value Semantics

In our distributed memory implementation, assigning an HTA to another that is distributed in a different way implicated data copying. The copy could be immediate or delayed using a lazy implementation, but the semantics was always that of a copy by value. In shared memory we can choose between copies

```
1  X = ...
2  hmap(... , X)
3  Z = X
4  X = ...
5  hmap(... , X)
```

Fig. 5. Copy Example

by value or by reference, also called deep and shallow copies, respectively. For example, a shared memory implementation could use a copy by reference model implemented through a copy-on-write strategy where a shallow copy that only copies the pointers is used until a write occurs, at which point a deep copy of all the data must occur. However, copy by reference introduces additional overhead into the library as proper reference counts must be kept to ensure that memory is de-allocated at the appropriate time. In addition, this scheme can potentially affect the affinity between tiles and processors as is illustrated by Figure 5. In this example, HTA X is initially assigned some values and then an operation is performed on it using hmap. Next, another HTA, Z, copies X. X is then changed again and another parallel operation occurs. Under the copy by value scheme, Z would be a new copy of X. When X is changed and then used by a computation, the tiles of X could still be in the caches of the processors that operated on them in the first hmap. However, under copy by reference, the second write to X would cause X to be the new copy, with Z continuing to point to the original data. The second hmap could then find that the tiles of X have changed affinity if the copy is not careful to preserve it. Intuitively, the easier implementation and lesser bookkeeping of copy by value leads us to believe that this is, on average, the faster strategy since one does not usually copy HTAs without modifying them afterwards. However, this conjecture would need to be experimentally validated.

3.5   New HTA Notations/Constructs

The greater flexibility of access to data by different threads in shared memory environments probably leads to programs with more complex patterns than those we have seen in distributed memory environments. As a result, it could be convenient to extend HTAs with notations to express these structures. For example, new ways to express task dependences, new operators (possibly domain-specific), etc. A very important question is whether these extensions would fit naturally in the clean semantics and array notation that characterize HTAs.

4   Conclusions

In this paper we have reviewed the different design issues that appear when considering a shared memory implementation for the HTA, a data type that allows to express data parallelism as well as locality. These issues can influence the performance and programming flexibility attained with the HTA. We are currently examining the trade-offs of the different options, considering several potential implementations. Our priorities are, in this order, to provide clear semantics to the programmer, to provide a notation as systematic as possible that enables most if not all HTA programs to run correctly in every kind of system, and finally to facilitate the effective parallelization of as many programs as possible using our class. In this process we should also consider their implications in hybrid memory systems.

References

1. Barnes, G.H., Brown, R.M., Kato, M., Kuck, D., Slotnick, D., Stokes, R.: The ILLIAC IV Computer. IEEE Transactions on Computers 8(17), 746–757 (1968)
2. McKellar, A.C., Coffman, J.E.G.: Organizing Matrices and Matrix Operations for Paged Memory Systems. Communications of the ACM 12(3), 153–165 (1969)
3. Wolf, M.E., Lam, M.S.: A Data Locality Optimizing Algorithm. In: Proc. of the Conf. on Programming Language Design and Implementation, pp. 30–44 (1991)
4. High Performance Fortran Forum. High Performance Fortran Specification Version 2.0 (January 1997)
5. Chamberlain, B., Choi, S.: The Case for High Level Parallel Programming in ZPL. IEEE Computational Science and Engineering 5(3), 76–86 (1998)
6. Carlson, W., Draper, J., Culler, D., Yelick, K., Brooks, E., Warren, K.: Introduction to UPC and Language Specification. Technical Report CCS-TR-99-157, IDA Center for Computing Sciences (1999)
7. Numrich, R.W., Reid, J.: Co-array Fortran for Parallel Programming. SIGPLAN Fortran Forum 17(2), 1–31 (1998)
8. Bikshandi, G., Guo, J., Hoeflinger, D., Almasi, G., Fraguela, B.B., Garzarán, M.J., Padua, D., von Praun, C.: Programming for Parallelism and Locality with Hierarchically Tiled Arrays. In: PPoPP 2006: Proc. of the ACM SIGPLAN Symp. on Principles and Practice of Parallel Programming, pp. 48–57 (March 2006)
9. Guo, J., Bikshandi, G., Fraguela, B.B., Garzarán, M.J., Padua, D.: Programming with Tiles. In: PPoPP 2008: Proc. of the ACM SIGPLAN Symp. on Principles and Practice of Parallel Programming, pp. 111–122 (February 2008)
10. NAS Parallel Benchmarks, http://www.nas.nasa.gov/Software/NPB/
11. Reinders, J.: Intel Threading Building Blocks: Outfitting C++ for Multi-core Processor Parallelism, 1st edn. O'Reilly, Sebastopol (July 2007)
12. Butenhof, D.R.: Programming with POSIX Threads. Addison Wesley, Reading (1997)
13. Chandra, R., Dagum, L., Kohr, D., Maydan, D., McDonald, J., Menon, R.: Parallel programming in OpenMP. Morgan Kaufmann Publishers, San Francisco (2001)

An Architecture and Protocol for the Management of Resources in Ubiquitous and Heterogeneous Systems Based on the SVP Model of Concurrency

Chris Jesshope[1], Jean-Marc Philippe[2], and Michiel van Tol[1]

[1] University of Amsterdam, Institute for Informatics
Kruislaan 403, Amsterdam 1098 SJ, Netherlands
[2] CEA, LIST, Boîte Courrier 94, Gif-sur-Yvette, F-91191, France
{jesshope,mwvantol}@science.uva.nl,jean-marc.philippe@cea.fr

Abstract. This paper proposes a novel hierarchical architecture and resource-management protocol for the delegation of work within a ubiquitous and heterogeneous environment. The protocol is based on serving an SVP place, where a component of work is delegated together with the responsibility for meeting any non-functional computational requirements such as deadline or throughput constraints. The protocol is based on a market where SANE processors bid for jobs to execute and selection is based on a cost model that reflects the energy required to meet the jobs requirements.

Keywords: concurrency models, heterogeneous systems, resource management, market models, ubiquitous systems.

1 Introduction

As CMOS nodes continue to shrink, the complexity of embedded systems grows. This progress enables the manufacturing of low-power and low-cost consumer electronic devices able to communicate through wired or wireless technologies. Embedding computing power in everyday consumer products leads to the possibility of having systems comprising networks of thousands of nodes near each user. This will provide everyone with the possibility of processing data any where and at any time, moving people into the pervasive computing era [1].

The design of such systems requires a dramatic shift at every level of the system as neither software nor hardware platforms are ready to face the issues raised by this exciting new research challenge. These ubiquitous systems may comprise a huge number of heterogeneous computing elements and will evolve around the users following their needs and habits. Thus, their optimisation will be highly dependant on their computing environment. Taking advantage of the huge computing power offered by this collaboration of elements will require the dynamic management of concurrency under conditions where computing elements may appear and disappear at will. This is a significant challenge.

M. Berekovic, N. Dimopoulos, and S. Wong (Eds.): SAMOS 2008, LNCS 5114, pp. 218–228, 2008.

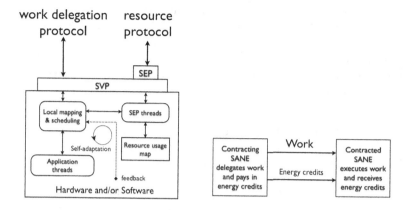

Fig. 1. Generic SANE (may be a collection of SANEs) responds to two protocols: one to perform work as families of threads the other to serve resources to external threads. The latter uses negotiation between SANES based on energy credits.

To solve these issues, a disruptive approach is being promoted in the ÆTHER European project, which embeds self-adaptivity at each level of the system[1], giving autonomy to the components and enabling the application designer to concentrate on the application instead of having to cope with all possible events in the lifetime of a computing resource in such a rapidly evolving environment. For this purpose, we have introduced the SANE concept (Self-Adaptive Networked Entity). This views the system as a collection of self-adaptive elements (software, hardware or both) that can observe their environment and their internal performance so as to autonomously modify their behaviour and improve some aspect of the overall system (e.g. performance, power used, etc.). These elements collaborate with each other and share information and resources in order to provide a global optimisation based on local and autonomous behaviour. This approach requires a new architecture and protocols to enable the dynamic sharing of resources and the consequent management of concurrency.

The mechanism that enables this distributed sharing of resources is the delegation of responsibility for the execution of units of work, where that responsibility includes meeting any performance constraints specified. We consider here a hierarchical cluster-based architecture, where each cluster presents a uniform interface to its environment defining it as a SANE processor (or cluster of SANEs). To be a SANE it must support the SVP model (SANE Virtual Processor) [2], see Figure 1. This paper describes the resource management protocol that enables delegation of work. SANEs are autonomous and from time to time may be given jobs to execute; a local user may submit a job or one may be delegated from its environment. In the latter case, the SANE will have contracted with an external thread to run that job and to meet certain expectations in its execution, for example performance. The contract is negotiated using a credit exchange, where

---

[1] More details can be found on the projects web site: http://www.aether-ist.org/

the cost of executing a job is initially assumed to be the energy expended by the contracted SANE. This can be measured in Joules. The contracting thread, which may be acting on behalf of another SANE, transfers credit for the agreed amount of energy to execute the work on the contracted SANE. In response, the contracted SANE agrees to meet the deadlines or performance constraints imposed by the contracting SANE.

2   The SVP Model and Its Resources

SVP is a dynamic concurrency model that defines a number of actions to enable the execution and control of families of identical blocking threads. It is a hier-archical model and any SVP thread may create subordinate families of threads. The family (and its subordinate families) is the unit of work that is delegated in a SANE system. Implementations of the SVP model have been demonstrated and evaluated in software [3], based on the $p$thread library and in hardware [4], based on instructions added to the ISA of a many-core processor. The SVP model is captured by the five actions listed below and their implementation will define the underlying protocol supporting the interfaces defined in Figure 1.

1. *create* - creates a family of indexed threads at a place with parameters $\{start, step, limit\}$ defining the index sequence. It is based on one thread definition and returns a family identifier that uniquely identifies that family for asynchronous control of its execution.
2. *sync* - blocks until the specified family of threads and all of their writes to memory have completed. It returns an exit code that identifies how the family terminated; in the case of break, it also returns a value from the breaking thread and in the case of squeeze, it returns a family index value.
3. *break* - only one thread in a family can succeed in executing a break, which terminates its family and all subordinate families. It returns a break value of a type specified by the thread definition to the family's sync action.
4. *kill* - asynchronously terminates a specified family of threads and all its subordinate families.
5. *squeeze* - asynchronously terminates a specified family of threads and any user-specified subordinate families so that it can be restarted at the squeeze point, which is returned via each squeezed family's sync action.

SVP has two essential roles. At the hardware level, it captures locality and regularity, which are key factors in mapping a computation to a set of resources, whatever those resources are. In the most efficient implementations, SVP threads will map onto wires or synchronisers to support blocking and hence support the scheduling of threads, instruction by instruction. Constraints in the model force compilers to analyse code and transform code to support the model's locality. This is important in managing the asynchrony and locality that will be required in future silicon systems. The model expresses this by restricting the commu-nication between threads. The first child thread created may synchronise only with the parent thread and other created threads their predecessor thread in the

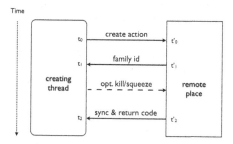

Fig. 2. Illustrates the SVP protocol between a thread and a place

family. Thus the model, rather than the program, exposes this to the compiler allowing it to statically map a computation onto hardware. Examples are compiling the language μTC to a multi-core ISA [5] or mapping and routing a family of SVP threads to FPGA hardware. Using novel self-adaptation techniques, these SVP hardware threads may be dynamically optimised using online-routing [6]. In all cases, the implementation will be captured as one or more binary modules that force locality in communication.

SVP's second role captures the dynamic distribution of work between different implementations of the SVP model. This is achieved by binding an abstract resource to a unit of work on the creation of a family of threads. That resource abstraction is the SVP *place* which is provided dynamically by a place server. An implementation of place provides a network address and a token for authentication when creating work there. For example, when a place is served, the address is used to implement the protocol, in whatever network setting the SANE exists. More importantly, to avoid unauthorised use of a place, the place server gives both the place and the thread requesting it a token, which must be matched during the SVP create protocol. Figure 2 illustrates the events in this protocol. It should be noted that the create action in this role is a form of a remote procedure call.

The use of place as an abstraction allows the dynamic binding of resources to code when creating a family of threads. The place also identifies a contract between two SANEs when delegating work, as illustrated in Figure 1, and hence it identifies a set of resources or virtual resources on which the work will be executed. This may be a partition of a multi-core chip, it may be a domain in an FPGA chip that is dynamically configured to execute the family of threads or it may even be a processor or cluster of processors in a Grid. Each will have its own implementation of the SVP actions and tools to compile μTC into that implementation. To achieve this abstraction, every implementation of SVP must deal with two pre-defined places and variables of type place:

– The *local* place is used to tell the SVP implementation that all threads in this family should be kept local to the creating thread, which may have different interpretations in different implementations.

- The *default* place is resource naive and the actual place will be determined by the mapping and scheduling algorithms of a SANE's implementation.
- A place variable has a meaning dependent on the specific implementation of SVP. It is set by a place server and used as a parameter of the create action.

The place concept is a heavily overloaded: it identifies a contract between a thread and a SANE, which will specify a level of service; it also embeds an address and a security key, which are used in the implementation of the create action to delegate the work. Once a SANE receives some delegated work, locally that work becomes resource naive and will be mapped and scheduled by the local mapping and scheduling threads (see Figure 1). These threads use the place to identify the contract negotiated and hence locate the specific constraints on execution agreed to. They must then organise the work to meet the constraints on the contract.

3   Resource Negotiation in SVP

A goal in designing SVP was to give a concurrency model that is as ubiquitous in its application as the sequential model. The two roles of SVP described above reflect a separation of concerns between algorithm design and concurrency engineering. Resource-naive code (using creates with the default place), like the sequential model, has properties of determinism and deadlock freedom under composition. An SVP implementation is therefore free to map and schedule threads as it likes. However, introducing specific places enables concurrency engineering and the model becomes quite general. The key element here is the introduction of mutually a exclusive place that sequentialises all work delegated to it. In implementing resource management we must also manage broadcast and deadlock induced in the model by resource failure. All of these issues are discussed below before the resource server protocol is presented.

Mutual exclusion in SVP. Non-deterministic choice is required to manage exclusivity of resource use in a distributed environment. The place server must offer its service to a number of client threads that all compete for the available resources. This and hence general concurrency engineering in SVP is implemented by providing mutually exclusive places. The processor resource rather than a memory lock is deemed more appropriate for ubiquitous concurrency and also allows a completely asynchronous memory model. A mutually exclusive place sequentialises concurrent requests to create a family of threads. As places abstract resources, this is just another overloading of the concept of place that can be mapped to its implementation. For example, in the *p*thread implementation of SVP [3], a mutually exclusive place simply uses a mutex. In the ISA version of SVP [4], mutual exclusion in a single processor is implemented by class bits in the place variable and corresponding state in the processor. The state indicates whether an exclusive family of that class is currently executing and hence sequentialises create actions in any of the classes. The resource management protocol is called the SEP (the *S*ystem *E*nvironment *P*lace), which is the mutually exclusive place at which external threads create the resource management protocol's threads to request and obtain places for their exclusive use in the delegation of work.

Broadcast in SVP. Because SVP is a deterministic model, which does not include any communication primitives, broadcast in the model must be implemented as a create action to one of a number of known places. For example, if a SANE cluster comprised n SANEs, where each SANE provided an SEP interface at a place, which was stored in the array of places SEP_cluster[n], then the μTC code below would broadcast a request to each SEP interface in the cluster. N.b. the create parameters are: (family id; place; start; limit; step; block) followed by a thread definition. In this code, n threads in family fo are created locally, each of which creates an SEP_request at an SEP interface.

```
int n; place SEP_cluster[n]; family fo;
...
create(fo;local;0;n-1;1;){
   family fi; index i;
   create(fi;SEP_cluster[i];0;0;1;) SEP_request(...);
   sync(fi);
   }
sync(fo);
```

Graceful degradation in SVP. Now consider what happens to this code if one of the SANEs in the cluster suddenly drops out before completing the request. The code deadlocks, as one thread in family fo will wait forever for its sync and hence family fo will never complete. One solution to this, and in general for any situation that requires graceful degradation, is a time-out on the create action, which allows family fo to wait a finite time before it completes. This can be implemented using a time-out thread, which kills family fo after a given time.

4   Resource Management Protocol

The implementation of the resource negotiation protocol in a SANE environment, like the SVP protocol over which it is implemented, is dependent on a SANE's level in its hierarchy. The generic protocol must provide for the requirements of systems at many different levels, from chip to board level and at many levels in a network hierarchy. The protocol comprises five stages: announce, request, bid, agree, delegate. Specific implementations may omit stages that are implicit in the design at that level. For example, the first stage requires a SANE processor to announce its capabilities to the rest of the system. In an on-chip environment, the capability of each SANE processor may be known a-priori and this stage may be omitted. However, for a SANE processor at the board level attached to a network or coming into range of a wireless network, this stage would be mandatory.

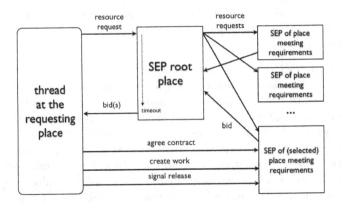

Fig. 3. Remainder of protocol, i.e. request, bid, agree and delegate, is undertaken when a thread requires resources to undertake a computation

Announce. In the first stage of the protocol, a SANE joining a cluster announces its capabilities using a common format for defining both resource capabilities and requirements. The protocol uses the concept of a *root SEP*, which is not necessarily a fixed place but a place variable via which all resource negotiation takes place. The root SEP and its possible implementations are described in more detail in Section 5. On joining a network, some low-level communication protocol will first be established and on top of that a protocol for implementing SVP. The latter will initialise the joining SANE with a place to initiate the SEP protocol; that place is the root SEP and is similar in concept to the router in a conventional network. The joining SANE announces its arrival by creating the SEP_announce thread at the root SEP. Only one parameter is required, which is a pointer to the record(s) defining its capabilities. Those capabilities are defined using a domained ID that defines a set of known functions on the network. The domained ID serves to identify the processing domain of the work (signal processing, image processing, etc.) and the particular function offered or required. The root SEP can filter any requests for resources by the capability requested and hence reduce the amount of communication required. It does not make sense, for example, to send a request based on image processing to a SANE that does not implement any image-processing algorithms. The capability is defined as a processing rate on this set of functions. Note that the domains may represent functions at various levels of granularity, i.e. from arithmetic operations to complex functions. This step is illustrated in the μTC code below. The SANE may also withdraw its capabilities from the pool using the SEP_withdraw thread. Of course it may also be withdrawn in a less graceful manner!

```
place root_SEP; family f_ann;
struct capability* my_capability;
...
create(f_ann;root_SEP;0;0;1;;) SEP_announce(my_capabilities);
```

Request. Having announced itself to its environment, a SANE may now make or receive requests for resources. These requests are again made to the root SEP, which will in turn forward the requests to any SANE in the environment that is capable of meeting the request. This is defined as a required performance on a given function but also includes an elapsed time for which the resources are required. A timeout is attached to each request, which is the validity of the invitation to tender from the contractor. The request (and subsequent bids) are identified by the family identifier of the thread created in making the request.

Bid. Each bid provides a yes/no response to the request and if yes, it will provide the overall cost for meeting the request, the time required to configure the resources, a lifetime (the provider will reserve these resources for this amount of time), the SEP to which agreement must be sent and a limit on the time the provider is able to provide resources, which may be less than or greater than the elapsed time requested. The use of energy as a cost measure allows the optimisation of the complete SANE system based on a (time, energy) couple. This step is illustrated below in μTC and illustrated in Figure 3.

```
place root_SEP; family req f;
struct resource* my_request; struct bid* my_bid, *good_bid;
...
create(req;root_SEP;0;0;1;;) SEP_request(my_request, my_bid);
```

Accept. When the requesting thread receives a list of bids, it will select one or more bids to meet its requirements and agree any required. In response, a provider will return a place that defines the contracted resources. The family identifier of the initial request for resources identifies the contract. This stage is equivalent to signing the contract and, in a full market system, will result in a credit transfer from the requesting SANE to the providing SANE.

```
place root_SEP work_place; family f_req, f;
struct bid* my_bid, good_bid;
...
create(f;good_bid*.place;0;0;1;;) SEP_agree(f_req,work_place);
```

Delegate. All that is left to do when the work_place has been returned is to create the delegated work at that place and to signal the release of that place when that work is complete.

```
place root_SEP work_place; family f_req, f;
struct bid* my_bid, *good_bid;
...
create(f; work_place;;;;;) my_work();
...
sync(f)
...
create(f;*good_bid.place;0;0;1;;) SEP_release(work_place);
```

5   The Root SEP

The root SEP is a conceptual place and admits many different implementations. It is first and foremost, the place to which a SANE announces itself and to which it directs requests for resources. It is assumed that directly or indirectly, all known SANEs in a cluster may be reached from this place. Two examples of its implementation are given below that illustrate the range of possibilities.

A unique root SANE. The root SANE is the physical root of the cluster and is given responsible for maintaining a complete picture of the capabilities of all SANEs that have announced themselves within the cluster. It also provides an interface to the next level of hierarchy, which is called the environment in this paper. In this case, the implementation is trivial, at initialisation this SANE provides any joining SANE with its root_SEP which is then used as a target for all announce and request threads. The only problem in this implementation is that it relies on the root SANE being fault tolerant, as it is a single point of failure in the entire system. Note that if a single root SEP becomes overloaded, its resources can easily be partitioned and allocated to two root SANEs known by two subsets of SANEs.

Every SANE is the root SEP. Here, every SANE in the cluster receives announcements from all SANEs joining the cluster. In this case, on initialisation, each SANE must receive the SEP of all SANEs in the cluster and is responsible for announcing itself to all of them. Now it can broadcast its own requests to the cluster. This solution has maximum redundancy.

Other solutions provide various forms of partitioning, e.g peer-to-peer style approaches, where a particular SANE may know only of its immediate neighbours and where broadcast may proceed in multiple hops over subsets of the cluster.

6   Related Work

The use of a distributed protocol for problem solving is not new. In 1980, Smith proposed the contract net protocol to specify distributed communication and control in a loosely-coupled, problem-solving environment [7]. In this protocol, task distribution used a negotiation process to decide which tasks were executed where. This protocol (and other work within ÆTHER [8]) adopted a managed approach to work delegation, i.e. one node, the manager, assumes responsibility for monitoring the execution of a task and processing the results of its execution. In the approach described here, both execution and the responsibility for meeting any execution constraints is delegated. The use of market models is not so new but we adopt a market model only required to provide modulation of a cost based on energy, where the market provides a distributed mechanism to detect and react to load. This is not discussed in detail in this paper, which focusses on the architecture and protocol. More information on market-based resource allocation can be found in the following thesis [14].

Mapping and scheduling workflows (a set of tasks with sometimes complex dependencies) onto gtrids, e.g. GridFlow [9] and Nimrod-G [10] has similar requirements. Here, a more pragmatic and coarse-grained approach is adopted, based on job-submission where communication between tasks uses files. These approaches typically use a cost/deadline resource management model. More recently, e.g. [11] and [12], there has been a trend towards using a just-in-time approach. Here, instead of analysing a workflow and trying to optimise a static schedule, resources are allocated on a first come, first served basis. The work described here differs from grid developments in a number of significant ways. Perhaps the first and most significant is that the ÆTHER project aims to build a complete programming solution to such distributed environments and in doing so, it has defined a model of concurrency that captures both work and resources in an abstract manner in a single integrated model [4]. We also adopts a just-in-time approach to scheduling but in our case this is required as the underlying SVP model is implemented at the level of instructions in a processors ISA and adaptations to load may occur at MHz rates, giving little time for planning a schedule. Also note that this just in time approach adapts to situations where there may be a significant latency in setting up a remote resource to perform a computation. Two examples are just-in-time compilation for different instruction sets and device configuration in FPGA like devices. In ÆTHER there is considerable interest in the design of run-time support for reconfigurable SoCs [13].

7   Summary

This paper has presented the architecture of a hierarchical SANE system, where resources are shared between SANEs by delegating both work and the responsibility to meet the deadline or requirements for that work. This architecture builds upon the SVP model of concurrency that provides an abstraction of work as a family of threads and an abstraction of resources as a place. The protocol provides a place server to define the place at which the family of threads is executed once the protocol has been completed. The protocol proposed for negotiating the use of resources is based on a cost model that uses the required energy as a baseline cost, to be modulated by market forces. A baseline implementation could use cost as simply a selection criteria with no credits being exchanged at all. In this way threads could collectively minimise energy consumption in the system. With a cost model however much richer scenarios can be envisioned, where the cost, although based on energy, is dependent on market conditions, such that at periods of high demand cost would rise. In such a scenario, one can imagine, as with our financial world, a number of SANEs cornering the market on energy credits by speculating in the market. Such cost policies and mapping strategies will be evaluated within the remaining period of the ÆTHER project in order to understand their emergent behaviour.

Acknowledgements

The authors acknowledge support from the European Community in funding the research undertaken in the ÆTHER project.

References

1. Krikke, J.: T-Engine: Japan's Ubiquitous Computing Architecture Is Ready for Prime Time. IEEE Pervasive Computing 04(2), 4–9 (2005)
2. Jesshope, C.R.: A model for the design and programming of multicores. In: Advances in Parallel Computing. IOS Press, Amsterdam (published, 2008), http://staff.science.uva.nl/~jesshope/Papers/Multicores.pdf
3. van Tol, M., Jesshope, C.R., Lankamp, M., Polstra, S.: An implementation of the SANE Virtual Processor using Posix threads. Journal of Systems Architecture (submitted, 2008), http://staff.science.uva.nl/~jesshope/Papers/Multicores.pdf
4. Jesshope, C.R.: Microthreading a model for distributed instruction-level concurrency. Parallel processing Letters 16(2), 209–228 (2006)
5. Bernard, T.A.M., Jesshope, C.R., Knijnenburg, P.M.W.: Strategies for Compiling μTC to Novel Chip Multiprocessors. In: Vassiliadis, S., Bereković, M., Hämäläinen, T.D. (eds.) SAMOS 2007. LNCS, vol. 4599, pp. 127–138. Springer, Heidelberg (2007)
6. Paulsson, K., Hübner, M., Becker, J., Philippe, J.-M., Gamrat, C.: On-Line Routing of Reconfigurable Functions for Future Self Adaptive Systems - Investigations within the AETHER Project. In: IEEE International Conference on Field Programmable Logic And Applications (FPL), Amsterdam, The Netherlands, Auguat 27-29, pp. 415–422 (2007)
7. Smith, R.G.: The Contract Net Protocol: High-Level Communication and Control in a Distributed Problem Solver. IEEE Trans. Comput. C-29(12) (1980)
8. Khodary, M.E., Diguet, J.-P., Gogniat, G.: Operating Environment on-line Metrics for Application Architecture Matching. In: 25th IEEE Norchip Conf., Aalborg, Denmark, pp. 19–20 (November 2007)
9. Cao, J., et al.: WorkFlow Management for Grid Computing. In: Proc. of the 3rd IEEE/ACM International Symposium on Cluster Computing and the Grid, pp. 198–205 (2003)
10. Buyya, R., Abramson, D., Giddy, J.: Nimrod/G: An Architecture of a Resource Management and Scheduling System in a Global Computational Grid. In: HPC Asia 2000, China (2000)
11. Deelman, E., et al.: Pegasus: Mapping Scientific Workflows onto the Grid. In: Across Grids Conference, Nicosia, Cyprus (2004)
12. Omar, W.M., Taleb-Bendiab, A., Karam, Y.: Autonomic Middleware Services for Just-In-Time Grid Services Provisioning. Journal of Computer Science 6, 521–527 (2006)
13. Marescaux, T., et al.: Run-time support for heterogeneous multitasking on recongurable SoCs. Integration, the VLSI journal 38, 107–130 (2004)
14. Lepler, J.H.: Cooperation and deviation in market-based resource allocation, University of Cambridge Technical report, UCAM-CL-TR-622 (2004) ISSN 1476-2986

Climate and Biological Sensor Network

Perfecto Mariño, Fernando Pérez-Fontán, Miguel Ángel Domínguez,
and Santiago Otero

University of Vigo
Vigo, Spain
jsotero@uvigo.es

Abstract. Biological research in agriculture needs a lot of specialised
electronic sensors in order to fulfil different goals, like as: climate monitoring, soil and fruit assessment, control of insects and diseases, chemical
pollutants, identification and control of weeds, crop tracking, and so on.
That research must be supported by consistent biological models able to
simulate diverse environmental conditions, in order to predict the right
human actions before risky biological damage could be irreversible. In
this paper an experimental distributed network based on climatic and
biological wireless sensors is described , for providing real measurements
in order to validate different biological models used for viticulture applications. First, the experimental network for field automatic data acquisition is introduced , as a system based in a distributed process. Following,
the design of the wireless network is explained in detail, with a previous
discussion about the state-of-the-art, and some measurements for viticulture research are pointed out. Finally future developments are stated.

Keywords: sensor systems, sensor networks.

1   Introduction

The experimental wireless network is deployed in a peninsula surrounded by
two large sea arms called "rias" in Spanish language. In that peninsula, located
in the northwest of Spain (near the northern border of Portugal), the vineyards
have four main productive zones called: Meaño, Cambados, Ribadumia and Meis
(Fig. 1).

Currently differences in productivity and quality of grapes are broadly related
with relative heights and sea proximity from each of four zones but nevertheless more rigorous biological and climatic research [1,2] must be done, in order
to provide accurate biological models for ecological simulations applied to viticulture. For that reason multidisciplinary work must be done among electronic
engineers, biologists and ecologists.

Each zone has an electronic zonal station (EZS), in order to bring differences
(microclimates), in measurements like: temperature, relative humidity, leave humidity, soil temperature, solar radiation, rain gauge (tipping bucket), and other
biological sensors. A data logger and a radio modem is included in each EZS in
order to sense, process and transmit the data, enabling the development of an

M. Berekovic, N. Dimopoulos, and S. Wong (Eds.): SAMOS 2008, LNCS 5114, pp. 229–237, 2008.
© Springer-Verlag Berlin Heidelberg 2008

Fig. 1. Peninsula photograph

automatic wireless sensor network (WSN), which nodes (the EZSs) are accessible from a wide area. These wireless communication capabilities allow that data could be remotely monitored. The implementation of a warehousing approach, allows the data to be stored in a centralized database that is responsible for query processing. The stored data will be used for biological and ecological models.

Firstly the paper describes the different elements employed in the experimental network. These include (a) the wireless nodes (b) the base station (c) the repeaters and (d) the data management. Finally some measurements from EZSs are depicted.

2   Data Acquisition System

The electronic zonal stations (EZSs) are connected with the base station (BS) by the UHF band (not licensed) between 869.4MHz to 869.65MHz, and the BS is also connected through Internet to the Data Base (DB), the biological and ecological models (BEMs), and to the Web access (Fig. 2). Each zonal station comprises an UHF radio modem that transmits the sensors information to the BS through a data call. A powering solar panel (PSP) is located near each EZS for feeding its circuits. In order to reduce costs, the BS makes a call to all the EZSs every 24 hours by means of a polling procedure [3]. During these calls the EZSs send all the information that has been stored on that period. Therefore the BS periodically executes the reading data process and later database storage of the received information, through an Ethernet local area network.

2.1   Data from Sensors

An electronic zonal station (EZS) is the basic acquisition equipment of the distributed system, that carries out the data registration (measurements and processing),

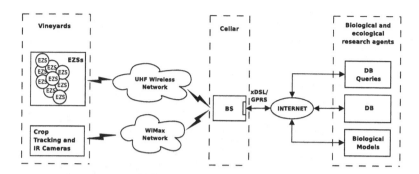

Fig. 2. Network architecture and database interfaces

and the communication with the base station (BS). In this way, each EZS comprises an automatic measurement unit with data transfer capability. The data acquisition process is made inside the EZS by the sensors and the data logger. Each EZS comprises the following sensors: temperature, relative humidity, leave humidity, soil temperature, solar radiation, rain gauge (tipping bucket), and other biological and ecological features depending on running models [4].

All that sensors are integrated in the data logger. The data logger is the EZS nucleus, it captures the data from each sensor, automates the measurements, synchronises the data and manages the communications. The data transmission is carried out by means of the data logger and the UHF radio modem connected to it. Next, the data captured by the EZS is sent to the database (DB), through the base station (BS), where they are saved. The communication process setting,

Fig. 3. EZS data acquisition and communications system assembled in the protection box

Fig. 4. Final assembly and EZS installation

through the UHF radio modem connected to the data logger, allows the control and programming of several tasks as well as the acquisition of stored data.

The data captured by the data logger are organised in registers. The registers comprise the sensor outputs as well as the time and date. These registers are then sent to the storage system where they are saved for a future access. The data logger is programmed for capturing and storing the sensors information each minute. Due to the limited capacity of the storage system integrated in the data logger, the data can only be stored during a day (24 hours). Figure 3 illustrates the data logger, the storage system, the UHF radio modem and connections with the sensors and electrical supply. Al these elements are placed inside a box which protects them from the weather conditions. This box and all the sensors are fixed to a metallic base located at the site (Fig. 4).

3   Global Data Management

The information obtained from the EZSs are collected by the BS and stored in the DB for later process, analysis and query. The BS requests and compiles the data from the different EZSs to store them in the DB. Also the BS is provided with an UHF radio modem to make the polling query of each EZS in the wireless network. Therefore the BS is a PC connected to a wireless network and Internet that executes the developed program to perform its operations flowchart. The figure 5 shows this flowchart.

Since all the measured data must have the same time reference for its later process, the BS obtains the system reference clock from a real time network server by the NTP synchronization protocol (Network Time Protocol). So after the date have been obtained, a time synchronization test is verified for the EZSs clocks,

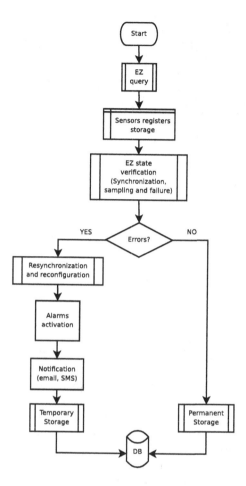

Fig. 5. BS operations flowchart

to determine if the collected data can be considered valid. If this is the case, the information is stored directly in the DB. Otherwise the problem is corrected (if it is possible), it is notified by e-mail and/or a message, and finally the data and the error information are stored. In this way is possible to know exactly when and what type of errors took place and, depending on this information data can be corrected.

The data from the EZSs are centralized in a relational database. This DB presents one interface with the BS through which all the system information is introduced, and three interfaces to access this information: general data access, access to interesting data to analyse viticulture features, and query of data for providing models (Fig. 5). The interface between BS-DB and queries-DB are executed directly by means of ODBC (Open Database Connectivity).

The general data access will directly take place through an Internet accessible Web page. Whereas for queries related to the analysis of viticulture features

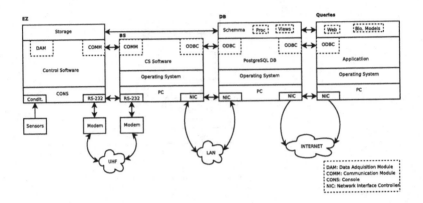

Fig. 6. Communication example between elements, interfaces and layers

and models, the access is made through specific views for each type of study [3]. Figure 6 shows an example of the EZS data management. This picture illustrates the structure of communications among equipments, interfaces and layers.

4   The State-of-the-Art and the Implemented Network

Past decade has been very fruitful in the development and application of several standards for mobile, nomadic and fixed wireless networks related with sensors [5,6,7]. Some specific problems about this kind of networks have been well studied, like: energy efficiency due to collisions, overemitting-receiving, control of packets and idle listening; scalability and changes adaptation in network size, node density and topology; communication paradigms like node-centric, data-centric and position-centric; and many others.

Nevertheless this great researching effort over wireless networks for sensors, there is no any accepted MAC for them, because this kind of sensor networks has a very big dependence of the application. Recent surveys about the most advanced wireless networks like MANETs [8,9] show poor real results in front of expected ones, because the great complexity involved in simulated MAC protocols, on big programming tools, was not after validated with implementation, integration and experimentation over real equipment (chips, microcircuits, modems, antennas, and others). In this way, a particular field of application, called "wireless sensor networks" (WSN) is proposed for environmental monitoring, industry and precision agriculture, among other sectors of activity. The WSNs are featured by a stronger interdisciplinary collaboration for creative projects, and a change in the communication paradigm from node-centric to data-centric one, because the main point is the transfer of data from the application field, and not the communication between all the network nodes.

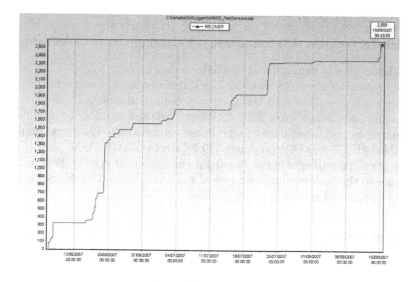

Fig. 7. Measured rain plot

4.1   The Wireless Sensor Network (WSN)

Several comparatives among general wireless standards like ZigBee [10,11], Ultra Wide Band (UWB) [12], Bluetooth [13] and WiFi [14] have been made in order to evaluate some examples of application included industrial wireless sensors. Also, more specific WSN applications could be found about environmental research like: hydrology [15], fire monitoring [16], deep ice [17], and others [18].

   Given the hilly nature of the vineyard zones (Section 1), the coverage challenges for linking the EZSs with the BS (Section 3) were founded in power, data speed and acceptable error ratio. For example, in the Meis zone the coverage area was over 5km, with difference in heights about 200m, very prone to interpose obstacles in the line-of-sight (LOS) among EZS-BS. In order to achieve a wireless network with very low cost and reduced power consumption, because static nodes are transmitting infrequently (low duty cycle) only two-way small data packets, the European ISM band (868-870MHz) was selected, where one channel with a data rate of 20kbps is available [13]. In this ISM band the used radio modems for linking EZS-BS, have the following features: 10-500mW of transmitting power, 25kHz of channel spacing, half-duplex communication, 10% duty cycle and 36 seconds of maximum emission time (must be controlled by the data logger, Section 2.1). To avoid an obstacle in the LOS between the BS and the EZS, a repeater station (RS) is inserted with other ISM radio modem and a directive antenna, linking the EZS (2,1km) with the BS (5,17km). Figure 7 shows an illustrative example of measured rain series carried out between EZS-RS-BS in the Meis zone.

5   Future Developments

Experimental work over the implemented WSN is being made in the following lines:

- Addition of new climatic and biological sensors to the EZSs.
- Deployment of new EZS over the four different vineyard zones for providing more spatial resolution to biological and ecological models.
- Design of a wireless broadband (20Mbps) network in order to provide crop tracking by real time images, and infrared cameras (zonal isotherm maps), by WiMax (IEEE 802.16) equipment [19,20] over the 5GHz ISM band (Fig. 2).
- Integrate those images in the global data management system (Section 3), for giving to the biological and ecological researchers new knowledge for future enhancement of models.

6   Conclusions

The authors have developed an experimental distributed network based on the WSN paradigm for wireless sensors. This WSN is based on the European ISM band for providing a low cost and low power consumption network, bringing real measurements to validate different biological and ecological models used for viticulture applications. Also a global data management system is designed to integrate consistently the measured data in the models. New developments in the experimental wireless network are being tested to add real time images and infrared cameras information, by means of broadband network standards.

Acknowledgment

This work has been sponsored by an R&D project from the Research General Directorate of the Galician Autonomous Government (Xunta de Galicia, northwest of Spain), Ref. PGIDIT06TIC052E. The authors want to thank the staff from MARTÍN CÓDAX CELLAR enterprise, for the kind permission to deploy the experimental wireless network in their properties and facilities.

References

1. Perry, T.S.: Capturing climate change. IEEE Spectrum 39(1), 58–65 (2002)
2. Gail, W.B.: Climate control. IEEE Spectrum 44(5), 20–25 (2007)
3. Mariño, P., Fontán, F.P., Machado, F., Otero, S.: Distributed sensors network applied to the rain impairment study on radiocommunication systems. In: Industrial Informatics, 2006 IEEE International Conference, Singapore, pp. 1036–1041 (August 2006)
4. Poza, F., Mariño, P., Otero, S., Machado, F.: Programmable electronic instrument for condition monitoring of in-service power transformers. IEEE Transactions on Instrumentation and Measurement 55(2), 625–634 (2006)
5. Akyildiz, I.F., Su, W., Sankarasubramaniam, Y., Cayirci, E.: Wireless sensor networks: a survey. Computer Networks 38(4), 393–422 (2002)

6. Niculescu, D.: Communication paradigms for sensor networks. IEEE Communications Magazine 43(3), 116–122 (2005)
7. Demirkol, I., Ersoy, C., Alagoz, F.: MAC protocols for wireless sensor networks: a survey. IEEE Communications Magazine 44(4), 115–121 (2006)
8. Conti, M., Giordano, S.: Multihop ad hoc networking: The theory. Communications Magazine, IEEE 45, 78–86 (2007)
9. Conti, M., Giordano, S.: Multihop ad hoc networking: The reality. Communications Magazine, IEEE 45, 88–95 (2007)
10. Prophet, G.: Is zigbee ready for the big time? EDN Europe (August 2004)
11. Wheeler, A.: Commercial applications of wireless sensor networks using zigbee. Communications Magazine, IEEE 45, 70–77 (2007)
12. Oppermann, I., Stoica, L., Rabbachin, A., Shelby, Z., Haapola, J.: UWB wireless sensor networks: UWEN - a practical example. IEEE Communications Magazine 42(12), 27–32 (2004)
13. Willig, A., Matheus, K., Wolisz, A.: Wireless technology in industrial networks. Proceedings of the IEEE 93(6), 1130–1151 (2005)
14. Kunz, M.: Wireless lan planning is a science, not an art! The Industrial Ethernet Book, pp. 32–34 (September 2006)
15. Moore, R.J., Jones, D.A., Cox, D.R., Isham, V.S.: Design of the hyrex raingauge network. Hydrology and Earth System Sciences 4, 521–530 (2000)
16. Ruiz, L.B., Braga, T.R.M., Silva, F.A., Assuncao, H.P., Nogueira, J.M.S., Loureiro, A.A.F.: On the design of a self-managed wireless sensor network. IEEE Communications Magazine 43(8), 95–102 (2005)
17. Guizzo, E.: Into deep ice [ice monitoring]. IEEE Spectrum 42(12), 28–35 (2005)
18. Cutler, T.: Case study: wireless, serial and etherner link for enviromental project. The Industrial Ethernet Book, pp. 37–40 (November 2005)
19. Ghosh, A., Wolter, D.R., Andrews, J.G., Chen, R.: Broadband wireless access with wimax/802.16: current performance benchmarks and future potential. IEEE Communications Magazine 43(2), 129–136 (2005)
20. Livingston, M., Franke, R.: Choosing a 802.16 radio for use in a wimax application. Embedded Systems Europe, 31–34 (July 2006)

Monitoring of Environmentally Hazardous Exhaust Emissions from Cars Using Optical Fibre Sensors

Elfed Lewis[1], John Clifford[1], Colin Fitzpatrick[1], Gerard Dooly[1],
Weizhong Zhao[2], Tong Sun[2], Ken Grattan[2], James Lucas[3], Martin Degner[4],
Hartmut Ewald[4], Steffen Lochmann[5], Gero Bramann[5],
Edoardo Merlone-Borla[6], and Flavio Gili[6]

[1] Department of Electronic & Computer Engineering, University of Limerick, Ireland
[2] School of Engineering & Mathematical Sciences, City University,
London EC1 0HB, UK
[3] Department of Electrical Engineering & Electronics, University of Liverpool,
Liverpool L69 3GJ, UK
[4] Institute of General Electrical Engineering, Albert Einstein Str. 2,
University of Rostock, D-18051, Germany
[5] Department of Electrical Engineering & Computer Science, Hochschule Wismar,
Philipp-Mueller Str, D-23952, Wismar, Germany
[6] Advanced Manufacturing and Materials, Centro Ricerche Fiat, Strada Torino 50,
Orbassano (TO), Italy

Abstract. Results are presented for on board sensing of the Gases NO, NO_2, SO_2 and CO_2. The optical fibre sensor was connected downstream of the Diesel Particle Filter (DPF) of a Fiat Croma and the measurements from the optical fibre sensors were recorded simultaneously using high specification reference instrumentation mounted in the boot of the car. In this way the results from the optical fibre sensors and the reference instrumentation could be directly compared. The results from the optical fibre sensors indicate that they are capable of measuring single ppm values of NO, NO_2 and SO_2 as required by the EURO IV standards and CO_2 up to a concentration of 15% which is more than adequate for in car monitoring. The optical fibre sensors therefore performed well when compared to the reference instrumentation in tests conducted on a rolling road and during "free driving" on an urban road.

Keywords: mid-infrared gas detection; UV gas detection; in-fibre Bragg grating temperature sensor; optical fibre sensor; vehicle emission detection.

1 Introduction

Automotive emissions typically consist of water vapour, carbon dioxide (CO_2), carbon monoxide (CO), oxides of nitrogen (NO_x), oxides of sulphur (SO_x), smoke particles (diameters of $0.05\mu m$ to $1\mu m$) and also particulate matter (diameters

M. Berekovic, N. Dimopoulos, and S. Wong (Eds.): SAMOS 2008, LNCS 5114, pp. 238–247, 2008.

greater than $1\mu m$). Under perfect combustion conditions the following relationship exists:

$$Fuel(C_xH_x) + Air \rightarrow CO_2 + H_2O \tag{1}$$

As carbon dioxide (CO_2) and water vapour (H_2O) are both present as trace gases in the atmosphere, no pollution would result from this process. However, in reality perfect combustion does not occur and the following relationship exists as fuel is burnt in an engine:

$$Fuel(C_xH_x) + Air \rightarrow CO_2 + H_2O + CO + SO_x + NO_x + PM + C_xH_x + smoke \tag{2}$$

Research has shown that each of these species is a threat to either human health or the environment [1]. Carbon monoxide (CO) is known to be poisonous to humans at concentrations above 400 parts-per-million. CO_2 is not strictly considered a pollutant as it exists naturally as a trace gas in the atmosphere. It is believed that the relatively high levels of CO_2 produced by combustion are a prime contributor to global warming [2]. CO and CO_2 have high absorption in the mid-infrared wavelength range [3], as shown in Fig. 1.

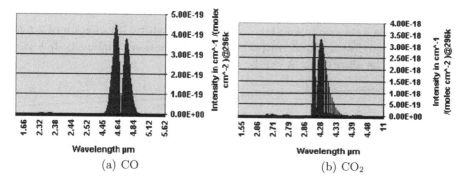

(a) CO   (b) CO_2

Fig. 1. Theoretical Absorption Spectra for CO and CO2 Gases [3]

Similarly, detection of the other gases namely SO_2, NO and NO_2 is possible in the UV/Visible part of the spectrum. The theoretical spectra for these gasses are shown in Fig. 2.

Optical fibre sensors are particularly well suited to monitoring vehicle exhaust emissions, as they can be made small, lightweight, and as they are made purely from glass (doped for high temperature measurement). This coupled with quartz lenses (for UV) or chalcogenide with Calcium Fluoride Lenses for Mid IR means that they can withstand the high temperature of the gases present in the car exhaust [4,5].

2   Theoretical Background

The Beer-Lambert Law is used to calculate how much incident radiation is absorbed by a sample and has been well documented in the literature [6]. The

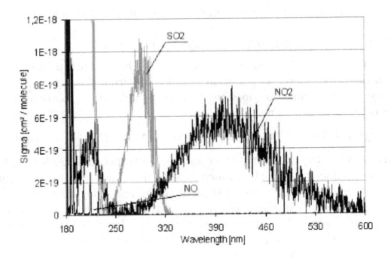

Fig. 2. Theoretical Absorption Spectra for NO, NO₂ and SO₂ Gases

sample may be an aqueous solution or a gaseous quantity. If radiation of intensity I_0 is directed at a sample of path length l, radiation of intensity I_t leaves the sample. The absorbance A can be defined as:

$$A = log_{10}\frac{I_0}{I_t} = \varepsilon cl \tag{3}$$

where ε is the molar absorption coefficient of the species and c is the concentration of the sample. The ratio I_t/I_0 is defined as the transmittance, T and from [6]

$$T = 10^{-\varepsilon cl} = \frac{I_t}{I_0} \tag{4}$$

This relationship was used to determine the concentration of the gas based upon experimental results of absorption observed in the mid infra red and UV part of the spectrum. The Reference Forward Model (RFM) was developed at Oxford University to simulate the absorption spectra of gases such as CO in the HITRAN Database [7]. These are calculated for different concentrations, pressures, and temperatures. It was possible to use the RFM to vary the path length of the sample and thus simulate the experimental results in the wavelength range of interest (i.e. within the pass band of the optical filter fitted to the pyroelectric detector).

Simulations were performed at various concentrations (1000ppm, 800ppm, etc) using RFM, the absorption spectra at these concentrations were then interpolated using MATLAB against the filter wavelength data over the same wavelength scale as the transmission spectrum of the band pass of the pyroelectric detector. The absorption spectrum was converted to a transmission spectrum and this was multiplied by the filter transmission spectrum. The resulting spectrum corresponds to the transmission by CO at a particular concentration over

Transmission

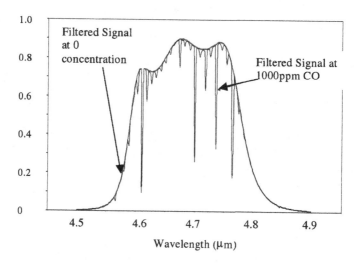

Fig. 3. A Comparison of the Transmission Spectra for CO at 0ppm and 7000ppm Calculated Using RFM

Transmission

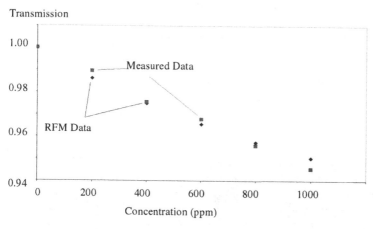

Fig. 4. A Comparison of the Transmittance Values Generated by the RFM Simulation and Those Produced Experimentally for CO

a path length of 360mm as measured by the pyroelectric detector. The results of the simulation are shown in Fig. 3 for concentrations of 0ppm and 1000ppm of CO for a path length of 360mm, at 23°C and 1 bar of pressure (i.e. ambient temperature and atmospheric pressure). By calculating the area under the curve at a particular concentration, the theoretical values for I_0 and I_t in Eq. 4 were calculated. The area under the curve at 0ppm corresponds to I_0, while the area under the curve at a particular concentration corresponds to I_t.

Fig. 4 shows the analysis of the experimental 200ppm step test. The transmittance was calculated as the concentration of CO in the cell was increased from 0ppm (when the cell was filled with N_2) to 1000ppm and then decreased in steps of 200ppm.

It is clear that the theoretical values are in close agreement with the measured values. The largest deviation (1%) is at a concentration of 1000ppm. The difference between the measured and theoretical results can be attributed to experimental uncertainty e.g. electrical noise on the outputs of the pyroelectric detectors. This could be reduced in future by improved the coupling of the emitter and detector to fibre which would increase the amount of radiant flux arriving at the detector which would increase the signal to noise ratio.

3   Experimental Results

3.1   Gas Concentration Measurement in the Mid Infra Red Range

The experimental set up for measuring CO_2 in the mid infra red region in the exhaust system of the demonstrator vehicle located in the test facility at CRF, Italy is shown in Fig 5. The components of the optical system and comparison to other research have been described in detail by Mulrooney et al [8]. A Dell Latitude D610 notebook equipped with a National Instruments PCIMCIA 6024E data acquisition card was used to acquire the data on site and a Lab View ®Virtual Instrument was used to store these voltages to a file.

The transmission mode optical fibre sensor (referred to as the straight sensor in Fig. 6) was connected to the exhaust system of the vehicle as in Fig. 5 and the output of the optical fibre sensor and reference instrument were recorded

(a) Close up: A) Fibre in, B) Gas Absortion Cell, C) Fibre out, D) Exhaust Pipe Section, Manufactured by CRF

(b) Relative to car showing the reference instrumentation

Fig. 5. Mid IR Sensor on the Exhaust Line of the Fiat Croma Demonstrator

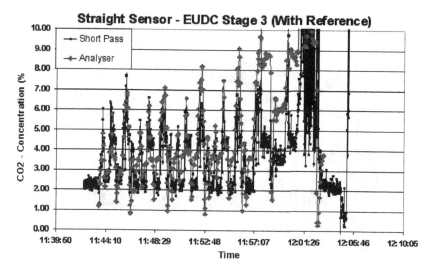

Fig. 6. CO_2 concentration recorded during the NEDC test cycle for the Fiat Croma on the roller test bench. Simultaneous measurements shown for the transmission mode optical fibre sensor and reference instrumentation.

simultaneously as the car was driven on roller test bench in compliance with a standard test known as the NEDC driving cycle. These results are shown in Fig. 6.

It is clear from Fig. 6 that the Optical Fibre Sensor is capable of faithfully reproducing the variation of CO_2 concentration over the whole NEDC cycle.

3.2 Gas Concentration Measurement in the Ultra Violet Range

The system for measuring the gases NO, NO_2 and SO_2 in the UV range is shown schematically in Fig. 7.

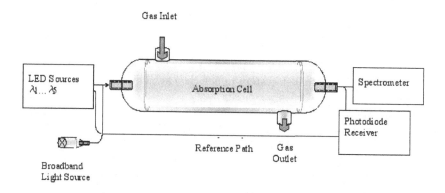

Fig. 7. The gas sensor for measuring in Ultra Violet range

Fig. 8. The UV gas sensor mounted underneath the car

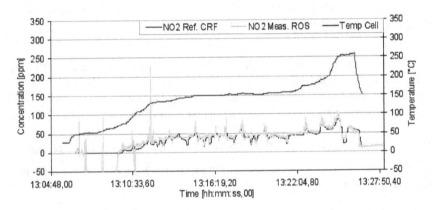

Fig. 9. NO$_2$ Test Results Under the Car With Simultaneous Reference Instruments Recording

The cell shown in Fig. 7 was enclosed in a steel flanged section which was inserted in line in the exhaust system under the car. This is shown photographically in Fig. 8.

The cell was used to record the levels of NO, NO$_2$ and SO$_2$ for a full cycle of the standard acceleration/ deceleration test with the car mounted on a rolling road at the test facility of CRF in Turin. The results of these tests corresponding to NO$_2$ are shown in Fig. 9.

It is clear from Fig. 9 that the value of NO$_2$ recorded on the optical sensor faithfully reproduces the values measured on the reference (lab based) instrumentation. The optical fibre sensor has therefore been proved to be capable of measurement within the exhaust of the vehicle.

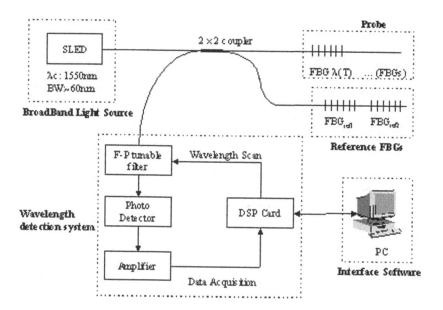

Fig. 10. The Optical Fibre Sensor for Measuring Temperature

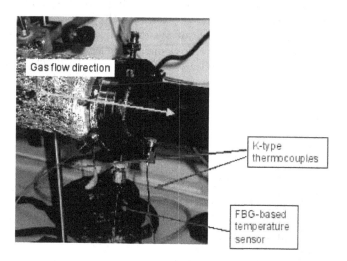

Fig. 11. The FBG Optical Fibre Sensor Mounted on the Experimental Exhaust System at the Laboratory of CRF, Turin

3.3 Optical Fibre Temperature Measurement

As well as measuring the gas concentrations using optical fibre technology, the OPTO-EMI-SENSE project has been concerned with the measurement of

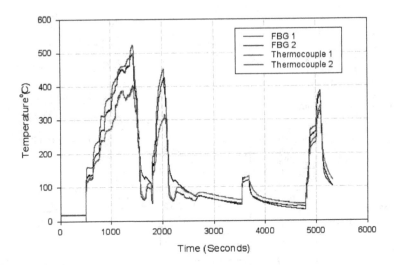

Fig. 12. Temperature Measurements on the Experimental Exhaust Test Facility with Simultaneous Reference Instruments Recording

temperature of the exhaust gases using in-fibre Bragg Gratings. The system for the temperature measurement is shown schematically in Fig. 10.

The FBG-based temperature sensor system utilizes a broad band (Superluminescent LED) light source (centred on a wavelength of 1550 nm) and a Fabry-Perot tunable filter for FBG wavelength interrogation. The temperature sensor located on the test exhaust system at the laboratory of CRF is shown photographically in Fig. 11 and the results of a typical temperature cycle corresponding to values encountered in a standard test cycle shown in Fig. 12.

4   Conclusions

Optical fibre sensors suitable for the detection of exhaust gas emissions and temperature have been described in this paper. The development of the sensors are novel as they uses a low cost and compact components coupled to optical fibre, to provide a practical solution for the measurement in the harsh environment of the car exhaust system.

This sensors have proved to be capable of detecting gas concentrations as low as single ppm values for NO, NO_2 and SO_2, and up to 20 % concentration of CO_2 in the exhaust of a car. An analysis of these results using the Reference Forward Model (RFM) and MATLAB indicated that the measured and theoretical values are in close agreement. Optical Fibre Temperature Measurements have been performed in the exhaust of a Diesel engine and these have demonstrated the sensors capability of accurately (to within one degree) measuring the exhaust gas temperature over a range of many 100s degrees centigrade (at least 800 °C).

Acknowledgments. The authors would like to thank the staff of the Emissions Group at Centro Ricerche Fiat for their assistance during testing. The authors would also like to acknowledge the support of the EU FP6 project Opto-Emi-Sense (Contract number: TST3-CT2003-506592) for funding this work.

References

1. Hillier, V.A.W.: Fundamentals of Motor Vehicle Technology. 4th edn., Thornes, Geltenham, UK (1991) ISBN 978-0-748705313
2. Energy Information Administration (Official Energy Statistics from the U.S. Government), http://www.eia.doe.gov/oiaf/1605/ggccebro/chapter1.html
3. Rothman, L.S., et al.: The hitran molecular spectroscopic database and hawks (hitran atmospheric workstation). Journal of Quantitative Spectroscopy & Radiative Transfer 96, 139–204 (2004)
4. López-Higuera, J.M.: Handbook of Optical Fibre Sensing Technology, pp. 286–287. John Wiley and Sons, Chichester (2002)
5. Stewart, G., Jin, W., Culshaw, B.: Prospects for fibre optic evanescent field gas sensors using absorption in the near-infrared. Sensors & Actuators B: Chemical 38(1-3), 42–47 (1997)
6. Banwell, C.M., McCash, E.M.: Fundamentals of Molecular Spectroscopy, 4th edn. McGraw Hill, London (1994)
7. Model, R.F.: http://www.atm.ox.ac.uk/RFM/
8. Mulrooney, J., Clifford, J., Fitzpatrick, C., Lewis, E.: Detection of carbon dioxide emissions from a diesel engine using a mid-infrared optical fibre based sensor. Sensors and Actuators A: Physical 136(1), 104–110 (2007)

Application Server for Wireless Sensor Networks

Janne Rintanen, Jukka Suhonen, Marko Hännikäinen, and Timo D. Hämäläinen

Tampere University of Technology, Department of Computer Systems
P.O. Box 553, FI-33101 Tampere, Finland
{janne.rintanen, jukka.suhonen, marko.hannikainen,
timo.d.hamalainen}@tut.fi

Abstract. Wireless Sensor Networks (WSN) can be used in various applications for home and industrial environments. The main challenges in these applications come from the requirement of collecting and presenting continuously changing sensor data. Powerful abstractions are required in order to support diverse WSN configurations and the varying user requirements for sensor data visualization. In this paper, we present the design of an application server for WSNs and the implementation of a server prototype referred to as TUTWSN Application Server (TAS). TAS offers services for permission management, information storing, visualization of sensor data, and messaging required for receiving sensor data from the WSNs in real-time.

1 Introduction

Wireless Sensor Networks (WSN) are emerging ad-hoc networks that may consist of thousands of sensor nodes combining wireless networking with environment sensing and data processing [1]. Sensors are autonomous devices that are capable of cooperatively monitoring physical and environmental conditions, such as temperature, sound, vibration and motion at different locations. The information from WSNs can be used in various applications for home and industrial environments. The WSN configurations are adjusted to the different environments with varying requirements for accessing and visualizing sensor data. In most cases the sensor data is not public. Especially in the industrial environment, means for altering the permissions to access information or a certain application is required. Due to the varying user requirements, a possibility to alter the WSN implementation and configuration without changes to the end user applications is required. On the other hand, it must be possible to present the sensor data with new methods without changing the underlying WSNs.

In this paper an application server for WSNs is designed. This server offers solutions to the varying user requirements and operates as a platform for sensor network applications. The main challenges of collecting and presenting continuously changing sensor data are solved in the server. This requires mechanisms for publishing information from the WSNs, solutions for scalable information storing and means for sensor data visualization. User groups recognized by the server are software developers, administrators and the end users. The end users can access sensor network applications implemented on top of the server platform through World Wide Web (WWW). For software developers the server provides a way to distribute applications and hasten development

M. Berekovic, N. Dimopoulos, and S. Wong (Eds.): SAMOS 2008, LNCS 5114, pp. 248–257, 2008.

by enabling the reuse of commonly required features of sensor network applications. The administrators are offered services for the administration of applications, permissions and users. The presented design is applied to a server prototype named TUTWSN Application Server (TAS). The work for this paper has been carried out by the DACI research group [2] in the Tampere University of Technology (TUT). The implementation of TAS is currently used and evaluated together with our own WSN technology called TUTWSN [3]. It should be noted that TAS does not depend on a particular WSN technology and can be used e.g. with ZigBee [4].

This paper is structured in the following way. Section 2 discusses research related to WSNs and sensor network applications. The design of TAS is presented in Section 3. The implementation of TAS is described in Section 4. Section 5 presents a case application named the Weather Service. Section 6 concludes the paper.

2   Related Research

Most of the WSN research concentrate on the low level properties of sensors such as energy consumption, hardware systems and communication protocols. Less research is related to the sensor network applications and application platforms.

Liferay Portal [5] and Joomla [6] are Web-based gateways for users to locate relevant content and applications. They support user management and permission management combined with administration applications but lack services for WSNs. CORIE [7], Glacsweb [8], PODS [9] and Wisden [10] are examples of standalone sensor network applications targeted to environmental monitoring. They do not concentrate on supporting different WSN implementations or permissions.

GSN [11] is a software middleware for a variety of WSNs. It aims to facilitate the programming of sensor network applications and provides means for abstracting from the implementation details of access to sensor data. NanoMon [12] is a sensor network monitoring software which provides visualization of sensor network topology and sensor data. NanoMon supports sensor data storing and provides plug-in capability for adding and removing custom user interface (UI) components. In the decentralized architectures of NanoMon and the GSN, the main functionality is implemented in a single application. This application operates as a server and a middleware software as well as handles information storing and visualization of sensor data. Neither GSN nor NanoMon provide user management or permission management, which are essential requirements for TAS.

TAS combines the functionality of a Web portal with features serving WSNs. Unlike NanoMon and GSN, TAS separates the middleware software from the information storing and visualization services. Also, TAS relies on a centralized architecture, where an application server handles information distribution and contains the main business logic. The centralized architecture provides ease of use for the user groups of TAS. New end users can register to TAS and the administrator can adjust permissions to sensor data by giving the end users access to a number of sensor network applications. All applications are accessed through TAS, and occasionally new applications emerge without any updating or other tasks required from the end user. Potential scalability problems are the down-side to using a centralized architecture.

3 Design of TUTWSN Application Server

On the highest level, TAS architecture is a three-tier client-server architecture. TAS users form the first tier. The functionality of TAS forms the second tier and the database the third tier. Data produced by the wireless sensors is distributed to the end users as shown in Fig. 1. TAS offers two abstraction layers between the end users and the wireless sensors. The first abstraction layer is formed by the WSN Gateways, which operate as message oriented middleware software between the WSNs and the application server. The WSN Gateways hide the low level hardware and communication details of the sensors. All communication between the WSNs and sensor network applications go through the WSN Gateways. Therefore, various types of WSNs can be integrated to TAS by implementing new middleware applications handling WSN specific messaging. The deployment of the WSN Gateways varies and the TUTWSN Gateway can run on the application server or on a remote PC connected to the Internet. The second abstraction layer is between the end users and TAS. It concerns the way of accessing sensor data and turning it into valuable services for the end users. TAS is responsible for distributing the sensor data received from the TUTWSN Gateways in a suitable form for different types of client applications including a Web browser, a cell phone and an email client.

Fig. 2 illustrates the layered architecture of TAS, which consists of the applications, service framework, server platform and the information storing layers. The server platform layer holds the communication, WSN management and permission management

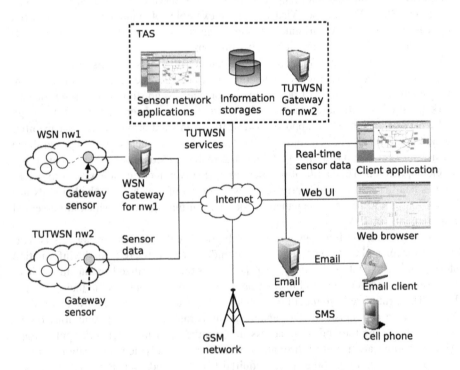

Fig. 1. High level architecture of the application server

modules. Applications are implemented on top of the service framework, which provides support for multiple types of client applications and means for separating the business logic from the data presentation.

TAS messaging enables loosely coupled, real-time messaging between sensor network applications. The design of TAS messaging uses the message dispatcher architecture. TAS handles registrations of new messaging components and dispatches messages to the registered message consumers. The benefit of the architechture is that it allows new sensor network applications, which are the messaging components, to be added and removed even at runtime.

A sensor application can use the TAS messaging directly or it can connect to an external WSN interface module referred to as gateway component. The separation of external WSN interfaces into multiple gateway components implies modular development and addresses performance problems, as the synchronously offered services form a potential pitfall on high network loads. An external WSN interface offers an alternative interface to the TAS messaging that is more suitable e.g. for Web browsers. An interface includes also additional functionality, such as refining stored sensor data into graphs and maps, the implementation of registration services and the management of users and permissions. This liberates developers from implementing these services separately for each application.

The WSN management consists of the SensorMaster component that implements the management interface. It allows applications running inside TAS to create new WSNs and query sensor data and information about sensors. When a new WSN is created, the SensorMaster initializes messaging channels for the WSN and inserts required information to the underlying databases.

Permission management allows managing permissions on user, group and role levels. For the end users, permission management shows as limited access to information.

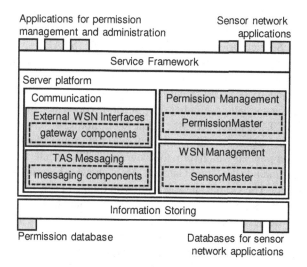

Fig. 2. The layered architecture of TAS

For the software developers, permission management offers interfaces for accessing and altering permissions. For the administrators, it means an easy way to administrate permissions to information and applications. The security is applied with the TAS messaging and permission management. Before dispatching a message, the TAS messaging component checks whether the source is permitted to send the message to the target from the PermissionMaster. If the permissions are insufficient, the message is dropped.

Scalability in information storing is taken into account by query optimization and architectural designing. The architectural solution for scalability is the separation of data into multiple databases and regular adjustments to the granularity of information. Information related to users, groups and services is stored in a permission database. Sensor data is stored in application specific databases, which are maintained by engine applications responsible for validating, filtering and storing sensor data. A vast amount of sensor data can make the data querying slower and slower by time. For instance, few applications require six temperature measurements per minute for the whole previous year from every sensor of the WSN. The engine applications in TAS create daily reports of the sensor data and then remove old data as time goes by. This keeps the sensor data querying fast without losing any important sensor data as only the granularity of saved information changes.

4   Implementation of TUTWSN Application Server

TAS is built on top of the JBoss application server [13]. Fig. 3 sums up the main technologies and their targets of use in TAS. The Java 2 Platform, Enterprise Edition (J2EE) [14] forms the core of the server-side implementation technologies. Extensible Markup Language (XML) technologies and Java 2 Platform, Standard Edition (J2SE) were used in the client-side implementation of sensor network applications. Hypertext Transfer Protocol (HTTP) with Secure Sockets Layer (SSL) are used to enable implementing services for light weight clients. Java Message Service (JMS) is used extensively internally in server-side, but also for communicating with more feature-rich Java-based client applications. Service Oriented Architecture Protocol (SOAP) [15] and XML were used due to their neutrality to the used programming language. They allow access to the stored information with third party software. The Structured Query Language (SQL), Java Database Connectivity (JDBC) and Open Database Connectivity (ODBC) were used when storing sensor data. A number of applications described in Table 1 were implemented on top of TAS, which serve the purpose of piloting different kinds of sensor network applications targeted to either public or selected groups of end users.

Four gateway components which form the external TUTWSN interfaces of TAS were implemented. They include the GraphGateway, MapGateway, ExternalServiceGateway and the JMSGateway. The GraphGateway returns an image of sensor data graph in response to HTTP requests containing a set of parameters. The MapGateway is similar to the GraphGateway but it returns images of maps representing WSNs. The ExternalServiceGateway can be used for querying information about users and their permissions using SOAP. The JMSGateway is responsible for receiving sensor data messages from the TUTWSN Gateways and delivering those messages to the sensor data alerts and other applications running inside TAS.

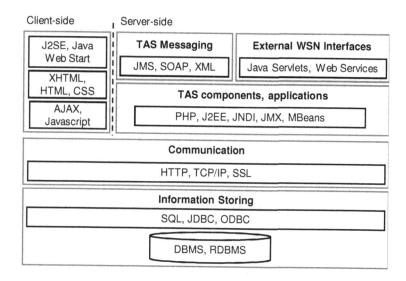

Fig. 3. Technologies and their targets of use

Table 1. Applications implemented on TAS

Application	Description
Administration Applications	
Administration	Manage permissions, users, user groups, roles and other applications.
Registration	Open registrations and create new end users.
Sensor Network	Create logical WSNs and manage WSN specific settings
UI Applications	
Sensor Alert Service	Create alerts when sensor reaches a certain value.
Weather Service	Observe temperatures on maps and graphs. A TUTWSN is tested for environmental monitoring purposes.
Truck Tracking Service	Monitor movements of trucks and temperatures inside a truck. A mobile TUTWSN is tested for object tracking.
TUTWSN Control Panel	End users can configure and monitor TUTWSN in real-time.
Engine applications	
TUTWSN Gateway	The message oriented middleware software for TUTWSN.
TUTWSN DBEngine	Stores diagnostic information and measurements from a TUTWSNfor analysis and research purposes.
WSDBEngine	Stores sensor data for a given set of sensors. Clears old sensor data and calculates daily reports of the sensor data. Used by the Weather Service.
Sensor Data Alerts	Receive and analyze sensor data. React by sending SMS and e-mail alerts when the received sensor data meets certain conditions. Used by the Sensor Alert Service.

The backbone of TAS messaging is the JMS. The goal of the implementation is to secure remote JMS connections using SSL and to provide custom permissions for messaging. Two virtual messaging channels are created for each WSN. Their purpose is to separate and limit access to sending and receiving messages with different natures in each WSN. The other channel is used for control messages and the other for monitoring messages. The monitoring messages contain sensor data produced by the sensors. The control messages alter the state of the sensors. The end users have different levels of permissions to the WSNs. Based on these permissions, the sensor network applications register as message consumers and producers to each messaging channel. This mechanism allows that, a user might have the permission to send control messages to his own WSN and only receive monitoring messages from other WSNs. When a new messaging component registers as a consumer or a producer of messages to a certain messaging channel, TAS will check permissions to the WSNs and either accept or deny the registration.

JMS technology was selected because the publish/subscribe messaging model provided by JMS matches well to the needs of TAS messaging. JMS implementation in JBoss also provides scalability and automatic load balancing features. SOAP over HTTP provides an alternative to JMS when implementing TAS messaging. The benefit of SOAP is interoperability, as SOAP implementations exist for a variety of programming languages and JMS is Java specific. The downside of SOAP compared to JMS is the request-reply nature of communication. Sensor network applications would be forced to do continuous queries for acquiring the real-time sensor data from TAS. Also the efficiency of SOAP is a liability, as XML parsing of SOAP messages is likely to be inefficient compared to the handling of serialized Java objects in JMS. Although JMS lacks the interoperability provided by Web Services and SOAP, it suits better to the requirements of TAS messaging.

5   Case Application: The Weather Service

The Weather Service is a sensor network application that reports measurements of air, water and ground using maps, graphs and textual summaries. End users can access both historical and current values of the measurements and browse daily reports of the minimum, maximum and average values. An engine application calculates the daily reports and collects sensor data from WSNs distributed to the end users. A TUTWSN given to an end user is formed by a hardware kit including a gateway sensor and a set of wireless sensors. Fig. 4 shows prototypes of these sensors. The wireless sensors are configured to measure targets such as the air and the ground. Using the administration applications of TAS, the administrator sets up the initial permissions and sensor properties before handing out the hardware kit. The new owner of the sensors must plug the gateway sensor into the Internet and deploy the wireless sensors. After that, he can optionally name the sensors and set their locations in the Weather Service application interface. End users of the Weather Service can contribute and offer content to the application by setting their sensors public. Initially only the owner of a sensor is able to observe it. As the amount of users increase, the Weather Service covers locations from ever wider areas.

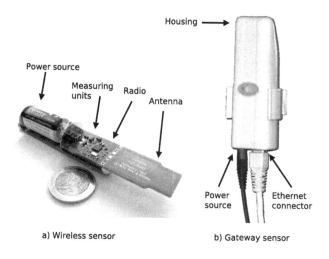

Fig. 4. TUTWSN sensor prototypes

The fetching of temperatures is presented in Fig. 5. A user requests a temperature report from the Weather Service application with a Web browser. The Weather Service forwards the request to the GraphGateway component of the external WSN interface, which in turn forwards it to the SensorMaster. Finally, the SensorMaster queries history data from the database. The GraphGateway accepts HTTP requests and returns replies in PNG format. The benefit of using a separate component to draw graphs is that the component can be reused in other services. The communication between the SensorMaster and the external service gateway use Java messaging.

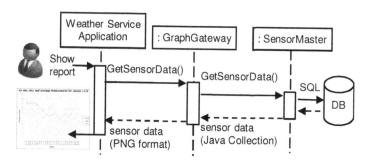

Fig. 5. The use of external WSN interfaces to fetch weather data

Fig. 6 shows the Map Page of the Weather Service. The maps are provided by the Google Maps API [16] with custom extensions for adding the measurement labels on the map. With the help of Asynchronous JavaScript and XML (AJAX), the UI works and feels as a desktop application.

A total of 6899 source lines of code was required to implement the Weather Service. Our experiments showed that using the precalculated daily reports in sensor data

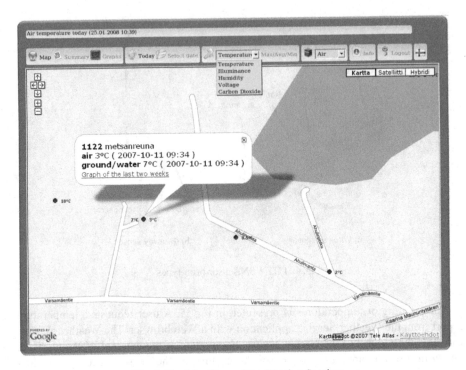

Fig. 6. The Map Page of the Weather Service

querying and graph drawing has a substantial effect on performance. A TUTWSN consisting of twenty temperature measuring sensors produced about 25 000 rows of sensor data in approximately one week. When using the precalculated reports, the query durations with varying time intervals up to 22 weeks remain nearly constant. When fetching the same information from the raw data, the query durations seem to grow exponentially. This proves that scalability should be taken into consideration when designing information storing for WSNs.

6   Conclusions

TAS is used as a platform for sensor network applications. These applications are used regularly by both public and selected groups of end users. The main challenges for designing TAS arouse from the goal of collecting and presenting continuously changing sensor data. This required support for variation in the WSN configurations and the user requirements, mechanisms for publishing information from WSNs, solutions for scalable information storing, and means for sensor data visualization.

Because functionality shared by many sensor network applications is already implemented in TAS, developers can focus on application specific problems, which leads to advances in WSN research. Emerging WSN technologies and various types of WSNs can be integrated to TAS by implementing new middleware applications handling the

WSN specific matters. Due to the proven functionality and the sensor network applications, TAS is in position to move to production state.

References

1. Culler, D., Estring, D., Srivastava, M.: Overview of sensor networks. IEEE Computer, Special Issue in Sensor Networks, 41–49 (2004)
2. DACI Research Group: Daci homepage, http://www.tkt.cs.tut.fi/research/daci
3. Kohvakka, M., Hännikäinen, M., Hämäläinen, T.D.: Ultra low energy wireless temperature sensor network implementation. In: Proc. 16th IEEE Int. Symp. Personal Indoor and Mobile Radio Comm (PIMRC 2005), Berlin, Germany, September 11–14 (2005)
4. ZigBee Standards Organization: ZigBee Specification, Document 053474r13 (December 2006)
5. Liferay, Inc.: Liferay portal (visited) (January 24, 2008), http://www.liferay.com/web/guest/products/portal
6. Joomla! Core Team: Joomla! (visited) (January 24, 2008), http://www.joomla.org/
7. Center for Coastal and Land-Margin Research: Corie about corie (visited) (January 24, 2008), http://www.ccalmr.ogi.edu/CORIE
8. Guizzo, E.: Into deep ice [ice monitoring]. IEEE Spectrum 42(12), 28–35 (2005)
9. Biagioni, E.: The remote ecological sensor network (visited) (January 24, 2008), http://www.pods.hawaii.edu
10. Paek, J., Chintalapudi, K., Cafferey, R., Govindan, R., Masri, S.: A wireless sensor network for structural health monitoring: Performance and experience. In: Proceedings of the Second IEE Workshop on Embedded Networked Sensors (May 2005)
11. Global Sensor Networks Team: GSN (visited) (January 24, 2008), http://gsn.sourceforge.net/
12. Yu, M., Junkeun, S., JinWon, K., Kee-Young, S., Pyeong, S.: Nanomon: A flexible sensor network monitoring software. Advanced Communication Technology. In: The 9th International Conference, vol. 2, pp. 1423–1426 (February 2007)
13. Red Hat Middleware, L.: Jboss application server (visited) (january 22, 2008), http://www.jboss.org/products/jbossas
14. Sun Microsystems: Java 2 platform, enterprice edition (J2EE) overview (visited) (January 24, 2008), http://java.sun.com/j2ee/appmodel.html
15. W3C: Soap specifications (visited) (January 28, 2008), http://www.w3.org/TR/soap
16. Google: Google Maps API (visited) (January 24, 2008), http://www.google.com/apis/maps/

Embedded Software Architecture for Diagnosing Network and Node Failures in Wireless Sensor Networks

Jukka Suhonen, Mikko Kohvakka, Marko Hännikäinen, and Timo D. Hämäläinen

Tampere University of Technology, Department of Computer Systems
P.O. Box 553, FI-33101 Tampere, Finland
{jukka.suhonen,mikko.kohvakka,marko.hannikainen,
timo.d.hamalainen}@tut.fi

Abstract. Wireless Sensor Networks (WSNs) consist of embedded and distributed sensor nodes that operate on harsh operating conditions and with limited energy resources. To ensure the desired level of service, it is essential to detect and correct occurring network and node problems. In this paper, we propose a diagnostics software architecture for WSNs consisting of self-diagnostics on embedded sensor nodes and management tools for network analysis. We define a minimum set of diagnostics information that needs to be collected for analyzing the network errors and performance. To minimize communication overhead, collected information is categorized and only needed categories are requested from nodes. The diagnostics architecture is verified with a practical WSN implementation.

1 Introduction

Wireless Sensor Network (WSN) may consist of thousands of randomly deployed embedded nodes that self-organize and operate autonomously. A WSN node combines environment sensing, data processing, and wireless networking with extremely low energy and cost. Sensed data is routed through multiple hops to a sink node that operates as user interface or gateway to other networks. The applications for sensor networks range from home and industrial environments to military uses [1].

Ideally, a WSN adapts to changing operating conditions autonomously. A network self-configures for optimal performance and lifetime, therefore making centralized maintenance unnecessary. In practice, a network experiences several issues that limit the self-configuration. For example, too long links between deployed sensor nodes or interferences from other wireless networks cause unreliability. While some of the issues can be eliminated with a careful deployment, a practical network might also encounter unexpected problems, such as software failures or logical errors in protocols and algorithms. As sensor networks become more complex, it is increasingly more important to collect diagnostics information that allows detecting the problems and identifying their causes. Rather than only informing problems after they already have occurred, the diagnostics should allow detecting arising issues.

Attaching cables to diagnose embedded nodes is not feasible and often not even possible. For example, a network might be deployed on hazardous or unaccessible environment. Therefore, a distributed mechanism to collect the diagnostics information is required.

M. Berekovic, N. Dimopoulos, and S. Wong (Eds.): SAMOS 2008, LNCS 5114, pp. 258–267, 2008.

Most of the reseach on WSN diagnostics concentrate on detecting node failures [2] or correcting sensor readings [2, 3].

A centralized approach that distinguishes a node failure from depletion is proposed in [4]. As nodes send their energy information to manager, a fault is assumed if a node does not reply to a query but should have energy left. [5] presents a reputation-based authentication mechanism that detects misconfigured or malicious nodes in the neighborhood. In [6], a distributed approach is used to detect faulty nodes. A node queries its neighbors and concludes that a neighbor has failed if it gives an invalid reply or fails to reply. The problem with these approaches is that they do not give a reason for the failure. Thus, if a failure is due to a network error, e.g. interference, replacing a failed node does not help as the new node will experience similar errors.

Collecting practical diagnostics information for network analyzation is barely researched for WSNs [7] and most of the existing approaches concentrate only on monitoring sensor readings and topology [8]. [9] concentrates on distributed debugging of sensor nodes but network performance is uncovered. When a fault, e.g. a deadlock or an application specific error, is detected, a node sends an error report to a sink and enters a mode in which a node can be debugged remotely. [10] presents a software architecture for monitoring and controlling WSNs. Only few collected diagnostics types are defined, comprising energy, neighbors, and link qualities. Diagnostics overhead is reduced with aggregation, although an exact method is not specified.

This paper presents WSN diagnostics targeted at measuring network and node performance and fault detection. As such, it is complementary with the research proposals that consider the reliability of sensor readings. The presented diagnostics comprise the collection of self-diagnostics information on sensor nodes and management tools for analyzing the data. While the related proposals concentrate only on detecting faults, our approach determines the reasons for misbehavior, therefore allowing correcting the problem. Unlike [10], our approach specifies exact metrics that are required for diagnosing a distributed wireless network. Instead of aggregating diagnostics and thus possibly losing invaluable measurement results, we propose minimizing the overhead by categorizing diagnostics and transmitting only categories that are required for analysis. The presented diagnostics is tested and implemented on a practical WSN environment.

This paper is organized as follows. Section 2 describes the design of the diagnostics architecture. Self-diagnostics collected on each node are described in Section 3. A prototype implementation is presented in Section 4. Finally, Section 5 concludes the paper.

2   WSN Diagnostics

2.1   Design Goals and Assumptions

The design goals for the diagnostics are to measure performance, detect node failures, and determine reason for the failures. As the primary purpose of a WSN is to collect sensor readings, diagnostics overhead must be minimized. Also, a light-weight implementation is required, because most of the memory and processing resources are required for the normal operation. Finally, the diagnostics must tolerate packet losses, as errors must be detected also during unreliable network conditions.

This paper assumes a synchronized, low duty cycle WSN using a clustered topology, because such WSN can be considered the most demanding in respect of collected diagnostics. Still, the proposed diagnostics is generalizable to other WSNs by disregarding irrelevant information. Duty cycling and clustering are used in WSNs to save energy. In a low duty cycle operation, transceiver is active only part of the time, while remaining time is spent on a low energy state. Clustering increases energy efficiency, because energy consuming forwarding is performed by a small subset of nodes that are referred to as *headnodes*, while the other nodes, referred to as *subnodes*, can sleep most of the time.

2.2 Diagnostics Architecture

The diagnostics architecture is shown in Fig. 1. Each node collects self-diagnostics information regarding the node itself and nodes in its neighborhood. The self-diagnostics enables measuring network Quality of Service (QoS), determine problems, and detect software failures. The information is stored for later analysis. The data can be stored in the WSN, e.g. on a node itself, or collected on a sink node, from which the information may be queried. In the implemented prototype, the data is stored in a database server to allow fast querying and maintaining longer history records. The management tools collect information for decisions that require human interaction. As detecting the reason for a problem from raw diagnostics values is hard, the management tools visualize the network status and emphasize the problematic behavior with graphs and alerts. Based on the analyzed performance, network parameters can be adjusted for refining the trade-off between performance and energy. However, such optimization is outside the scope of this paper. In this paper, configuring denotes instructing the self-diagnostics on sensor nodes to select the collected diagnostics information and the collection interval.

To avoid complexity on resource constrained nodes, a node pre-processes diagnostics data is only slightly. As extensive analyzation requires global knowledge and computational resources, complex analysis is performed on the management tools that are run outside the sensor network. The approach does not significantly increase overhead on network, because an intensive diagnosing is switched on only on-demand.

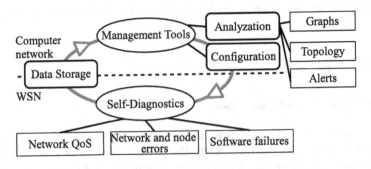

Fig. 1. Design of the distributed WSN diagnostics

3 Self-diagnostics on Embedded Nodes

Each node collects self-diagnostics information about its operation and transmits the data to a sink node as shown in Fig. 2. It should be noted that the design does not limit the number of sinks that monitor the network. Because the information required for diagnostics is related to several layers, each layer maintains information about its state and operation. In the physical layer, diagnostics information comprises battery voltage, and hardware status of sensors and other peripherals that is determined based on performed self-tests. Self-test information allows disregarding invalid sensor readings and replacing misbehaving nodes, whereas voltage enables an early warning before depletion. Medium Access Control (MAC) layer maintains connectivity information to the neighbors and active routes are recorded on the routing layer. Forward queue information required for analyzing network load and delays is maintained in between MAC and routing layers.

A self-diagnostics control module is used to collect and combine the data from different layers to get extensive information about the state of the node. The control module also maintains statistics from individually measured parameters that is used quantify resources status, e.g. average link reliability. Self-diagnostics application communicates with a sink node by utilizing the underlying protocol stack. The application receives commands from the sink that determines the content of collected data and instructs the control module to gather the requested information. Then, the application reports back to the sink. The sink may command the application to perform one-shot queries or generate diagnostics packets periodically.

The architecture requires only minimal changes a typical sensor code, because WSN nodes usually use diagnostics information internally to make operational decisions. For example, link reliability information is crucial when selecting highest reliability route.

3.1 Diagnostics Categories

As all of the self-diagnostics information may not be needed at the same time, the diagnostics data is divided into several categories. Diagnostics data on each category is generated in a separate packet. The benefit of this approach is that only the categories of interest are transmitted and different transmission intervals may be used for each packet. For robustness, most of the diagnostics are expressed as counter values, thus

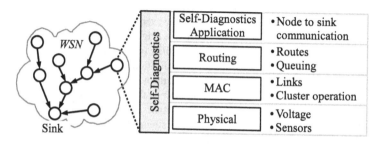

Fig. 2. Collection of network diagnostics on embedded sensor nodes

allowing missing a packet without the loss of information. The categories and collected statistics are summarized in Table 1.

Node information category collects generic information about a node. If the node information shows symptoms of misbehavior, more extensive diagnostics are switched on. *Network and node events* assign a reason for occurred events that allows evaluating the behavior of a node. Traffic information is collected in *cluster traffic* and *node traffic* categories. Knowledge about the traffic is essential when determining throughput and reliability. The node traffic gives more detailed information by detailing per link traffic, but has a higher overhead. *Network topology* category gives an overview of network structure. The topology information is collected separately, because it can be collected infrequently when network is static.

3.2   Node Information

The node information packet is used to get an overall impression of the performance. It allows detecting the symptoms of misbehavior and thus, the need for collecting other diagnostics categories. Additionally, if a node does not perform sensing, the node information is regarded as a keep-alive message indicating that a node is still available.

Voltage information is used to determine when to replace a node. A comparison against stored voltage values gives the rate of voltage drop and thus energy depletion. Too high depletion rate indicates performance problems and a requirement for deeper examination of the node. Queue usage and delay are used to detect forwarding problems. High queue usage increases delays and is usually an indication of a performance bottleneck. However, if the delays are high while queue usage is low, a next hop link might not be reliable which causes retransmissions.

Table 1. Collected self-diagnostics and diagnostics categories

Category	Statistics	Description
Node information	Voltage	Latest voltage measurement
	Queue statistics	Average and maximum queue usage and delays
	Role	Indicates headnode or subnode
	Boots	Boot counter
	Network scans	Network scan counter
	Route changes	Cumulative number of route changes
Network and node events	Event	The descriptor of an occurred event
	Reason	A reason for the event
	Neighbor	A reference to a neighbor node relating to the event
Network topology	Neighbor	Neighbor identifier (e.g. unique address)
	Link quality	Link quality indication
	Channel	Frequency that the neighbor operates on
	Sleep schedule	Duty cycle timing relative to the sender
Cluster traffic	Channel usage	Average and maximum channel usage
	RX/TX counters	The number of attempted and failed operations
Link traffic	Neighbor	Neighbor identifier
	RX/TX counters	The number of attempted and failed operations

A role parameter tells whether a node acts as a headnode or saves energy as subnode. The information is crucial when evaluating the used clustering algorithm and determining network coverage as only headnodes forward traffic. Boot, network scan, and route change counters are used to detect instability. The boot counter is stored in a non-volatile memory and incremented on every boot. An increase in the boot counter is always an indication of severe hardware or software problems. Network scans, route changes, and role changes are a part of the normal network activity. However, too frequent changes indicate instability that decrease performance and increase energy usage.

3.3 Network and Node Events

Network and node events are used to express the reasons for performed operations on a sensor node. A diagnostic event identifies the performed operation, reason, and a neighbor reference. The operation is a network scan, a synchronization loss, a route change, a role change, or a boot. The reason is a simple integer value with a predetermined meaning that describes the cause for an event, thus giving an information why the sensor software performed a certain operation. The neighbor reference identifies neighbor address that relates to the event, for example the neighbor to which a synchronization was lost. Communication overhead is minimized by fitting several events into one packet.

3.4 Network Topology

Network topology is constructed by requesting each node to send diagnostics regarding their neighbors. An average link quality to each neighbor is used to detect weak and therefore unreliable links. If a node has only neighbors with weak links, user interaction is required to add new nodes that can forward traffic more reliably.

Simultaneous transmissions within an interference range cause collisions and thus performance degradation. For detecting overlapping communication periods and evaluating channel assignment algorithms, nodes send channel and sleep schedule information of their neighbors acting as a headnode. As sleeping often causes a significant forwarding delay, the sleep schedule information also enables evaluating end-to-end latencies.

3.5 Cluster and Link Traffic

The traffic information is divided into as cluster traffic and link traffic. The main difference between these is that the cluster traffic handles aggregates, whereas the link traffic maintains separate counters for each neighbor. Thus, cluster traffic has less overhead and is useful for identifying bottlenecks or clusters that have low reliability. Then, the collection of link traffic counters can be switched on in the neighborhood of the problematic cluster to get detailed traffic profile and identify badly behaving nodes.

The traffic counters comprise transmission (TX) and reception (RX) successes and failures. A transmission failure is detected when an acknowledgment is not received. However, reception failures cannot be detected directly, because a receiver does not usually know when to expect a transmission with contention based channel access.

Therefore, the reception failure counter is increased when either a missed sequence number is detected or a duplicate is received. A duplicate means that a sender did not receive acknowledgment packet and had to retransmit. The reasons for unreliability can be concluded together with the neighbor information, e.g. low Received Signal Strength Indication (RSSI) is a possible reason for unreliability. However, if link has high RSSI, the unreliability might be caused by interference.

In addition to the traffic counters, the cluster traffic contains channel that describes the utilization of the wireless channel. A high channel usage indicates a bottleneck and thus the requirement to add more headnodes to balance the load. Only a headnode sends the cluster traffic information.

4   Prototype Implementation

WSN diagnostics architecture is implemented on Tampere University of Technology Wireless Sensor Network (TUTWSN) platforms consisting of energy-efficient protocol stack [11] and sensor hardware [12] that are optimized with cross-layer design. The TUTWSN embedded sensor node that is used in the implementation is presented in Fig. 3. The platform uses a PIC18F8722 [13] MicroController Unit (MCU) that executes 2 Millions Instructions Per Second (MIPS). The node is powered with two 1.5 V AA batteries. The MCU includes an Analog-to-Digital Converter (ADC) that is used to measure battery voltage and read analog sensors. For environmental monitoring, a node is fitted with temperature, accelerometer, and carbon dioxide sensors. The platform contains a Nordic Semiconductor nRF24L01 RF transceiver that operates at 2.4 GHz frequency and supports transmit powers of -20 dBm...0 dBm.

The implementation architecture is shown in Fig. 4. The collected self-diagnostics are transmitted through gateway nodes to a WSN server. Instead of accessing the WSN directly, User Interfaces (UIs) connect to the WSN server. The benefits of this approach is that WSN server provides a centralized access control with authentication. Additionally, the server hosts several web applications that allow monitoring the sensor network

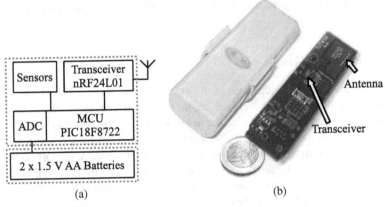

Fig. 3. TUTWSN embedded sensor node a) hardware architecture, b) prototype and its weatherproof casing

without installing special software on a client computer. Diagnostics data is stored to a database, which allows evaluating long term performance on the network.

The operation of management tools is divided between the WSN server and configuration and monitoring UIs on a client computer. The WSN server pre-processes the received data for the database and utilizes back-end services for sending threshold based alerts to network administrator with e-mail. A client UI shown in Fig. 5 combines the analyzation and configuration.

4.1   Memory Requirements and Communication Overhead

The self-diagnostics implementation takes 4 kB program memory and 300 B data memory. The self-diagnostics application and the self-diagnostics control module are included in the memory requirements. However, the memory requirements for collecting per protocol layer diagnostics are not included, because the information is needed for a normal node operation in any case. For example, MAC layer needs to maintain link information even when the self-diagnostics are not transmitted to a sink.

The self-diagnostics information is transmitted in five packets types that correspond with the self-diagnostics categories. Due to transceiver limitations, a fixed packet size of 32 B is used, which leaves 18 B per packet for payload after MAC and routing headers. For fully utilizing the available payload, network and node events are included in the node information packet.

To reduce the payload requirements, the size of a counters in bits (b) is optimized as

$$b = \log_2 e \cdot (1 + m) \cdot i, \tag{1}$$

where e is the maximum number of measured events per second, m is the maximum allowed number of consecutively missing packets, and i is the maximum transmission interval. The counters are optimized to allow 5 minutes interval between received packets and one missed packet. With these optimizations, the size for of a diagnostic counter ranges from 8 to 12 bits.

For simplicity, diagnostics data is transmitted periodically. Fig. 6 compares the resulting diagnostics per node overhead against the amount of sensor data. Diagnostics overhead is increased, when more accurate diagnostics are switched on. Collecting all

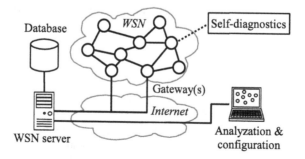

Fig. 4. Implemented architecture of WSN diagnostics

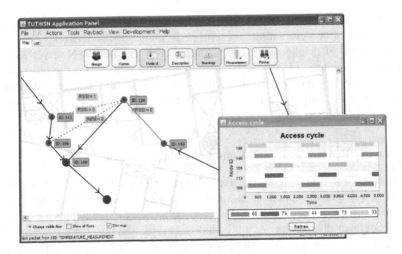

Fig. 5. User interface visualizing network topology and connectivity between nodes. The dialog shows the communication periods of selected clusters.

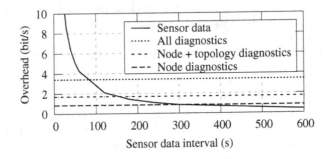

Fig. 6. Diagnostics against sensor data overhead on the implementation

diagnostics requires sending 4 packets periodically. As packet sizes are fixed, diagnostics and sensor data overheads are equal when sensor data interval is 5 minutes. When sensor data is sampled often, the diagnostics overhead is insignificant. To further reduce the overhead, it would be possible to transmit diagnostics packets only when diagnostics counters have changed.

5 Conclusions

This paper presents a diagnostics software architecture for diagnosing node and network errors in resource constrained embedded distributed systems, such as WSNs. The architecture consists of self-diagnostics on embedded nodes and management tools for analyzing network.A minimum set of diagnostics information that needs to be collected for analyzing the network errors and performance is defined. To minimize communication overhead, the self-diagnostics information is categorized and only needed categories are requested from nodes. According to prototype implementation, only slight communication overhead is required.

References

1. Karl, H., Willig, A.: Protocols and Architectures for Wireless Sensor Networks. John Wiley & Sons Ltd, Chichester (2005)
2. Yu, M., Mokhtar, H., Merabti, M.: Fault management in wireless sensor networks. IEEE Wireless Communications 14(6), 13–19 (2007)
3. Zohra, F.A., Selmic, R.R.: Fault aware wireless sensor networks. In: Int'l Conf. on Networking, Sensing and Control, April 15–17, pp. 30–35 (2007)
4. Ruiz, L.B., Siqueira, I.G.: Fault management in event-driven wireless sensor networks. In: 7th ACM Int'l Symposium on Modeling, Analysis and Simulation of Wireless and Mobile Systems (MSWiM 2004), pp. 149–156. ACM, New York (2004)
5. McCoy, D., Sicker, D., Grunwald, D.: A mechanism for detecting and responding to misbehaving nodes in wireless networks. In: 4th IEEE Communications Society Conf. on Sensor, Mesh and Ad Hoc Communications and Networks (SECON 2007), June 18–21, pp. 678–684 (2007)
6. Elhadef, M., Boukerche, A., Elkadiki, H.: Diagnosing mobile ad-hoc networks: two distributed comparison-based self-diagnosis protocols. In: 4th ACM Int'l Workshop on Mobility Management and Wireless Access (MobiWac 2006), pp. 18–27. ACM, New York (2006)
7. Wang, Y., Liu, X., Yin, J.: Requirements of quality of service in wireless sensor networks. In: Int'l Conf. on Systems and Int'l Conf. on Mobile Communications and Learning Technologies (ICN/ICONS/MCL), April 23–29, pp. 116–120 (2006)
8. Yu, M., Song, J., Kim, J., Shin, K.Y., Mah, P.S.: NanoMon: A flexible sensor network monitoring software. In: 9th Int'l Conference on Advanced Communication Technology, February 12–14, vol. 2, pp. 1423–1426 (2007)
9. Krunic, V., Trumpler, E., Han, R.: NodeMD: diagnosing node-level faults in remote wireless sensor systems. In: 5th Int'l Conf. on Mobile Systems, Applications and Services (MobiSys 2007), pp. 43–56. ACM, New York (2007)
10. Sun, L., Sun, Y., Shu, J., He, Q.: MotePlat: A monitoring and control platform for wireless sensor networks. In: Grid and Cooperative Computing Workshops (GCCW 2006), pp. 452–458 (October 2006)
11. Suhonen, J., Kuorilehto, M., Hännikäinen, M., Hämäläinen, T.D.: Cost-aware dynamic routing protocol for wireless sensor networks - design and prototype experiments. In: 17th Annual IEEE Int'l Symposium on Personal, Indoor and Mobile Radio Communications (PIMRC 2006), Helsinki, Finland, pp. 1–5 (September 2006)
12. Kohvakka, M., Hännikäinen, M., Hämäläinen, T.D.: Ultra low energy wireless temperature sensor network implementation. In: 16th Int'l Symposium on Personal Indoor and Mobile Radio Communications (PIMRC 2005), Germany, pp. 801–805 (September 2005)
13. Microchip Technology Inc.: PIC18F8722 Family Data Sheet (2007), http://ww1.microchip.com/downloads/en/DeviceDoc/39646b.pdf.

Signature-Based Calibration of Analytical System-Level Performance Models

Stanley Jaddoe and Andy D. Pimentel

Computer Systems Architecture group
Informatics Institute, University of Amsterdam, The Netherlands
{vjaddoe,andy}@science.uva.nl

Abstract. The Sesame system-level simulation framework targets efficient design space exploration of embedded multimedia systems. Even despite Sesame's efficiency, it would fail to explore large parts of the design space simply because system-level simulation is too slow for this. Therefore, Sesame uses analytical performance models to provide steering to the system-level simulation, guiding it toward promising system architectures and thus pruning the design space. In this paper, we present a mechanism to calibrate these analytical models with the aim to deliver trustworthy estimates. Moreover, we also present some initial evaluation results with respect to the accuracy of our calibration mechanism using a case study with a Motion-JPEG encoder.

1 Introduction

The increasing complexity of modern embedded systems, which are more and more based on (heterogeneous) MultiProcessor-SoC (MP-SoC) architectures, has led to the emergence of system-level design. A key ingredient of system-level design is the notion of high-level modeling and simulation in which the models allow for capturing the behavior of system components and their interactions at a high level of abstraction. As these high-level models minimize the modeling effort and are optimized for execution speed, they can be applied at the early stages of design to perform, for example, architectural Design Space Exploration (DSE). Such early DSE is of eminent importance as early design choices heavily influence the success or failure of the final product.

With our Sesame modeling and simulation framework [1,2], we target efficient system-level design space exploration of embedded multimedia systems, allowing rapid performance evaluation of different architecture designs, application to architecture mappings, and hardware/software partitionings. Key to this flexibility is the separation of application and architecture models, together with an explicit mapping step to map an application model onto an architecture model.

Although Sesame's system-level simulation allows for efficiently evaluating different application/architecture combinations, it would fail to explore large parts – let alone the entire span – of the design space. This is because system-level simulation is simply too slow for comprehensively exploring the design space, which is at its largest during the early stages of design. For this reason, Sesame uses analytical models [3,4] to provide steering to the system-level simulation, guiding it toward promising system architectures and therefore allowing for *pruning* the design space. These analytical models,

M. Berekovic, N. Dimopoulos, and S. Wong (Eds.): SAMOS 2008, LNCS 5114, pp. 268–278, 2008.

which include models for performance, power and cost estimation, are used for quickly searching the design space by means of multi-objective optimization using evolutionary algorithms. So far, this analytical modeling stage lacked a systematic method for deriving the model parameters that specify application requirements and architecture capabilities. Clearly, the accuracy of these analytical models is highly dependent on the correct determination of these parameters.

In this paper, we focus on the performance estimation part of our analytical models (i.e. the power and cost models are not addressed) and present a technique based on execution profiles, referred to as *signatures*, that allows for deriving the application and architecture specific parameters in these analytical performance models. Using a preliminary experiment with a Motion-JPEG encoder application and an MP-SoC architecture, we also show initial results of the accuracy of our approach by comparing the estimations of our signature-based analytical model with those from simulation.

The remainder of the paper is organized as follows. In the next section, we introduce the basic analytical system model [3,4] for which we want to derive the model parameters. Section 3 describes how we determine application specific model parameters via a profiling mechanism based on signatures. Section 4 describes how architecture specific parameters are derived using a comparable mechanism. In Section 5, we put together the pieces of the puzzle presented in Sections 3 and 4 to actually construct signature-based analytical performance models. Section 6 presents initial results of the evaluation of the accuracy of our approach using an experiment with a Motion-JPEG encoder application. Section 7 describes related work, and Section 8 concludes the paper.

2 Basic Analytical System Model

In the Sesame framework, applications are modeled using the Kahn Process Network (KPN) [5] model of computation in which parallel processes communicate with each other via unbounded FIFO channels. By executing the application model, each Kahn process records its actions in order to generate its own *trace of application events* which is necessary for driving an architecture model. There are three types of application events, divided in two groups: *execute* events for computational behavior and *read* and *write* events for communication behavior.

The architecture models in Sesame simulate the performance consequences of the computation and communication events generated by an application model. Architecture models are constructed from building blocks provided by a library containing template models for processing cores, and various types of memories and interconnects.

Since Sesame makes a distinction between application and architecture models, it needs an explicit mapping step to relate these models for co-simulation. In this step, the designer decides for each application process and FIFO channel a destination architecture model component to simulate its workload. This is an important step in the design process, since the final success of the design can be highly dependent on these mapping choices. To decide on an optimum mapping, many instances need to be considered (and thus simulated). In realistic cases, in which the underlying architecture is also varied during the process of design space exploration, simulation of all points in the design space is infeasible. Therefore, analytical models are needed to prune the design space, steering the designer towards a small set of promising design points which then can be simulated. The remainder of this section elaborates on the basic analytical performance model [3,4] we use in Sesame for design space pruning, after which the subsequent sections present our signature-based mechanism to 'calibrate' this analytical model.

The application models in Sesame are represented by a graph $KPN = (V_K, E_K)$ where the set V_K and E_K refer to the Kahn processes and the directed FIFO channels between these processes, respectively. For each process $a \in V_K$, we define $B_a \subseteq E_K$ to be the set of FIFO channels connected to process a, $B_a = \{b_{a1}, \ldots, b_{an}\}$. For each Kahn process, we define a computation requirement, shown with α_a, representing the computational workload imposed by that Kahn process onto a particular component in the architecture model. The communication requirement of a Kahn process is not defined explicitly, rather it is derived from the channels attached to it. We have chosen this type of definition for the following reason: if the Kahn process and one of its channels are mapped onto the same architecture component, the communication overhead experienced by the Kahn process due to that specific channel is simply neglected. For the communication workload imposed by the Kahn process, only those channels that are mapped onto different architecture components are taken into account. So our model neglects internal communications and only considers external communications. Formally, we denote the communication requirement of the channel b with β_b. To include memory latencies into our model, we require that mapping a channel onto a specific memory asks computation tasks from the memory. To express this, we define the computational requirement of the channel b from the memory as α_b. Here, it is ensured that the parameters β_b and α_b are only taken into account when the channel b is mapped onto an external memory. The actual determination of the above model parameters, which is the contribution of this paper, will be addressed in the next section.

Similarly to the application model, the architecture model is also represented by a graph $ARC = (V_A, E_A)$ where the sets V_A and E_A denote the architecture components and the connections between the architecture components, respectively. In our model, the set of architecture components consists of two disjoint subsets: the set of processors (P) and the set of memories (M), $V_A = P \cup M$ and $P \cap M = \emptyset$. For each processor $p \in P$, the set $M_p = \{m_{p1}, \ldots, m_{pj}\}$ represents the memories which are reachable from the processor p. We define processing capabilities for both the processors and the memories as c_p and c_m, respectively. These parameters need to be set such that they reflect processing capabilities for processors, and memory access latencies for memories. The determination of these parameters will be addressed in Section 4.

The above model needs to adhere to a number of constraints, such as that each Kahn process has to be mapped to a processor, each channel has to be mapped to a processor (in case of local communication) or memory, and so on. For a formal description of these constraints, we refer to [3,4].

3   Application Requirements

As indicated in the previous section, we need to determine the model parameters for application requirements (α_a, α_b and β_b) and architecture capabilities (c_p and c_m). To this end, we present an approach based on execution profiles of application events, referred to as *signatures*, to determine these model parameters. In the remainder of this section, we focus on the derivation of the model parameters – via these signatures – for application requirements. As will become clear, our approach strictly adheres to the separation of concerns concept [6], separating application (requirements) from architecture (capabilities) signatures.

A signature of a Kahn process represents its computational requirements. These process signatures describe the computational complexity at a high level of abstraction using an Abstract Instruction Set (AIS). Currently, our AIS consists of the small set of abstract instruction types as shown in Table 1(a)[1]. To construct a signature, the real machine instructions that embody the computation, derived from an Instruction Set Simulator (ISS), are first mapped onto the AIS, after which a compact execution profile is made. This means that the resulting signature is a vector containing the instruction counts of the different AIS instructions. The first column in Table 1(a) shows the signature (vector) index that each AIS instruction type corresponds to.

To illustrate the process of determining the process signatures, consider Table 1(b) which shows an example event trace of Kahn process k_1. When deriving the signature of process k_1, only the *execute* events in its event trace are considered. Each *execute* event comes with an identifier of an operation, to indicate which operation was executed. The signature of k_1 is the sum of the signatures of the operations executed by k_1. In the example of Table 1(b), operations op_1 and op_2 have signatures that describe the computational requirements of these operations. Now, assume that an ISS generates the trace of (in this case, ARM) instructions as shown in the first column of Table 1(c) for op_1. The next step is to classify these instructions (is it a basic integer instruction, or a memory operation, or a branch instruction, etc.). In other words, the assembly instructions have to be mapped to the AIS instructions defined for our signatures. The result of this classification is shown in the second column of Table 1(c). Then, a signature for op_1 can be generated based on the counts of the AIS opcodes. For op_1, this gives

$$op_1.\text{signature} = [3, 15, 1, 0, 3, 9, 0, 0] \tag{1}$$

with the AIS counts ranked according to the first column of Table 1(a). Using the same method, a signature for op_2 can be generated. Assume that its signature is:

$$op_2.\text{signature} = [8, 17, 8, 0, 2, 29, 2, 0] \tag{2}$$

Then, using these signatures we can answer the original question, that is, calculate the signature of process k_1 (i.e., α_{k_1}). According to the event trace of process k_1, op_1 was executed two times, op_2 one time. Thus,

$$k_1.\text{signature} = 2op_1.\text{signature} + op_2.\text{signature} = [14, 47, 10, 0, 8, 47, 2, 0] \tag{3}$$

An important thing to note is that in practice, if an operation is executed more than once, the derived signatures for each execution of the operation may not be equal (due to data dependencies, or pseudo-random behaviour of the operation). In that case, the operation's signature becomes the average signature of all executions of that operation.

---

[1] In this paper, we focus on programmable cores as processor targets, but the AIS also consists of a special "co-processor" instruction that can be used for modeling dedicated HW blocks.

Table 1. Table (a) shows the currently defined AIS instructions with their index in the vector-based process signatures. Table (b) lists the event trace of process k_1, and Table (c) shows an execution trace of op_1 as obtained by an ARM ISS (left column) and the corresponding AIS instructions (right column).

Signature index	AIS opcode	Description
1	AIS_BMEM	Block memory transfers
2	AIS_MEM	Memory transfers
3	AIS_BRANCH	Branches
4	AIS_COPROC	Co-proc. instructions
5	AIS_IMUL	Int. multiplications
6	AIS_ISIMPLE	Simple Int. arithmetic
7	AIS_OS	Software interrupts
8	AIS_UNKNOWN	Non-mappable instruction

(a)

read	f_2
execute	op_1
write	f_1
read	f_2
execute	op_2
write	f_1
execute	op_1
write	f_1
write	f_1

(b)

ARM instruction	AIS opcode	ARM instruction	AIS opcode
bl 0x81c4;	AIS_BRANCH	str r3, [fp, #−16];	AIS_MEM
mov ip, sp;	AIS_ISIMPLE	ldr r2, [fp, #−20];	AIS_MEM
stmdb sp, fp, ip, lr, pc;!	AIS_BMEM	ldr r3, [fp, #−16];	AIS_MEM
sub fp, ip, #4;	AIS_ISIMPLE	mul r3, r2, r3;	AIS_IMUL
sub sp, sp, #12;	AIS_ISIMPLE	str r3, [fp, #−24];	AIS_MEM
ldr r2, [fp, #−16];	AIS_MEM	ldr r2, [fp, #−16];	AIS_MEM
ldr r3, [fp, #−20];	AIS_MEM	ldr r3, [fp, #−24];	AIS_MEM
add r2, r2, r3;	AIS_ISIMPLE	add r2, r2, r3;	AIS_ISIMPLE
ldr r3, [fp, #−24];	AIS_MEM	ldr r3, [fp, #−20];	AIS_MEM
rsb r3, r3, r2;	AIS_ISIMPLE	mul r3, r2, r3;	AIS_IMUL
str r3, [fp, #−24];	AIS_MEM	str r3, [fp, #−16];	AIS_MEM
ldr r2, [fp, #−16];	AIS_MEM	sub sp, fp, #12;	AIS_ISIMPLE
ldr r3, [fp, #−20];	AIS_MEM	ldmia sp, {fp, sp, pc};	AIS_BMEM
add r2, r2, r3;	AIS_ISIMPLE	mov ip, sp;	AIS_ISIMPLE
ldr r3, [fp, #−24];	AIS_MEM	stmdb sp, fp, ip, lr, pc;!	AIS_BMEM
mul r3, r2, r3;	AIS_IMUL		

(c)

A signature of a FIFO channel describes the load induced by the channel on memory components (i.e., α_b and β_b from Section 2). This communication requirement of a FIFO channel depends on the size of the token (in bytes) sent via the channel, and the total number of tokens sent. In our application models, the size of the tokens sent via a FIFO channel is fixed. The number of tokens sent via a FIFO channel can be extracted from the Kahn process' event trace. Each *write*-event in an event trace contains data about to which communication port the token was sent. So, the signature of a FIFO channel f is a two-element vector containing the number of tokens sent via the channel and the size of each token:

$$f.\text{signature} = [n_{tokens}, n_{size}] \tag{4}$$

For example, assume the event trace of process k_1 in Table 1(b) and a token size for channel f_1 of $n_{size} = 12$ bytes. Since process k_1 writes four times a token of 12 bytes to f_1 (see Table 1(b)), the signature of f_1 thus becomes:

$$f_1.\text{signature} = [4, 12] \tag{5}$$

4 Architectural Capabilities

Previously, the computational and communication *requirements* of an application have been defined. In this section, the computational and communication *capabilities* of processors and memories will be defined. These capabilities will also be encoded as (vector-based) signatures.

If a Kahn process k_1 is mapped onto a processor p_1, then the number of cycles p_1 is busy processing k_1 (denoted as $\mathcal{T}(p_1)$) can be calculated as a function of the signatures of k_1 (the computational requirements) and p_1 (the processor capabilities):

$$\mathcal{T}(p_1) = f(k_1.\text{signature}, p_1.\text{signature}) \tag{6}$$

The aim is to find or define both p_1.signature and the function f in (6). With these, we can calculate the number of cycles a processor is busy processing the *execute* events emitted by Kahn processes mapped onto the processor.

Using an ISS, we can measure how many cycles a certain operation takes when executed on a specific processor (like an ARM). If this is repeated for many operations, a *training set* can be built. Using this training set, the computational capabilities of a processor (i.e., its signature) can be derived by, for example, linear regression, or techniques used in the field of machine learning.

Using the example from the previous section, a (very small) training set can be made. This training set consists of the signatures of op_1 and op_2 and the associated cycle counts. Let us assume that executing op_1 took 185 cycles, and that op_2 took 369 cycles when executed on an ARM processor. Since a training set consists of a list of vectors (operation signatures), and a list of cycle counts, this problem can be solved using the least-squares method. For example, let SM be the matrix with the signatures of operations op_1 and op_2 as rows, p_1.signature be the weight vector we want to calculate for processor p_1, and c be the vector with cycle counts for each row in SM. Then, $SM \cdot p_1.\text{signature} = c$ is solved using the least squares method.

$$\begin{pmatrix} 3 & 15 & 1 & 0 & 3 & 9 & 0 & 0 \\ 8 & 17 & 8 & 0 & 2 & 29 & 2 & 0 \end{pmatrix} \cdot p_1.\text{signature} = \begin{pmatrix} 185 \\ 369 \end{pmatrix} \tag{7}$$

The signature of p_1 is the the vector consisting of weights for each AIS instruction. The unit of the elements in the vector is 'cycles per instruction'. Note that these weights can be adapted in order to perform high-level architectural design space exploration for the given processor (e.g., make multiplications more/less expensive, etc.).

$$p_1.\text{signature} = [2.19, 7.11, 1.62, 0.0, 1.19, 7.4, 0.33, 0.0] \tag{8}$$

Given an operation signature s that is not included in the training set, the estimated number of cycles on p_1 for that signature is simply the inner product of s and p_1.signature.

The signature (and thus the communication capability) of a memory component (i.e., c_m) is a two-element vector $[r_{read}, r_{write}]$ that only consists of the (average) read and write latencies. So far, in contrast to processor signatures, we have not developed any methods to get reliable memory signatures. Instead, a designer may use values from memory data sheets to create a memory signature.

5   Analytical Performance Estimation

In the previous sections, portions of a (signature-based) analytical performance model were presented. In this section, these portions will be forged together to get an analytical performance model for an architecture.

$\mathcal{T}^c(p) \leftarrow 0$

foreach $k \in X_p$ **do**

    foreach $f \in FIFOChannels_{k,ext}$ **do**

        $b \leftarrow f.\text{signature}[n_{tokens}] \cdot f.\text{signature}[n_{size}]$

        $m \leftarrow \mathcal{M}(f)$

        if f is an incoming channel of k **then**

            $\mathcal{T}^c(p) \leftarrow \mathcal{T}^c(p) + b/m.\text{signature}[r_{read}]$

        end

        if f is an outgoing channel of k **then**

            $\mathcal{T}^c(p) \leftarrow \mathcal{T}^c(p) + b/m.\text{signature}[r_{write}]$

        end

    end

end

Algorithm 1. Calculation of $\mathcal{T}^c(p)$

First, some definitions have to be made. The set X_p is the set of processes that are mapped onto processor p. A similar definition applies to X_m, the set of channels mapped onto memory m. $\mathcal{M}(f)$ denotes the memory onto which channel f is mapped and $FIFOChannels_{k,ext}$ is the set of channels of process k that are mapped onto an external memory.

The time $\mathcal{T}^e(p)$ a processor p is spending on executing operations is the inner product of the sum of the signatures of all processes mapped on p, with the signature of p.

$$\mathcal{T}^e(p) = \left\langle \left(\sum_{k \in X_p} k.\text{signature} \right), p.\text{signature} \right\rangle \tag{9}$$

The time $\mathcal{T}^c(p)$ the processor is communicating depends on the number of bytes sent and received via FIFO channels that are mapped on an external memory. This quantity can be calculated by Algorithm 1.

The total time processor p is busy processing *read*, *write*, and *execute* events is

$$\mathcal{T}(p) = \mathcal{T}^e(p) + \mathcal{T}^c(p) \tag{10}$$

The number of cycles $\mathcal{T}(m)$ a memory m is busy sending or receiving data is calculated in Algorithm 2, in a similar way as $\mathcal{T}^c(p)$.

The maximum processing time of an architecture with a certain mapping depends on the architecture component with the largest processing time. Therefore, we need to solve

$$\min \max \left(\max_{p \in P} \mathcal{T}(p), \max_{m \in M} \mathcal{T}(m) \right) \tag{11}$$

6   Experimental Results

In this section, mapping exploration results of the signature-based analytic method will be compared to simulation results using a Motion-JPEG (M-JPEG) encoder application. The target MP-SoC architecture we used in this experiment consists of four ARM processors with local memory and a crossbar interconnect. The design space we considered for this experiment consists of all possible mappings of the M-JPEG tasks (i.e. processes) on the processors in the MP-SoC platform.

$b \leftarrow 0$

foreach $f \in X_m$ **do**

$\quad b \leftarrow b + f.\text{signature}[n_{tokens}] \cdot f.\text{signature}[n_{size}]$

end

$\mathcal{T}(m) \leftarrow b/m.\text{signature}[r_{read}] + b/m.\text{signature}[r_{write}]$

Algorithm 2. Calculation of $\mathcal{T}(m)$

Before the M-JPEG application model was mapped on the architecture model, the application was compiled using an ARM C++ compiler, and executed within the SimIt-ARM instruction set simulator environment [7]. The generated ARM instruction traces were used to create the application and architecture signatures. These signatures were subsequently used for determining the parameters in our analytical performance model, as was previously explained. Note that this process is only a one-time effort.

Since the design space in our experiment is relatively limited (consisting of 4096 different mappings), it was possible to evaluate all of these mappings, both analytically as well as by simulation using our Sesame framework. The analytical and simulation results are shown in Figure 1. Note that only the first fifty mappings are depicted due to space limitations (to avoid cluttering in the graph). Each mapping gets a certain index. The order of the mappings in Figure 1 is more or less arbitrary. Mappings with successive indices are not necessarily related to each other. In this experiment, we measured an average relative error of our analytical model compared to simulation of only 0.1%, with a standard deviation of 0.2. From this, it can be concluded that the performance estimates of our analytic method are promising since they show small errors with respect to the simulation-based estimates.

It should be noted however that this is only a preliminary evaluation, using some simplified assumptions and circumstances: we obtained the signatures by training with the application itself, and the application used in this case study is still a fairly static, pipeline-based application of which the workload is well suited for prediction. Also, the application does not cause any contention on the interconnect. In an additional experiment, we artificially generated excessive network contention for the M-JPEG application. As a result, the error increased to an average of 14% with a standard deviation of 26. But since in this case the analytical estimates were optimistic and still showed the correct performance trends, we believe that these results are still very promising in the scope of high-level design space pruning (the pruning does not throw away possible good candidate mappings). We also stress that the evaluation time of our analytical performance models is several orders of magnitude smaller as compared to Sesame's system-level simulations.

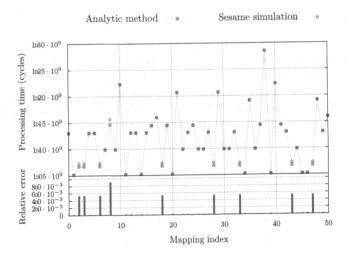

Fig. 1. Comparison between simulation and analytical methods of M-JPEG mappings on a crossbar-based multiprocessor architecture

7   Related Work

Much work has been performed in the area of software performance estimation [8], including methods that use profiling information, typically gathered at the instruction level. For example, in [9] a static software performance estimation technique is presented which uses profiling at the instruction level and which includes the modeling of pipeline hazards in the timing model. In [10], a source-based estimation technique is proposed using the concept of "virtual instructions". These are similar (albeit a bit more low level) to our AIS instructions, but which are directly generated by a compiler framework. Software performance is then calculated based on the accumulation of the performance estimates of these virtual instructions. The idea of convolving application and machine signatures, where the signatures contain coarse-grained system-level information, has also been applied in the domain of performance prediction for high-performance computer systems [11]. In [12], a workload modeling approach based on execution profiles is discussed for statistical micro-architectural simulation. Because they address micro-architectural simulation, their profiles include much more details (such as pipeline and cache behavior), while we address the system level at a higher level of abstraction. In [13], the authors suggest to derive a linear model from a small set of simulations. This method tries to model the performance of a processor at a meso-scopic level. For example, cache behaviour and pipeline characteristics are taken into account. The significance of all cache and pipeline related parameters is determined by simulation-based linear regression models. This may be comparable with the 'weight' vector discussed in Section 4. Another interesting approach is presented in [14], in which the CPI for in-order architectures is predicted using a Monte Carlo based model.

8 Conclusions

In this paper, we presented a technique for calibrating our analytical performance models used for system-level design space pruning. More specifically, we introduced the concept of application and architecture signatures, which can be related with each other to obtain performance estimates. Using a preliminary case study with a Motion-JPEG encoder application, we showed that our signature-based analytical performance model shows promising results with respect to accuracy. But since this application still is relatively static in its behavior, we need to extend our experiments in the future to also include more dynamic applications. Moreover, we need to further study the (off-line) generation of training sets for deriving processor signatures, as well as to investigate extending our signatures to better capture micro-architectural behavior.

References

1. Pimentel, A.D., Erbas, C., Polstra, S.: A systematic approach to exploring embedded system architectures at multiple abstraction levels. IEEE Trans. on Computers 55, 99–112 (2006)
2. Erbas, C., Pimentel, A.D., Thompson, M., Polstra, S.: A framework for system-level modeling and simulation of embedded systems architectures. EURASIP Journal on Embedded Systems (2007) doi:10.1155/2007/82123
3. Erbas, C., Cerav-Erbas, S., Pimentel, A.D.: A multiobjective optimization model for exploring multiprocessor mappings of process networks. In: Proc. of the int. conference on Hardware/Software Codesign & System Synthesis (CODES+ISSS), pp. 182–187 (2003)
4. Erbas, C., Cerav-Erbas, S., Pimentel, A.D.: Multiobjective optimization and evolutionary algorithms for the application mapping problem in multiprocessor system-on-chip design. IEEE Trans. on Evolutionary Computation 10, 358–374 (2006)
5. Kahn, G.: The semantics of a simple language for parallel programming. Information Processing 74, 471–475 (1974)
6. Keutzer, K., Malik, S., Newton, A., Rabaey, J., Sangiovanni-Vincentelli, A.: System level design: Orthogonalization of concerns and platform-based design. IEEE Trans. on Computer-Aided Design of Integrated Circuits and Systems 19 (2000)
7. Qin, W., Malik, S.: Flexible and formal modeling of microprocessors with application to retargetable simulation. In: Design, Automation and Test in Europe (DATE) Conference, pp. 556–561 (2003)
8. Bammi, J.R., Harcoun, E., Kruijtzer, W., Lavagno, L., Lazarescu, M.: Software performance estimation strategies in a system level design tool. In: International Conference on Hardware Software Codesign (CODES), pp. 82–87 (2000)
9. Beltrame, G., Brandolese, C., Fornaciari, W., Salice, F., Sciuto, D., Trianni, V.: An assembly-level execution-time model for pipelined architectures. In: Proc. of Int. Conference on Computer Aided Design (ICCAD), pp. 195–200 (2001)
10. Giusto, P., Martin, G., Harcourt, E.: Reliable estimation of execution time of embedded software. In: Proc. of the Design, Automation, and Test in Europe (DATE) Conference, pp. 580–588 (2001)
11. Snavely, A., Carrington, L., Wolter, N.: Modeling application performance by convolving machine signatures with application profiles. In: Proc. of the IEEE Workshop on Workload Characterization, pp. 149–156 (2001)

12. Eeckhout, L., Nussbaum, S., Smith, J., De Bosschere, K.: Statistical simulation: adding efficiency to the computer designer's toolbox. IEEE Micro 23, 26–38 (2003)
13. Joseph, P., Vaswani, K., Thazhuthaveetil, M.: Construction and Use of Linear Regression Models for Processor Performance Analysis. In: Proc. of the Int. Symposium on High-Performance Computer Architecture, pp. 99–108 (2006)
14. Srinivasan, R., Cook, J., Lubeck, O.: Performance Modeling Using Monte Carlo Simulation. IEEE Computer Architecture Letters 5 (2006)

System-Level Design Space Exploration of Dynamic Reconfigurable Architectures

Kamana Sigdel[1], Mark Thompson[2], Andy D. Pimentel[2], Todor Stefanov[1], and Koen Bertels[1]

[1] Computer Engineering, EEMCS, Delft University of Technology, The Netherlands
{kamana,stefanov,koen}@ce.et.tudelft.nl
[2] Computer Systems Architecture Group, University of Amsterdam, The Netherlands
{mthompsn,andy}@science.uva.nl

Abstract. One of the major challenges of designing heterogeneous reconfigurable systems is to obtain the maximum system performance with efficient utilization of the reconfigurable logic resources. To accomplish this, it is essential to perform design space exploration (DSE) at the early design stages. System-level simulation is used to estimate the performance of the system and to make early decisions of various design parameters in order to obtain an optimal system that satisfies the given constraints. Towards this goal, in this paper, we develop a model, which can assist designers at the system-level DSE stage to explore the utilization of the reconfigurable resources and evaluate the relative impact of certain design choices. A case study of a real application shows that the model can be used to explore various design parameters by evaluating the system performance for different application-to-architecture mappings.

1 Introduction and Related Work

In recent years, reconfigurable architectures have received ever increasing attention due to their adaptability and short design time. The main advantage of reconfigurable computing is its ability to increase performance with accelerated hardware execution, while possessing the flexibility of a software solution. Reconfigurable systems can speed up the application's execution time by mapping selected application kernels onto reconfigurable hardware. In the context of heterogeneous reconfigurable systems, to make early design decisions such as mapping of an application onto reconfigurable hardware, it is essential to perform Design Space Exploration(DSE). DSE environments assist designers in rapid performance evaluation of various parameters such as: architectural characteristics, application-to-architecture mappings, scheduling policies and hardware/software partitioning. This enables a designer to identify design candidates that satisfy functional and non-functional design constraints, e.g: performance, chip area, power consumption etc. DSE environments and methodologies help traversing (typically) huge design spaces efficiently, thus performing DSE at a high level of abstraction facilitates design decisions to be made at very early design stages, which can significantly reduce the overall design time of a system.

M. Berekovic, N. Dimopoulos, and S. Wong (Eds.): SAMOS 2008, LNCS 5114, pp. 279–288, 2008.

Though system-level DSE modeling and simulation of reconfigurable system has been touted for quite some time, there are not many tools and models available for system-level DSE for reconfigurable systems. Authors in [1] have presented a modeling methodology for dynamic scheduling of run-time reconfigurable architectures based on discrete event systems. Papers [2] and [3] present a system-level modeling framework for performance evaluation and rapid exploration of different reconfiguration alternatives. Similarly, authors in [4] present an approach for simulating and estimating the performance of reconfigurable architectures based on SystemC. However, these tools and methods are quite limited in number and their level of maturity is not yet very high. Typically, either such tools are not generic enough to be used for every kind of reconfigurable architectures, or they have a restricted focus and therefore cannot exploit simultaneously all the potential aspects of dynamic reconfiguration (such as area usage, reconfiguration overheads and obtainable speedup). In order to fill this gap, in this paper, we present a model for system-level DSE for reconfigurable systems, which can simulate and estimate performance for reconfigurable architectures at a higher abstraction level. For this, we use the Sesame framework [5] as a modeling and simulation platform and the Molen architecture [6] as an example of a reconfigurable architecture. The main contributions of this paper are as follows:

– Extension of the Sesame framework to support partially dynamic reconfigurable architectures.

– Construction of a Sesame model for Molen, which captures the most important behavioral aspects of the architecture and can assist a designer to evaluate the performance of the Molen architecture at the early stage of system-level DSE.

– Initial experimental validation of DSE for a real application - which shows various kinds of explorations and validations that can be performed with the proposed model.

2   The Molen Architecture

The Molen polymorphic processor is established on the basis of the tightly coupled co-processor architectural paradigm [6][7]. It consists of two different kinds of processors: the core processor, which is a general-purpose processor (GPP), and the Reconfigurable Processor (RP). The reconfigurable processor is further subdivided into the $\rho\mu$-code unit and *custom configured unit* (CCU) (see Figure 1). These two processors are connected to one arbiter. The arbiter controls the

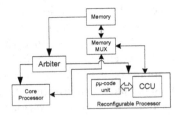

Fig. 1. Molen Architecture

co-ordination of the GPP and RP by directing instructions to either of these processors. In order to speed up the program by running on reconfigurable hardware, parts of the program code running on a GPP can be implemented on the CCU. The code to be mapped onto the RP is annotated with special pragma directives. When the arbiter receives the pragma instruction for RP, it initiates an operation in the reconfigurable unit, gives the data memory control to the RP and drives the GPP into a wait state. When the arbiter receives an end signal from the RP, it releases the data memory control back to the GPP, which can then resume its execution. An operation executed by the RP is divided into two distinct phases: *set* and *execute*. In the *set* phase, the CCU is configured to perform the required operation and in the *execute* phase the actual execution of the operation is performed.

3   Sesame Modeling Approach

The Sesame modeling and simulation environment [5] is geared towards fast and efficient exploration of embedded multimedia architectures, typically those implemented as heterogeneous MPSoCs. Sesame adheres to a transparent simulation methodology where the concerns of application and architecture modeling are separated. An application model describes the functional behavior of an application and an architecture model defines the architectural resources and constraints. For application modeling, Sesame uses the Kahn Process Network (KPN) model of computation [8], which consists of concurrent processes that communicate data using blocking read/non-blocking write synchronization over unbounded FIFO channels.

The processes contain functional application code together with annotations that generate events describing the actions of the process. Communication events Read (R) and Write (W) describe FIFO channel communication and the Execute (EX) event describes computation performed by a Kahn process (typically a function). These events are collected into event traces that are mapped, using an intermediate mapping layer, onto an architecture model (see Figure 2; note that the mapping layer is not shown in detail). Unlike the application model, which is un-timed, the mapping and architecture layers are modeled together in a timed simulation domain. The mapping layer consists of Virtual Processors (VPs) and bounded size FIFO channel components which are connected using the same network topology as the application model. The main purpose of the mapping layer is to forward the event traces to components in the architecture model (application processes onto processors and communication channels onto communication structures) according to a user-specified mapping. The components in the mapping layer simulate synchronization of communication events in such a way that forwarded events are "safe" meaning they do not cause any deadlock due to unmet data dependencies when mapped onto shared resources.

In the architecture model, the architectural timing consequences of the events are modeled. Interconnection and memory components model the utilization and the contention caused by communication events. Processor components model processor utilization using a lookup table that relate computational (EX) events to an execution latency. These latency values may be obtained from literature, hardware measurements, rough estimates or from more detailed simulators such as described in [9].

4   The Molen Model with Sesame

In this section, the Sesame model for the Molen architecture will be described in detail. To create a model with correct Molen reconfiguration behavior, we need to add three extra synchronization mechanisms: one at each Sesame layer, i.e. application, mapping and architecture. In the following sections we describe how these synchronizations are modeled in the different Sesame layers.

4.1   Application Modeling

The Molen architecture exhibits a tightly coupled co-processor paradigm and allows CCUs to run as a co-processor, which adds control dependencies between the GPP and CCUs. Moreover, in Molen, due to its reconfigurable nature, there can be extra dependencies between the tasks mapped to CCUs due to the resource constraints imposed by the FPGA. In some cases, these added dependencies can lead to a deadlock situation in the architecture model. To avoid this deadlock, we have restricted the KPN graphs in the application layer to be static and acyclic. Additionally, to make sure only safe events are forwarded from the mapping layer to the architecture models, we modified the application by adding a Kahn channel from the application's output (or sink) node to its source node(s). Furthermore, we also added a token channel between each pair of communicating processes (see the dashed arrows in the application layer of Figure 2). Unlike the other channels in the Kahn network (which communicate data), these channels only carry a token that needs to be read by the source node before each iteration. For a streaming application, such as depicted in Figure 2, this means that after node A has written data to node B, A has to wait for the token from sink-node F before it can write a new data item to the stream. To achieve this, Kahn processes code has been slightly adapted to read and write the token channels, which adds special read(R_T) and write (W_T) events to the application trace.

   This way the pipeline parallelism is removed from the application which avoids two data-dependent tasks to be active simultaneously on the architecture model. This will prevent the deadlock situation in the Molen model that might occur due to the co-processor behavior and the resource constraints. It is important to note that the sink-to-source channel does not remove all the parallelism in the application, particularly "fork-and-join" parallelism still remains available between tasks that are not data dependent such as between the task pairs (C,D) and (E,D). To enable reconfigurability in the architecture model, one additional change to the application model is required. At the end of each iteration of a task, we add a special *execute(pragma)* event. Similar to the pragma directive in Molen, this event indicates that if the task is mapped onto FPGA, the FPGA can be reconfigured to execute another task after its completion. We use the

KPN graphs generated by PN-gen tool[10], for which an iteration is defined as a set of read (R), execute (EX) and write (W) events for a particular task.

4.2 Mapping Layer

The mapping layer forwards the events (read, execute and write) from the application model as soon as their dependencies are met. To avoid the deadlock mentioned earlier, we also need to perform an additional synchronization in the mapping layer. This synchronization will guarantee that events for a certain task will only be forwarded once *all* its input data is available. To this end, the virtual processors(VP) in the mapping layer are extended such that a VP first checks the availability of all its input data by checking a special token channel for all of its inputs. When all data is available, it proceeds as normal and forwards R,W and EX events to the architecture. Finally, it writes a token to all of its output token channels to signal to all subsequent nodes that data is available. Since VPs have no knowledge of the structure of an application, they cannot autonomously determine when all input is available or when to signal "output available" to other nodes. Therefore reading and writing of token channels is managed explicitly by the application model and the events created by the special reads(R_T) and writes(W_T) are used by the VPs in the mapping layer to perform the extra synchronization in the timed simulation domain.

Note that these synchronization events are not forwarded to the architecture model: only timing consequences of normal R,W or EX events are modeled there. The modifications to the application model essentially allow the mapping layer to dynamically determine a valid, deadlock-free schedule for application events, which is needed to successfully drive the underlying Molen architecture model. However, these modifications limit the class of Kahn process networks that can be run, because not all Kahn networks can be extended easily with the required token channels. This is another reason why currently we restrict the KPN graphs to be static and acyclic. In the future, the model can be refined and these restrictions can be relaxed.

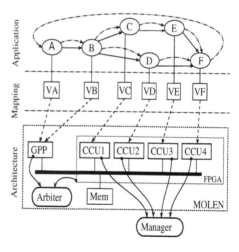

Fig. 2. Three layers in Sesame's infrastructure for Molen

4.3 Architecture Modeling

Architecture models in Sesame are constructed from generic building blocks provided by a library, which contains templates for processors, memories, buses, on-chip networks and so on. We created a model for the Molen architecture using these components and by instantiating processor components with different parameters to model the respective properties of the GPP and the RP (i.e. CCUs). In addition to the general behavior of a processor, CCUs have been given some extra parameters such as area occupancy and reconfiguration delay. In Figure 2, this architecture is shown together with the mapping of an application. In the following sections we describe the GPP/FPGA synchronization mechanism to model co-processor behavior and the modeling of reconfigurable hardware. These are the components that would cause the simulation to deadlock, without the modifications described above.

Modeling the Arbiter

As mentioned before, the Molen pragma directive has been modeled as a special execution event in the application layer which is passed to the architecture model. The arbiter has been modeled as a component in the architecture layer which controls the execution of the GPP and CCUs (see Figure 2).

When a processor (GPP or CCU) receives the special pragma event, it requests a lock from the arbiter. The arbiter coordinates the co-processor behavior by granting exclusive control to either the GPP or the CCUs. To illustrate the interaction between the GPP, CCUs and the arbiter, consider Figure 3. The figure shows these interactions in the case where GPP and CCUs want to execute at the same time. In this particular case, GPP gets the lock to execute at T0. At time T1,

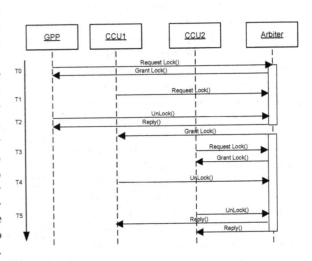

Fig. 3. GPP/CCU, Arbiter Interaction

CCU1 requests execution. Since the GPP is still executing, CCU1 goes to a wait mode. When the GPP finishes its execution, it returns the lock at time T2 and execution is granted to CCU1. At time T3, CCU2 requests execution. Since CCU1 and CCU2 both execute in parallel on the FPGA, CCU2 also gets the lock and can start execution. At time T4, CCU1 finishes its execution, but CCU2 is still executing on the FPGA and only finishes its execution at time T5. At time T4, if the GPP was to request the lock for execution, then it has to wait until time T5. In this way, the arbiter guarantees that all the CCUs finish their execution before it releases the lock.

Modeling Reconfiguration

The Molen architecture supports dynamically reconfigurable FPGAs with partial reconfiguration capability. By reconfiguring part of the FPGA while other parts continue execution normally, it is possible to significantly reduce the impact of the (large) reconfiguration overhead on the total execution time. To capture this behavior in our model we model reconfiguration as follows. A CCU component represents the implementation of a Kahn process in hardware, which means that there are as many CCUs as the number of processes mapped onto the FPGA. Each CCU has an associated reconfiguration delay to configure the task and the percentage of area it occupies. In the current version of our model, we assume a static mapping which means we know in advance which tasks are mapped onto the CCUs. The CCUs are synchronized by a reconfiguration manager (see Fig. 2). The reconfiguration manager is responsible for configuring and releasing CCUs based on the availability of the area on the FPGA. When a CCU wants to execute a task, it sends a request to the reconfiguration manager to be configured; the manager checks for the availability of area on the FPGA and decides whether or not to configure a particular CCU. If there is enough area available immediately, then the CCU will be configured, otherwise it will be blocked until sufficient area is available. Once the necessary area is available and the CCU is configured, the CCU will be blocked to model its reconfiguration delay before it starts the real execution of the events. In this way, the effects of the reconfiguration delay on the system performance is modeled. The interaction between CCUs and the reconfiguration manager is shown in Figure 4 where Fschd is the

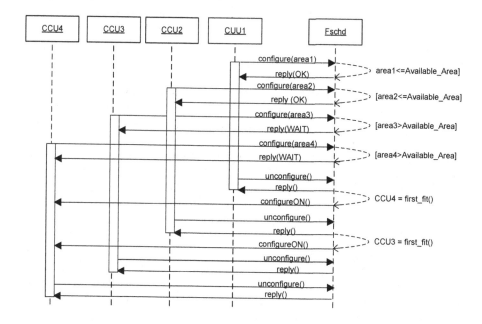

Fig. 4. Interaction between CCUs and Reconfiguration Manager

reconfiguration manager. For experimental purposes, in this paper, we have implemented a simple first fit placement algorithm. In our first fit algorithm, the first CCU which fits onto the available FPGA area will be scheduled first. However, any kind of task placement and scheduling algorithm for the reconfigurable hardware can be implemented as a plugin to the reconfiguration manager.

5   Case Study and Preliminary Results

In this section, we will describe a case study using the previously described Molen model and we will discuss our preliminary results. Our aim is to show what kind of experiments and results can be obtained from the model and what conclusions can be drawn from it. We do not discuss the accuracy of the model, since model validation and calibration is left as future work. In this case study, we use a

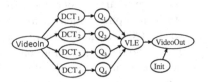

Fig. 5. Application model

data parallel Motion-JPEG encoder application which is mapped onto the Molen architecture. Figure 5 shows that the DCT and Quantizer tasks of the Motion-JPEG application are divided into 4 parallel streams (synchronization channels are not shown in this figure). We instantiate the Molen model with 8 CCU units. This allows us to make optimal use of the parallelism available in the application by mapping each of the DCT and Q tasks onto a CCU. Also, note that as discussed in Section 4.3, a CCU is represented as an implementation of a Kahn process. The computational latency values that the GPP model component associates with the computational events, are initialized using estimated (but non-Molen specific) values. For the CCUs, we use the same values divided by 10, implying that the same computational event would execute 10 times faster on the reconfigurable hardware than on the GPP. We realize that in reality the latency of the CCU is different and does not show any dependency with the latency of the GPP. We use this simplified assumption here for illustration purposes. Similarly, we assume an estimated value for the reconfiguration delay and area for each CCU.

In the first experiment, we look at the impact of different task mappings on the total execution time in terms of simulated clock cycles. In this case, we assume each task takes almost the whole area on a FPGA and we fix the size of each CCU to 95%, thus forcing reconfiguration every time for each CCU. At first, we map all the tasks to GPP and in each successive mapping we move one task (either DCT or Q tasks) from GPP to CCUs. Figure 6 shows the results for these mappings. The mapping column lists the successive mappings(1st mapping: all tasks are mapped to GPP, 2nd mapping: DCT1 to CCU and rest to GPP, 3rd mapping: DCT1 & DCT2 to CCUs and rest to GPP and so on). The "cycle time" column lists the total execution time for each mapping and the last column lists the speedup for each mapping compared to the first mapping. Because of the lower execution latency of CCUs as compared to the GPP, we

No	Mapping	Cycle Time	Speedup
1st	First	371150560	1.000
2nd	prev+DCT1	331948000	1.118
3rd	prev+DCT2	292745440	1.267
4th	prev+DCT3	253542880	1.463
5th	prev+DCT4	217906240	1.703
6th	prev+Q1	199425856	1.861
7th	prev+Q2	200145472	1.854
8th	prev+Q3	194465088	1.908
9th	prev+Q4	188784704	1.965

Fig. 6. Results Experiment 1

Area	Delay	Slow Reconf	Cycle Time	Speedup
95	25000	1792	188784704	1.965
75	18750	1792	175984704	2.108
50	12500	1536	137532992	2.698
30	7500	1280	140418784	2.643

Fig. 7. Results Experiment 2

might expect this to significantly increase the system performance. However, the results show that in fact there is a non-linear trade-off. This is because, moving the tasks to CCUs will add to the latency for reconfiguring the CCUs each time.

In the second experiment, we explore the impact of varying the CCU sizes. Once again we simplify the model by assuming the area for DCT and Q is the same. We scale the reconfiguration delay proportional with the CCU area, which is true property of most current reconfigurable hardwares. As a reference mapping, we use the mapping that has all DCT and Q tasks on CCUs and all others on the GPP. Figure 7 shows the results for different area and reconfiguration delay values. It lists the cycle times and number of "slow reconfigurations". This is the number of times the CCU has been reconfigured when there is not enough area for immediate execution. Moreover, it lists the speed-ups in each case when the area varies. As it can be inferred from the results, there is a clear relation between area and time. When CCUs occupy more area, less CCUs can be executed simultaneously hence more reconfigurations are required implying longer reconfiguration delay and thus longer execution time. At the same time, when CCUs occupy less area, there are less reconfigurations and reconfiguration delay, hence faster execution.

Finally we note that all the above system-level simulations (with the given input consisting of 8 picture frames of 128^2 pixels) can be executed in less than 0.5 second, thus allowing for extensive design space exploration.

6   Conclusion and Future Work

In this paper we have created a model for the Molen reconfigurable platform using the Sesame framework. The case study in this paper has shown that various design parameters such as area, reconfiguration delay and task mappings can be explored with the current model. Due to fast execution times it can be used to efficiently explore and evaluate different design choices of the reconfigurable architecture. Moreover, the model is easily extensible and only few modifications are required to the existing model for modeling various other design options.

The current version of the model assumes static mapping (i.e. we know in advance which tasks are mapped onto FPGA). In the future, we want to extend the model to support dynamic (run-time) mapping of application tasks onto reconfigurable and non-reconfigurable hardware. Additionally, we will validate the current Molen model against a real Molen implementation to allow for final calibration of the model in order to increase its accuracy.

References

1. Noguera, J., Badia, R.M.: System-level power-performance trade-offs in task scheduling for dynamically reconfigurable architectures. In: CASES 2003: Proceedings of the 2003 international conference on Compilers, architecture and synthesis for embedded systems, pp. 73–83. ACM, New York (2003)
2. Hsiung, P., Lin, S., Chen, Y., Huang, C.: Perfecto: A SystemC-based performance evaluation framework for dynamically partially reconfigurable systems. In: FPL 2006: Proceedings of the Conference on Field Programmable Logic and Applications, pp. 1–6. IEEE, Los Alamitos (2006)
3. Rissa, T., Vasilko, M., Niittylahti, J.: System-level modelling and implementation technique for run-time reconfigurable systems. In: FCCM 2002: Proceedings of the 10th Annual IEEE Symposium on Field-Programmable Custom Computing Machines, p. 295. IEEE Computer Society, Washington (2002)
4. Qu, Y., Soininen, J.P.: Systemc-based design methodology for reconfigurable system-on-chip. In: DSD 2005: Proceedings of the 8th Euromicro Conference on Digital System Design, pp. 364–371. IEEE Computer Society, Washington (2005)
5. Erbas, C., Pimentel, A.D., Thompson, M., Polstra, S.: A framework for system-level modeling and simulation of embedded systems architectures. EURASIP J. Embedded Syst. 2007(1) (2007)
6. Vassiliadis, S., Wong, S., Gaydadjiev, G.N., Bertels, K., Kuzmanov, G., Panainte, E.M.: The molen polymorphic processor. IEEE Transactions on Computers 53(11), 1363–1375 (2004)
7. Vassiliadis, S., Gaydadjiev, G.N., Bertels, K., Panainte, E.M.: The molen programming paradigm. In: Pimentel, A.D., Vassiliadis, S. (eds.) SAMOS 2004. LNCS, vol. 3133, pp. 1–10. Springer, Heidelberg (2004)
8. Kahn, G.: The semantics of a simple language for parallel programming. In: Proc. of the IFIP Congress 74 (1974)
9. Pimentel, A.D., Thompson, M., Polstra, S., Erbas, C.: Calibration of abstract performance models for system-level design space exploration. Journal of Signal Processing Systems for Signal, Image, and Video Technology 50(2), 99–114 (2008)
10. Verdoolaege, S., Nikolov, H., Stefanov, T.: PN: a tool for improved derivation of process networks. EURASIP Journal on Embedded Systems 2007(1), 13 (2007)

Intellectual Property Protection for Embedded Sensor Nodes

Michael Gora, Eric Simpson, and Patrick Schaumont

Virginia Polytechnic Institute and State University,
Secure Embedded Systems Group,
302 Whittemore Hall (0111), Blacksburg VA 24061, USA
{gora,esimpson,schaum}@vt.edu
http://www.ece.vt.edu/schaum/research.html

Abstract. Embedded Sensor Networks are deeply immersed in their environment, and are difficult to protect from abuse or theft. Yet the software contained within these remote sensors often represents years of development, and requires adequate protection. We present a software based solution for the Texas Instruments C5509A DSP processor which uses object-code encryption and public-key key exchange with a server. The scheme is tightly integrated into the tool flow of the DSP processor and compatible with existing embedded processor design flows. We present performance and overhead metrics of the encryption algorithms and the security protocols. We also describe the limitations of the solution that originate from its software-only, backwards-compatible nature.

1 Introduction

Securing intellectual property in embedded applications is an ever growing concern for developers. These concerns are even more prevalent when such applications are deployed in unsecure and hostile environments as is often the case with sensor networks. Code utilized on such nodes can represent a major investment on the part of the developer, yet the code is often left unprotected. A common fear is that such an unsecured product, discarded or stolen, appears on the black market where it can be obtained by a competitor. Code stored in plain text could easily be copied and deployed on a competing platform damaging the original developers market position. Even worse in the case of critically important networks, code could be reverse engineered to aid in the disruption of service or theft of sensitive data. Solutions lend themselves to hardware based approaches for securing newly developed systems [1]. However, this leaves a great deal of older systems that run on a legacy platform vulnerable. Rather than opting for costly hardware retrofits for such systems, a software approach may extend the platforms useful application life.

Our work presents such a solution for securing firmware-based intellectual property (FIP) on embedded sensor nodes. The solution is geared to be compatible with the existing design flow for the Texas Instruments C5509A DSP (C55). Figure 1 illustrates the two parts of our solution. First, tight integration

M. Berekovic, N. Dimopoulos, and S. Wong (Eds.): SAMOS 2008, LNCS 5114, pp. 289–298, 2008.

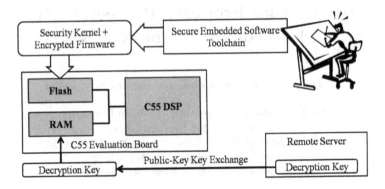

Fig. 1. IP security schema overview

of IP encryption and the software tool-chain provides a novel and streamlined method for the protection of firmware. This is extended with a security kernel which provides a platform for the authentication and decryption of secured code at boot.

Second, the security kernel negotiates a firmware based intellectual property (FIP) decryption key from a key server at startup. The use of a key server is required as the C55 does not posses any secure nonvolatile memory. Under the generic nature of the implementation it can not be assumed there is hardware present that does. However, the introduction of a key server requires an authentication procedure, in order to avoid man-in-the-middle attacks. This is further addressed in Section 6. Here, we assume that the sensor node can be reliably authenticated by the key server. We use a public-key exchange protocol based on an Elliptic Curve Diffie-Hellman (ECDH) protocol. The approach of storing the key off of the sensor node prevents the simple decryption of the FIP by reverse engineering of the firmware. The firmware key can only be obtained by booting the node and completing the key-exchange. The retrieved FIP key is utilized internally on the processor to decrypt the firmware. As the key exchange and decryption can occur only at boot there is no required runtime overhead. Once the ECDH key exchange has completed, the firmware decryption service has a footprint of only 7.3 Kbyte. To our knowledge this is the first published result of a complete end to end implementation of a firmware encryption scheme combined with an ECC public-key exchange on a DSP. We have verified our approach by building an end-to-end prototype of the entire system, including sensor node and key exchange server.

The paper is organized as follows. Section 2 outlines the assumptions that shaped our design decisions. Section 3 covers the methodology for the encryption and decryption of the firmware object code. Section 4 presents the implementation details of ECDH on the C55. The performance of both ECDH and firmware encryption are reported in Section 5 and compared to other platforms. Section 6 analyzes strengths and weaknesses of our solution while Section 7 summarizes the project and indicates areas for future work.

2   Constraints

Our primary focus is the creation of a software-only protection mechanism to secure intellectual property in firmware on a Texas Instruments C5509A DSP, a 16-bit processor. In addition, maximal flexibility is ensured in development, by creating portable code in C, and by integrating the firmware encryption flow in the C55s software development environment, Code Composer Studio 3.1 (CCS). All additions to the tool-chain to facilitate this are also written in portable C code for the GNU Compiler Collection 4.2.0. All encryption schemes are developed with a minimum of 128bit AES secret key security or equivalent [3] as specified by the NSA guidelines [2].

Given the constraints outlined above, we opted for a combination of firmware encryption with a remote key-exchange. Indeed, as this is only a software based solution the addition of a specific hardware component to securely store or generate this key is not an option. We therefore use a public-key key exchange mechanism to retrieve the firmware decryption key. The resulting arrangement is divided into two distinct components, IP encryption/decryption, and key transmission.

3   IP Encryption and Decryption

3.1   Identification and Encryption

Identification and encryption are a tightly coupled step in our implementation. The final binary requires plain text code sections. These perform such tasks as key exchange, authentication, firmware decryption, and traditional boot up tasks. Identification of the sensitive IP and non-critical code sections is accomplished during development through the built in code section pragmas made available by CCS. The net effect of singling out only the critical IP allows code to be selectively encrypted allowing for smaller decryption times.

Encryption of the selected code sections occurs after the compilation and linking of the design results in a complete binary and is a post processing step. As we have adopted the strategy of allowing individual sections of firmware to be encrypted it is necessary that these sections are logical entities handled by the DSP compiler and linker. As such we obtain tight integration between firmware encryption and firmware production. A development tool included with CCS, OFD55, provides detailed information on each section contained in a binary file, including the size and offset of each. Figure 2 demonstrates how a compiled binary file resulting from CCS is encrypted.

The Object Encryptor (OE) is a utility we developed that encypts a plain text binary. The developer can choose what sections in the binary should be encrypted by providing a sections file. The sections file only contains the names of the identified sections to be encrypted. The offset and length of the sections are provided by the OFD55 utility from the CCS tool chain (OFD file). The OE next uses a designer-provided key (Key file) and an arbitrarily generated nonce to encrypt the designated code sections. For additional security the OE allows the use of different Keys and nonce to be used on different code section. This

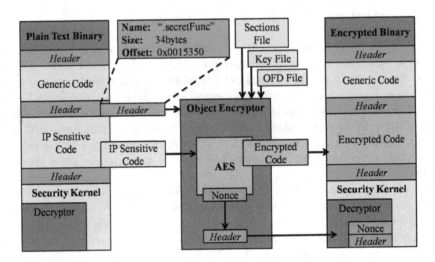

Fig. 2. Object Encryption

provides a greater flexibility in key and IP management by allowing the developer to specify different key management policies for each section. Generating the encrypted key stream is accomplished through AES in Counter Mode [11]. An AES key length of 128 bits is used as to satisfy the requirements for secret level clearance specified by the NSA standard [2]. The AES Counter mode allows the use of a key-stream in blocks of 16 bits, as is needed for the native word length in the C55 processor. At the same time, it also avoids the requirement that code sections need to be a multiple of 128 bits.

Besides the encryption of firmware sections, the OE also creates an additional data section in the resulting encrypted binary. Space for this data section is allotted in the security kernel. The plain text data section holds the offset, size, and nonce information for each IP sensitive code section that was encrypted. This data section is used by the Security Kernel at boot time to locate encrypted firmware and decrypt it into executable object code. After the OE concludes the resulting binary will contain both encrypted and plain text code sections. Any standard methods of deploying the binary may be then used.

3.2   Decryption in the Security Kernel

Decryption may be handled in two ways, a one time cost to decrypt all encrypted firmware at boot or a distributed run time cost to decrypt individual sections when needed. Regardless, decryption follows the same general methodology and should only be performed on internal DSP memory. At any time unprotected code only exists in the C55, where it is assumed to be secure, as the abundance of fast and tightly controlled memory alleviates the necessity of utilizing chip ram. JTAG and other security concerns are further addressed in Section 6 of this paper.

The actual decryption routines in the security kernel are always present in plain text. However except for software integrity issues, which are addressed in Section 6, this is not of concern. During decryption the section information stored in the security kernel by the OE is used to set up encrypted sections for decryption. The only missing information for decryption is the 128bit key, which must be brought from a secure external source.

3.3   C55 Design Flow

One of the primary goals of this work is to provide an IP encryption solution that is easily utilized across a wide series of potential target applications. As such it is necessary to consider the development suite, design flow, and deployment for a typical C55 implementation. A generic implementation containing assembly and C code is compiled or assembled before being placed as dictated by the memory map. These placed code sections are then linked appropriately before being written to a binary output file. Any post processing is then performed before the binary is flashed to the C55 and executed. The only additions to the design are the addition of the security kernel which is developed with only low level C code and assembly functions as to have as minimal impact. Inclusion of the OE is the only addition to the flow and will generate encrypted code sections as identified by the designer. No other design alterations are required after these initial steps. The only remaining step is to change the boot vector of the C55 to run the security kernel upon processor reset.

4   Key Transmission

4.1   Overview

Communication between the C55 and the key server occurs over an open unsecure channel in our implementation. As such the establishment of a secure channel is required before any key exchange may occur. A public key protocol such as Diffie-Hellman is perfectly suited to such a task. Diffie-Hellman (DH) is a well known mechanism for public key cryptography across many different platforms. We utilize Diffie-Hellman over Elliptic Curves, which is well suited for embedded applications. Indeed, an implementation of Elliptic Curves over a 256 bit prime field provides equivalent security compared to an RSA key of 3072 bits, which corresponds to an 128-bit secret key. Thus, a 256-bit prime field provides secret-level security according to the NSA standard [2].

While other highly portable C code implementations of ECDH exist (such as LibTomCrypt [5]) these are not suited to deployment on the C55. An embedded implementation of ECDH, TinyECC [6], requires the use of TinyOS and the nesC compiler in the tool chain. We opted against using TinyECC as to maintain compatibility with the existing design path. After careful consideration it was deemed necessary to implement ECDH from the ground up. This includes the extended precision finite field (GF) arithmetic necessary to implement EC, the math functions to implement an EC point multiplication and the DH protocol that relies on EC point multiplications to derive public and secret keys.

4.2 Diffie-Hellman Protocol

ECDH is a well known exchange protocol and as such only its specific implementation will be covered. For the purpose of this implementation only one ECDH exchange will occur during boot of the target system. During this single cycle a public key is derived and transmitted between the DSP and server systems. Each public key is used to derive a 128 bit private key that can be used to transmit the IP decryption key through an AES block cipher as summarized in Fig. 3.

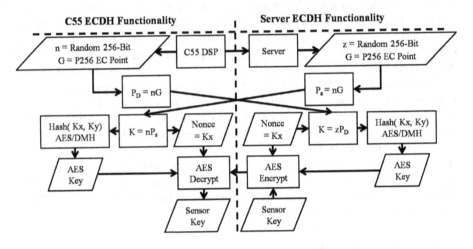

Fig. 3. Diffie-Hellman public key exchange and AES key derivation

Deriving a public key requires that both DSP and server sides of the scheme use the same base point. We use the IEEE standard for the 256 GF(p) field [7]. A single EC scalar multiplication creates the desired public key whose bit stream including its degree is transmitted over the insecure channel. Each public key once received by the opposite platform requires an additional scalar multiplication against that platforms previously determined number. The result is an identical private key on both server and DSP sides of the implementation. The private key is represented as a point (X,Y) of two 256 bit fields. The same AES 128 bit implementation used to decrypt the IP sensitive sections of code is utilized to transmit the key. To generate the key it is necessary to reduce the 512 bits of private key into a 128 bit AES key. This compression is obtained through a Davies Meyer hash implementation.

4.3 Elliptic Curve Arithmetic and Finite Field

Elliptic Curve arithmetic is built on top of modular arithmetic, and creates public and secret keys by multiplying a point on an elliptic curve by a scalar value. By default, points are represent in the affine (X,Y) coordinate system. For efficiency reasons, embedded system implementations internally apply projective format (X,Y,Z) for points, and include conversions from/to affine to projective format as needed. The IEEE standard [7] provides generic implementations for addition, subtraction, doubling, conversion between affine and projective, and scalar multiplication.

The modular arithmetic for point operations are based on finite field arithmetic of either the prime (GF(p)) or binary (GF(2P)) type. We used the GF(p) scheme, in part because an easily accessible open-source implementation was available that could be used as a golden reference [5]. Field length for the finite arithmetic is another system parameter to choose. According to Table 1, a secret equivalent protection for a 128-bit private key required us to use a 256-bit prime field. GF(p) requires an efficient embedded implementation of multi-precision arithmetic operations. However for the lowest level of these such as addition and multiplication there is no easy access to the carry bits and leads to large and complex implementation. To combat this problem addition, subtraction, shift operations, and comparisons are written in assembly.

5 Results

5.1 Demonstrator Components

The demonstrator hardware contains a Spectrum Digital C55 Development System and a server running the key-server functionality. The communications link between the C55 board and the server is based on USB, but easily replaceable with other technologies. The software on the C55 DSP board includes a USB communications library, the security kernel containing the ECDH protocol and the Object Decryptor, and finally an encrypted C55 application. The server server contains a similar USB library, a matching ECDH protocol and the secret key that can decrypt the object code. Software for the C55 kit is developed in CCS on a development system, which also contains the Object Code Encryptor. Once the application is generated and encrypted, it is downloaded into the Flash memory of the C55 board. The key used to encrypt the application is installed on the Server. Next, the C55 board can be booted and will go through a complete key exchange and application decryption sequence.

5.2 Encryption Performance for the C55

Through testing on our demonstrator components we obtained an average performance of approximately 21 million cycles or 105 milliseconds for one ECDH exchange on the C55 processor. This value is obtained by performing several different key exchanges with different 256-bit scalar values. We then compared this performance with several different published implementations. The comparison is done in seconds normalized over the operating frequency of the platform. The results of this comparison are captured in Fig. 4. This demonstrates that our implementation on a 16-bit platform compares favorable to some of the published 32-bit platforms. We also evaluated the symmetric-key encryption performance

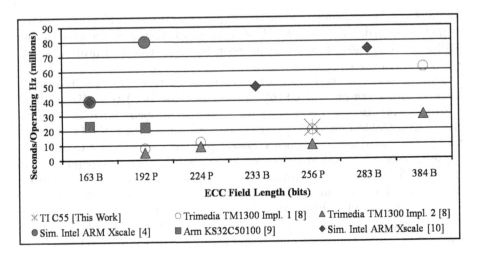

Fig. 4. ECDH speed comparison

on the C55 and evaluated that to be 2023 cycles per 128 bits. We can also observe that the symmetric-key encryption speed is 3 orders of magnitude faster then public-key encryption.

For the complete protocol, we evaluated that the ECDH handshake and subsequent decryption of 128 Kbytes of firmware takes about 40 million cycles on the C55. Since ECDH consumes 20 million cycles, it thus takes roughly the same amount of time to decrypt a block of 128 Kilobytes of code as it takes to perform two ECC point multiplications (one complete ECDH handshake). The complete on-chip memory space of the C55A contains 256 Kilobyte, and the security kernel will never decrypt more than this during boot. Hence, it would be necessary to optimize the current symmetric-key decryption speed before improving ECDH protocol implementation. The memory footprint for the security kernel is approximately 17.3Kb or merely 6.7% of available onboard memory for the C55. This is broken up between two sections AES and ECDH which respectively have footprints of 7.1Kb and 13.3KB. It should be noted that ECDH also utilizes the Rijndael algorithm to perform a Davies Meyer hash on the private key value to generate an AES transmission key. This represents the 3.1 K byte discrepancy in size between the two footprints. Upon retrieving the firmware key ECDH may be discarded leaving a run time footprint of 7.1Kb for AES decryption, or 2.7% of available memory.

6   Security Analysis

In this section, we discuss the challenges of implementing a firmware protection technique using only software techniques. We are interested in securing off-chip object code. Once the off-chip object code is loaded from nonvolatile memory onto the processor and decrypted, it is no longer protected. Hence, we assume that the C55 processor package itself can be protected from external inspection or tampering. This requires additional precautions, such as security measures for the chip JTAG interfaces [12]. Securing such vulnerabilities on an existing system is not reasonably done in a generic implementation and if possible would require tight integration with the end application. We also assume that the encrypted firmware itself can be trusted. Any vulnerability in this code such as buffer overflows or unchecked data access would lead to an additional security breach.

6.1   System Authentication and Integrity

System authentication and integrity are of crucial concern to a software only solution. Due to the nature of the C55 and its lack of secured nonvolatile memory these issues present themselves outside the scope of such a solution. For the purposes of this paper we thus assume that the end-user of the system is able to guarantee the integrity of the security kernel. This is required to thwart an attack that would compromise the platform by code injection, or through hardware emulation. Booting with a compromised security kernel or in software that was running on an emulated system would leave the decrypted code sections vulnerable. Solutions that provide security kernel integrity can either rely on physical protection, or else use a hardware-based hashing facility [13]. Processors with on-chip non-volatile memory are able to store the security kernel on-chip [14]. For a RAM-only processor such as the C55, an add-on SHA-1 hardware module with a write-only hashing facility can be used as a building block for integrity verification. A secure hash can be combined with an encryption key into a keyed-Hash Message Authentication Code (HMAC). This can be used to both verify the integrity and the authenticity of the node simultaneously [15]. A failure to respond correctly to such a response would result in the denial of a decryption key as per a key management scheme. Finally, we emphasize that the limitations are all originating from the desire to support firmware protection on legacy platforms. Part of our efforts has been to identify exactly those risks mentioned above, and to analyze possible countermeasures.

7   Conclusions

We have presented a complete demonstrator for firmware code encryption on embedded sensor nodes. Our results show that such a mechanism can be systematically integrated into a TI C55 software production flow, and that the resulting overhead on system resources is minimal. We have achieved software-only code security by storing secrets off-platform in a key-server. While this may not be an option for all embedded sensor situations, it did fit the purpose of our project. The code encryption flow is presently being adopted by our industrial partner. We are considering further improvements on the protocol and its implementation, including hardware authentication of the C55 platform to the server and the protection of C55 interfaces and debug ports which could affect the sensor node at runtime.

References

1. TCG Mobile Trusted Module Specification v 1.0 (June 2007), http://www.trustedcomputinggroup.com
2. CNSS: National Policy on the Use of the Advanced Encryption Standard (AES) to Protect National Security Systems and National Security Information. ICNSS Policy No. 15 Fact Sheet No. 1, Ft. Mead (2003)
3. Giry, D.: Recommended Cryptograph Keylength, http://www.keylength.com
4. Branovic, I., Giorgi, R., Martinelli, E.: A Workload Characterization of Elliptic Curve Cryptography Methods in Embedded Environments. In: ACM SIGARCH workshop on Memory Performance, pp. 27–34. ACM, New York (2003)
5. LibTomCrypt, http://libtom.org
6. TinyECC, ECC for Sensor Networks, http://discovery.csc.ncsu.edu/software/TinyECC/
7. Microprocessor and Microcomputer Standards Committee of the IEEE Computer Society: IEEE Standard Specifications for Public Key Cryptography. IEEE-SA Standards Board, New York (2000)
8. Hu, Y., Li, Q., Kuo, C.-C.: Efficient Implementation of Elliptic Curve Cryptography (ECC) on VLIW-Micro- Architecture Media Processor. In: 2nd IEEE ICME, pp. 181–184. IEEE Press, New York (2004)
9. Wollinger, T., Pelzl, J., Wittelsberger, V., Paar, C.: Elliptic and Hyperelliptic Curves on Embedded P. In: 3rd ACM TCES, pp. 509–533. ACM, New York (2004)
10. Bartolini, S., Branovic, I., Giorgi, R., Martinelli, E.: A Performance Evaluation of ARM ISA extensions for Elliptic Curve Cryptography Over Binary Finite Fields. In: 16th IEEE CAHPC, pp. 238–245. IEEE Press, New York (2004)
11. Ferguson, N., Schneier, B.: Practical Cryptography. Wiley Publishing, Inc., Indianapolis (2004)
12. Buskey, R.F., Frosik, B.B.: Protected JTAG. In: IEEE Parallel Processing Workshop, p. 8. IEEE Press, New York (2006)
13. Dallas Semiconductor: White Paper 8: 1-Wire SHA-1 Overview (September 2002), http://www.maxim-ic.com/
14. Suh, G., O'Donnel, C., Sachdev, I., Devadas, S.: Design and Implementation of the AEGIS Single-Chip Secure Processor Using Physical Random Functions. In: 32nd IEEE ISCA, pp. 25–36. IEEE Press, New York (2005)
15. Bellare, M., Canettiy, R., Krawczykz, H.: Message Authentication using Hash Functions: The HMAC Construction. In: 2nd CryptoBytes, RSA Laboratories, Bedford, vol. 1, pp. 25–36 (1996)

Author Index

Lecture Notes in Computer Science

Sublibrary 1: Theoretical Computer Science and General Issues

For information about Vols. 1–4847
please contact your bookseller or Springer

Vol. 4988: R. Berghammer, B. Möller, G. Struth (Eds.), Relations and Kleene Algebra in Computer Science. X, 397 pages. 2008.

Vol. 4985: M. Ishikawa, K. Doya, H. Miyamoto, T. Yamakawa (Eds.), Neural Information Processing, Part II. XXX, 1091 pages. 2008.

Vol. 4984: M. Ishikawa, K. Doya, H. Miyamoto, T. Yamakawa (Eds.), Neural Information Processing, Part I. XXX, 1147 pages. 2008.

Vol. 4981: M. Egerstedt, B. Mishra (Eds.), Hybrid Systems: Computation and Control. XV, 680 pages. 2008.

Vol. 4978: M. Agrawal, D. Du, Z. Duan, A. Li (Eds.), Theory and Applications of Models of Computation. XII, 598 pages. 2008.

Vol. 4975: F. Chen, B. Jüttler (Eds.), Advances in Geometric Modeling and Processing. XV, 606 pages. 2008.

Vol. 4974: M. Giacobini, A. Brabazon, S. Cagnoni, G.A. Di Caro, R. Drechsler, A. Ekárt, A.I. Esparcia-Alcázar, M. Farooq, A. Fink, J. McCormack, M. O'Neill, J. Romero, F. Rothlauf, G. Squillero, A.Ş. Uyar, S. Yang (Eds.), Applications of Evolutionary Computing. XXV, 701 pages. 2008.

Vol. 4973: E. Marchiori, J.H. Moore (Eds.), Evolutionary Computation, Machine Learning and Data Mining in Bioinformatics. X, 213 pages. 2008.

Vol. 4972: J. van Hemert, C. Cotta (Eds.), Evolutionary Computation in Combinatorial Optimization. XII, 289 pages. 2008.

Vol. 4971: M. O'Neill, L. Vanneschi, S. Gustafson, A.I. Esparcia Alcázar, I. De Falco, A. Della Cioppa, E. Tarantino (Eds.), Genetic Programming. XI, 375 pages. 2008.

Vol. 4967: R. Wyrzykowski, J. Dongarra, K. Karczewski, J. Wasniewski (Eds.), Parallel Processing and Applied Mathematics. XXIII, 1414 pages. 2008.

Vol. 4963: C.R. Ramakrishnan, J. Rehof (Eds.), Tools and Algorithms for the Construction and Analysis of Systems. XVI, 518 pages. 2008.

Vol. 4962: R. Amadio (Ed.), Foundations of Software Science and Computational Structures. XV, 505 pages. 2008.

Vol. 4961: J.L. Fiadeiro, P. Inverardi (Eds.), Fundamental Approaches to Software Engineering. XIII, 430 pages. 2008.

Vol. 4960: S. Drossopoulou (Ed.), Programming Languages and Systems. XIII, 399 pages. 2008.

Vol. 4959: L. Hendren (Ed.), Compiler Construction. XII, 307 pages. 2008.

Vol. 4957: E.S. Laber, C. Bornstein, L.T. Nogueira, L. Faria (Eds.), LATIN 2008: Theoretical Informatics. XVII, 794 pages. 2008.

Vol. 4943: R. Woods, K. Compton, C. Bouganis, P.C. Diniz (Eds.), Reconfigurable Computing: Architectures, Tools and Applications. XIV, 344 pages. 2008.

Vol. 4942: E. Frachtenberg, U. Schwiegelshohn (Eds.), Job Scheduling Strategies for Parallel Processing. VII, 189 pages. 2008.

Vol. 4941: M. Miculan, I. Scagnetto, F. Honsell (Eds.), Types for Proofs and Programs. VII, 203 pages. 2008.

Vol. 4935: B. Chapman, W. Zheng, G.R. Gao, M. Sato, E. Ayguadé, D. Wang (Eds.), A Practical Programming Model for the Multi-Core Era. VI, 208 pages. 2008.

Vol. 4934: U. Brinkschulte, T. Ungerer, C. Hochberger, R.G. Spallek (Eds.), Architecture of Computing Systems – ARCS 2008. XI, 287 pages. 2008.

Vol. 4927: C. Kaklamanis, M. Skutella (Eds.), Approximation and Online Algorithms. X, 289 pages. 2008.

Vol. 4926: N. Monmarché, E.-G. Talbi, P. Collet, M. Schoenauer, E. Lutton (Eds.), Artificial Evolution. XIII, 327 pages. 2008.

Vol. 4921: S.-i. Nakano, M.. S. Rahman (Eds.), WALCOM: Algorithms and Computation. XII, 241 pages. 2008.

Vol. 4919: A. Gelbukh (Ed.), Computational Linguistics and Intelligent Text Processing. XVIII, 666 pages. 2008.

Vol. 4917: P. Stenström, M. Dubois, M. Katevenis, R. Gupta, T. Ungerer (Eds.), High Performance Embedded Architectures and Compilers. XIII, 400 pages. 2008.

Vol. 4915: A. King (Ed.), Logic-Based Program Synthesis and Transformation. X, 219 pages. 2008.

Vol. 4912: G. Barthe, C. Fournet (Eds.), Trustworthy Global Computing. XI, 401 pages. 2008.

Vol. 4910: V. Geffert, J. Karhumäki, A. Bertoni, B. Preneel, P. Návrat, M. Bieliková (Eds.), SOFSEM 2008: Theory and Practice of Computer Science. XV, 792 pages. 2008.

Vol. 4905: F. Logozzo, D.A. Peled, L.D. Zuck (Eds.), Verification, Model Checking, and Abstract Interpretation. X, 325 pages. 2008.

Vol. 4904: S. Rao, M. Chatterjee, P. Jayanti, C.S.R. Murthy, S.K. Saha (Eds.), Distributed Computing and Networking. XVIII, 588 pages. 2007.

Vol. 4878: E. Tovar, P. Tsigas, H. Fouchal (Eds.), Principles of Distributed Systems. XIII, 457 pages. 2007.

Vol. 4875: S.-H. Hong, T. Nishizeki, W. Quan (Eds.), Graph Drawing. XIII, 402 pages. 2008.

Vol. 4873: S. Aluru, M. Parashar, R. Badrinath, V.K. Prasanna (Eds.), High Performance Computing – HiPC 2007. XXIV, 663 pages. 2007.

Vol. 4863: A. Bonato, F.R.K. Chung (Eds.), Algorithms and Models for the Web-Graph. X, 217 pages. 2007.

Vol. 4860: G. Eleftherakis, P. Kefalas, G. Păun, G. Rozenberg, A. Salomaa (Eds.), Membrane Computing. IX, 453 pages. 2007.

Vol. 4855: V. Arvind, S. Prasad (Eds.), FSTTCS 2007: Foundations of Software Technology and Theoretical Computer Science. XIV, 558 pages. 2007.

Vol. 4854: L. Bougé, M. Forsell, J.L. Träff, A. Streit, W. Ziegler, M. Alexander, S. Childs (Eds.), Euro-Par 2007 Workshops: Parallel Processing. XVII, 236 pages. 2008.

Vol. 4851: S. Boztaş, H.-F.(F.) Lu (Eds.), Applied Algebra, Algebraic Algorithms and Error-Correcting Codes. XII, 368 pages. 2007.

Vol. 4848: M.H. Garzon, H. Yan (Eds.), DNA Computing. XI, 292 pages. 2008.